Seeing into the Life of Things

Stephen Seleman

SEEING INTO THE LIFE OF THINGS

Essays on Literature and Religious Experience

Edited with an introduction by

JOHN L. MAHONEY

Fordham University Press
New York
1998

Copyright © 1998 by Fordham University Press
All rights reserved
LC 97–45736
ISBN 0–8232–1732–9 (hardcover)
ISBN 0–8232–1733–7 (paperback)
ISSN 1096–6692
Studies in Religion and Literature, No. 1

Library of Congress Cataloging-in-Publication Data

Seeing into the life of things : essays on literature and religious
experience / edited with an introduction by John L. Mahoney.
    p.   cm. — (Studies in religion and literature : 1)
  Includes bibliographical references and index.
    ISBN 0-8232-1732-9 (alk. paper). — ISBN 0-8232-1733-7 (pbk. :
alk. paper)
    1. Religion and literature.   2. Religion in literature.
3. Literature—History and criticism.   I. Mahoney, John L.
II. Series: Studies in religion and literature (Fordham University
Press) : 1.
PN49.S38   1998
809'.93382—dc21   97-45736
                                                        CIP

Printed in the United States of America

While with an eye made quiet by the power
Of harmony, and the deep power of joy,
We see into the life of things.

Wordsworth, *Tintern Abbey*

CONTENTS

ACKNOWLEDGMENTS

The editor must acknowledge first the talent and enthusiasm which all the contributors brought to their work. Their commitment to a difficult assignment and to the deadlines set by their often tyrannical colleague was a great source of inspiration. As he completed the reading and editing of their splendid essays, he realized what a rich bounty he had gathered and could only echo Dryden's praise of Chaucer's *Canterbury Tales* with the proverb, "here is God's plenty."

Special thanks to Michael Buckley, s.j., Director of the Jesuit Institute of Boston College, for his encouragement and for the good offices of the Institute. The many discussions connected with the planning of the new journal *Religion and the Arts* had a great influence on the planning of this volume. My colleagues Joseph Appleyard, s.j., Dennis Taylor, and Judith Wilt, whose launching of a sequence of courses on Religion and Literature in the English Department of Boston College inspired the work, provided never-failing advice, and support. And, as always, Professor Richard Schrader has been most helpful on bibliographical and editorial matters.

Elaine Tarutis, editorial assistant, critic, and adviser, was indispensable in every phase of preparing the essays for publication. Heather Lynch's and James Thompson's sharp gazes caught many of the editor's mistakes. I am grateful to Boston College for a Faculty Undergraduate Research Grant that made her assistance possible. I am also grateful to the Rattigan Research Fund and to the Graduate Research Fund of Boston College. Jackie Cain and Roy Kral, and Harry Locke brought their precious gifts of friendship and music to the enterprise. And, as always, Ann Dowd Mahoney made all things possible.

J. L. M.

COPYRIGHT ACKNOWLEDGMENTS

Permission to reprint "The Need for a Religious Literary Criticism," which appeared in *Religion and the Arts* (Vol. 1, No. 1 [1996]: 124–50), has been granted by the author, Dennis Taylor, and by the Trustees of Boston College.

Permission to reprint short specified excerpts from Wallace Stevens's *Opus Posthumous*, *The Letters of Wallace Stevens*, *The Necessary Angel*, and *The Palm at the End of the Mind* has been granted by Alfred A. Knopf, Inc., and by Faber and Faber, Ltd.

Permission to print an adaptation of Professor Richard Kearney's "Poetry, Language, and Identity; A Note on Seamus Heaney," which originally appeared in *The Dublin Journal* (Winter 1986), has been granted by the author.

Excerpts from "East Coker," "Little Gidding," and "The Dry Salvages" in *Four Quartets*, copyright 1943 by T. S. Eliot and renewed by Esnie Valeris Eliot, have been reprinted with the permission of Harcourt, Brace and Company. Excerpts from *Murder in the Cathedral* by T. S. Eliot, copyright 1935 and renewed 1963 by T. S. Eliot have been reprinted with permission of the publisher.

A version of Stephen Fix's essay "Prayer, Poetry, and Paradise Lost: Samuel Johnson as Reader of Milton's Christian Epic" appeared in substantially similar form in the *Journal of English Literary History* 52 (1985): 649–681. Permission to reuse material from that essay has been granted by the editors of *ELH*.

Permission to reprint specified excerpts from the *Collected Poems of Stevie Smith* has been granted by New Directions Publishing Corp. and by Professor James MacGibbon.

Special thanks to Professor J. Robert Barth, S.J., for the cover photograph of Tintern Abbey.

PREFACE

As the discourse of contemporary cultural studies has brought questions of race, nationality, and gender to the center of the critical enterprise, there is in some circles a strong sense that religion, or perhaps religious experience, should likewise command the attention of the academic and of the larger critical community. Certainly one important aspect of the cultural situation of men and women—from primitive to modern and postmodern societies—has been the response to or questioning of some higher force or power beyond the quotidian. It need not be the special language of Christian or Jew or Moslem or Buddhist, although such traditions have produced their own special stories. It may even be the wildly exuberant quest of André Gregory of the remarkable screenplay *My Dinner With André* for a purpose in his life, for a new kind of experience that required his learning "how you can go through a looking-glass into another kind of perception, in which you have that sense of being united to all things, and suddenly you understand everything."

Or it may be the more measured response of the physicist Sir Arthur Eddington in *The Nature of the Physical World*:

> We all know that there are regions of the human spirit untrammeled by the world of physics. In the mystic sense of the creation around us, in the expression of art, in a yearning towards God, the soul grows upward and finds the fulfillment of something implanted in its nature. The sanction for this development is within us, a striving born with consciousness of an Inner Light proceeding from a greater power than ours. Science can scarcely question this sanction, for the pursuit of science springs from a striving which the mind is impelled to follow, a questioning that will not be suppressed.

Whether this force or presence becomes the occasion for some sort of institutional configuration or for some less formal, more personal expression of celebration, adoration, petition, or even doubt or loss, it has certainly found articulation, however fleeting at times, in the metaphor or symbol of story, drama, or poem. Whether one sees the passage from ritual to art as progress or decline, says J. Robert Barth, s.j., in the *Encyclopedia of Religion*, "it remains true that religion has continued to be seen as part of the poetic experience. While no one would claim an identity of religion and poetry, a relationship between them has often been affirmed, even as new theories of poetry have emerged."

It may be that the subject requires no elaborate discussion. Weren't the origins of the great Greek tragedies —with their rare blending of music, dance, and poetry—ultimately religious, part of celebrations honoring the god Dionysus? Haven't the earliest prayers and stories of the Bible taken a poetic form, finding in language and imagery a way to translate the untranslatable, to articulate the heart's deepest desires? The larger question perhaps relates to the compatibility or companionability of literature and religious experience. To what extent do they intersect? When does one so dominate the other as to rob it of its integrity? What is it that accounts for an abundance of simply bad religious literature? Should artist and priest, art and theology simply go their separate ways?

There are, of course, impressive voices that have recognized problems and raised objections. Samuel Johnson, a Church of England man and a major Enlightenment literary figure, contended in a famous passage in his *Life of Edmund Waller* that "the ideas of Christian theology are too simple for eloquence, too sacred for fiction and too majestic for ornaments." And William Wordsworth, lover of nature and one of the great Romantic poets, while finding an "affinity between religion and poetry," nevertheless contended that "no poetry has been more subject to distortion than that species the argument and scope of which is religious; and no lovers of art have gone further astray than the pious and the devout." Even T. S. Eliot, whose *Four Quartets* strike many readers as major works of religious art, in his early-career essay "Religion and Literature," described the religious poet as one "who is dealing with a confined part of the subject matter: who is leaving out what men consider their major passions and thereby confessing their ignorance of them." And Jonathan Culler, distinguished contemporary theorist and critic, has taken a remarkable tack in his sharply negative observation, "Recently, there has been a striking revival of interest in the sacred. Instead of leading the critique of superstition, comparative literature is contributing to the legitimation of religious discourse" (*Profession 1984*: Modern Language Association).

At the same time there are many eloquent tributes to poetry's religious power. There is Sir Philip Sidney's memorable 1595 Renaissance *Apology for Poetry*, with its combining of classical and Christian strains. Citing Aristotle as his authority, he describes poetry as "an art of imitation . . . that is to say, a representing, counterfeiting, or figuring forth; with this end, to teach and delight." His major examples, "both in antiquity and excellence, were they that did imitate the inconceivable excellencies of God—the Psalms of David, Solomon's Song of Songs, others." Percy Bysshe Shelley, in the Romantic rhetoric of his 1821 *Defense of Poetry*, broadens the vocation of poet to include all those "who bring into a certain propinquity with the beautiful and true, that partial apprehension of the invisible world which is called religion." With proper respect for the great canonical statements, some of the axioms articulated by the modern American poet Richard Eberhart at the 1968 meeting of the Modern Language Association of America catch quite nicely the points of intersection of literature and religious experience. "Poetry," he says in one, "orders our imaginings!" And in another, "Poetry makes the spiritual real. It erects value and substantive meaning." Engaging axioms—and especially engaging given the current culture wars with deeply divided camps arguing, on the one hand, for the unique beauty and transcendence of works of art and, on the other, for the same works of art as material objects.

This volume has grown out of an awareness of interesting recent developments in the broad but, I think, relatively undeveloped field of Religion and Literature—small programs in English, Theology, and Religious Studies Departments, interdisciplinary ventures, conferences, and a small but growing number of impressive journals in the field. Such a volume could introduce broad and more focused areas of discussion, and could enrich college and university courses, adult education and discussion groups, and the reading experience of those readers who find the field a source of interest and reflection. Many of us have, of course, already benefited greatly from the pioneering efforts of scholars like Amos Wilder, Nathan Scott, Northrop Frye, T. R. Wright, and others, and we hope to build on such strong foundations.

This is, at least it is the hope of the contributors, a different kind of book. Given the large body of critical discourse that has developed around New Historicism and Feminism—to take just two prominent contemporary theoretical strategies—there seems to be a genuine need for fresh and original voices who can contribute to the fuller development of a similar body of discourse about the intersections of religion and literature. Part One of this volume will attend to some of the large theoretical issues.

Dennis Taylor, editor of the newly launched scholarly journal *Religion and the Arts*, introduces and addresses in Part One that central and compelling question of how the critic finds the kind of discourse adequate to religious experience, how that critic can avoid the vagueness and sentimentality that weakens much contemporary writing. After a wide-ranging yet penetrating survey of the contemporary critical scene, he offers specific examples of a religious view of poems by Yeats and Stevens, stories by Flannery O'Connor and Sandra Cisneros, a film of Ingmar Bergman, a novel of Dostoyevsky, and a journal of Ettie Hillesum. This introductory probe reveals Taylor's attempt to define a difficult field and to, at one and the same time, underline his sense of the religious and to bring to the process an appropriate critical rigor.

J. A. Appleyard, a specialist in reading theory, traces the levels of developing maturity in readers, and, with Thomas Merton's *The Seven Storey Mountain* as his exemplary text, focuses on parallels between reading and spiritual development, specifically on the psychological dimensions of reading religious texts. Philip Rule, drawing on the work of a feminist theorist like Anne Mellor, warns of the "stereotyping of male and female cognitive operations." Using two biographies of John Keats—one by W. J. Bate, the other by Aileen Ward—and two major texts—the Mount Snowdon passage in Wordsworth's *Prelude* and Elizabeth Barrett Browning's *Aurora Leigh*—he underlines the gender issue and its vitality for any inclusive critical discussion of religious writing.

John Boyd brings a more specifically theological dimension to bear on the question of the volume, focusing sharply on the Paschal action—death and resurrection—in religious writing, in T. S. Eliot's *Murder in the Cathedral* and the *Four Quartets* and in Graham

Greene's *The Power and the Glory*. And Charles and Jane Ranney Rzepka offer a fascinating perspective on the current cultural climate, a climate of cross-dressing, of role reversal with the literary theorist and critic becoming the preacher and the preacher, especially in mainline Protestant denominations, generally neglecting the "amoral secularism traditionally associated with literary studies."

Part Two brings together a number of critics/teachers offering somewhat more practical approaches to questions of literature and religious experience in particular texts. Robert Kiely, a Victorian scholar with special interests in the genre of saints' lives, offers what he calls a post-Modern reflection on the *Rule* and *Life* of Saint Benedict. Sounding very much like the New Historicist returning to a classic text, he cites the celebrated Abbess Hildegard of Bingen and her interesting reply to the question of a monastic community of men on how best to follow the *Rule* and a section of Pope Gregory the Great's "Life and Miracles of Saint Benedict," and calls attention to how flexible the *Rule* is for both. Hildegard emphasizes the reality of a monastery of men, focusing on an "insignificant detail" like sleeping arrangements and especially underclothing as a "protection against the temptations of the flesh." Gregory, responding to an ingenuous questioner, regards the *Rule* of Benedict as a great way of spreading the faith. Yet at the same time he has doubts about its becoming too harsh and legalistic, and reminds the questioner about God's continuing presence and the importance of a good monk's knowing and being true to himself.

Stephen Fix, currently editing the "Life of Milton" for the Yale Works of Samuel Johnson, stresses how inadequate sharply defined critical categories can be in one's attempt to come to terms with a religious work. For Fix, Johnson's response to *Paradise Lost*—both its subject matter and its rhetoric—shaped his seemingly quirky critique. Long though the great religious epic is, removed as it seems from human interest, Johnson saw the reading of it as a duty. Critical rules cannot adequately explain how we are "held captive by Milton's sublime greatness," how we are provoked to "confront the story of our lost innocence; and finally, we break down." For Johnson, Fix argues, we need not just "recreation" but "re-creation," "something more than literature can give."

A number of essays in Part Two deal with particular writers and texts as they reveal the intersection of literature and religion. Kevin Van Anglen underlines the religious dimension in Emerson's and Thoreau's Transcendentalism. Using what he regards as "a less pre-programmed approach to the question of secularization and the persistence of religious traditionalism" will enable us to read Transcendentalist texts like Emerson's *Divinity School Address* and Thoreau's *Walden* with greater sensitivity to their complexity for embodying contradictions in matters of belief and unbelief. John Mahoney, intrigued by the often bleak portrait of religious questions in the poems of Stevie Smith, uses that very skepticism as a way of approaching works like "Not Waving But Drowning," "God Speaks," and "No Categories."

J. Robert Barth, who has written extensively about the Coleridgean imagination, views Hopkins's poetry in the tradition of the great Romantics, especially Wordsworth and Coleridge, emphasizing Hopkins's "awareness of the relationship between the created world and the world of transcendent reality," "the sacramental sense." Through poems like "The Wreck of the Deutschland," "God's Grandeur," and "The Windhover," Barth demonstrates, "we draw close not only to creation but to the Creator." Michael Raiger ranges over several Flannery O'Connor stories, commenting that they reveal not so much Hopkins's "enjoyment of the natural as the sign of God's presence" as moments of "extremity" where grace is revealed. Raiger traces in stories like *The Artificial Nigger, Revelation*, and *A Good Man Is Hard to Find* creatures "blasted by sin beyond the recognition of God's image, but nevertheless held in the superabundance of God's gift of being." In O'Connor the grotesque leaves "space for the sublime vision."

John Anderson, noting how a kind of canonical bias against religious poetry has contributed to the exclusion of certain kinds of poets, especially women poets, sees the challenge of reading and studying such poets and with them important religious poetry. Working closely with the nineteenth-century British poet Charlotte Smith and with sections of her epic *The Emigrants* and the so-called Middleton sonnet from her collection of *Elegiac Sonnets*, he views Smith as addressing religious matters from the "social role of the Church to psychological portraits of a woman's struggle between faith and despair."

Henry Louis Gates, Jr., using as his text "the Fathers have eaten sour grapes" passage from Ezechiel, finds it a stunning cautionary tale on the "notion of the heritability of guilt across generations and across time." Discussing Jewish–African American relations and highlighting a recent New York conference that looked for common ground on such issues as slavery and social justice, he vigorously uses Ezechiel's words to protest "score-settling" and to view the past as a "wellspring of moral courage." Richard Kearney, philosopher and literary theorist, takes Seamus Heaney, a recent Nobel Prize winner for poetry, as his subject. Rejecting a narrow image of Heaney as remaining "faithful to the primacy of the provincial" or as a "good old homespun Catholic," Kearney sees the poet before the Irishman, and explores in the poetry the "pivotal motif of homecoming." In a remarkable comprehensive overview of a range of poems, he gives notable attention to Heaney's *Station Island* (Lough Derg in the North is a familiar place of pilgrimage and of spiritual meditation), calling special attention to the ways in which the poet keeps returning to "an exploration of the homing instincts of religious and political reverence."

Melinda Ponder, continuing the concern with gender and literary theory raised by Philip Rule, brings to the fore a woman poet more famous for having written the words of "America the Beautiful" in 1893, her prayer for a badly fractured country. But the chief concern of her essay is Bates's figuring of Katharine Coman, her Wellesley College friend, faculty colleague, and role model, as a female Savior who rescued her from spiritual anguish. Bates's sonnets, greatly influenced by Christina Rossetti, capture vividly, Ponder argues, "Coman's ministering presence in her spiritual life."

Dorothy Judd Hall, currently writing extensively on the poetry of Wallace Stevens, takes a cue from Louis Martz's emphasis on Stevens's "meditative temperament," his links with the "monastic tradition," and follows what she describes as his spiritual journey in poems like "Sunday Morning," "Sailing After Lunch," "The Snow Man," and "Final Soliloquy of the Interior Paramour." Hall's special concern is the coming together of two religious traditions in Stevens, "the tao of Zen meditative detachment and the Christian contemplative path, the *via negativa*."

In two wide-ranging essays on literature–religion connections,

David Leigh and Judith Wilt pursue long-standing and engaging interests that seem vitally connected to the overarching concerns of this volume. Leigh, who has recently completed a book on spiritual autobiography, offers a new method of reading and thinking about the genre. It is a method that approaches such autobiographers "separated from the mediation of a religious community" using "the methods of prose fiction." In books as different as Gandhi's *Autobiography*, *Black Elk Speaks*, Dorothy Day's *The Long Loneliness*, Nelson Mandela's *Long Walk to Freedom*, and others, Leigh locates the life-writer as narrator and deals with the plot as a kind of "spiral pilgrimage," arguing that the "modern Augustine or Teresa must also be a Faulkner or Woolf."

Judith Wilt's versatility as a scholar-teacher active in the fields of Religion and Literature and Film Theory is demonstrated in "Acts of God: Film, Religion, and 'FX.' " Tracing her own rich moviegoing experience from the blockbuster days of *Quo Vadis* to the homey worlds of *Going My Way* and *The Bells of St. Mary's* and on to the more domestic settings of *Places in the Heart* and *Household Saints*, she has come to see film not as a vehicle for religion, but film, with all its wondrous special effects, as religion. Film is religion, she contends, "in the sense that it does for the mass audience the cultural work that religions have done, supply models for ethical action and provide grounding images for ideals and desires." Film is most effective when at its most mature, offering "the sacralization of the mundane, the miracle of ordinary dailiness."

By combining the theoretical and the practical, *Seeing into the Life of Things* should serve an important need as both scholarly contribution to a developing field and valuable guide for those who read, reflect on, and discuss the literature of religious experience.

JOHN L. MAHONEY

I

Some Theoretical Perspectives

1

The Need for a Religious
Literary Criticism

Dennis Taylor

A GREAT CRITICAL NEED of our time is for ways of discussing religious or spiritual dimensions in works of literature. We live in an age of critical discourses that are expert in discussing the dimensions of class, gender, textuality, and historical context. Yet an important part of the literature we read goes untouched by our discourses, or is deconstructed, historicized, sexualized, or made symptomatic of covert power relationships. The negative hermeneutic of such reductive discourse has been thorough and successful. Attempts at a more positive non–reductive hermeneutic tend to be soft discourses, appealing to general unexamined values and a pre-converted audience. There is a need in our time for religious interpretations that are substantial enough to enter into a productive and competitive relation with the reigning critical discourses. The answer to the dilemma of skepticism and softness may simply be a sense of the intricacy of the subject. The need for a religious literary criticism not only is reflective of a current scholarly void, but also comes out of a spiritual hunger, felt by many teachers and students, for a way of discussing the intersections of their own spiritual lives with what they read. These two needs, scholarly and spiritual, reflect the extreme difficulty of the subject which invites intellectual short-circuiting and collapse at a number of points.

To say there is a great vacuum in discussions of spirituality in literature is, of course, unfair to those who have long been working in this field, and whose work might be associated with jour-

An earlier version of this essay appeared in *Religion and the Arts* 1. 1 (Fall 1996): 124–49.

nals like *Religion and Literature, Christianity and Literature, Literature and Theology, Renascence, Religion and the Arts,* and others. But even the editors and writers of these journals would probably agree that their discourse is not yet one of the major discourses of the academy.

In this essay, I point to some examples of moments in literature which cry out for a sophisticated critical treatment that has been lacking in recent decades. I list seven such moments, and with them allude to some relevant contemporary work that may contain the seeds of the discourse or discourses that we seek.

(1) Yeats's "The Man who dreamed of Faeryland" begins:

> He stood among a crowd at Dromahair;
> His heart hung all upon a silken dress,
> And he had known at last some tenderness,
> Before earth took him to her stony care;
> But when a man poured fish into a pile,
> It seemed they raised their little silver heads,
> And sang what gold morning or evening sheds
> Upon a woven world-forgotten isle
> Where people love beside the ravelled seas;
> That Time can never mar a lover's vows
> Under that woven changeless roof of boughs:
> The singing shook him out of his new ease.

The poem continues through three more stanzas, each of them representing a stage in the man's life: young love, prosperous middle age, rancorous old age, and death. And each stage is interrupted by a strange intrusion: a fish singing about a land of faithful love, a lug-worm singing about a gay exulting race, a knot-grass singing about a rich silence where lover next to lover is at peace, a worm proclaiming that God has laid his fingers on the sky. I am concerned not with interpreting this interesting and layered poem, but simply with pointing to some elements we need to find critical languages for. One element is the development of a person's life. There is an industry of psychological study on development; "character development" used to be a major category in literary criticism, but no longer. Our current discourses can do interesting things with Yeats's "Man who dreamed of Faeryland." Feminism can see the distortions of a patriarchal system controlling the man's life; Marxist analysis can see the bourgeois economic structures; new historicists can see Yeats controlled by a romantic consciousness that displaces the reality of Yeats's own placement in the power system.

But what is left over is a nagging spiritual question about the man, about the worth of his life as we see it, and as he sees it. There are the questions of where he is going, what stages he arrives at, and what is his life's meaning, in a sense of "meaning" too intellectually murky to be of interest to the semioticians. (Ogden and Richards's treatment of the "meaning of meaning" is typical of that tradition.) Even our current developmental sciences have missed some of the spiritual richness we might still find in nineteenth-century romantic *Bildungsroman*, in eighteenth-century notions of gained wisdom, in ancient Christian notions of spiritual pruning. We no longer know how to discuss wrong turnings and right turnings, achieved insights, persistent blindnesses, breakthrough moments. We shrink from defining the rich possibilities of human development.

Meanwhile, Yeats's man's life, however we define its development, is cut athwart by another dimension. At each moment when the shape of his life seems to have taken a final satisfactory shape, he experiences an interruption which perplexes and confounds. What interrupts is not another system but something that challenges all systems, something as questioning and unsettling as the best deconstructive scalpels of our critics, but suggesting something unconditioned, all-demanding, and ultimately unevadable. The grotesque triviality of the images suggests the fragile yet persistent nature of these revelations. We need to talk about the experience of a person's developing life and these odd turnings to which it is subject, as rendered in intricate detail in the literary work. What is this intimation that comes crashing into a life and upsetting its carefully constructed schemes?

To find modes of criticism that address these issues, we might look in different places. Of course, there are the developmental theorists: Erikson with his life stages and his followers with their discussions of mid-life crises, William Perry with his description of intellectual stages, Lawrence Kohlberg with his description of moral stages, James Fowler with his description of faith stages. But their schemes are relatively abstract next to the extreme intricacy of an accomplished literary work. (The 'Enneagram' system of character types may be something literary critics need to consider.) Secondly, there are the phenomenological and historical critics who simply trace the ways in which writers struggle with religious or spiritual issues: J. Hillis Miller in *The Disappearance of God: Five Nineteenth-Century Writers*, Geoffrey Hartman in *Wordsworth's Poetry, 1787–1814*, Robert Ryan in *Keats: The Religious Sense*. Ryan, for example, watches the play of Keats's mind with and within certain defined Christian positions—rejecting, accommodating, developing those positions. Ryan gives his account with no sense that he (Ryan) has a vested interest for or against the Christian positions. At the same time, there is a passionate interest at the heart of the book, which gives the discussion vitality and drama. This combination of interest and detachment is probably necessary for the kind of criticism we seek. Miller's position is certainly detached, but in *The Disappearance of God* he carefully charts the systoles and diastoles of his writers' spiritual struggles. Hartman's theme, which focuses on Wordsworth's apocalyptic imagination and his attempt to naturalize it, may be allegorical of something else, unnamed, but is explored with a thorough sense of the scholarly contexts so necessary to a successful religious criticism. For the field we seek, these books by Hartman and Miller were among their best. Ryan has not published a book since (but another is about to appear). Religious literary discourses cannot develop if there is no audience to receive and advance them.

The terms "religious," "spiritual," to which we can add the word "ethical," slide over a wide range of literary material and overlap in ways difficult to sort out. The spiritual seems to reside at the place where the religious collides with the ethical, the place where "The singing shook him out of his new ease." We need critical languages that can make these discriminations.

(2) Wallace Stevens's "The House Was Quiet and the World Was Calm" reads:

> The house was quiet and the world was calm.
> The reader became the book; and summer night
>
> Was like the conscious being of the book.
> The house was quiet and the world was calm.

The words were spoken as if there was no book,
Except that the reader leaned above the page,

Wanted to lean, wanted much most to be
The scholar to whom his book is true, to whom

The summer night is like a perfection of thought.
The house was quiet because it had to be.

The quiet was part of the meaning, part of the mind:
The access of perfection to the page.

And the world was calm. The truth in a calm world,
In which there is no other meaning, itself

Is calm, itself is summer and night, itself
Is the reader leaning late and reading there.

Frank Lentricchia, an accomplished postmodern critic with
Marxist sympathies, has been undergoing a strange pilgrimage of
late. Something, he says, has been happening to him: "these—
what?—had always the same prelude: solitude, perfect quiet in
the late morning, the end of a period of work on the writing of
the day, an empty house with not even the two cats around, and
me gazing aimlessly through the rear windows into the backyard,
a dense enclosure of trees and bushes" (41), and an extraordinary
sense of a kind of happiness comes over him. I am interested in
these moments of insight that occur in the quiet, a quiet of the
mind, a quiet of the world. What is this rich quiet, and how does
one account for its richness? At the English Institute, 1994, where
the language of Cultural Studies dominates, Barbara Johnson gave
a paper entitled "Muteness Envy," on Keats's "Ode on a Grecian
Urn." The paper argued (among other things) that the celebration
of quietness in Keats was a male celebration of female silence, a
symptom therefore of male oppression which is then projected as
an ideal form upon a female object, the silent poem or urn. Cultural Studies is very good, here in its feminist mode, at symptom-
ological readings of high cultural artifacts. But I am left with a
question: Is there an idea of muteness which is still a value to be
sought, and to be distinguished from the gagging of women? Can
Lentricchia's moment be described in a way that resists easy re-
duction (he is a white male well-paid professor). "Quiet time" is
one of our precious domestic categories; and high culture talks

about moments of being, the still point of the turning world. Can
we not distinguish (*a*) the stillness which nourishes us, from (*b*)
the stillness that is a symptom of inflicting silence on the oppressed?—so perhaps we can see both these things operating in
Keats? Or are these two readings simply at war, never to be adju-
dicated?

"It," the moment of spiritual quiet, in its many kinds and versions, is often narrated with a full sense of the moment's ironic
context, all that challenges its spiritual claims. Thus Yeats in "Vacillation" describes such a moment, the source of so much meditative energy in the poem:

> My fiftieth year had come and gone,
> I sat, a solitary man,
> In a crowded London shop,
> An open book and empty cup
> On the marble table-top.
>
> While on the shop and street I gazed
> My body of a sudden blazed;
> And twenty minutes more or less
> It seemed, so great my happiness,
> That I was blessed and could bless.

A sudden moment of digestion, like a baby's burp which produces a smile? Or something more? What are these moments of
happiness? "Happiness" is both a soft and an ultimate word,
which, with words like "joy," "sadness," "despair," "ennui,"
etc., is avoided by our current rigorous criticism. But the rigor
avoids questions of ultimate import, of primary interest to many
readers. What is an eternal moment that lasts for twenty minutes?

Some criticism helps us to approach the topic: for example,
discussions of the structure of the meditative lyric moment, as in
Louis Martz's *The Poetry of Meditation* and Meyer Abrams's adaptation of this to romantic poetry in "Structure and Style in the
Greater Romantic Lyric." Recently, Henry Weinfield (in *The
Poet Without a Name*) has followed the ins and outs of Gray's
meditation in the "Elegy." I would contrast Weinfield's approach
with the more telling but simplistic eloquence of a Roland
Barthes in "The Great Family of Man" (a classic postmodern attack on the sentimentalism of humanism). Like Barthes, Gray

(and Weinfield) knows that meditations about the universal problems of death and blight can be evasions for seeing the role of social injustice; but Gray knows that social analysis and social progress do not, in turn, solve the universal problems. One can be concerned with both kinds of problem.

What makes a lyric meditation successful? What are its distractions? Where does it get one? In a meditative moment, one may come to a profound insight into gender relations which might lead to a paper on the gender distortions of Keats. But what about the meditation itself, its structure, the phenomenon of its outcome, the sheer quality of its insight? These questions applied to the lyric meditation are like the questions we posed for the individual life in discussing Yeats's "The Man who dreamed of Faeryland." The (old) New Criticism of Brooks and Warren and company was expert at detailing the paradoxical nature of such meditations, their ironic contexts, and often drew upon religious notions of earned visions, as in Robert Penn Warren's famous essay "Pure and Impure Poetry":

> Poetry wants to be pure, but poems do not. . . . They mar themselves with cacophonies, jagged rhythms, ugly words and ugly thoughts, colloquialisms, clichés, sterile technical terms, head work and argument, self-contradictions, clevernesses, irony, realism—all things which call us back to the world of prose and imperfection. . . . The saint proves his vision by stepping cheerfully into the fires. The poet, somewhat less spectacularly, proves his vision by submitting it to the fires of irony—to the drama of his structure—in the hope that the fires will refine it. In other words, the poet wishes to indicate that his vision has been earned, that it can survive reference to the complexities and contradictions of experience. (229–30, 252)

For a number of reasons, this formulation lost respect, as the newer criticisms developed more historical insights into the "complexities and contradictions of experience" and of texts. But once criticism has entirely eliminated the vision, or reduced it to compromising historical forces, what is left? At the end of *Renaissance Self-Fashioning*, Stephen Greenblatt describes a process of conversion in which he perceived the power and necessity of new historical criticism (256–57). He "perceived" it, but what is this seeing, this vision? Is it entirely lost in the object seen? We need to stay longer with Lentricchia's puzzlement about the sheer experience of the spiritual moment. And we may need to wonder what other disciplines, represented for example in Lonergan's *Insight*, Balthasar's *The Glory of the Lord: A Theological Aesthetics*, and other texts, say about such moments.

What strange creatures we are: strings of biology which come up with insights. Our criticism needs to ponder such oddities more.

(3) In Flannery O'Connor's "The River," the following scene occurs:

> "If I baptize you," the preacher said, "you'll be able to go to the Kingdom of Christ. You'll be washed in the river of suffering, son, and you'll go by the deep river of life. Do you want that?"
> "Yes," the child said, and thought, I won't go back to the apartment then, I'll go under the river.
> "You won't be the same again," the preacher said. "You'll count." (168)

Well, there it is, the Southern Baptist language. How can such language be penetrated? We may think of it as language to be accepted as gospel, or dismissed as rant, depending on where we are on the religious spectrum. But our responses are often much more complicated than our stereotyping allows; and it would be interesting to discriminate how various religious types and nonreligious types respond to such language. Admittedly, to one group, such discrimination might seem impious; to another, it might seem bad taste. We know of at least one person who penetrated such language: O'Connor herself, a Catholic fascinated by Baptist rhetoric, who rendered it in all its grotesqueness (as she saw it) and yet with great respect. Respect for what? What content does a word like "salvation" have in our critical language, except as a term of sectarian narrowness and religious club membership? In the Baptist's speech, there is a sliding between traditional religious language and the language of psychology ("You'll count"). Is the latter something the Baptist preacher would actually say? Is it O'Connor's intrusion into the language to make it more weighty for urbane readers? (Or is it technical Calvinist terminology about the 'elect'?) In any event, are there places in which traditional religious language intersects with secular language in mutually invigorating ways? And what would such invigoration mean? Do we have a way of discussing any of these questions? Admittedly, the religious/secular relation has been much discussed in relation to British romantic poetry and the American renaissance. Abrams's *Natural Supernaturalism* for one side of the ocean, Matthiessen's *American Renaissance* for the other are magisterial accounts. But are the issues of much importance in our contemporary criticism? It is curious that Tolstoy's 'Christian' tracts seem so narrowly ideological next to his major novels; yet does the vitality of these novels have some connection with the remarkable religious development he was undergoing?

Some criticism relevant to this topic of religious/secular intersections would be criticism concerned with competing voices in a society. The problem of the religious voice is that it used to be the hegemonic standard and now is occluded by the current standard. But a criticism which simply traces the interaction of voices in a text, in the manner of Bakhtin, helps reinstate the interest of these once dominant and now despised languages. One promising result of our current discourses is to make us suspicious of the hegemony of mainstream secular discourse, and seek its cracks and flaws, and also the places where other kinds of language may have been suppressed, distorted, and dismissed, as religious language increasingly has been, at least since Nietzsche. Sociolinguistic examination of the Arnoldian standard, mainstream urbanity, is an example of such suspicion. Two examples of recent criticism unearth an occluded 'Catholic' voice in scholarly and powerful ways. One is Eric Griffiths's *The Printed Voice of Victorian Poetry*, chapter 4, which traces how Hopkins manages the relation between establishment 'Leavisian' English and the alien voice of Roman Catholicism. Another is the work of Paul Giles and Jenny Franchot tracing the Catholic 'other' in the culture of Protestant Emersonian America. These is, of course, an enormous body of work in medieval, Renaissance, and Victorian literature which carefully constructs the religious contexts. Nevertheless this criticism does not tend to enter into the major discourses of our time, or at most is used as a material to be retooled in the higher criticism of Cultural Studies. Again, there is an enormous body of American studies exploring the complex religious influences on the politics of the Founding Fathers. Liberty may in fact be a religious notion. The point is made, and then left to lie.

I have not yet mentioned the more important part O'Connor's story, the world of the little boy, the conflict of the secular parents and the evangelical baby sitter, the effect on the boy of his experience at the healing service, his transformation, and his drowning. For one of my students, the boy experiences salvation; for another, he is a cult-induced suicide. How do we get these two camps talking to each other?

There are other features in O'Connor's passage which our criticism is no longer able to discuss. For example, the theme of the "apartment" which we can call the "Waste Land" theme. Eliot mesmerized the century with his diagnosis in the most influential poem of the century. "The Waste Land" is a poem whose morality (and form) has been fiercely resisted. Its claim to make universal moral judgments has been attacked. Curiously, we live in what is probably the most judgmental era of literary criticism and yet an era in which the right to make judgments is ritually denied. Current literary discourse takes on a multitude of social oppressions and social distortions, but in a curiously narrow way, with a single focus, say, on patriarchalism, on homophobia, on racial prejudice, on child abuse. But there is a curious fanaticism and diffidence in such focuses, as though the critic declines to be pressed on his or her ultimate belief about the nature of the whole mess. Traditional religious discourse, which Eliot relied on, took on the whole mess; but this discourse is now seen as a narrow discourse of its own, based on fundamentalist religious assumptions. We have no way now of talking about widespread social ill, moral decline, anomie, lovelessness. The best lack all conviction; the worst are full of passionate intensity. A great challenge to the discourse we seek is how to avoid the puritanism and intolerance and religious violence of the past, and regain some of the scope and power of older discourses.

Of course some of our criticism, feminist, Marxist, does attempt a global overarching diagnosis of an entire civilization. But what these movements decline to consider is: what would it be like to exist in Utopia? Once the genders are made equal, and the classes eliminated, what might then happen? Ancient religious traditions are expert in treating what can happen to a promised land experience, and how it can fall prey to the seven devils of the well-fed mind. Indeed, we need an entire reconsideration of the tendencies of the mind which lead to patriarchalism, homophobia, racial prejudice, child abuse, and the rest of it. Mill's "A Crisis in My Mental History, One Stage Onward," chapter 5 of his *Autobiography*, may stand for the point where the well-balanced, reasonable mind collapses into something else:

> In this frame of mind it occurred to me to put the question directly to myself, "Suppose that all your objects in life were realized; that all the changes in institutions and opinions which you are looking forward to, could be completely effected at this very instant: would this be a great joy and happiness to you?" And an irrepressible self-consciousness distinctly answered, "No!" At this my heart sank within me: the whole foundation on which my life was constructed fell down. All my happiness was to have been found in the continual pursuit of this end. The end had ceased to charm, and how could there ever again be any interest in the means? I seemed to have nothing left to live for. (81)

Juxtapose this, for example, with a passage by Fredric Jameson in *The Political Consciousness*, a passage admirable for taking the risk it does, but a passage which does not take into account the elements that constituted Mill's crisis:

> For Marxism, indeed, only the emergence of the post-individualistic social world, only the reinvention of the collective and the associative, can concretely achieve the "decentering" of the individual subject called for by such diagnoses; only a new and original form of collective social life can overcome the isolation and monadic autonomy of the older bourgeois subjects in such a way that individual consciousness can be lived—and not merely theorized—as an "effect of structure" (Lacan). (125)

No wonder that our critics rarely risk such "positive" passages, all too easily subject to the postmodernist knife. A positive hermeneutic must engage all the things that make mockery of it and threaten to make it null and void. Mill's attempt to recover from his crisis by using Marmontel, Carlyle, and Wordsworth is less interesting than his posing the question that knocks his world into a vacuum. We need some way of talking about these ultimate dissatisfactions. Jameson probably cannot 'see' Mill's point because for Jameson the point is immediately suspect as a wrong diagnosis, a false consciousness controlled by an unreflected bourgeois mentality. Even the question "what if?" (all your objects is life were realized) is assumed to be out of court. But questions like this have a way of recurring.

(4) One of Ingmar Bergman's darkest films, *Through a Glass Darkly*, ends:

> MINUS (full of anxiety): Give me some proof of God.
> Silence.
> MINUS: You can't.
> DAVID: Yes, I can. But you must listen very carefully to what I'm saying, Minus.
> MINUS: That's just what I need, to listen.
> DAVID: It is written: *God is love.*
> MINUS: For me that's just words and nonsense.
> DAVID: Wait a moment and don't interrupt. (60)

The moment is a delicate one; the language cries out to break down into cliché and inadequacy. David walks a tightrope with his son, and tries to find some way to speak of the love he believes in, in order to give his son a reason for living. He succeeds for the moment.

Do we have a language to talk about the delicacy of a spiritual conversation, its perils, its successes, its implications? Going on, do we have a language to talk about spiritual quest? Do we have a language to talk about love? One of the difficulties of the topic is untangling the relation of the religious and the spiritual; or, better perhaps, the religious and the ethical, with the spiritual some kind of linking category. Can we discriminate these dimensions at work in a literary passage in the way Kierkegaard recommended. If we cannot, what happens to such passages?

Often literature has these climactic spiritual moments; the penultimate paragraph of O'Connor's "The Artificial Nigger" is a preeminent example, yet it is often attacked as religious pabulum. The last sentence of Carver's "Cathedral" is another, though no one attempts to explain it. It merely reads: " 'It's really something,' I said" (17), and yet the story explodes with some immense illumination in that last line. The end of *My Dinner with*

André is another, though Wally's transformation is so minimalist it might not be noticed; and it is keyed by André's final question: "A wife. A husband. A son. A baby holds your hands, and then suddenly there's this huge man lifting you off the ground, and then he's gone. Where's that son?" (112–13). What kind of questions are these? Because we cannot talk about any such moments, we cannot discriminate more difficult ones, like that experienced by Charles Ryder in *Brideshead Revisited*. When he finds himself praying that Lord Brideshead make the sign of the cross on his deathbed, if only out of courtesy to the family, how do we assess such a moment, which arouses such intensely opposed readings—as a religious breakthrough or a religious breakdown? The end of *Babette's Feast* is another, though the tipsy general's toast ("that which we have chosen is given us, and that which we have refused is, also and at the same time, granted us") (60) is so laced with irony and humor that it has resisted negative commentary. But what does it mean? Some mystical nonsense, best left untouched? Or some deep paradox needing to be explored?

The (old) New Critics were expert in paradoxes, and they were expert in dealing with body/spirit dichotomies, virtue/corruption dichotomies, heaven/earth dichotomies. With the New Critics' decline in reputation, these dichotomies were theorized as the surface tensions produced by the hidden conflicts of a bourgeois capitalist economy, a sort of fiddling with paradoxes while the poor burned. But the paradoxes may not have been destroyed, simply moved and rehidden. The positive terms in the New Critical paradoxes, spirit, virtue, heaven, have now no positive content. ("What, on the level of the ideologeme, remains a conceptual *antinomy*, must now be grasped, on the level of the social and historical subtext, as a *contradiction*" [Jameson 117].) Yet the old terms have powerful content for many people. The problem afflicts the artist as well as the reader. Bergman originally hoped that the end of "Through a Glass Darkly" would be a near-Paradiso moment in secular terms, but looking back he rejected the ending (a sort of reverse Chaucerian recantation). It is curious how such terms sometimes have great vitality, and at other times fall flat. The whole question of how such terms are used in literature, the question of tone, is one of the great questions for religious literary analysis; but where is such analysis to be had? What would it mean to say "Love is real. You must listen

very carefully" so that it had a full and rich content, to be expli-
cated by a sophisticated criticism?

But careful analysis, and debate, about the way in which spiritual terms are used in literature, are what our criticism needs.
Here the multiple new historicist conversions, Miltonists seeing
through Milton at last, Wordsworthians seeing through Wordsworth at last, are helpful, if only in highlighting language which
now needs to be re-debated. Kierkegaard's mode of talking about
marriage rhetoric in the second volume of *Either/Or* may be
worth returning to, if we can get around Nietzsche. And then
perhaps we can get further to Kierkegaard's recantation of 'or,'
his teleological suspension of the ethical, in *Fear and Trembling*.

(5) Sandra Cisneros's story "Little Miracles, Kept Promises" is
simply a list of prayer notes left at a shrine; for example:

> Dear Niño Fidencio
>   I would like for you to help me get a job with good pay, benefits,
> and a retirement plan . . . Many thanks
> > César Escandón
> > Pharr, Tejas

> Father Almighty,
>   Teach me to love my husband again. Forgive me.
> > s.
> > Corpus Christi

> Virgencita de Guadalupe. For a long time I wouldn't let you in my
> house. I couldn't see you without seeing my ma each time my
> father came home drunk and yelling, blaming everything that ever
> went wrong in his life on her. (118–19, 127)

Cisneros's story is a rich example of how a writer's interest in
religious language and objects can bypass negative hermeneutics,
and simply rest fascinated in the spectacle of the religious details
and behaviors of a mainstream religion, here a Spanish-American
community in the southwest United States. Also, this minority
religious culture, complete with its prayers, devotions, religious
formulas, superstitions, and idolatries (can we distinguish the last
two from the first two?) is then connected with the type of hero-
ine we expect in a *New Yorker* short story, a self-motivated average

sensuous woman, who uses the language of her people to express her own desires.

The remarkable quality of the last prayer is a sort of feminist appropriation of traditional religious language, but without doing great violence to that language, and without subsiding into the comfortable formulas we might associate with New Age and modern goddess religion. (One difficulty with our language, or lack thereof, is that it invites stereotypical phrases like "New Age," when in fact the interior dynamics of New Age, and its complicated contact with traditional religion, are of extreme interest.) Somehow Cisneros leaves both sides invigorated, the language of piety and the language of personally appropriated piety. What is this life that both sides have? How does such language lead to personal enrichment, when supposedly it should suppress? 'Personal enrichment,' of course, is a phrase belonging to another language, that of psychology and pop psychology. We need a tough critical language which can trace the issues and nature of personal enrichment in the complex embodiment of a work of literature. This leads to a number of themes which our critical languages need to explore.

First, the great difficulty in writing about religious language, or in religious language, is that no language is more subject to parody. It is extremely difficult to scalpel through the parodic distortions of a religious language to seek the right tone which Bergman, with controversial success, sought in "Through a Glass Darkly." Our examples so far have struggled with distortions of sectarian points of view: the Southern Baptist rhetoric of O'Connor, the Dutch Reform rhetoric of Dinesen, the secular European piety of Bergman, the Spanish Catholic language of Cisneros; and all four suggest a truth of some sort in these languages. What is this truth? Is it a universal truth that cuts across all four, some lowest common denominator (with all the perils, as a result, of being bland)? Or is it a truth to be found only in that particular denomination, as it seeks to articulate its own religious language (and thus only an ideology)?

Second, one of the promising areas of critical religious research is the way in which religious traditions, until recently considered as supporting colonialist and capitalist structures, in fact have supported the aspirations of minority cultures and races and genders. Some of the most exciting work now may well be in explorations of the use of religion by enslaved Negroes, by inhabitants of ghettos, by poor frontier women or by women generally. Thus Jameson again: "the work of Eugene Genovese on black religion restores the vitality of these utterances by reading them, not as replication of imposed beliefs, but rather as a process whereby the hegemonic Christianity of the slave-owners is appropriated, secretly emptied of its content and subverted to the transmission of quite different oppositional and coded messages" (86). Completely subverted? Maybe. In "The Little Black Boy," does Blake entirely subvert Christian doctrines? But the point about appropriation is a very good one, and accounts for one of the vital parts of current Cultural Studies. As to the depth and nature of the subversion, I would say that the issue is worth discussing.

In Cisneros we smile at the religious language, but the satire is not destructive, but rather part of a complex exploratory presentation of human desire and anguish. The religious objects are simply presented as an integral part of the experience. Cultural Studies is often focused on the material object of culture; and 'materialism' is a term often put forth as though it explained something. One discovery of Giles's book is that of a Catholic communal materialism which reminds us that our reverence for material practices can derive from both religious and anti-religious sources. In the current work of art historians, the role of icons is being discussed without being tied to the old Protestant/Catholic, or Christian/pagan, controversies. There is a freshness in the air, a willingness simply to see how religious objects work.

Other interesting ways of assimilating religious language include Kathryn Stockton's *God Between Their Lips*, where the lesbian agenda does not replace but in fact reopens for us the intrinsic interest of Victorian religious language. John Maynard brings together the competing but also cooperating discourses of Victorian erotics and Victorian religion, to their mutual invigoration. Philippe Sollers's novel *Women* is one of the more notable examples of novels fascinated by the vitality of Catholic religious language, and the way it intersects with one's own sensual life. Etty Hillesum's *An Interrupted Life* eventually integrates her experience with an eclectic religious language composed of Jewish, Christian, and other elements.

(6) In *The Brothers Karamazov*, Alyosha is with Grushenka, and Dostoyevsky writes:

This woman, this "dreadful" woman, had no terror for him now, none of that terror that had stirred in his soul at any passing thought of woman. On the contrary, this woman, dreaded above all women, sitting now on his knee, holding him in her arms, aroused in him now a quite different, unexpected, peculiar feeling, a feeling of the intensest and purest interest without a trace of fear, of his former terror. (III.vii, 419–20)

We glimpse briefly—and it is surprising how brief such glimpses are in such a long novel written to expand on such glimpses—the point where a personality experiences an upheaval that leads to spiritual growth. When we think of narrative and story, "spiritual growth" is a central issue. Yet nowhere is the limitation of our current discourses more visible than when it comes to thinking about this notion. The Victorian novel is more or less organized around moments of spiritual growth, or spiritual failure, moments in which a character breaks through, or does not, into a new level of generosity, understanding, compassion, honesty, remorse, forgiveness. *He Knew He Was Right* and *Can You Forgive Her?* are titles pointedly designed by Trollope to highlight this tradition. Thomas Hardy rejected the religious argument that suffering is somehow worth it if it leads to spiritual growth. But he found the topic of central importance. Our current discourse does not. What is spiritual growth? What impedes it? What furthers it? Does it have beginning points and end points? Is individual spiritual growth part of a larger system of some sort? What is its importance if, meanwhile, thousands are being bombed? What is the relation between spiritual growth and social justice? We need the language to discuss these things.

As to hints and directions, the new ethical criticism (from Wayne Booth to Hillis Miller) may provide one kind of model. But there can be something potentially static and resented in ethical criticism: "such sinister and silent collusion between particular, concrete arrangements of power and an abstract and 'universal' style of representation seemed to many to be the peculiar speciality of ethics" (Harpham 388). Political criticism has shown how the humanistic 'subject' of ethics is constructed by discourses that often exclude others. We need a more dynamic notion of the spiritual subject in its many varieties. We need a way to place the ethical view within a larger structure, like that of developing spiritual lives. Another productive model is Rosemary Haught-on's *The Transformation of Man*, the most interesting part of which is its four stories, the first about two siblings who have a fight but as a result 'get somewhere.' Haughton represents a number of theologians who have become interested in the role of "story" in religious experience, the story we tell of ourselves to others, the story a society tells about itself, a story with parts and implications. The idea of "story" brings together the individual and the social, as in Lévi-Strauss's account of the way myths finesse contradictions in social life: new historicism, like Jameson's, is expert at unearthing hidden contradictions, but not so good at discussing how these are negotiated by the individual, and to what effect. Is there a right story for the individual, a story as 'seen by God,' however changeable moment by moment and adaptable to new circumstances? 'Getting somewhere' is a notion explored in Etty Hillesum's *An Interrupted Life*, the most articulated interior account of a spiritual journey and transformation since St. Thérèse's *Story of a Soul*. (When has *that* book been discussed in our criticism, or how could it be, except, as it has, in an eerily fascinated Freudian manner?). Is there such a thing as getting somewhere into greater goodness, greater truth, greater beauty, greater justice, a getting somewhere, for the individual and society, that is not prescriptive and universalist in a bad sense? Are some stories more clarifying than others? Cultural Studies is expert at unearthing cultural stories, but is unable to discriminate better from worse. What we need for spiritual growth is the kind of criticism we saw at its best in Miller's *The Disappearance of God* and Hartman's *Wordsworth's Poetry*, books not particularly concerned with the concept of spiritual growth, but showing careful phenomenological tracings of the spiritual life; yet these works seem to exist in a late new critical time warp of little relevance to today. Alyosha's breakthrough when he recovers his religion is described in terms very similar to Stephen Dedalus's breakthrough when he rejects his religion, and both are rooted in Pauline and Augustinian moments of conversion. How do we render such moments to ourselves in our own terms?

The great obstacle to much of these considerations may be the claims of Cultural Studies for an extreme relativism and particularism. If in present religious articles, positive terms like "transcendental," "spiritual," "divine," "numinous," "mystical" are coded words with little content, the same applies to the negative terms common in Cultural Studies: "essentialism," "totalizing," "humanism," "universalism," etc. An informed religious criticism can help clarify the conceptual blur in both these negative and these positive terms. "Universalism," for example, may be attacked on social or epistemological grounds: on social grounds, when a narrow class value (Arnoldian culture) is promoted as universal; on epistemological grounds, when any concept is shielded from deconstruction. The religious answer to both "universalisms" (which confusingly appeal to each other) is that social universals have continually to be reexamined to get to the real universals associated with the poor, and that epistemological universals have continually to be questioned in the light of the religious challenge suspicious of intellectual substitutes for God. Several 'religion and literature' essays are currently exploring the 'mystical' dimension of Derrida, with his sense of how terms take over, dissolve, recombine, and tie a religious experience to an endlessly receding horizon.

There are also interesting intersections now occurring among the various discourses which try to reinstate "presence" against the Derridean deconstruction or, better, by means of the pruning first demanded by such deconstruction. Some critics are converging on a material presence called "the body," Joyce's poor dogsbody, the body of the poor, the tortured body. In some orthodox Christian sects, Christ is material man. Conrad's *Heart of Darkness* pursues its deconstructive sense of lost metaphysical presence, but for all its horrific rhetoric may miss a more concrete presence, the persons of the natives: how much of this blindness is Marlow's and how much Conrad's? And a treatise could be written on the curious intersection between Christian pragmatism and Rortyan pragmatism, each oddly distrustful of universalisms: how can you love God whom you cannot see if you cannot love your neighbor whom you can see?

(7)
> Whose spirit is this? we said, because we knew
> It was the spirit that we sought and knew
> That we should ask this often as she sang.
>   —Wallace Stevens, "The Idea of Order at Key West"

The phrase has been ringing in my ears for several weeks: you need courage to put that into words. God's name. S. [Spier] once said to me that it took quite a long time before he dared to say "God," without feeling that there was something ridiculous about it. Even though he was a believer. And he said he prayed every night, prayed for others. And, shameless and brazen as always, wanting to know everything there is to know, I asked, "What exactly do you say when you pray?" And he was suddenly overcome with embarrassment, this man who always has clear, glass-bright answers to all my most searching and intimate questions, and he said shyly: "That I cannot tell you. Not yet. Later—"

—Etty Hillesum, *An Interrupted Life* 76

This enterprise of seeking a religious critical language may come tumbling down around this topic. We have no way of talking about God in literary criticism. Yet the lesser terms we use, 'meaning of life,' 'getting somewhere,' 'spiritual development,' if we use them at all, tend inexorably to raise the God-question. And if they do not, they tend to revert to reductive modes of discourse. And because God comes tumbling in behind these questions, literary criticism avoids them—but to its cost, the result often being an evasive Pyrrhonian skepticism. Of course our literary historians can talk about writers' conceptions of God, and can do so in very distinguished and helpful ways, usually by avoiding the God-term and replacing it with "religion." "God" is the place in the discourse where scholarly neutrality slips into something else, negative, positive, evasive. It is the place where historical scholarship meets a major issue, and steps back so that the historical structure will not be endangered (often a good move). It is the place where the critic, like Spier the Jungian analyst who is Etty's mentor in *An Interrupted Life*, is most embarrassed, most exposed, most naked. It demands talk about ultimate questions, indeed the ultimate question. Yet if such talk is excluded, we miss the pith and core and "Ahnung" of the literary drive in many cases. From Ingmar Bergman to Woody Allen, from James Joyce to John Updike, the God-question haunts and perplexes and burns, as much as it did for Augustine. But we are unable to talk about the essential thing. Why?

For the historical critic, the question of the existence of God evokes various responses: (*a*) rejection, which reveals itself in the hostility of the critic and shows up as anti-religious agenda in many new historicist works; (*b*) acceptance, which reveals itself in bland acceptance as in the high Victorian mode, and marginal religious 'criticism' today; (*c*) suspension of the question, as in the best of historical scholarship cited above. "C" usually leaves us with a haunted feeling and at the edge of questions like: What do we really think of this God business, or of Keats's, or Fitzgerald's, or Emerson's ultimate view? The question is thought to be best avoided, but doing so can vitiate the scholarship. For example, E. P. Thompson's interpretation of the working movement and its attendant literature in *The Making of the English Working Class* is hurt by his excessive hostility to the Methodist theology and theology itself. Walter Haughton's magisterial *Victorian Frame of Mind* is flawed by its identification of Christianity with Puritan Christianity, and so misses the complexity of religious history. Cultural Studies and its attendant disciplines are hard-edged with ultimate evaluation, though evaluation of a 'this goes without saying' nature. We need to bring up from the depths the ghosts of what we are evaluating, and to evaluate them in the open. The biggest ghost is God. And here Edward Said's anger (at that "religious" veering toward "the private and hermetic over the public and social") and Jonathan Culler's dismay (that religious criticism is undermining the energetic demythologizing of comparative literature) become relevant. At least these critics are willing to talk about the question, and demand that we talk about a subject politely excluded from serious conversation. Paradoxically, religious critics are not ready to talk, except to the already converted.

Spier is afraid to talk about prayer, because it would require him to talk about God. How can one use the word "God" in a sentence in a literary critical work? We can at least be aware of the number of quotation marks we use, as in the case of the Victorian congregation, some of whom heard the preacher speak literally (without quotation marks), others who heard single quotations marks, and others who heard double quotation marks. The believer's 'God,' the questioner's "God," the skeptic's "God" all represent voices needing to be heard. (Imagine Newman, Arnold, and Mill sitting in the same congregation.) The intricacy and brilliance of a modern religious poem like Geoffrey Hill's "The Mystery of the Charity of Charles Péguy" is partly due to its management of these various voices.

One of the many reasons for avoidance is that the God-issue introduces an enormous host of problems (and suddenly makes relevant two thousand years of theologizing—what an immense load to add to our already overloaded graduate students). If there is no God, everything is permitted, says Ivan Karamazov. But if there is a God, everything goes crazy. Also, all the worst bogies seem to be reintroduced: resignation, superstition, religious wars, questions of old morality. Also, a critic's entire life is suddenly at stake, his or her whole long, often painful, relation to a religious tradition which may have penetrated at vulnerable times, often via parents, into one's deepest sense of self, of sex, of life vision.

We seem in a terrible dilemma: we cannot talk about it, but if we don't, we ignore something fundamental at the heart of the work. So our powerful critical languages go on poking at what seem to be edges, until we decide (as in a common new historicist conversion) that the edge is the center. But like Melville's whale, the God-question rises up from the displaced edge and threatens to overwhelm us.

Of all the topics in my laundry list, this is the most important and the most difficult. I cannot imagine what such a language would look like in our culture. But we could at least talk about remnants of God, or hungers for God, or 'experiences' of God, as they occur in literary works and in our experience of literary works; and in fact this is what my seven examples do. If religious language is a language of desire, what is the desire for? For a lost womb, for a classless society, for no death, for God? When is the desire misshapen? How is the desire fulfilled? How does the language of desire become distorted, and religious phrasing a distortion? A form of literary criticism I find interesting is Kierkegaard's *Fear and Trembling* which manages to talk, not about God, but about Abraham's faith, in a witty and circumambient manner, circling the fort, trying out theories of the case, coming up with paradoxical formulations, and in the end at least opening up to us the fascination and the mystery and the power of Abraham. Perhaps there are ways of talking about things we really cannot talk about very well. Deconstructive criticism is notorious for a sometimes frolicky consciousness about itself, because of its self-consciousness about its own vulnerability to deconstruction. And in talk about God, self-consciousness is put to its most intense test.

Religious critical discourse, when it is 'God-talk,' may be some personal form of musing as in Lentricchia; it may be reinvesting marginalized religious discourse as in Cisneros; it may be playing with the edges of religious and secular discourse as in Bergman and O'Connor; it may be some further kind of history writing that finesses passionate interest into objective reporting. Harold Bloom's *The American Religion* is an interesting case for its historical insight into some of our least fashionable religions, and its odd agenda. Bloom's own theology of God as a version of the autonomous imagination is strongly engaged and thus strongly subject to exposure. Another place to look is to our recent 'literary' biblical criticism, as practiced by Frye and Kermode, Alter and Hartman, Girard and Bloom. The oddest of these, again, is Bloom with his theory of the J writer and her version of the uncanny pre-priestly Yahweh who creates and murders. Bloom's strong "misreading" again represents at least an engaged criticism which dares to frame the fearful symmetry of the issue. Whatever an adequate discourse might be, we need a mode of analysis, a tough and critical mode of proceeding, which takes into account all sides of the case, which is neither dismissive nor gullible, which seeks to "explore" in Eliot's sense and in a manner which is of interest to feminists, new historicists, politically engaged writers, and to all who have a pressing interest in the culture of our time.

The above seven passages make little sense if the God-question is put aside. Yeats's dream is illusion, Stevens's quiet is non-noise, O'Connor's preacher man is a con, Bergman's David is playing word games, Cisneros's prayers are superstitions, Alyosha's change of heart is a mood-swing, and Stevens's 'spirit' is honorific rhetoric. Etty's Spier *should* be ashamed of himself for lending an otherwise honest mind to ancient hocus-pocus. Of course, a theological approach to these moments can flatten them out as fully as the non-theological approach; and a non-theological approach then leads to other ways to make the passages interesting, through deconstruction, through political interpretation, through a feminist analysis, etc. But my argument is that if we are not able somehow to keep the God-question open, we are poor readers, because the question is open for the writers we study.

Another interesting hint for such discussion is the controversial ending of Jameson's *The Political Unconscious*. Jameson's final question has similarities to the question behind this essay:

how is it possible for a cultural text which fulfills a demonstrably ideological function, as a hegemonic work whose formal categories as well as its content secure the legitimation of this or that form of class domination—how is it possible for such a text to embody a properly Utopian impulse, or to resonate a universal value inconsistent with the narrower limits of class privilege which inform its more immediate ideological vocation? (288)

Or more positively:

The achieved collectivity or organic group of whatever kind—oppressors fully as much as oppressed—is Utopian not in itself, but only insofar as all such collectivities are themselves *figures* for the ultimate concrete collective life of an achieved Utopian or classless society. (291).

I like Jameson's interest in the Utopian glints in nasty bourgeois literature. His suspicions of its distortions, and his interest in its leavening role, are not unlike what I would imagine in a religious literary criticism. In an astonishing act of generosity, Jameson allows: "The preceding analysis entitles us to conclude that all class consciousness of whatever type is Utopian insofar as it expresses the unity of a collectivity," which presumably applies to Irish Revivalists and Gaelic peasants, monks and professors, Baptist preachers and their audiences, Swedish film companies, Catholic cults, and literary critics. Jameson warns us that his Utopian glints allude "to the as yet untheorized object—the collective—to which they make imperfect allusion"(294). A religious literary criticism might agree and substitute a God-term for "the collective." In any event, the object is as yet untheorized.

Interestingly, Jameson's gap between the ideological distortion and Utopian depth of literary works is rather like Wayne Booth's gap between the conventional surface and the humane depths of an Austen text. On the surface, Austen argues that a woman's happiness consists in a perfect marriage; underneath, she shows the inadequacy of any such simplistic ideal and the norm of a much richer human ideal. Similarly, David Parker's distinguished *Ethics, Theory, and the Novel* reinvokes D. H. Lawrence's notion of the ways in which novels ethically "question the moral systems they might superficially be taken to be supporting" (147). How we reconcile such 'prophetic' insights with our equally passionate commitments to pluralism and multiculturalism is one of the great questions for a religious literary criticism.

For an adequate reading of the religious dimensions of literary texts, we need languages that are critical and passionate, ecumenical and committed, detached and empathic. Such a language needs to enter into productive dialogue with our reigning discourses. It needs to appeal not only to the converted, but also to those with no pronounced commitments, and also to be helpful to those who are hostile to religion. The problem with many of the offhand attacks on religious criticism is that they have little to attack except fundamentalist simplicities, which makes their own attacks seem simplistic. The subject of religious experience, and of course religion itself, is a profoundly divisive and disturbing subject, and for that reason famously avoided in polite conversation. Nevertheless, we need to take on these dark currents, and begin to talk about them. As Jonathan Culler says:

> The political and intellectual health of our nation requires, I submit, that the religious justifications of political positions and thus religious discourse be as much a subject of debate and critique as other ideological formations and discourses. (31)

A thousand years seem to separate Culler from Lentricchia's odd recovery at the end of "En Route to Retreat: Revisiting Mepkin Abbey":

> I ran across this passage in Merton: "When a man enters a monastery he has to stand before the community, and formally respond to a ritual question: *Quod petis?* 'What do you ask?' His answer is not that he seeks a happy life, or escape from anxiety, or freedom from sin, or moral perfection, or the summit of contemplation. The answer is that he seeks *mercy*." I try to, but cannot imagine what the secular world would have to become for that ritual to obtain, for it to be one of ours. (60)

The conversation between Culler and Lentricchia is indeed unimaginable; for that matter, the conversation between Lentricchia and traditional faith is almost unimaginable. And yet some conversation must begin if we are to be adequate readers of Yeats's man who dreamed of faeryland, of Stevens's quiet, of O'Connor's preacher, of Bergman's rhetoric, of Cisneros's milagrito girl, of Alyosha on Grushenka's lap, of Stevens's untheorized object.

WORKS CITED

Abrams, Meyer. "Structure and Style in the Greater Romantic Lyric." *From Sensibility to Romanticism*. Ed. Frederick Hilles and Harold Bloom. Oxford: Oxford UP, 1965.

————. *Natural Supernaturalism: Tradition and Revolution in Romantic Literature*. New York: Norton, 1971.

Alter, Robert. *The Art of Biblical Narrative*. New York: Basic Books, 1981.

Bakhtin, M. M. *The Dialogic Imagination: Four Essays*. Trans. Caryl Emerson and Michael Holquist. Austin: U of Texas P, 1981.

Balthasar, Hans Urs von. *The Glory of the Lord: A Theological Aesthetics*. 1961. Trans. T. Clark. San Francisco: Ignatius, 1982.

Barthes, Roland. "The Great Family of Man." *Mythologies*. Trans. Annette Lavers. New York: Noonday, 1990.

Bergman, Ingmar. "Through a Glass Darkly." *Three Films*. Trans. Paul Austin. New York: Grove, 1970. Trans. of *En Filmtrilogi*. 1963.

Bloom, Harold. *The American Religion*. New York: Simon & Schuster, 1992.

————. *The Book of J*. Trans. David Rosenberg. Commentary by Harold Bloom. New York: Grove Weidenfeld, 1990.

Booth, Wayne. *The Company We Keep: An Ethics of Fiction*. Berkeley: U of California P, 1988.

Carver, Raymond. *Cathedral*. New York: Knopf, 1983.

Cisneros, Sandra. *Woman Hollering Creek and Other Stories*. New York: Random House, 1991.

Culler, Jonathan. "Comparative Literature and the Pieties." *Profession 86* (1988): 30–32.

Dinesen, Isak. "Babette's Feast." *Anecdotes of Destiny*. New York: Random House, 1958.

Dostoyevsky, Fyodor. *The Brothers Karamazov*. Trans. Constance Garnett. New York: Random House, 1950.

Eliot, T. S. *The Complete Poems and Plays*. New York: Harcourt, Brace, 1952.

Erikson, Eric. *Childhood and Society*. New York: Norton, 1950.

Fowler, James. *Stages of Faith: The Psychology of Human Development and the Quest for Meaning*. San Francisco: Harper & Row, 1981.

Franchot, Jenny. *Roads to Rome: The Antebellum Protestant Encounter with Catholicism*. Berkeley: U of California P, 1994.

Frye, Northrop. *The Great Code: The Bible and Literature*. New York: Harcourt Brace Jovanovich, 1982.

Giles, Paul. *American Catholic Arts and Fictions: Culture, Ideology, Aesthetics*. Cambridge, Eng.: Cambridge UP, 1992.

Girard, René. *Violence and the Sacred*. Baltimore: Johns Hopkins UP, 1977.

Greenblatt, Stephen. *Renaissance Self-Fashioning*. Chicago: U of Chicago P, 1980.

Griffiths, Eric. *The Printed Voice of Victorian Poetry*. Oxford: Clarendon, 1989.

Harpham, Geoffrey. *The Ascetic Imperative in Culture and Criticism*. Chicago: U of Chicago P, 1987.

Hartman, Geoffrey. *Wordsworth's Poetry, 1787–1814*. New Haven: Yale UP, 1964.

Haughton, Rosemary. *The Transformation of Man: A Study of Conversion and Community*. Springfield, IL: Templegate, 1967, 1980.

Haughton, Walter. *The Victorian Frame of Mind, 1830–1870*. New Haven: Yale UP, 1957.

Hill, Geoffrey. *New and Collected Poems, 1952–1992*. Boston: Houghton Mifflin, 1994.

Hillesum, Etty. *An Interrupted Life: The Diaries of Etty Hillesum, 1941–43*. Trans. Arno Pomerans. New York: Pantheon, 1983.

Jameson, Fredric. *The Political Consciousness: Narrative as a Socially Symbolic Act*. Ithaca, NY: Cornell UP, 1981.

Johnson, Barbara. "Muteness Envy." The English Institute: Harvard University (2 September, 1994).

Kermode, Frank. *The Genesis of Secrecy: On the Interpretation of Narrative*. Cambridge, MA: Harvard UP, 1979.

Kierkegaard, Søren. *Either/Or*. Trans. David Swenson and Lillian Swenson. Garden City, NY: Doubleday, 1959.

———. *Fear and Trembling*. Trans. Walter Lowrie. Princeton, NJ: Princeton UP, 1941.

Kohlberg, Lawrence. *The Philosophy of Moral Development*. San Francisco: Harper & Row, 1981.

Lentricchia, Frank. "En Route to Retreat: Making it to Mepkin Abbey." *Harper's Magazine* (January 1992): 68–78. Rpt. in *The Edge of Darkness*. New York: Random House, 1994.

Lévi-Strauss, Claude. *Tristes Tropiques*. Trans. John Russell. New York: Athenaeum, 1961.

Lonergan, Bernard. *Insight: A Study of Human Understanding*. New York: Philosophical Library, 1956.

Martz, Louis. *The Poetry of Meditation*. New Haven: Yale UP, 1954.

Maynard, John. *Victorian Discourses on Sexuality and Religion*. Cambridge, Eng.: Cambridge UP, 1993.

Matthiessen, F. O. *American Renaissance: Art and Expression in the Age of Emerson and Whitman*. New York: Oxford UP, 1941.

Mill, John Stuart. *Autobiography*. Ed. Jack Stillinger. Boston: Houghton Mifflin, 1969.

Miller, J. Hillis. *The Disappearance of God: Five Nineteenth-Century Writers*. Cambridge, MA: Harvard UP, 1963.

———. *The Ethics of Reading: Kant, de Man, Eliot, Trollope, James, and Benjamin*. New York: Columbia UP, 1987.

———. *Poets of Reality: Six Twentieth-Century Writers*. Cambridge, MA: Harvard UP, 1965.

O'Connor, Flannery. *The Complete Stories*. 1962. New York: Farrar Straus Giroux, 1974.

Ogden, C. K, and I. A. Richards. *The Meaning of Meaning*. 1923. New York: Harcourt, Brace, 1959.

Perry, William. *Forms of Intellectual and Ethical Development in the College Years*. New York: Holt, Rinehart and Winston, 1970.

Ryan, Robert. *Keats: The Religious Sense*. Princeton, NJ: Princeton UP, 1976.

Said, Edward. "Conclusion: Religious Criticism." *The World, the Text, and the Critic*. Cambridge, MA: Harvard UP, 1983.

Shawn, Wallace, and André Gregory. *My Dinner with André*. New York: Grove, 1981.

Sollers, Philippe. *Women*. Trans. Barbara Bray. New York: Columbia UP, 1990. Trans. of *Femmes*. 1983.

Stevens, Wallace. *Collected Poems*. New York: Knopf, 1954.

Stockton, Kathryn. *God Between Their Lips: Desire Between Women in Irigaray, Brontë, and Eliot*. Stanford, CA: Stanford UP, 1994.

Thérèse de Lisieux, Saint. *The Story of a Soul*. Trans. John Clarke. Washington, DC: ICS Publications, 1976.

Thompson, E. P. *The Making of the English Working Class*. New York: Pantheon, 1963.

Warren, Robert Penn. "Pure and Impure Poetry." *Kenyon Review* 5 (1943): 229–30, 252.

Weinfield, Henry. *The Poet Without a Name: Gray's "Elegy" and the Problem of History*. Carbondale: Southern Illinois UP, 1991.

Yeats, William Butler. *Collected Poems*. Ed. Richard Finneran. New York: Macmillan, 1989.

Waugh, Evelyn. *Brideshead Revisited*. Boston: Little, Brown, 1945.

2

Imagination's Arc: The Spiritual Development of Readers

J. A. Appleyard, S.J.

EIGHTEEN-YEAR-OLDS ARE MORE LIKELY to encounter Virginia Woolf's *To the Lighthouse* or William Faulkner's *The Sound and the Fury* in a college literature course than to take them to the beach for summer reading. Left to themselves, if they read fiction for enjoyment, they might be preoccupied with John Grisham or Anne Rice. The variety of books young adults might read, the different circumstances in which they read, and their varied motives for reading all suggest the possibility of describing a developmental trajectory that moves from simple and familiar forms and rewards to novel and challenging ones. There is good reason to think that a similar trajectory exists in the changes that young adults go through in their religious lives. I want to suggest that these two trajectories are related, that they can influence each other, and that it will be useful for teachers of literature to understand something about what could be happening in the spiritual lives of their students.

The premise underlying this thesis is that reading deals with the same issues that are the terrain of spiritual growth: identity, relationships with others, what it means to love, the nature and limits of truth and knowing, manners and morals, mortality, evil, death, what we hope for beyond our lives. Teachers take this premise for granted, I suspect, though they might not use the terminology of spiritual development, and they recognize intuitively that their students undergo changes over time in their ability to deal with these issues, as readers and as human beings.

There is, however, more than intuitive support for these points of view. There is considerable empirical evidence for them and a number of theoretical accounts that fill in our understanding of what these developmental changes involve and how they occur.[1] Let us look first at reading and at some of the key characteristics of reading from a psychological point of view, as they illuminate the developmental issues college students are likely to be dealing with.

READING DEVELOPMENT

I have described elsewhere a sequence of stages that readers seem to go through from childhood to adulthood. The general picture is this: At age two or three a child has only an intermittent grasp of the boundary between fantasy and actuality, so that the story world and the real world are scarcely distinguished. The structures of stories and the motivations of characters in them that children can grasp at this age are extremely simple. By age ten or eleven, however, the same child can hold together much more compli- cated story-forms and themes. He or she has begun to master the lessons of school and of apprenticeship in the larger world and now enjoys identifying with the heroes and heroines of endless versions of the timeless story about the conflict of good and evil. At seventeen, though, this same reader is likely to have moved further, to have discovered that romance is only one way of imag- ining the world and that important truths are complicated, so he or she becomes a rather critical seeker of wisdom about the world and human life in the stories he or she reads. Still later, say at twenty, this reader may have become a student of literature, who realizes that stories are not just narratives to get lost in or to think about but also texts that require us to think about how and by whom they have been put together, their effects on us, the issues they raise in the world of contemporary intellectual discourse, and the kinds of meaning they can plausibly claim to offer. In middle age this same reader may discover that the keenest pleasure of reading now lies less in understanding how books work than in seeing the ironies and complexities of his or her own experience explored in the predicaments of fictional characters. And, finally, even this reading stance may itself be transcended by the discov- ery that all these ways of reading are choices we make in how we

---

[1] A useful overview of the theories is contained in Kurfiss.

want to read and that we shift among them for our own purposes as we discover our mature selves.

To best understand how this process works, we need to begin with an interactional or transactional view of reading such as we might put together from the works of Wolfgang Iser, Louise Rosenblatt, and Norman Holland, centering on the historically situated encounter between a reader and a text. In this view the text is a system of response-inviting structures that the author has organized by reference to a repertory of social and literary codes shared by author and reader. The reader brings to bear on this text expectations derived from literary and life experience. The text feeds back these expectations or challenges them. The reader filters this feedback through characteristic defenses, imbues these data with fantasies, tests them against his or her canons of value and belief, and transforms the event into a coherent experience. The reading process is thus a dialectic of reader, text, and world, with the reader's developing self-appropriation at the center of the process (Iser; Rosenblatt; Holland).

Cognitive Dimensions of Reading Development

The first thing to say about this process is that it has an indispensable cognitive element, the main lines of which can be fairly well explained by a theory such as Jean Piaget's.[2] In his view, to know is to construct meaning out of our interaction with the world of experience, using the cognitive structures at our disposal. From infancy onward, these structures develop and change, as experience of our social and physical environment grows and our physiological capacities unfold. We acquire new cognitive schemas, combine simpler ones into larger and more adequate ones for dealing with our experience, and interiorize this knowledge in increasingly abstract forms. Piaget's distinctive contribution to the epistemology of development was to divide this process into stages—periods of equilibrium in the learning process when thinking is characterized by stable structures that are qualitatively different from those of the stages that precede and follow—and to argue that these stages unfold according to an innate groundplan, are therefore universal in human beings, and are irreversible,

---

[2] A useful overview of Piaget's account of development can be found in Piaget and Inhelder. See also Piaget.

since each one fundamentally transforms the accomplishment of the previous one. Learning, that is, movement from one stage to another, occurs when the learner acts to resolve discrepancies between new experiences and the ways of knowing that made sense in an earlier stage. Instead of "assimilating" new experience into previous modes of knowing, the learner "accommodates" his or her modes of knowing to the demands of the new experience.

For example, a ten-year-old reader grasps only a certain kind of story, one with characters clearly defined as good or evil, whose inner lives are uncomplicated, a story without structural complexities such as flashbacks and sub-plots, and with a happy ending. The same reader at age sixteen is likely to find this kind of story boring. Adolescents want to read instead about complex characters who face moral dilemmas and are involved in intricate plots and may not come at all to happy endings. The difference is a difference of cognitive stage.

From a Piagetian perspective, the chief cognitive issues college students face have to do with the late residue of the transition from concrete-operational to formal-operational thinking. The distinction between these stages is simple, but the implications are enormous. In the concrete-operational stage, students reason in terms of particular objects and their concrete relationships here and now; they rely on partial observations, memorize, follow rules, interpret literally, make only rudimentary generalizations, are puzzled by disconfirming evidence (if they notice it at all). In the formal-operational stage, however, students think in terms of formal or logical relationships that exist between propositions about objects. They can reason hypothetically about possible outcomes (therefore they can speculate, imagine and test alternatives, think about the consequences of what-if hypotheses). They can imagine alternative futures, construct theories, understand others' points of view. They can consider several variables and their interaction simultaneously, which means that they are much more likely, for example, to grasp the interrelationships of the elements of a text (e.g., how the words and images of a poem modify each other). They can solve complex problems and are not surprised by the challenge of having to change their accustomed ways of thinking in order to incorporate unexpected data. Their thinking is general, abstract, and complex. They can reflect critically about their own thinking.

College teachers will recognize most of their students some-where in this sketch. The problems of freshmen are easily corre-lated with the concrete-operational stage; the virtues we want in senior English majors are evident in the later position. Empirical data suggest that college students are squarely in the middle of this conflict (Kurfiss 10). Few seniors reach the full development of formal-operational thinking, and most freshmen are "transi-tional," reasoning formally in areas that interest them and where they have experience, or using a mix of concrete and formal strat-egies. The task of college instructors is clearly to teach in ways that challenge students to move beyond their familiar ways of making sense of the world while supporting them in this often awkward and painful growth.

Affective and Psychosocial Dimensions of Reading

Important as cognitive issues are, however, there is much more to reading. Piaget's theory is fundamentally an account of how logical and relational thinking develops in individual learners. In his view, fantasy and imagination are simply part of the muddle out of which more adequate and orderly ways of thinking will emerge—a severe handicap for any theory that wants to give a positive account of the power that stories have over us. Moreover, his picture of the child "going it alone" neglects the social context that mediates and facilitates the development of the individual (Bruner 61). For these dimensions of reading we have to look elsewhere.

Psychoanalytic theory would seem to provide a useful comple-ment, since it focuses so much on feeling and on the determina-tive influence of childhood experience on later development. Sigmund Freud's account of how fantasy gives expression to un-conscious desires and fears does help us to understand something of the power of certain kinds of thematic imagery in childhood reading. But Freud's theory has its own limitations for our pur-poses: its dependence on a particular view of infantile sexuality, and the conflict-filled picture of childhood it derives from its clin-ical orientation. Carl Jung's more controversial but positive view of the role of the unconscious in affective development and his notion of an unconscious that is more than personal—a kind of well of the inherited experience of the race which the images of

art embody—suggest something further about why reading matters so much to us on the level of feeling as well as knowing.

The most useful framework for understanding the affective and
social dimensions of reading in relation to developmental issues is
Erik Erikson's account of development.[3] His map of the life-cycle
originates in a psychoanalytic view of the tension between psychological needs and social constraints. This results in a framework of stages defined by the issues that evolving inner capacities
and changing social relationships set as the agenda specific to each
period of development. Thus, one's "identity," the distinctive
way an individual perceives the self and relates to the world, is
reorganized as one confronts and weathers the critical issues
proper to each stage of growth and learns through social interaction the distinctive roles that the culture makes available to the
developing individual. For Erikson, unlike Piaget, development
does not move inevitably in a straight line and by a series of irreversible jumps. The issues of each stage are resolved more or less
successfully, the balance among them becomes the foundation on
which the next stage builds, but the unresolved issues may have
to be renegotiated later. The process may fail to go forward, or
growth may be advanced in some areas of one's life, slowed down
in others. The identity achieved at each stage, then, is a provi-
sional set of abilities and vulnerabilities, a distinctive way of per-
ceiving the self and of relating to the world. The inclusiveness
and flexibility of Erikson's view of development suits a discussion
of reading better than Piaget's does, since maturity in reading does
not occur independently of other kinds of development. It involves cognitive structures, affective issues, interpersonal relationships, and particular social roles which the dominant culture
proffers to the developing reader.

In Erikson's view, the issue of identity, implicit in the earlier
stages of development, comes to the fore in the adolescent years,
so the central agenda for the college student is likely to be achieving a confident sense of self-identity. Who am I? What roles do I
play in my relationships with others? What ideals are really worth
my commitment? What values and behaviors are truly authentic
for me? These are questions that are likely to be on students'
minds, whether they are explicitly brought into the classroom or

---

[3] See both *Childhood* and *Identity*.

not. They arise in part because adolescents have only recently discovered their own subjectivity and the multiplicity of truth, in part because society offers them conflicting values and roles and identities (e.g., major fields of study, career choices, sexual identities, religious beliefs, political agendas, etc.) and pushes them to chose among these. Erikson proposed the idea of a "moratorium" to help explain how young adults often deal with this situation, by avoiding commitments while exploring alternatives. A developmental moratorium can also turn into psychological paralysis for some students, who postpone commitment entirely, drift along, play the game of satisfying or avoiding authority figures, and may even fall into cults and ideologies that offer simple and unambiguous answers to life's questions.

In some respects college is our culture's institutionalized form of adolescent moratorium, a safe place for students to experiment, rebel, and explore self and world. For better or worse, literature deals so centrally with issues of identity and its implications that teachers seldom have to decide whether or not to raise them. When they do come up, though, teachers may appear to have choices about whether to encourage students to pursue these issues or to insist on focusing on more objective matters of literary study (such as textual structures, the critical implication of an author's ideas, authors' biographies, the historical and social context in which a work was produced, etc.). But is this choice even meaningful if the students one is teaching are preoccupied with questions of identity and respond to what they read through the filter of these issues? This does not mean that the instructor has to abandon his or her agenda and allow students to wallow in self-absorption. Students, after all, need precisely to test alternative ways of looking at questions, to explore the implications of different commitments, and, above all, to confront experiences and points of view different from their own, to accommodate realities that may be refractory as well as congenial, and to learn to think systematically about these matters. They will be most helped, therefore, by approaches that are sympathetic to their questions *and* that bring these into relation with what writers and their works say about these questions, alternative views they present, the historical circumstances that condition the formulation of the questions in a particular work, etc.—in other words, by combining the implicit agenda of the student with the instructor's explicit one. For the college teacher the fundamental lesson of the step Erikson takes beyond Piaget in conceiving of how development works is that learning occurs in a matrix of emotional and inter-personal needs. If we want students to mature academically, we have to be sensitive to the issues that influence how and what they are learning.[4]

Cultural Dimensions of Reading Development

To fill in this picture of the social dimensions of the development of readers we need to say something more about a topic that is implicit in Erikson's account: namely, to what extent we can speak of *the reader's experience as socially constructed*, an artifact both of the history of literary invention and of the particular cultural experiences that prepare a reader to read. The claim that particular kinds of cultural experiences have a significant influence in form-ing the reader's sensibility is the subject of much current investi-gation. Some of the studies focus on the determinative effects of factors such as social class, economic level, race, and ethnocentric bias on the responses of particular groups of readers.[5] Of these, gender has been the most frequently cited cultural factor in claim-ing a distinctive development for different groups of readers.[6] An-other group of studies has investigated how ideologies may be embedded in the experience of reading, as part of the content of a story, in the formal structures of setting or character or plot (Davis[7]); or in the expectations readers bring to the interpretation of narrative conventions (Rabinowitz). Ideology spills over into the realm of all the value-laden attitudes through which we orga-nize our experience. Where do these come from? Clearly, any answer will be inadequate that does not include the interaction of our developing egos with the cultural institutions, language codes, social rituals, customs, and especially the whole universe of fantasy in which we are educated from the first songs and games

---

[4] William G. Perry, Jr., gives a very helpful description of the issues college students are likely to be dealing with and the transitions they experience in *Forms*. See also "Cognitive and Ethical Growth."

[5] For example, Heath, Robinson; Scollon and Scollon; Taylor and Dorsey-Gaines.

[6] There is a review of the discussion on this topic in *Gender and Reading*

[7] Davis also offers a useful history of the development of the concept of "ide-ology" in literary analysis.

we learn in our parents' arms to the most recent TV shows and movies we have seen. But this invented universe is not just a storehouse of accumulated data and signs available for use by our developing consciousness; it is more like a matrix which provides the structures in which our consciousness comes to maturity. Northrop Frye has given us one map of the literary portion of this world, in a detailed taxonomy of motifs, archetypes, symbols, myths, and genres. This fictional world has been accumulating since the origins of the human race; our history has sifted and laminated it in countless ways; we are initiated into it as infants, and our consciousness of ourselves grows to maturity in and through it. In its content this fictional universe resembles Jung's archetypal collective unconscious, but its transmission through social learning mechanisms seems more plausible than Jung's innate psychic structures.

In its strong forms this conception of culture as a social artifact would appear to contradict the psychodynamic account of the reader's education we have been exploring. A genetic view of development, after all, conceives of growth as a process which occurs from within the individual, whose skills and capacties flower in adjustments which operate in ever more finely tuned ways on the data of the outer world. A social-construction perspective, on the other hand, locates the significant factors in the social world's ideologies and values, and imagines that the culture imprints itself from the outside on the blank slate of individual consciousness. How can we keep both claims in fruitful tension?

Bernard Lonergan points out that we get both kinds of education simultaneously and dialectically: we grow up as individuals whose capacities unfold and become more sophisticated, but we are simultaneously initiated into the world's meaning mediated to us by our parents, friends, the communities and social institutions we live in, and the culture that embodies our values. These are not two different movements. There is a two-way traffic between them, and a forward movement toward an equilibrium.[8] This kind of dialectical view of development enables us to hold to-

---

[8] Lonergan's two principal works are *Insight* and *Method in Theology*. The basis for this notion of a double development is implicit in *Method* (see chap. 4, especially 115–18), but was worked out only in later essays, particularly in the ones reprinted as chaps. 6, 12, and 13 of *Third Collection*. A helpful study of Lonergan's views on development and education is *Old Things and New*.

gether all the different kinds of data that are potentially relevant
to a description of how a reader's sensibility changes across the
lifespan: the maturing central nervous system, the evolving psy-
chodynamics of our inner lives, the changing social roles available
to us as we mature, the values we absorb from our families and
communities, the kinds of books we read, the kinds of readers our
educational institutions encourage us to be, the fictional universe
which is the cultural matrix in which our development occurs,
and the judgments and moral commitments by which we shape
our lives as we mature. Our development as readers is no less
complex or subtle a matter than our development as human beings, and simple theories will not do it justice.

SPIRITUAL DEVELOPMENT

In considering the complexity of readers' psychological development we have come close to issues that bear upon spiritual development. It remains now to look explicitly at some of them. The
terms 'spiritual' and 'spirituality' have been used in a variety of
meanings. The starting point is Paul's distinction between a
merely natural human being and a 'spiritual person' who is under
the influence of the Spirit of God (1 Co 2:14–15). In the seventeenth century "spirituality" came to be applied to the interior
life of the Christian, eventually to the life of perfection as distinguished from the "ordinary" life of faith. Contemporary usage
includes meanings that range from the Christian life of grace to a
generic concept of the kind of engagement with experience that
leads to a richer human life. Sandra Schneiders, whose analysis I
am borrowing from here, constructs an inclusive definition of
spirituality: "the experience of consciously striving to integrate
one's life in terms not of isolation and self-absorption but of self-
transcendence toward the ultimate value one perceives" (684).
One's horizon of ultimate concern may be God revealed in Jesus
Christ and experienced through the gift of the Spirit within the
Church (in which case one is talking about Christian spirituality),
but it may also be another system of value, religious or secular.
Schneiders points out, however, that in practice there is no such
thing as "generic spirituality." As lived experience, a spirituality
is always determined by a particular horizon of value, entailing a

relatively coherent and articulated understanding of both the human being and the horizon of ultimate value, some historical tradition, some symbol system, and so on (684). This is worth keeping in mind when students talk about the "spiritual" dimensions of their lives. They may mean a vague apprehension of the immaterial dimension of all human life, or they may mean lived experience that actualizes this dimension within a horizon of ultimate value. In speaking of a reader's spiritual development, therefore, we ought to think at least of growth oriented to an horizon of ultimate concern, which at some point will become a conscious attempt to integrate one's life in relation to this horizon. This will ordinarily be in a religious context, and in our culture most commonly the religious context will be Christian, though, of course, how well–filled–in a person's understanding and experience of any religious context is in our society will vary enormously from person to person.

How do we develop spiritually? This topic is less well schematized than cognitive and psychosocial development. A helpful framework for thinking about it comes from James Fowler's study of faith development. He proposes a series of stages which describe the structural features of faith considered as a way of understanding and responding to contingency, finitude, and ultimacy in our lives. Though not identical with spirituality, this understanding of faith overlaps it considerably, and the trajectory of development that Fowler describes must underlie the growth of any explicit relationship with a God or a value system that defines ultimacy in our lives.

(1) In Fowler's view, primal faith begins in the infant's intimate trust in the love and wisdom of its first caregivers, experienced through their presence and nurturing. (2) At about age two, language emerges to mediate relations to the world and others; perceptions, feelings and imaginative fantasy blend in symbols and stories that embody meaning and reassurance. (3) Then, at about school age, thinking becomes more orderly, less dependent on fantasy, and faith becomes a matter of reliance on the rules and implicit values of the family's community of meanings, which are typically experienced in rituals and practices and in narratives about the community and its beliefs. Adolescents often still have this kind of faith and many adults too, though further stages may develop. (4) The next stage often emerges in early adolescence

and is rooted in the new self-consciousness and interest in interiority typical of teenagers and their determination to find both a satisfactory identity and a world-view. The result is a set of beliefs and values newly synthesized, conventional in that they are drawn largely from significant others, and tacit in that they are not yet critically examined though they may be passionately held. (5) The transition to the next stage, Fowler says, is occasioned by experiences that lead people to examine and make critical choices about the defining elements of their identity and faith. Two movements are at the heart of this transition: the sense of self shifts from one's relations and roles to a new awareness of the person behind these masks for whom one now takes responsibility, *and* previously unexamined convictions and beliefs become matters of more explicit choice, commitment, and accountability. Sometimes people will work through only one of these shifts, critically examining their beliefs but not coming to a new sense of self-authorization, or the reverse may be true. If one arrives at this stage at all, it may only be in one's thirties or forties. (6) At mid-life—because of new awareness of the complexity and fragility of life, the reality of aging and death, the problematic nature of our own certitudes, and the powerful examples of people of other faiths and beliefs— the firm sense of identity and the clear boundaries of this stage may crumble, and we may move to an experience of ultimate reality that is marked by contradictions, polarities, or paradoxical elements. Our felt sense of this reality and our receptivity to its influence may deepen even while its conceptual clarity diminishes. (7) Finally, the tensions and contradictions of this stage may disappear because of a radical decentering of the self. This decentering, which has led us to see the world through the eyes of a widening circle of family, friends, groups we identify with, and our own mature convictions and commitments, now leads us to see the world from a perspective that includes people quite different from ourselves, through the eyes of all humankind. The values that give our lives meaning have also been expanding, and this process reaches a completion when we decenter to such an extent that we value things and people the way the Creator values them or as they are valued at the ultimate horizon of meaning we acknowledge. This is the *kenosis* or emptying-out of self that moves beyond finite centers of value and power and trusts solely in the radical Other.

Young men and women of college age are likely to be negotiating the transitions from the third of these stages into the fourth and on to the fifth. That is, some may still be rooted in a rules orientation, unreflectively taking for granted the religious beliefs and practices of the communities in which they have grown up. Or, more likely, their religious attitudes will exhibit the features of the fourth stage: self-conscious preoccupation with some degree of interior quest, interest in ideas and even ideologies, proneness to take on the views of influential individuals or groups, tentativeness and revisability of commitments. Some may even be entering the fifth of these stages, coming to a deeper sense of themselves in relation to an horizon of value and taking responsibility for the choices and commitments that embody this identity.

Fowler's stages are rooted in a cognitive-structural account of development. They aim at clarifying how we make faith-meaning in our lives. Does spiritual development involve more than these cognitive stages describe? Yes, in the sense that, as I have indicated in citing Sandra Schneiders, an adequate notion of spirituality and of spiritual development includes the idea of consciously striving to integrate one's life experience with one's beliefs and to transcend imperfect versions of integration in favor of more inclusive ones. In Fowler's terms, the first three stages (and even the fourth) may be said to happen to one without much conscious volition, through the ordinary experiences of growing up and being taught a system of values and, implicitly at least, an horizon of ultimate meaning. Conscious efforts at spiritual development would seem to be possible only in the stages that begin with adolescence. Whether Fowler's higher stages of faith development describe adequately what spiritual writers would consider spiritual development I am not qualified to say, but I do not think the matter needs to be fully clarified for our purposes here. It does need to be said, however, that Fowler's stages are meant to describe a development that can occur within both religious and non-religious frameworks of meaning, whereas a large number of instances of spiritual development we are likely to encounter among U.S. college students will involve relationship to a personal God. The dynamics of this relationship will fit within the categories Fowler describes, but they are likely to be expressed less in terms of meaning and more in terms of feelings, personifications, consciousness of unworthiness and the sense of being loved, movements of attraction and withdrawal, and affect-laden imagery (Barry 61–71).

One Reader's Spiritual Development

Granted the similarities between reading development and spiritual development, how shall we talk about the relationship between them? I suggest that the two are clearly parallel (enough has been said to demonstrate this) and that the two can influence each other. A remarkable illustration of the interplay is to be found in the autobiography of Thomas Merton, *The Seven Storey Mountain*. Merton became known as a spiritual writer, poet, and essayist, but before he was any of these he was an undergraduate and graduate student of English literature, an apprentice writer, and a wide-ranging reader. Walter Conn gives an extended analysis of Merton's account of his college and graduate school days, in the course of exploring the cognitive, affective, and moral dimensions of religious conversion (esp. 159–77). I shall borrow liberally from Conn and also from Merton's autobiography to show how some key moments in Merton's experience illustrate the movement from Fowler's third to his fourth and fifth stages:

- As a boy Merton moved between France, England, and Long Island because of his parents' travels and subsequently their illnesses and early deaths. His schooling was mostly in England. He had been baptized in the Episcopal Church, but his parents were not regular churchgoers. As a young teenager, he went through a "religious phase" at one school, where prayer was attractive because country churches and good food and the green countryside made it so. Later, at Oakham, a large public school, he found religion meant little more than gentlemanly conduct and dry arguments and he became an intellectual rebel. Finishing school, he traveled to Rome, where the mosaics in the church of Saints Cosmas and Damian moved him to think about Christ and the faith of the craftsmen who made them. He was carrying the poems of D. H. Lawrence in his knapsack and found himself disgusted with the ones about the four Evangelists and how little Lawrence understood the New Testament. He began reading the Gospels instead and then tried to pray in the churches he visited, but it was a short-lived enthusiasm.
- Merton spent a year at Cambridge University, where he reveled in his freedom and in opportunities for a profligate life. The only

grace of that year, he said later, was that he read Dante closely. When he returned to New York in 1934 to go to Columbia, he had dismissed religion from his life, had gotten a woman pregnant and on his guardian's insistence had left her (she and the baby later died in the bombing of London), and had found a temporary spiritual home where so many other intellectuals did in the 1930s, in Communism. Here was an ideal of changing the world, if not himself.

- College was a full life for Merton. He wrote for the school paper and the humor magazine, edited the yearbook, ran cross-country, worked at Rockefeller Center, partied with a precocious undergraduate literary crowd, and was profoundly unhappy. His grandfather and grandmother, with whom he lived, died, and Merton himself had a nervous and physical collapse.

- In a course on French Medieval Literature he had to read Étienne Gilson's *The Spirit of Medieval Philosophy*, where he came upon the first concept of a God he ever had that was not a simplistic anthropomorphism—not a jealous, limited God, but one who transcended all concepts, who might conceivably be believed and loved. He began to go to the local Episcopal church in Southampton on Sundays.

- He found his way into Mark Van Doren's course on Shakespeare, the only place, he said, where he "ever heard anything really sensible said about any of the things that were really fundamental—life, death, time, love, sorrow, fear, wisdom, suffering, eternity" (*Mountain* 180). One of Van Doren's great virtues, he thought, was that he did not talk about literature as though it were economics or philosophy or sociology or psychology, and yet the material of literature is chiefly human acts—that is, free acts, moral acts—and literature makes statements about these acts that can be made in no other way, so it is always commenting on ethics and psychology and metaphysics and theology. Van Doren's class was one of the few things that could persuade him to get on the train and go to Columbia at all.

- A friend gave him Aldous Huxley's *Ends and Means*, published in 1937 in the midst of worldwide depression and gathering political turmoil in Europe. Huxley's theme was how an ideal society is to be achieved, and he argued that only a commitment to disinterested virtue and detachment from the things of this world could overcome the materialism of modern life and give access to the spiritual order of love. The book had a deep influence on Merton, tapping into his guilt about his earlier misconduct and his sense of the hollowness of much of his present life.

- In February 1938 Merton began a master's degree in English. He took as a thesis topic "Nature and Art in William Blake." The key insight he came to about Blake was that his poetry, far from being a celebration of passion and natural energy, represented a rebellion against naturalism not only in the aesthetic order but in the moral order as well. It glorified the transfiguration of man's natural love in the refining fire of mystical experience. These ideas fed Merton's growing sense of himself as a divided soul, sick and torn, but drawn to the notion of a virtuous life that was ordered toward God. He recognized this with his head, he said, but only slowly came to desire it with his heart.
- One Sunday morning in September of the same year he entered a Catholic church near Columbia and stayed only for the sermon—on the Incarnation—but afterward knew that he saw the world with different eyes. He could not understand why he was so happy. Days later he borrowed a biography of Gerard Manley Hopkins. Reading about the young poet's correspondence with John Henry Newman and his indecision about entering the Catholic Church, he suddenly found he was asking himself "What are you waiting for?" He went to the nearby parish church and told the priest who answered the door that he wanted to become a Catholic. In November of that year he was baptized.
- The story did not end there, of course. Baptism did not change Merton all that much. His faith was still very much an intellectual experience, he later thought. His treasures were still success and reputation as a writer. When a friend asked him what he really wanted to be, he gave what he considered the lame answer that he wanted to be a good Catholic. When his friend told him that what he should say is that he wanted to be a saint, Merton said he could not be a saint (he thought of his sins, his false humility, his cowardice). His friend's response—"All that is necessary to be a saint is to want to be one. Don't you believe that God will make you what He created you to be, if you will consent to let Him do it?"—left him disturbed (*Mountain* 238). In subsequent months he came to the realization that he might become a priest, decided to enter the Franciscans, experienced serious doubt (while reading the Book of Job) that he had a true vocation, in any event was turned down by the Franciscans, went to teach literature at St. Bonaventure's College, wrestled with the decision to declare himself a conscientious objector to military service (flunking the medical exam settled that), made a retreat at the Trappist monastery at Gethsemani in Kentucky where he prayed for a vocation to join the monks there, worked part of a

summer among the poor in Harlem, and finally—a few days after Mark Van Doren in the Columbia Faculty Club put the question directly to him about his old notion of becoming a priest—found that he could not get out of his head the image of the Gethsemani bell calling him and decided "The time has come for me to go and be a Trappist." Nor did the story end, even there, but we shall stop at this point.

Merton's growth in these years exhibits the distinctive themes of the middle stages in Fowler's schema: the conventional religious piety and equally conventional intellectual rebellion of early adolescence; the self-conscious attempts to find connections among the disparate experiences of early manhood, to take seriously his inner life and find out where his searching was leading;[9] and finally the kinds of experience of God that led him to make choices and commitments that entailed substantial consequences for the way he would live.

I do not want to suggest that Merton's spiritual development can be explained simply, by pigeonholing it into categories. The numberless tiny roots of the dispositions and attitudes that made his religious experiences possible would be immensely difficult to identify and map. Anyone's religious imagination is, and is bound to seem, complex and all but unique. Nonetheless, there are observable commonalities in how people develop. Any teacher makes use of this assumption to think about how to challenge a class and individuals in it.

In Merton's account of this part of his conversion story we can see some of the ingredients that are apt to be elements in the less dramatic life transitions (religious or not) that our students undergo in their early adult years. First, there is the existential context, marked by disquiet of soul, cognitive and moral

---

[9] At some point Merton's view of his situation turned into the conviction of a conscious quest for a new identity. In *My Argument with the Gestapo*, a thinly disguised and highly personal autobiographical novel he wrote in 1941 (it was published only after his death) the principal character says to British officers who are questioning him: "If you want to identify me, ask me not where I live, or what I like to eat, or how I comb my hair, but ask me what I think I am living for, in detail, and ask me what I think is keeping me from living fully for the thing I want to live for. Between these two answers you can determine the identity of any person. The better answer he has, the more of a person he is. . . . I am all the time trying to make out the answer as I go on living" (160–61).

disequilibrium. Part of this, in Merton's case, is aroused by guilt about his behavior and his treatment of others. Part of it is caused by new ideas he cannot readily assimilate in books he is reading. Part of it is brought on by challenges to discover his best self, from close friends who know him best and can reach into his soul with their questions. The result is an experience of his divided self, which may even be characterized as a full-blown crisis of identity. What comes to his aid in this predicament? In part it is the very ideas he struggles to assimilate from his reading. They become means of self-knowledge. A mentor plays a crucial role, prodding his movement forward, modeling desirable attitudes. Reflectiveness, inner exploration, outward-turning contemplation are the pot in which these ingredients are stirred (in Merton's case we should call these prayer). The result comes as moments of insight, disclosure, decision, a reorientation whose outcomes are new commitments, new behaviors, a new sense of identity and of the fit of the world's meaning.

All stories of spiritual development do not end in baptism and the monastery, but they are likely to go through stages similar to the ones Fowler schematizes, where at some point conventional attitudes give way to self-conscious searching and this eventually turns into choices and commitments that embody a new sense of who one is in relation to a trustworthy, transcendent Other.

THE OVERLAP BETWEEN READING AND SPIRITUAL DEVELOPMENT

Merton's story of his student days, though we look back at it from the angle of his later eminence as a spiritual writer, is not so very different in its details from the experiences any talented undergraduate or graduate student might have today in a good university. The issues are the same: experiencing the breakdown of conventional beliefs, negotiating moral and intellectual confusion, consciously probing one's inner life, deciding who are true and false friends, discovering that even appealing ideas need to be questioned, finding good mentors, experiencing the slow unveiling of one's true self, making tentative commitments and finally firm ones. And literature class is often the venue where students contest these issues, identifying passionately with characters and causes, being challenged by authors and ideas, fitting together old habits of reading and new knowledge and skills, trying hard to connect it all in a stable sense of identity.

Teachers of literature might be helped to see how far the activity of reading reaches into themes they are more likely to consider in relation to spiritual development by looking briefly at some psychological accounts of the mind's operation in the reading process and some maps of the issues involved in it.

Psychoanalytically oriented theorists, for example, would argue that reading involves affective processes that reach into the center of our self-organization. Bruno Bettelheim's thesis about fairy tales is well known: that children are attracted to them because they deal directly with the existential problems of growing up, "overcoming narcissistic disappointments, Oedipal dilemmas, sibling rivalries, becoming able to relinquish childhood dependencies, gaining a feeling of selfhood and of self-worth, and a sense of moral obligation" (6). Literary theorists such as Simon Lesser and Norman Holland make a similar claim about all fiction. Although its overt subject is the world we live in, human relationships, and social and moral issues, the underlying and real sources of the energy with which we experience literature are emotional, because it deals with the profound desires and fears we have for ourselves, which these themes can tap. As important as thematic content, however, are the formal structures at work in both storytelling and reader response, which both secure our affective involvement and control it so that it is unthreatening and tolerable. On the one hand, Holland suggests, a work of literature lures us willingly into its world by offering us the promise of gratification on the most basic oral level, of "taking in" in open-mouthed wonder the fantasies it contains, of reexperiencing the undifferentiated fusion of ourselves and the world around us that we knew as infants before we learned to separate ego from external world (74–79). But this fusion threatens to overwhelm us with the loss of self, so the formal organization of a story must safeguard us from engulfment. Form—that is, everything from the sound pattern of the words to the structure of the narrative—controls the experience, and therefore gives us permission to enjoy our feelings safely, reassures us that they are acceptable and still within our control, and integrates them into a vision of order, a process not unlike the one Aristotle long ago labeled catharsis (Lesser 248). It does this, Lesser proposes, through a double strategy. It gratifies our lust for the experience of the story by telescoping time and sustaining the forward movement of events, but by focusing our attention on one central action and clarifying the pattern of events, form permits us simultaneously to stand outside and beyond the death-bound movement of time as onlookers (169–70). Thus, though fiction magnifies and intensifies the issues it deals with, its formal characteristics control our anxiety by devices that distance and frame–in Lesser's term "bind"—the emotions it causes, so that they do not reach disturbing proportions as we read or threaten to merge with our world after we are done (Lesser 183–84).

Implicit in psychoanalytic theory, of course, is the claim that the space where this kind of activity occurs is much broader than simply reading. D. W. Winnicott, for example, argues that childhood play is an example of a strategy that is a permanent feature of our psychic lives. The blanket or toy that is the child's first possession is a "transitional object" that is neither wholly outside nor wholly inside; it overcomes the child's confusion between desires and realities, between what is subjectively conceived and what is objectively perceived. We continually renegotiate this need as we grow older. It is the wellspring of human creativity. In the arts, religion, scientific work, and imaginative living generally we mediate between the inner world of our needs and desires and the outer world of shared and verifiable experience.

Sharon Parks, a developmental psychologist, uses the terminology of imagination and images, more typically associated with literature and other forms of artistic creativity, to explain growth in religious faith. Her work in campus ministry led her to study the faith development of young adults. This is the critical time of life, she argues, for forming a vision of the possibilities that lie beyond immediate existence and a passion for worthy ideals that can guide one's life. The likelihood of doing so depends on two factors, the capacity for critical reflection on experience (a common point among cognitive-developmental theorists) and the ability to adequately name an ideal or a good that is worth our commitment. The latter can occur, she thinks, only by means of images.

Drawing on a Coleridgean notion of the imagination as an active power that struggles to unify contingent experience, conscious thought, and the creative guidance of a transcendent Spirit within us, she argues that faith is constituted through moments of revelatory insight into the meaning of existential situations that are expressed and embodied in images. These may be the symbols of a faith community (e.g., a concept—God—or an event— Passover—or a person—Muhammed—or a thing—bread and wine) or, more broadly, the particular images we use to compose the significance of our individual lives. She notes H. Richard Niebuhr's likening of such revelatory images to a luminous sentence in a difficult book, "from which we can go forward and backward, and so attain some understanding of the whole" (Niebuhr 93). The new image or insight enables us to see the whole of life in ways that previously eluded us. Occasions of such insight are the purpose of all truly liberal education, she observes. Education and the journey of faith are inextricably linked (Parks 125).

Faith—whether religious or the primal force of belief, promise, and fidelity that shapes all existence and is not specifically religious—is a life of the imagination, William Lynch argues. It is not the case that faith comes after and adds something to human knowledge (the great modern separation). Rather, faith is a form of imagining and experiencing the world. Its images change the way we see the world (Lynch says: to believe that the poor are *blessed* puts an entirely different light on things). The most significant accomplishment of faith, however, is that its images can hold together "ironically" (that is, in ways that can include the profoundest contradictions of experience) reality, history, and revelation.

The views of imagination offered by Parks and Lynch make clear that our affective investment in images is accompanied by an equally important cognitive involvement. The psychologist D. W. Harding offers an important distinction between the "participant" and the "spectator" roles to account for both these elements in readers' responses to stories (300–17). No matter how much we are immersed in a story, no matter how much we identify with the participants in their experiences or live vicariously through their experience, we are always standing aside and evaluating—though perhaps unconsciously—the significance of characters and of events, their modes of representation, and their meaning for us. Fictional images allow us empathic insight into ways of life beyond our own range. In them we can imagine potentialities that have remained rudimentary in ourselves, recognize types of experience that we know in our own, enlarge the range not only of our experience but also of our understanding. Moreover, the sophisticated reader not only evalutes while participating, but also is aware of the process, knows that he or she "is in social communication of a special sort with the author, in which the represented participants are only part of a convention by which the author discusses, and proposes an evaluation of, possible human experience" (Harding 317). A literary education, one might say, is largely a training in articulating the further reaches of this distinction.[10]

Finally, we can locate these psychological considerations within a map of the full range of activities involved in reading a literary text by looking at the description Robert Scholes gives in his admirable book about teaching literature, *Textual Power.* His schema has the advantage of demonstrating how much is at stake when we undertake to help students do something as apparently simple as reading.

Scholes distinguishes three levels of activity. The first, called simply "reading," is the largely unconscious engagement with the text by which we "construct characters, situations, and a world out of words, by means of cultural codes and generic codes that enable us to process these words so as to construct from them a story" (27). This is the basic process of assembling out of the words on the page characters, situations, and a story. It involves knowledge as much as skill. We have to know the generic codes (such as what a story is and how character is indicated in a text) and especially the cultural codes (such as the denotation and connotations of significant words, the meanings of important actions) that were operative in the composition of the text and the historical situation in which it was composed. Competent mature readers process these codes unconsciously, however, and do not think twice about it. Only when they encounter difficulty do they shift to the next level of activity.

The next level, "interpretation," depends on failures of reading, Scholes proposes, on a reader's feeling of incompleteness.

---

[10] The simultaneous performance of "participant" and "spectator" roles by the reader might be compared to the double activity that would be typical of someone engaged in the Spiritual Exercises of Ignatius Loyola: growth in experiencing God in prayer and growth in the ability to "discern" the movements of desire in one's soul in relation to that experience.

Something has not been understood, or the text has a concealed or non-obvious level of meaning that can be found only by an active, conscious process of interpretation. Typically, this involves a shift from summarizing events to discussing the meaning of a work. The move is triggered, Scholes says, by some excess of meaning in a text or some deficiency of knowledge in the reader. Its goal is to formulate the themes of the text, the attitudes the writer takes toward them, and the strategies the writer uses to accomplish the thematizing. This is a much more complicated activity than simple reading, and it is what we spend most of our time teaching. We explain the rules of the interpretive game and the principles and procedures that lead to strong interpretive positions, so that students can see how it is done and learn how to do it themselves.

But such interpretation is incomplete without a further extension into what Scholes calls "criticism." If interpretation arises because of some excess of meaning in a text or some deficiency of knowledge in the reader, the reverse of this situation—some deficiency in the text or some excess in the reader—leads to the activity of "criticism." This involves a critique of the themes developed in a given fictional text, or a critique of the codes themselves out of which a given text has been constructed. It is essentially a process of making value judgments about the themes in the text or the codes at work in the text, but the important point is that these judgments are made by an individual reader not on his or her own behalf but on behalf of a class or group in which he or she has membership. The reader's social and political responses to a text, having been shaped by membership in groups defined by shared values and interests, lead to a critical evaluation of the text. The most striking recent examples of this kind of criticism come from feminists, but any group that has identified its interests as a class can mount a critical attack on a story's codes and themes from the position of its own system of values. Texts, in this perspective, are not products of an isolated realm of "art." They embody world-views with social consequences, and seeing the relationship between textual strategies and social consequences is an important aspect of maturity in reading. We have to open a dialogue, Scholes says, between the literary text we read and the social text in which we live.

If this is a true dialogue, it has to be open to the possibility of working both ways. Acts of criticism evaluate texts from the perspective of our interests and commitments, but texts can also interrogate our values and change us. And the territory susceptible to this give-and-take in the act of reading is not limited to the political, the social, or the ethical. It potentially includes the whole compass of meaning that we call spiritual. Scholes says elsewhere, speaking of the development (and decline) of our physical and mental powers as readers:

> We humans are the animals who know that we shall die. We know that our lives are shaped like stories, with a beginning, a middle, and an end, that that the end is inevitable. Reading, I am contending, consists, among other things, in recognizing and facing the signs of this pattern, too. We read life as well as books, and the activity of reading is really a matter of working through signs and texts in order to comprehend more fully and powerfully not only whatever may be presented therein but also our own situations, both in their particularity and historicity and in their more durable and inevitable dimensions. (*Protocols* 18)

George Steiner speaks of our "answerability to the meaning of the world" that is at stake when we read. The hermeneutic quest is to achieve an "answerable understanding" of the author's construct. Steiner does not allow us the fashionable distance from resolution that so much contemporary theory assumes. History and experience may be impenetrable, but it is the function of literature and art to tell us precisely of their obstinacies. We make a "wager on the meaning of meaning," which is, finally, a wager on transcendence and its accessibility to us (Steiner 4).

One of the fascinating similarities between reading development and spiritual development is that, while the fact that both will occur is fairly predictable through their early stages, neither kind of development necessarily continues much beyond the level it reaches in early adolescence (Appleyard 121–23; Fowler 161, 172). In both areas development can stop with conventional ways of making meaning out of experience and conventional forms of commitment. Whether they go further depends on capacities an individual is equipped with, on the kinds of experiences a person has, and on how he or she responds to them. For reading, the most significant factor in development after adolescence is the kind of education one undergoes. While I would be reluctant to make the same claim for spiritual development, it is clear that college is one of the prime environments in which the quality and extent of one's spiritual development is in play, precisely because of the moral and intellectual challenges that are predictable parts of the overall growing up that occurs during the college years. If college can be the setting for this kind of development, and if it overlaps with reading development, and if the latter is sometimes even the vehicle of the former (as we saw in Merton's case), and if both are exercises of imagination, then the attitude of the teacher of literature toward both kinds of development in the lives of students in the classroom may be a crucial dimension in what happens to them.

Sharon Parks remarks, at the end of her study of the faith development of young adults, that "every professor is potentially a spiritual guide and every syllabus a confession of faith" (134). In today's academic culture, which enshrines (and, Parks aptly suggests, is tyrannized by) a distinction that goes back at least to Kant, between what can be talked about empirically and what must be left to the realm of personal opinion and belief, most teachers of literature might be reluctant to go so far. We have no difficulty understanding the immediate object of the teacher of literature. Looking at Scholes's three levels from the perspective of theories of psychological development, we can see that a particular kind of reader is implied by each one: at the lowest level, an immature reader who has mastered basic reading skills but uses them simply to absorb uncritically the narrative on a page; on the next level, a much more competent reader who can synthesize complex information from a variety of sources in order to understand the meanings of a text and how it has been constructed; at the highest level, a reader who understands how text and world are interconnected, who can evaluate texts and be evaluated by them in order to recognize the signs and images in which some part of the reliable meaning of his or her life is disclosed. The teacher's task is to help the student become each of these readers, to deepen his or her capacity for critical reflection until it embraces the full range of issues that are involved in reading texts.

How does a teacher lead students through these transitions? The conventional advice of developmentalists is to find the right combination of challenge and support for the particular stage a student is at. Development occurs because the meaning-making strategies that work in one stage are challenged by new and disconfirming experiences, a healthy disequilibrium that is resolved only when the student arrives at more inclusive strategies of meaning-making that can contain both old and new experiences. The teacher does this by creating appropriate challenges, by arousing curiosity, by clarifying what is mysterious, by helping students attend to the interconnections among truths, by paying attention to their accounts of their experience, by designing assignments that enlarge that experience, and by supporting students as they struggle to find ways to be answerable to the meaning of their lives. If this answerability entails a spiritual dimension, it may not be the teacher's primary responsibility to facilitate it, but it may be irresponsible to ignore it.

In the end, perhaps it is not persuasive to claim more than the possibility that reading *can* be a means to spiritual development or that the two *may* proceed in tandem and illuminate each other. Sophisticated reading does not necessarily entail spiritual maturity; nor is the reverse the case. Reading development is fundamentally a matter of knowledge, perhaps self-knowledge—an affectively toned knowledge, but knowledge still. Spiritual development is about one's relationship to God or at least to a transcendent horizon of value, partly about knowing but also about trusting and being acknowledged by whom and what one trusts. But the fact that the two may unfold through similar stages, are frequently driven by the same experiences and focus on similar issues, and that both are apt to employ the currency of imagination to embody their steps forward may strike us as wonderful and worth thinking about as we encounter our students and become involved in their lives.

Works Cited

Appleyard, J. A., s.j. *Becoming a Reader: The Experience of Fiction from Childhood to Adulthood*. Cambridge, Eng.: Cambridge UP, 1990.

Barry, William A., s.j. *Spiritual Direction and the Encounter with God: A Theological Inquiry*. New York: Paulist, 1992.

Bettelheim, Bruno. *The Uses of Enchantment: The Meaning and Importance of Fairy Tales*. New York: Knopf, 1976.

Bruner, Jerome. *Actual Minds, Possible Worlds*. Cambridge, MA: Harvard UP, 1986.

Conn, Walter. *Christian Conversion: A Developmental Interpretation of Autonomy and Surrender*. New York: Paulist, 1986.

Crowe, Frederick E., S.J. *Old Things and New: A Strategy for Education*. Atlanta, GA: Scholars, 1985.

Davis, Lennard J. *Resisting Novels: Ideology and Fiction*. New York: Methuen, 1987.

Erikson, Erik H. *Childhood and Society*. 2nd ed. New York: Norton, 1963.

————. *Identity, Youth, and Crisis*. New York: Norton, 1968.

Flynn, Elizabeth A., and Patrocinio P. Schweickart, eds. *Gender and Reading: Essays on Readers, Texts, and Contexts*. Baltimore: Johns Hopkins UP, 1986.

Fowler, James M. *Stages of Faith: The Psychology of Human Development and the Quest of Meaning*. San Francisco: Harper & Row, 1981.

Frye, Northrop. *Anatomy of Criticism: Four Essays*. Princeton, NJ: Princeton UP, 1957.

Harding, D. W. "Psychological Processes in the Reading of Fiction." In *Aesthetics in the Modern World*. Ed. Harold Osborne. New York: Weybright and Talley, 1968. 300–17.

Heath, Shirley Brice. *Ways with Words: Language, Life, and Work in Communities and Classrooms*. Cambridge, Eng: Cambridge UP, 1983.

Holland, Norman N. *The Brain of Robert Frost: A Cognitive Approach to Literature*. New York: Routledge, 1988.

————. *The Dynamics of Literary Response*. New York: Oxford UP, 1957.

Iser, Wolfgang. *The Act of Reading: A Theory of Aesthetic Response*. Baltimore: Johns Hopkins UP, 1978.

Kurfiss, Joanne. "Intellectual, Psychosocial, and Moral Development in College: Four Major Theories." *Manual for Project QUE (Quality Undergraduate Education)*. Washington, DC: Council for Independent Colleges, 1983.

Lesser, Simon O. *Fiction and the Unconscious*. Chicago: University of Chicago P, 1957.

Lonergan, Bernard, S.J. *Insight: A Study of Human Understanding*. New York: Philosophical Library, 1957.

————. *Method in Theology*. New York: Herder & Herder, 1972.

————. *A Third Collection: Papers by Bernard Lonergan, S.J.* Ed. Frederick E. Crowe, S.J. New York: Paulist, 1985.

Lynch, William F., S.J. *Images of Faith: An Exploration of the Ironic Imagination*. Notre Dame, Ind.: U of Notre Dame P, 1973.

Merton, Thomas. *My Argument with the Gestapo: A Macaronic Journal*. Garden City, NY: Doubleday, 1969.

————. *The Seven Storey Mountain*. New York: Harcourt Brace Jovanovich, 1948.

Niebuhr, H. Richard. *The Meaning of Revelation*. New York: Macmillan, 1952.

Parks, Sharon. *The Critical Years: The Young Adult Search for a Faith to Live By*. San Francisco: Harper & Row, 1986.

Piaget, Jean. "Intellectual Evolution from Adolescence to Adulthood." *Human Development*, 15 (1972): 1–12.

Piaget, Jean, and Barbel Inhelder. *The Psychology of the Child*. New York: Basic Books, 1969.

Perry, William G., Jr. "Cognitive and Ethical Growth: The Making of Meaning." In *The Modern American College: Responding to the New Realities of Diverse Students and a Changing Society.*" Ed. Arthur Chickering. San Francisco, Jossey-Bass, 1981.

————. *Forms of Intellectual and Ethical Development in the College Years: A Scheme*. New York: Holt, Rinehart & Winston, 1970.

Rabinowitz, Peter J. *Before Reading: Narrative Conventions and the Politics of Interpretation*. Ithaca, NY: Cornell UP, 1987.

Robinson, Lillian S. *Sex, Class, and Culture*. Bloomington: Indiana UP, 1978.

Rosenblatt, Louise M. *The Reader, the Text, the Poem: The Transactional Theory of the Literary Work*. Carbondale: Southern Illinois UP, 1978

Scholes, Robert. *Protocols of Reading*. New Haven, CT: Yale UP, 1989.

————. *Textual Power: Literary Theory and the Teaching of English*. New Haven, CT: Yale UP, 1985

Scollon, Ron, and Suzanne Scollon. *Narrative Literacy and Face in Interethnic Communication*. Norwood, NJ: Ablex, 1981.

Schneiders, Sandra M., i.h.m. "Spirituality in the Academy." *Theological Studies*, 50 (1989): 676–97.

Steiner, George. *Real Presences*. Chicago: U of Chicago P, 1989.

Taylor, Denny, and Catherine Dorsey-Gaines. *Growing Up Literate: Learning from Inner-City Families*. Portsmouth, NH: Heinemann, 1988.

Winnicott, D. W. *Playing and Reality*. New York: Basic Books, 1971.

3

The Gendered Imagination in Religion and Literature

Philip C. Rule, S.J.

FUNDAMENTAL TO THE INTERDISCIPLINARY STUDY of religion and literature are two concepts, experience and imagination. Literature and religion alike arise out of human experience grasped and shaped by the imagination. Experience may be simply defined as the raw stuff of living, our day-to-day, minute-by-minute encounter with the world. Imagination is more elusive, as many writers are quick to point out even as they assert its central role in faith and religion, precisely because imagination is involved in any understanding of imagination.[1] The elusive nature of the imagination is further compounded by the fact that feminist studies (in both theology and critical theory) have shown us that men and women experience differently and therefore, one must conclude, imagine differently. We must realize, then, that in a real sense, the imagination is gendered. This must be understood, as feminist writers point out, in a very carefully nuanced sense lest one fall into the traditional stereotyping of male and female cognitive operations.[2] Nevertheless, there are differences and those difference are, as I hope to show, significant.

Contemporary studies in religion and literature therefore must take into consideration the growing body of writing in both theology and critical theory produced by feminist writers. This was not the case twenty years ago when Vernon J. Ruland attempted a nearly definitive survey of "the acclaimed landmarks and exciting uncharted frontiers of interdisciplinary religious studies" (vii). His book covers some 344 writers, only fifteen of whom were

---

[1] See, for example, Hart 184; Haight 25–27, 41; and Brooker.

[2] In the area of theology, see Ross and Hilkert, and Parsons.

women, none of whom wrote from a formally feminist point of view. The canon of creative writers studied was, of course, also predominantly male.

We must consider these new theological and literary critical approaches because theory colors the way one experiences, imagines, and reflects. As theology and critical theory are born of critical reflection on religious experience (believing) and literary experience (both writing and reading), they in turn become part of the process that structures our consciousness, of which imagination is a key part. As Harold Bloom has long argued, subsequent writers inform our reading of earlier writers. More important in the present context, as Thomas Kuhn has pointed out in his classic study of paradigm shifts, systems or methods are notoriously resistant to change, as we witness everywhere today in the world of literary studies.

In order to show how feminist writing has provided "exciting uncharted frontiers of interdisciplinary religious studies," I would like to consider briefly the following: first, two classic biographies of Keats and some current feminist readings of Keats; secondly, Wordsworth's struggle in *The Prelude* to grasp the nature of the imagination; thirdly, an explicitly male and female engagement with the epic form as seen in *The Prelude* and *Aurora Leigh*; and, fourthly, and very briefly, a few examples of feminist voices in critical reflection on religious experience.

In 1963, Walter Jackson Bate and Aileen Ward published biographies of John Keats. Both were highly respected and both were favorites of differing admirers. By general consensus Bate's life, which won him the first of two Pulitzer Prizes for biography, became the critical study. In 1985, reviewing Keats studies for the MLA research volume on the Romantics, Jack Stillinger gives Ward's life qualified praise, concluding that it "obviously maintains its usefulness." He goes on to say that "Bate's biography . . . is *of another order of magnitude* and has claims to be one of the *best critical biographies ever written of any poet*" (672; emphasis added). In the light of this "official" assessment, what is one to think when Marjorie Levinson acknowledges her indebtedness to "Aileen Ward's unsurpassed biography and to the important work of Walter Jackson Bate and Robert Gittings" in her study of Keats's "life of allegory" (7). Are these two, somewhat contradictory evaluations merely political infighting of the sort common to the literary profession, or is there some other explanation? It is precisely this question that set me thinking about the topic of this essay. Reading Levinson and other recent writers on Keats, I began to realize that Ward's biography may have opened up for them "exciting uncharted frontiers."

Biography, too, is a work of the imagination. Having meticulously assembled and studied the details of a subject's life and writings, biographers must imagine the person whose narrative they will shape. The biographer must come up with a central insight into the subject which will act as an organizing principle of the narrative material. I suggest that the core of Bate's life is the chapter on Negative Capability, which was also the subject of his own Harvard College essay on Keats. As a young boy in school at Enfield, Keats possessed "qualities rarely found together—courage, sensitivity, and generosity" (17). At this early stage of life there was "a union of energy, courage, and absorption in something outside himself," a "generous capacity for commitment, for imaginative identification" (27). He is a "virile, relatively unbookish poet" (73) taken by the "virile, penetrating idiom" of Shakespeare's verse (85). Bate consistently uses terms like "virile," "manly," "masculine" to describe both Keats and his poetry. When Bate comes to treat the concept of "negative capability," he explicitly relates it to Keats's youthful, manly qualities when he says that "what strikes us most in his capacity for sympathetic identification, starting with the school days at Enfield, is its inclusiveness" (253).

The question Bate leaves unexplored is what made the man become the poet. This is precisely the question Aileen Ward sets out to answer.[3] Her more explicitly psychological reading contextualizes Keats's poetic growth within the process of his psychosexual development beginning with his mother and following more fully than Bate his relations with women and the final tragic courtship of Fanny Brawne. Keats's inability or unwillingness to commit himself to a relationship with a woman seems rooted in his ambivalent feelings about his beautiful, affectionate, young mother who abandoned him and his siblings. This carries over into a subsequent tension between two kinds of women, "flirta-

---

[3] See Ward's *John Keats: The Making of a Poet*. It is interesting to note that a later paperback edition of Bate's book bears the subtitle *The Growth of a Genius*.

tious young beauties and serious young ladies, sexually much less challenging, often several years older than himself" (13). In *Endymion* personal self-exploration merges with the nature of creativity, for "around the original core of his myth were gathering meanings which he was still struggling to formulate to himself: the birth of the poetic consciousness, now somehow linked with a dream of fulfillment in sexual love" (92). Beneath this lies a deepening and maturing awareness that after love comes death, "you cannot eat your cake and have it too," as Keats himself gradually realized.

Ward was not writing as a feminist critic. She speaks easily of Keats's "sober masculine style" (50) and Chapman's "hard masculine strength of phrase" (74), but she is intensely sensitive to the gender issues involved in Keats's sexual and poetic growth. During the writing of *Endymion* he began "to recognize in himself a rhythm of energy and indolence, of alternation between the masculine imposition of self upon experience and feminine surrender to it" (166). Unlike Bate who characterizes negative capability as rooted in a quickly maturing masculinity, Ward sees it as growing gradually out of his relationships with women and defined ultimately as feminine in its characteristics. Anne Mellor points out that "above all, Keats defines the true poet as empathetic, a quality everywhere identified with femininity in the eighteenth century." Keats is moving toward an understanding of creativity, of the imagination, that bears remarkably feminine qualities, qualities like self-negation and passivity rather than domination. Keats's constant identification of food and love and the mention in *Endymion* of "sexual pleasure as feeding at the breast" and in his letters to Fanny Brawne of "trying to wean himself from her" (309) suggest to Ward the psychosexual complexity of Keats's thinking about poetic consciousness.

Such an approach has opened doors to recent writers like Marjorie Levinson, Anne Mellor, Karen Swann, Karla Alwes, and others who read Keats anew from a feminist perspective.[4] Thus, while not recognized as such at the time of its publication, Ward's biography appears to be the basis for exciting alternate readings of

---

[4] Mellor's treatment of the relation between Keats's psychosexual maturing and his critical theorizing is a superb development of ideas latent in Ward's biography. See also Alwes and Swann.

Keats's poetry. And many of these alternate readings confirm the fact that the imagination is gendered however complexly and ambivalently. Because imagination is central to religious experience, clearly anyone now wishing to explore the religious dimensions of Keats's thought and poetry must take these new readings into consideration.

My next point concerns an interesting contrast in *The Prelude*, the poem in which Wordsworth struggles to grasp the nature of the imagination, tracing it from earliest youth up to, possibly, the date of the final revisions of the poem. In that great autobiographical epic there are two striking moments, moments when Wordsworth is engaged in the very typically masculine activity of climbing a mountain. Yet in the retrospective act of writing about these moments, which are personal epiphanies about the imagination, the imagery becomes significantly feminine. What occurs in these passages is an example of what Alan Richardson has called the "colonization of the feminine," a process by which "male writers drew on memories and fantasies of identification with the mother in order to colonize the conventionally feminine domain of sensibility."

While my analysis of the two key passages (Book 6.592–616 and Book 14.33–62) and the subtle differences in wording between the 1805 and the 1850 versions must perforce be brief, it will show that gender is central to Wordsworth's grasp of the imagination. In recalling the moment of crossing the Alps, Wordsworth describes imagination "like an unfathered vapour" simply "lifting up itself / Before the eye" (1805). This is later expanded to: "That awful Power rose from the mind's abyss / Like an unfathered vapour" (1850). The "mind" and "its prowess" later become "the soul" and "her prowess." The original version closes with: "Which hides it [the mind] like the overflowing Nile." This is expanded into: "That hides her [the soul], like the mighty flood of the Nile / Poured from his fount of Abyssinian clouds / To fertilize the whole Egyptian plain." "Unfathered" clearly suggests an act of parthenogenesis, exclusively a female phenomenon. Rising "from the mind's abyss" rather than simply "lifting up itself / Before the eye" adds an additional note of a womb-like origin which is subtly echoed in the revision of the passage in Book 14.

What is notable in the climbing of Mt. Snowdon is the simple fact that the original purpose of climbing the mountain to see the rising of the sun, a male figure, is lost in the moment of encountering the moon, a female figure, irradiating the mist. In the original "the moon looked down upon this shew / In single glory" like some passive presence. In the revisions the moon takes on an active, dominant role. Whereas in the original the poet sees the mist "Which meek and silent rested at my feet," in the revised text the mist stretches "Into the main Atlantic, that appeared / To dwindle and give up his majesty / Usurped as far as the sight could reach." It is now the "presence of the full-orbed Moon, / Who, from her sovereign elevation, gazed / Upon the billowy ocean, as it lay / Meek and silent." The "abyss" of the passage in Book 6 is quietly echoed in "A fixed, *abysmal*, gloomy, breathing-place" (emphasis added).

Two final examples bring out the gendering process at work here. In lines only slightly revised from the original, Wordsworth describes his search for imagination thus: "we have traced the stream / From the blind cavern whence is faintly heard / Its natal murmur," repeating the womb-like analogy. And the person who has "risen / Up to the height of feeling intellect" is described in domestic, female terms. For he

> Shall want no humbler tenderness; his heart
> Be tender as a nursing mother's heart;
> Of female softness shall his life be full,
> Of humble cares and delicate desires,
> Mild interests and gentle sympathies. (225–31)

Clearly Wordsworth's language in recording these two crucial episodes in *The Prelude* bears out Jean Hagstrum's assertion that "if Empson is right—and I think he is—that in Wordsworth 'Sensation and Imagination interlock,' it then must follow that sexuality remains an ever-present force even in transcendental moments, for there is simply no intellectually honest way of excluding it from so comprehensive sensationism as Wordsworth's own literary and political criticism establishes" (82). My contention, obviously, is that the changes and rearrangements in the 1850 text thematically relate the two moments of transcendental experience and explain the nature of imagination deliberately, and successfully I think, in gendered terms. Such a reading goes against that of Jonathan Wordsworth, who, assuming the artistic superiority of the 1805 text, says that in making changes like those I have pointed out, "Wordsworth does not merely destroy one of his greatest pieces of poetry, he weakens precisely those aspects which had made it the fitting climax to his poem" (328).

In spite of his couching the imagination in terms of female activities of birthing and nursing in these key passages of *The Prelude*, Wordsworth was with great confidence writing an epic, a traditionally male preserve; and he describes himself throughout the poem as a solitary figure moving toward moments of prophetic inspiration and missioning. The epic dimensions of Wordsworth's narrative elevate his private and personal experience to the level of the public and general. Barrett Browning's *Aurora Leigh*, like *The Prelude*, is an autobiographical narrative about the growth of a poet's mind. And she establishes the Wordsworthian note immediately as Aurora says:

> I, writing thus, am still what men call young;
> I have not so far left the coasts of life
> To travel inland, that I cannot hear
> That murmur of the outer Infinite
> Which unweaned babies smile at in their sleep
> When wondered at for smiling. . . .

The indirect allusion to nursing is not unintentional as we shall see.

The main plot line eventually brings Aurora and her cousin Romney Leigh together in marriage but not until each pursues separate careers, she as a poet, he as a social activist. She rejects his initial, very Miltonic sounding proposal of marriage which belittles her poetic aspirations:

> "Write woman's verses and dream woman's dreams,
> But let me feel your perfume in my home
> To make my sabbath after working days,
> Bloom out your youth beside me—be my wife." (2.831–34)

At the end she accepts him when he is humbled by the failure of his social projects and, like Jane Eyre's Rochester, blinded in a fire which destroyed his ancestral estate. Throughout the poem the two characters represent the traditionally perceived dichotomy between man the doer and thinker and woman the nurturer and feeler. It was in fact this very cultural dichotomizing of the male and female roles that consigned women writers to turning out lyrics and novels and left the writing of epics to men. A modern reader can hardly suppress a smile when reading a passage like this one culled from an gynecology textbook published in the United States a decade before the appearance of *Aurora Leigh*:

> The great administrative faculties are not hers. She plans no sublime campaigns, nor leads armies into battle, or fleets to victory. The Forum is no theatre for her silver voice, full of tenderness and sensibility. She discerns not the course of the planets, Orion with his belt, and Arcturus with his Suns are naught to her but pretty baubles set up in the sky. She guides no ships through the night and tempest across the trackless sea to some far-off haven half round the world. She composes no *Iliad*, no *Aeneid*. The strength of Milton's poetic vision was far beyond her fine and delicate perceptions. (Meigs 49–50)

While the plot line of *Aurora Leigh* pursues the question of contemporary gender roles, thematically the focus is on Aurora's development of what Holly Laird calls an "epical *Ars Poetica*." These projects intertwine. One of Browning's tenets is that poetry should deal with the present, not the past, precisely because contemporary society needs what poets do best—mediation between the worlds of spirit and matter. Furthermore, the lure of the epic and heroic past is misguided, for

> All actual heroes are essential men,
> And all men possible heroes; every age,
> Heroic in proportions, double-faced,
> Looks backwards and before, expects a morn
> and claims an epos. (5.151–55)

So, at the plot level, Aurora describes vividly the contemporary clashes between both the sexes and the social classes. Two other characters crucial to her portrayal of the contemporary scene are Marian Erle, a poor, working-class girl whom Romney decides to marry as a symbol of the union of the classes, and Lady Waldemar, a beautiful, wealthy, and very buxom woman hot in pursuit of Romney.

After narrating her own struggles for social and financial independence and the gradual achievement of a poetic reputation, Aurora expounds the poetics that grounds her conviction both about the fusion of epic mode and contemporary events and about a reconciliation between active service and poetic contemplation.

This poetics is presented in Book 5, sandwiched between two significant encounters, one with Romney at the end of Book 4 and one with Lady Waldemar at the end of Book 5. Meeting for the first time since they went their separate ways, Aurora and Romney take up again the argument about the usefulness of poetry. She reflects,

> "What is art
> But life upon the larger scale, the higher,
> When, graduating up in a spiral line
> Of still expanding and ascending gyres,
> It pulses toward the intense significance
> Of all things, hungry for the Infinite?
> Art's life—and where we live, we suffer and toil." (4.1151–57)

Through poetry Aurora will feed this universal hunger of men and women for the Infinite. In the process she will find an unfulfilled particular hunger in herself—for human love.

Book 5 opens with a remarkable panorama of creation that echoes Michaelangelo's creation and Chaucer's vibrant and sensual portrait of spring in *The Canterbury Tales*. She asks whether her poetry will be "in mysterious tune / With man and nature?" (3–4) and, as her litany of attunements reaches a climax, whether it will be in tune

> With all that strain
> Of sexual passion, which devours the flesh
> In a sacrament of souls? with mother's breasts
> Which, round the new-made creatures hanging there,
> Throb luminous and harmonious like pure spheres? (14–18)

Having painted creation in rich images of fertility, procreativity, and nurturing, she then surveys her poems and finds them lacking, precisely because what is needed is a treatment of contemporary life in an epic mode. Precisely because "every age, / through

being beheld too close, is ill-discerned / By those who have not
lived past it" (166–68), she says:

> poets should
> Exert a double vision: should have eyes
> To see near things as comprehensively
> As if afar they took their point of sight,
> And distant things as intimately deep
> As if they touched them. (183–88)

Certainly this "double vision" entails combining a divine and a
human perspective which is one of the goals of religion—to try
to see things as God sees them even while we are immersed in
the particularity of human experience. So, echoing the imagery
of the opening lines of the book, she exhorts herself:

> Never flinch,
> But still unscrupulously epic, catch
> Upon the burning lava of a song
> The full-veined, heaving, double-breasted Age:
> That, when the next shall come, the men of that
> May touch the impress with reverent hand, and say
> "Behold—behold the paps we all have sucked!
> This bosom seems to beat still, or at least
> It sets ours beating: this is living art,
> Which thus presents and thus records true life." (5.213–20)

The double vision must be matched by a double life, for

> "While Art
> Sets action on the top of suffering:
> The artist's part is both to be and do,
> Transfixing with a special, central power
> The flat experience of the common man,
> And turning outward, with a sudden wrench,
> Half agony, half ecstasy, the thing
> He feels inmost—never felt the less
> Because he sings it." (366–73)

Like Wordsworth she will play a mediatorial role turning the raw
particularities of personal experience into something of universal

significance for all people, ultimately feeding the hunger of all created beings for the Infinite.

However complete as a poet, she suddenly finds herself incomplete as a person because she has no one to love, no one who loves her. Her encounter with Lady Waldemar, immediately after enunciating her poetics, is tightly related to both theme and plot. Reflecting on her rival's "alabaster shoulders and bare breasts, / On which the pearls, drowned out of sight in milk, / Were lost" (619–21), stunningly showcased to attract male admirers, Aurora echoes the opening passage again and suggests that the Lady has forgotten Nature's purpose for her endowments. At the end, the marriage of Aurora and Romney is a union of poetic creativity and love, which is precisely where Wordsworth ends *The Prelude*—establishing the relationship between love and imagination. This union is in religious terms a fusion of art and service, described in language echoing the Book of Revelation, which will give birth to "New churches, new economies, new laws / Admitting freedom, new societies / Excluding falsehoods: He shall make all new" (9.947–49). Here one clearly hears echoes of the essentially religious apocalyptic visions of both Wordsworth and Shelley.

Browning has thus successfully[5] used a traditionally male genre to articulate a feminist poetics which is not exclusively for women but, as Holly Laird says, "it is a poetics for everyone, feminist in that it sees everyone as gendered, and everyone as in need of re-education about women's capacities" (362). Laird says that "Browning's terminology enacts embrasure, enfolding possibilities, multiplying choices, permitting alternatives" (360). Does not such language evoke the descriptions of Keats's negative capability and Wordsworth's poetic empathy? A parallel to this can be found in Philip Keane, a contemporary Christian ethicist writing about the need for re-imaging and re-imagining moral questions, who advises that "to reflect on our moral images, to really think about them, we need to let go, to open ourselves up to the full power and meaning of images. Religious contemplation, when properly understood, is a leisurely or playful action. Moral contemplation must have the same play aspect" (106–107). This

---

[5] Deirde David comments somewhat acerbically that Browning "afflicted herself with a traditionally masculine genre" (102).

marks a dramatic shift from centuries of exclusively rational analysis and deductive reasoning. It is an openness to, an unfearful embracing of, the complexity of experience which undergoes its first organization in the imagination. Were one to pursue the religious implications of the various views of imagination looked at here, I think they would converge in what theologian Roger Haight sees as one of the fundamental objects of existential faith: "the benign nature of ultimate reality as a whole." Central to the experiencing of God is a certain "wise passivity," a willingness to be "done unto" rather than to do—a negative capability, if you will. Feminist critical theory may have opened doors for a fuller exploration of this basic human experience.

Certainly modern feminist theological thought has made us keenly aware that there are different ways of looking at religious experience. In defending a gender-inclusive translation of the Bible against the closed-mindedness of some Christians, Richard Clifford insists on the need to be sensitive to reader response, for linguistic studies have shown that "men and women hear the same words differently and process them differently" (15). Sister Francis Teresa, writing about celibacy (both mandatory and voluntary) points out that "Church documents on the subject are still sprinkled with words like mastery, dominance, and self-control and, to the discerning female eye, reveal in every line that they have originated in the male brain" in spite of the fact that "women enormously outnumber celibate, consecrated men." From a feminist point of view, by reducing celibacy to abstinence from sex one loses sight of the fact that it must be rooted in the love of God (986). Finally, and only by way of a closing example, Letty Russell has shown how the self-consciousness of women is changing the face of the churches particularly in the area of social justice. In imagining differently, these women's writings provide a different set of images for the critical reflection which is theology.

I trust I have made my point that the impact of feminist critical thought on literature and religion has made it imperative for scholars today approaching the interdisciplinary study of literature and religion to familiarize themselves with this rich intellectual gift of the last twenty years.

WORKS CITED

Alwes, Karla. *Imagination Transformed: The Evolution of the Female Character in Keats's Poetry.* Carbondale: Southern Illinois UP, 1993.

Bates, Walter Jackson. *John Keats*. Cambridge, MA: Belknap P of Harvard UP, 1963.

Bloom, Harold. *The Anxiety of Influence: A Theory of Poetry*. New York: Oxford UP, 1973.

Brooker, Jewel Spears. "Imagination: A Mystery Re-viewed." *Christianity and Literature* 42 (1992): 157–63.

Browning, Elizabeth Barrett. *Aurora Leigh*. Ed. Karry McSweeney. Oxford: Oxford UP, 1993.

Clifford, Richard. "The Bishops, the Bible, and Liturgical Language." *America* 172 (1995): 15.

David, Deirdre. "Elizabeth Barrett Browning: 'Art as Service.'" *Intellectual Women and Victorian Patriarchy: Harriet Martineau, Elizabeth Barrett Browning, George Eliot*. Ithaca, NY: Cornell UP, 1987.

Hagstrum, Jean. *The Romantic Body: Love and Sexuality in Keats, Wordsworth, and Blake*. Knoxville: U of Tennessee P, 1985.

Haight, Roger. *Dynamics of Theology*. New York: Paulist, 1990.

Hart, Ray. *Unfinished Man and the Imagination*. New York: Herder, 1968.

Keane, Philip. *Christian Ethics and Imagination*. New York: Paulist, 1984.

Kuhn, Thomas. *The Structure of Scientific Revolutions*. Chicago: U of Chicago P, 1962.

Laird, Holly A. "Aurora Leigh: An Epical *Ars Poetica*." *Writing the Woman Artist: Essays on Poetics, Politics, and Portraiture*. Ed. Suzanne W. Jones. Philadelphia: U of Pennsylvania P, 1991.

Levinson, Marjorie. *Keats's Life of Allegory: The Origins of a Style*. Oxford: Blackwell, 1988.

Meigs, Charles D. *Woman: Her Diseases and Remedies—A Series of Letters to His Class*. 2nd ed. Philadelphia: Lee & Blanchard, 1847.

Mellor, Anne. *Romanticism and Gender*. New York: Routledge, 1993.

Parsons, Susan. "Feminist Ethics after Modernity." *Studies in Christian Ethics* 8 (1995): 77–94.

Richardson, Alan. "Romanticism and the Colonization of the Feminine." *Romanticism and Feminism*. Ed. Anne Mellor. Bloomington: Indiana UP, 1988. 13–25.

Ross, Susan A., and Mary Catherine Hilkert, o.p. "Feminist Theology: A Review of Literature." *Theological Studies* 56 (1995): 327–52.

Ruland, Vernon J. *Horizons of Criticism: An Assessment of Religious-Literary Options*. Chicago: American Library Association, 1975.

Russell, Letty. *Church in the Round: Feminist Interpretation of the Church*. Louisville: Westminster/John Knox, 1993.

Stillinger, Jack. "John Keats." *The English Romantic Poets: A Review of Research and Criticism*. Ed. Frank Jordan. 4th ed. New York: MLA, 1985.

Swann, Karen. "Harassing the Muse." *Romanticism and Feminism*. Ed. Anne Mellor. Bloomington: Indiana UP, 1988. 81–92.

Teresa, Sister Francis. "The Trouble with Men." *The Tablet* (August 5, 1995): 986.

Ward, Aileen. *John Keats: The Making of a Poet.* New York: Viking, 1963.

Wordsworth, Jonathan. *William Wordsworth: The Borders of Vision.* Oxford: Clarendon P, 1982.

4

The Paschal Action and the Christian Imagination

John Boyd, S.J.

THE STUDY OF RELIGION (or theology) and literature is healthiest, it seems to me, when the differences and not merely the similarities in the analogy of the two are respected. The uniqueness and autonomy of each should be kept clear. Each should be treated for precisely what it is. I find equally unsatisfactory Matthew Arnold's absorption of religion into poetry, in his "the strongest part of our religion today is its unconscious poetry" (299), and Paul Tillich's absorption of culture into religion in making all serious art religious: "religion is the substance of culture, culture is the form of religion" (42).

With this in mind, though it is quite legitimate and often illuminating to approach literature by studying themes such as hope, alienation, conscience, and the like, I prefer to seek out evidences of belief, and in the present study, of Christian belief, in the precisely literary structures of the poem, play, or novel, that is to say, in plot, imagery, and the like. In this way such influences can be found imaginatively transformed into aesthetic or poetic analogues, for literary structures are the embodiment of theme, voice, and point of view, which, in turn, bear some analogy to real-life perspective and conviction, granted all that should be granted about literary convention and persona. In this essay I am seeking those structures that reflect the Christian doctrine of the Incarnation and its redemptive implications.

It is a commonplace of orthodox Christian belief that mankind was redeemed through the human action of Christ, the God-Man. The Word of God, the Second Person of the Blessed Trinity, became human in Jesus Christ. The divine and human natures were united in His Person without their confusion or their can-

celing each other out. But it is too readily forgotten or muted
that the pattern of the redeemed imitates by analogy the life of
the Redeemer in the same manner of incarnation, the immersion
of the divine into the thoroughly human. In this respect the nature of the Church in its hierarchic and corporate pattern, the
sacraments, the development of Christian doctrine in providential
dependence upon human psychological laws, manifested in accordance with the exigencies of history and the evolutionary revelation itself of divine Providence, all immediately come to mind.
In all these, as in other areas of Christian experience, the pattern
is fully human, yet never merely human, much less humanitarian.
Always at work are a divine transformation of the human, a divine
vitality being shared with men and women, and a divine control,
reflecting a penetration of the human by the Son of God, which
once for all established our solidarity with Him. Other religions
do not claim in their beliefs such a firm solidarity. It is natural
enough, then, to expect and actually to find forms and patterns in
Christian art, of patterns of belief in the incarnation and awareness
of its implications for Christian living, forms and patterns, however, which are genuinely and characteristically artistic because
human.

It is also a commonplace of Christian belief that we were redeemed by Christ's sufferings, death, and resurrection. That these
form one single human action is a favorite theme of F. X. Durrwell, a Redemptorist priest and prominent theologian of the redemption. In his book *The Resurrection* he discusses the idea with
great care and perceptiveness; and it is this action and its essential
unity that we refer to in these pages as the Paschal Action. In it
the death and resurrection comprise a single action, not mere
human death with a reward attached. The Risen Christ is not
merely the term of the death but also the sum of it all and its
crown, the goal that set the pattern of the entire Paschal Action
and toward which it moved from the very beginning. His wounds
were glorious in His rising, because victory burned in them as He
died.

Durrwell writes: "According to St. John, Christ was accustomed to have envisaged both events together, as two aspects,
dark and light, of his messianic destiny. He saw them as the final
point of his life, linked together in that one 'hour' " (35). The
passion is the hour of the prince of this world (John 14:30), the

hour of humiliation which Christ fears (12:27). It is only a glorious hour, because His resurrection is to come as the conclusion of His death: "The hour is to come that the Son of Man should be glorified," He cries, when He is told of the Gentile proselytes who have asked to see Him (12:20–23). Durrwell then recalls Christ's immediately adding: "Truly, truly I say to you, unless a grain of wheat falls into the earth and dies, it remains alone; but if it dies, it bears much fruit. He who loves his life loses it, and he who hates his life in this world, will keep it for eternal life" (12:24–25). The theme and its image are importantly paradoxical. "Thus," adds Durrwell, "Christ's unique hour encompasses both his death and his resurrection." And the reason: "because they are joined together in a single action" (36). Another image in John's gospel, referring to the death and resurrection, is that of the journey. Speaking of the most important action of his life, Christ says, "I am going to the Father" (16:10). Durrwell comments: "Our Lord was not so much going to his death as by way of it; it was a mortal journey whose end was with the Father" (37). Durrwell also refers to two Church Fathers' opinions on the matter. He quotes St. Augustine as saying: " 'Therefore does the Father love me because I lay down my life that I may take it up again.' What is he saying? 'My Father loves me because I am dying in order to rise again.' The resurrection is the goal towards which Christ is working" (36). St. Jerome's translation (the Latin Vulgate) of the Emmaus story in Luke sees not only the necessity of the death and the resurrection, but the glorification of Christ as well, as the end toward which the death is subordinated: "and so enter into his glory" (Luke 24:26) (35).

St. Paul constantly parallels the death and resurrection of the Savior. On many occasions he does this by way of their application to the redeemed, that if we have died with Christ, so we must rise with Him. In the famous passage in the fifteenth chapter of First Corinthians, he speaks of those who deny the resurrection of the redeemed as tantamount to denying Christ's own resurrection; and the consequence of this would be that they would still be in their sins. "But in fact Christ has been raised from the dead, the first fruits of those who have fallen asleep. For as by a man came death, by a man has come also the resurrection from the dead" (25:20–22). In this passage and its larger context, the efficacy of the resurrection both of Christ and of the redeemed as part of the Paschal Action is intrinsically linked to the passion and death. Paul's well-known text in Philippians about the mind of Christ and our sharing in it is most explicit about the matter of the single action of the death and resurrection of Christ: "He emptied himself, taking the form of a servant, being born in the likeness of men. And being found in human form, he humbled himself and became obedient unto death, even to death on a cross. Therefore God has highly exalted him . . ." (Phil. 2:5–11). "*Therefore*" is used to link the two events. The kenosis, or self-emptying, is the point, and the resurrection is part of it. Further, when Paul speaks of the redeemed as sharing in Christ's death, it is not in a temporal sense, but in sharing in the mystery through baptism, a symbol of both the death and the resurrection (Rom. 6:3; Col. 2:11ff.). "From this point of view," concludes Durrwell, "the death of Jesus is welded together with his resurrection in the one mystery. The crucifixion and the resurrection are not so much two separate events as one mystery with two facets" (54). This argument has great imaginative power, as we shall soon see.

The Paschal Action, the central action of the redemption, comprising the death and resurrection of Christ linked in unity, is an action unique in all history. It is unique in kind. Though completely human, this action of Christ in His human nature manifests the power of God, Who alone is lord of life and death. This action of weakness, suffering, and defeat in a human view becomes the medium of triumph and victory, and the model of true Christian wisdom for the redemption of the world. Through the power of God the same humanity that suffers is triumphant. The action is unique in pattern. These disparate elements of life and death are united, as we have seen, into one action, the resurrection being the end toward which the sufferings and death moved from the beginning, the finality and goal of the entire action. This is the fuller view of the wisdom of the cross, which Christ urged upon all who would follow Him. It speaks for the victory of life over sin and its progeny of death, both temporal and eternal. Finally, this action is historically unique. It is not to be assimilated to the pattern of the dying and rising god of mythology. It is an historical action and not one ideally projected by the mythographer. It has happened once for all, not to be historically repeated. This pattern of action is not ironic but paradoxical, a point to be made more explicit later in this essay.

This Paschal Action of Christ Himself is the exemplar, the pattern for imitation in at least three ways. It is the model of the Christian life of the redeemed. The grain of wheat must die, and if it does, it is vitalized. The amount and kind of suffering vary in each life, as does the tasting of the real victory even now. But this victory is built into the suffering, and makes all the difference. And, more important, the reality of the heavenly reward matters absolutely. It is important, then, to see that the Christian life imitates Christ's Paschal Action in a very earnest way. Even if sufferings are minimal in one's life, there is always a death to die, and this is to be accomplished in the image of Christ and incorporated into Him in grace. This brings us to the second way in which Christ is exemplar for the redeemed. It is in the life of the liturgy and of the sacraments. The incorporation, spoken of just now, comes about through baptism, which not only produces it but is modeled on the death and resurrection of Christ, the plunging into the water of death to sin and the rebirth through Christ's rising and our own. The sacrifice of the Mass is the ritually ontological repetition of the very Paschal Action we are discussing. Christ's death and resurrection are made present to us in a remarkable way. The other sacraments as well are reminders of their origin in this Paschal Action, as are many of the minor actions and rubrics of the liturgy. As I mentioned at the outset, it can too easily be forgotten that the redemption not only is effected by this Paschal Action but also is modeled on its exemplarity. The third way of imitating the Paschal Action is the work of the Christian imagination attuned to its ways.

The approach we are taking in this essay involves seeing literature as an imitation or miming of human life. This is the work of imagination. In the case of the Paschal Action it is an imitation of Christ's own experience or of the experience of others already imitating Him, viewed in the perspective of faith deriving from Him. I mean literature as imitation in the better understanding of that classical term, surely not as the mere copy or faithful expression of some idea or the appearances of things to form the "content" of a play, poem, or novel, but rather as an artful, creative structure that reveals in its pattern the deeper themes of human life that it mimes (Boyd, *Function* 18–26). If the Christian life of faith and grace is achieved in the image of the incarnate Redeemer (though uniquely so in each case), Christian literature, in reflecting a redeemed point of view and awareness of human life, carries imitation further, into the imaginative order, and hence can readily be achieved through analogous structures. The Scholastic concept of exemplary causality can throw some light on all this. By imitation of the exemplar or archetype, a person or thing shares, participates in, the perfection of the exemplar or archetype, yet only by achieving their own form. According to the exigencies of art, literature participates in what it mimes only by achieving its own structure or form. In this way the autonomy of art and its self-sufficiency are not diluted the way they seem to be in much modern myth criticism and in Robertson's allegorism (see Betherum). Such Christian literature as we are concerned with here partakes of the method of the incarnation in its specific Paschal Action by imaging forth aesthetic patterns that reflect this central Christian doctrine and its implications for the life of the redeemed.

Relating this action to the dramatic patterns of tragic and comic plots reveals that it is neither of these, while evidencing a complete transformation of the ingredients of each. Christ's triumphant death absorbed all the bitterness of the tragic human condition, but His rising utterly outstripped the most sanguine hopes of human reconciliation and of a happy ending. The Paschal Action embodies the paradox of life gained through death, of the divine influence achieved through the human; and all tragic and comic ironies must pale in the face of this paradoxical manifestation of the power of God.

Compared with tragedy, the suffering of the Paschal Action is quite different. It is not due to a tragic fault or flaw; it is not self-caused but sacrificial and atoning in nature. In the long run it is not self-destructive but asserts a value that in the plot's final state brings victory. The grain of wheat must die to beget new life; the cross must take life in order to gain it at a higher level. This victory and vitality, implied in the suffering, are evident in themselves in the final glory, transcending all natural expectation of a comic happy ending. This ending has a permanence and security that supersedes comedy's possible need to repeat its struggle at a future date, and there is no need of a comic purging. But the final thing to remember is that, in the Paschal Action, whether of Christ or of one in imitation of Him, the plot is redemptive and symbolic of the union of life and death, of new life emanating from the suffering and death, the triumph of the life of grace, "the heaven-haven of the Reward." The second part of this essay will test the ideas above in four well-known examples of Christian literature: in T. S. Eliot's *Murder in the Cathedral* and in his *Four Quartets*, and in Gerard Manley Hopkins's *The Wreck of the Deutschland*, and in Graham Greene's *The Power and the Glory* (also called in Britain *The Labyrinthine Ways*).

The general or gross structure of *Murder in the Cathedral* is relatively simple. There is the portrayal of the situation in Canterbury prior to the present return of Thomas à Becket from exile, the temptations of Thomas on his return, the attack on him, and then his slaying, with an added dialogue in modern form of the knights who killed him. It is the simple presentation of the martyrdom common to martyrdom plays: the sufferings, including the temptations against his dignity, dedication, and ascetical ways; death; and the final accepted glory of the saint.

In some detail we witness the fourfold temptation of Thomas, after the chorus of women describes the state of affairs during the past seven years because of Thomas's exile after his conflict with the king, Henry. Thomas is tempted, first of all, to resume his former life, prior to his consecrated life as priest and bishop: "Remembering all the good times past" (23). "Fluting in the meadows, viols in the hall, / Laughter and apple-blossom floating on the water, / Singing at nightfall, Whispering in chambers" (23). And when the temptation does not work, the Tempter says to Thomas: "If you will remember me, my Lord, at your prayers, / I'll remember you at kissing-time below the stairs" (25). The second temptation is to resume the chancellorship and serve Henry this way:

> Think, my Lord,
> Power obtained grows to glory,
> Life lasting, a permanent possession,
> A templed tomb, monument of marble.
> Rule over men reckon no madness. (26–27)

The third tempter urges him to back the king of France—"You and I, my Lord, are Normans" (32). A revolution against the king of England would favor the Church and this would benefit him.

> Shall I who ruled like an eagle over doves
> Now take the shape of a wolf among wolves?
> Pursue your treacheries as you have done before:
> No one shall say that I betrayed a king. (34)

The final temptation is to think selfishly of the glory of martyrdom:

> But think, Thomas, think of glory after death.
> When king is dead, there's another king,
> And one more King is another reign.
> King is forgotten, when another shall come:
> Saint and martyr rule from the tomb.
> . . . . . .
> Think of pilgrims, standing in line
> Before the glittering jewelled shrine. (37–38)

Thomas:

> The last temptation is the greatest treason:
> To do the right deed for the wrong reason. (44)

In the Christmas homily, which occurs as an Interlude between the two "Parts" or acts of the play, Thomas is discoursing about St. Stephen, the first Christian martyr, whose feast is the next day. He says, in the spirit of the Paschal Action, that we both grieve and rejoice at his martyrdom, but ultimately we rejoice because of his heavenly glory. His part in the sacrifice of Christ is commemorated in the Mass, the memorial of Calvary. "For who in the World will both mourn and rejoice at once and for the same reason" (48)?

> A martyr, a saint, is always made by the design of God, for His love of men, to warn them and to lead them, to bring them back to His ways. A martyrdom is never the design of man; for the true martyr is he who has become the instrument of God, who has lost his will in the will of God, not lost it but found it, for he has found freedom in submission to God. The martyr no longer desires anything for himself, not even the glory of martyrdom. So thus as on earth the Church mourns and rejoices at once, in a fashion that the world cannot understand; so in Heaven the Saints are most high, having made themselves most low, seeing themselves not as we see them,

but in the light of the Godhead from whom they draw their being. (49–50)

And he adds: "I do not think I shall ever preach to you again; . . . it is possible that in a short time you may have yet another martyr" (50). This is the essential state of the action, death ending in glory.

The second "Part" reveals the gradual unfolding of the attack on Thomas and his final killing. His undoing, after the "purification of the motive," is his rising to glory. The four knights then discuss in modern idiom the wisdom of his slaying. The chorus in prayer then begin to realize what has happened: "We thank Thee for Thy mercies of blood, for Thy redemption by blood. For the blood of Thy martyrs and saints, / Shall enrich the earth, shall create the holy places. . . . Blessed Thomas, pray for us" (84, 86).

While imaginative or artful imitation *per se* best fits drama and the narrative, it is also applicable to lyric and philosophic poetry. This comes about by the shape or pattern of the theme through imagery, sound, and language. After all, literary imitation has to do with the probability of action or theme and the resultant likeness to life they achieve. Eliot's *Four Quartets* is a massive and subtle poetic achievement, informed by the philosophical and the theological. Little can adequately be said in a short space about the themes of the poem. It is a discussion of time and change and a consequent proper evaluation of the place of a limited reality vis-à-vis the infinite God, with respect to perception and/or memory, art, and religion. Again the Incarnation of the Word of God in Christ is the key to a solution for the first two lesser themes as well as the last, the major one. The theme of the religious redemption of mankind is generally developed and overlays the first two, the minor themes, without canceling them out, since they are seen as dependent upon the eternal, the intersection of the timeless with time in the Incarnation.

The poem, all quartets taken together, is a unit, ultimately a single poem, but each quartet singly reflects the Paschal Action in its development of the religious theme. There is a general purification for the sake of a fuller expression of the self that reflects the Paschal Action. This is intricately done by the purification of the four elements and of other quaternities. To see this fully, one

requires detailed analysis of each quartet. But there is another ver-
ification of the Paschal Action, of death and resurrection united,
in the poem as a whole, gradually and more explicitly developed
as each quartet succeeds another. What is implicit in the first quartet—the religious, incarnational solution—becomes more explicit
as we move through each of the others. The solution is quite
muted at the outset, much more attention being given to the
problem to be solved, but by the last quartet the solution of new
life is seen to be more sure, self-confident, and celebratory, with
the price of suffering and death being given more emphasis in the
middle two quartets (Boyd, "Paschal Action" 186–87). Only a
growth within the pattern of the main theme, the religious one,
can account for such a unity and its sustained achievement.
Throughout, paradox is evident in the service of the redemption
through the Paschal Action.

Paradox is also quite amply used in specific sections throughout—for example, in something as minor as in "The menace and
caress of wave that breaks on water" (*The Dry Salvages*, 1.31). At
this point we shall examine two passages as part of the Paschal
Action developing throughout the poem as a whole, and gradually unifying it. The first is from "East Coker," dealing with the
passion and death of Christ and our participation in it.

> The wounded surgeon plies the steel
> That questions the distempered part;
> Beneath the bleeding hands we feel
> The sharp compassion of the healer's art
> Resolving the enigma of the fever chart.
>
> Our only health is the disease
> If we obey the dying nurse
> Whose constant care is not to please
> But to remind of our, and Adam's, curse,
> And that, to be restored, our sickness must grow worse.
>
> The whole earth is our hospital
> Endowed by the ruined millionaire,
> Wherein, if we do well, we shall
> Die of the absolute paternal care
> That will not leave us, but prevents us everywhere.

The chill ascends from feet to knees,
The fever sings in mental wires.
If to be warmed, then I must freeze
And quake in frigid, purgatorial fires
Of which the flame is roses, and the smoke is briars.

The dripping blood our only drink,
The bloody flesh our only food:
In spite of which we like to think
That we are sound, substantial flesh and blood—
Again, in spite of that, we call this Friday good.

(4.1–25).

This passage supplies rich paradoxes, stressing the efficacy of Christ's suffering and the image of this in the redeemed. He is presented as sharing in the weakness of humanity, our wounded nature needing redemption. Though He is humanly pure and sinless, He took to Himself our ability to suffer and so transformed our lot. Throughout this entire lyric, the union of suffering and death with new life is intensely manifest, as a sign of the success of the Paschal Action, yet always muted in the overall mood of the first three quartets.

The second passage is the prelude to *Little Gidding*, the passage about the season of the Holy Spirit, Pentecost, in and out of time, standing for the fulfillment of the resurrection.

Midwinter spring is its own season
Sempiternal though sodden towards sundown,
Suspended in time, between pole and tropic.
When the short day is brightest, with frost and fire,
The brief sun flames the ice, on pond and ditches,
In windless cold that is the heart's heat,
Reflecting in a watery mirror
A glare that is blindness in the early afternoon.
And glow more intense than blaze of branch, or brazier,
Stirs the dumb spirit: no wind, but pentecostal fire
In the dark time of the year. Between melting and freezing
The soul's sap quivers. There is no earth smell
Or smell of living thing. This is the spring time
But not in time's covenant. Now the hedgerow
Is blanched for an hour with transitory blossom

Of snow, a bloom more sudden
Than that of summer, neither budding nor fading,
Not in the scheme of generation.
Where is the summer, the unimaginable
Zero summer? (1.1–20)

In Christian doctrine the Ascension and the feast of Pentecost are
of a piece in finally seeing the redemption as a success that is
complete. The frequent use of paradox secures the season as in
and out of time, signifying the completeness of the Paschal Action.

The pattern of the Paschal Action occurs frequently in Hopkins's poetry, but it is especially evident in the main structure and
particular sections of *The Wreck of the Deutschland*. Its theme is that
of the supernatural life of heaven deriving from human sufferings
and death—it is Hopkins's, theology of history: "It rides time like
riding a river" (Stanza 6). It characterizes what he has to say about
his own conversion and religious dedication: "over again I feel
thy finger and find thee" (Stanza 1). It also underlies his return to
writing poetry; but most of all the theme deals with the experience of the five nuns, and, in and through them, with that of the
whole human race—mercy through mastery (see Stanza 10). All
action ends in the last stanza, as deriving from all that has gone
before:

Dame, at our door
Drowned, and among our shoals,
Remember us in the roads, the heaven–haven of the Reward:
Our King back, oh, upon English souls!
Let him easter in us, be a dayspring to the dimness of us, be a
    crimson-cresseted east,
More brightening her, rare-dear Britain, as his reign rolls,
Pride, rose, prince, hero of us, high-priest,
Our hearts, charity's hearth's fire, our thoughts, chivalry's
    throng's Lord. (Stanza 35)

In the last four lines of this stanza, the victory of the resurrection
is most richly celebrated in the elaborate paraphrasing of what is
implied in Reward and King, namely unity and triumph with the
Risen Christ, and in Him even now.

Besides this large and over-arching structure, there are other evidences of the Paschal Action locally in the many paradoxes used, the natural image of mystery generally, and of the death and resurrection of Christ:

> Be adored among men,
> God, three-numbered form;
> Wring thy rebel, dogged in den,
> Man's malice, with wrecking and storm,
> Beyond saying sweet, past telling of tongue,
> Thou art lightning and love, I found it, a winter and warm;
> Father and fondler of heart thou hast wrung:
> Hast thy dark descending and most art merciful then. (Stanza 9)

A word about Greene's *The Power and the Glory*. The title is enough to remind us that the plot's action is the work of God in the victory of his power. It will be recalled that the novel has to do with activity of a hunted priest in Mexico during the persecution in the 1920s. He is struggling to be a help to his people, while on the run from the officers of the government. The hunt is also God's hunt directed toward him and those with whom he works. Hence the title of the novel in Britain, *The Labyrinthine Ways*, a reference to Francis Thompson's *The Hound of Heaven*, in which the creature flees from God's love until he gives in. The pattern of the Paschal Action takes place in the gradual victory of God's hunt inside that of the police. At the same time the priest is plagued with all his troubles of the past: adultery, with a child from the union; and chronic alcoholism, which makes him seem to himself unworthy of his mission to his flock. Grace and divine life grow gradually for him as both the hunts grow to an intensity and end with his capture. He is executed as a martyr to the Faith and to his priestly profession. It all ends in a glorious victory for the cause of the priest and of the Church; and this is signaled by the welcoming of a new priest at the door by a young boy, who then enters into the work of God in harboring the priest. The life of grace has triumphed, and the images of the labyrinthine ways and the power and the glory fuse into one.

As a final comment, let us look at the difference between irony and paradox, and especially between tragedy and comedy on the one hand and the drama of the Paschal Action on the other. I would begin by saying that irony is the issuing of a single reality as completely opposite to what is expected. The tragic issue of Oedipus's recognition of his terrible guilt is quite contrary to his initial quest to solve the plague in his city. Or it can be of a comic sort, where malice threatens to undo society, as in the case of the plotting against Prospero both by the nobles and by Caliban and his rowdy fellows. The rebels are defeated and are replaced by Prospero's victory, owing to the agency of magic and laughter. In paradox we have the coexistence of two realities, and this especially in the Paschal Action. These two realities are nature and grace, the human and the divine. In the Paschal Action the supernatural power of God, made evident in grace and new life, redoes the human situation in its own image. The human, the locus of death, is remade in the image of God's power and grace.

From this brief distinction between irony and paradox, it is clear that no play—or other genre—that is essentially about the Christian life fully considered, that is, no piece in the form of the Paschal Action, can be tragic. Tragedy has no place where the Paschal Action is meant to be shown. But can there be a tragedy about Christian life at all? Yes, it would seem so. It could be about a Christian who is a failure as a Christian. I think of Alan Paton's *Too Late the Phalarope* in which there is an heroic-sized, attractive man meeting his downfall in adultery amid a culture of miscegenation. He becomes an outcast of his people—the story is set in apartheid South Africa—because of their falsely condemnatory attitude, that can only be called a failure in Christian charity. The book is not about redemptive suffering. Graham Greene's *Brighton Rock* would seem to be another such tragedy. Nor is the Paschal Action, despite its happy ending, a comedy, even in the serious sense. A comedy's plot is different, once again without Christian redemptive suffering; and a comedy usually ends with an implied, at least, concern for further earthly life, with new adventures to be faced on the morrow. Yet there can be Christian comedies, as we find in Christopher Fry's work, a slice of Christian life that is comic. Be these conjectures as they may, it is interesting to consider another kind of dramatic action, verifiable by extension in other genres, expressive of the central concern of Christians, namely, that of the Paschal Action. It is genuinely human in every way, being modeled on the incarnation and focused on its central and characteristic redemptive concern. "Was it not necessary that the Christ should suffer these things and so enter into his glory?" (Luke 24:26).

WORKS CITED

Arnold, Matthew. "The Study of Poetry." *The Portable Matthew Arnold.* Ed. Lionel Trilling. New York: Viking, 1949.

Betherum, Dorothy, ed. *Critical Approaches to Medieval Literature: Selected Papers from the English Institute, 1958–1959.* New York: Columbia UP, 1960.

Boyd, John D., s.j. *The Function of Mimesis and Its Decline.* Cambridge, MA: Harvard UP, 1968.

———. "Christian Imaginative Patterns and the Poetry of Thomas Merton." *Greyfriar: Siena Studies in Literature* 13 (1972): 3–14.

———. "The Paschal Action in Eliot's *Four Quartets.*" *Renascence: Essays on Values in Literature* 40 (1988): 176–88.

Durrwell, F. X., C.SS.R. *The Resurrection.* Trans. Rosemary Sheed. New York: Sheed & Ward, 1960.

Eliot, T. S. *Four Quartets.* New York: Harcourt, Brace, 1943.

———. *Murder in the Cathedral.* New York: Harcourt, Brace, 1935.

Greene, Graham. *The Power and the Glory.* New York: Viking Press, 1940.

Hopkins, Gerard Manley. *The Poems of Gerard Manley Hopkins.* Ed. W. H. Gardner and N. H. MacKenzie. 4th ed. London: Oxford UP, 1970.

Paton, Alan. *Too Late the Phalarope.* New York: Scribner's, 1953.

Tillich, Paul. *Theology of Culture.* Ed. R. C. Kimball. New York: Oxford UP, 1959.

NOTE

I wish to thank the editor of *Greyfriar: Siena Studies in Literature* for permission to use in this essay parts of my article "Christian Imaginative Patterns and the Poetry of Thomas Merton." I wish also to thank the editor of *Renascence: Essays on Values in Literature* for permission to use in this essay parts of my article "The Paschal Action in Eliot's *Four Quartets.*"

5

Moral Cross-Dressing: Contemporary Trends in Liberal Preaching and Literary Criticism

Charles J. Rzepka and Rev. Jane R. Rzepka

> The odd thing, in fact, about literature as an imagined territory is that there are apparently no natural limits—and hence, it would seem, there are apparently no natural limits to the field of literary criticism (Greenblatt and Gunn 6).

IF STEPHEN GREENBLATT AND GILES GUNN ARE RIGHT, the territory jointly administered by literature and religion should be colonized mainly by natives of literature. Their homeland, after all, has no natural limits, while we suspect that the inhabitants of religion are still posting border-guards at strategic check-points. However the case may be, the territory in question is largely uncontested at present. Theologians and preachers coexist peacefully with poets and critics, all engaged in a brisk barter in texts, sacred and secular, as well as ideas hermeneutical, metaphysical, and mythopoetical. Recently, critics and preachers have even begun to exchange academic gowns for ministerial robes, and vice versa. This professional cross-dressing is taking place principally between the mainline Protestant or "liberal" denominations and literary cultural studies in the academy, and it is confined, largely, to one particular professional function: moralizing. To an ever-increasing degree, academic critics are expressing moral judgments or taking moral positions on writing practice and practitioners, while ministers are abandoning their traditional homiletic mandate to chastise and correct.

According to one study, mainline Protestant religion has all but stopped using the vocabulary of wrongdoing, let alone the traditional concepts of "sin," "evil," and "hell." Now preachers are inclined to talk about "errors in judgment," "emotional problems," or "dysfunctional families" (Witten, "Accommodating" 2), and to cite ameliorating social forces such as "structures of political and economic oppression" or "discrimination" (Peters 2). Instead of saying, "You are sinners—filthy, miserable, greasy sinners!" today's minister is more likely to say, "I'd just like to share that we need to target holiness as a growth area" (Plantinga 102).

The person on the street once knew what a sermon was: doctrine and moralizing.[1] Traditionally, the sermon spoke of religious faith, appropriate personal behavior, duties and obligations, and public order. Sin was important, as well as the need for God, a source of moral authority. Indeed, sermons were expected to be moralistic. As Harold Bosley points out in his description of early American preaching styles, "Novels like *The Scarlet Letter* and *Saints and Strangers*, taken together with the thousands of records of trials in churches in which members are made to answer for unjust weights in their store, lying about service rendered, loose living, etc., spell out the concrete ways in which the gospel was focused on life" (30).

In the nineteenth century, Calvinists, Evangelicals, and Liberals alike preached morality. Calvinists, of course, approached the subject from the standpoint of original sin and natural depravity. The famous preacher and evangelist D. L. Moody, for example, who achieved remarkable success both in America and in England during the 1870s and 1890s, believed that the neglect of religion was what made people "the miserable failures they knew they had become" (Wagenknecht 181). Liberals, on the other hand,

---

[1] Most students coming into the college classroom for the first time think they know what literary criticism is: aesthetic appreciation, the enhancement of what Richard Harter Fogle once called the "permanent pleasure" of reading. Both the title and the motto of Fogle's book on the English Romantics, *The Permanent Pleasure*, were taken from chapter 14 of Coleridge's *Biographia Literaria*: "Nothing can permanently please which does not contain in itself the reason why it is so, and not otherwise." For the most part, secondary education in England and America still teaches this version of literary interpretation, promoted since the inter-war period by the New Critics and deriving, ultimately, from Coleridgean notions of organic form.

preached a morality of character development, as shown in Henry Ware, Jr.'s tract *On the Formation of the Christian Character: Addressed to Those Who Are Seeking to Lead a Religious Life*. According to Ware, the moral sense was a faculty that could be developed through education, training, practice, and skill. "Be on your guard against setting your mark too low. . . . The higher you aim, the higher you will reach" (107–108).

It was during the Victorian period, against the rising tide of moralizing, middle-class, Evangelical culture on both sides of the Atlantic, that the efforts begun by many of the Romantics to define literature in opposition to moral or philosophical didacticism began to make inroads in the academy. By the turn of the nineteenth century, despite Matthew Arnold's rear-guard action on behalf of poetry as "a criticism of life" (an action mirroring the liberal religious emphasis on building moral character), literature's efficacy in encouraging moral conduct, improving character, and reforming evil had begun to slip off the critical agenda, leaving in place the goal of enhancing aesthetic pleasure. Critics were to give us, in the words of Walter Pater, not abstract moral wisdom, "not the fruit of experience, but experience itself," and to enable us "to burn always with [a] hard, gemlike flame, to maintain [the] ecstasy" of aesthetic perception (319).

In part, this was simply a matter of criticism catching up with the growth of an aesthetic movement rooted in Kant's *Critique of Judgment* and Keats's pugnaciously sensuous verse. "We hate poetry that has a palpable design on us," Keats wrote (61). His experiential poetics was kept alive by Tennyson, Rossetti, and the Pre-Raphaelites, among others. As M. H. Abrams argued in *The Mirror and the Lamp*, critical reflection on the creative process, which had shifted its focus from imitation to expression by the end of the eighteenth century, shifted focus again with the advent of modernism, this time to the literary work itself, Wimsatt's "verbal icon" (3–29).[2] With few exceptions, for the first half of the twentieth century and well into the second half, the notion of the essential amoralism of great literary works and, accordingly, of sound commentary and literary interpretation held sway in Anglo-American academies. Formalism and "close reading" took

---

[2] The phrase "verbal icon" comes, of course, from the title of W. K. Wimsatt Jr.'s *The Verbal Icon: Studies in the Meaning of Poetry*.

for granted the organic, integrated, and self-sustaining form of the literary work (a view first posited, in the English tradition, by Coleridge). As a delicate and complex balance of ironic tensions and contraries, the text was now considered "intrinsically" worthy of study, without reference, necessarily, to "extrinsic" facts of production, reception, or biography.[3] By the mid-twentieth century religion and poetry, as well as preaching and criticism, had come to administer largely separate moral and aesthetic domains.[4] As this narrative suggests, most of the impetus in the post-Romantic evolution toward a separation between moralism and literature originated with modernist poets and critics, who sought to rid literature of the last vestiges of moral purpose granted it by the Victorians. Religious leaders, meanwhile, had not greatly budged from their long-standing suspicion of literature's moral and doctrinal relativism. "Traditionally," writes Northrop Frye, "religious scholarship is the most anti-literary of all verbal disciplines. For Christian scholars since New Testament times . . . poetry and fables were what other religions had: [Christians] had the 'truth,' and while truth might be conveyed in descriptive or conceptual or rhetorical language, it could never be conveyed in literary language" (xiv). Emerson's injunction to new preachers, in the "Divinity School Address," to follow the example of Jesus as Poet and "convert life into truth" (109)[5] was the exception that proved the general rule exemplified by the great nineteenth-century American preacher Lyman Beecher, who prided himself on never recommending any book but the Bible. Beecher's attitude toward poets, even those he most admired, like Byron, is perhaps best summarized by his response to the news from Missolonghi: "Oh, I'm so sorry that Byron is dead. I did hope he would live to do something for Christ" (Wagenknecht 14).

---

[3] "Extrinsic" and "intrinsic" are the two categories of approach that essentially subdivide the argument of René Wellek and Austin Warren's *Theory of Literature*.

[4] This is not to deny New Critical affiliations with groups such as the Agrarian Movement of the American South, led by critics like Allen Tate and John Crowe Ranson, who emphasized the role of poetry in returning society to a Christian, anti-industrial outlook. The impact of such critics on the Anglo-American academy as a whole, however, was neither a religious nor a moral one.

[5] "Always the seer is a sayer," writes Emerson (108), and of Jesus's teachings in particular he says, "The understanding caught this high chant from the poet's lips. . . . [But] the idioms of his language and the figures of his rhetoric have usurped the place of his truth; and churches are not built on his principles, but on his tropes" (105).

While religionists tended to distrust the moral equivocation of literature and literary pursuits, literary critics came to see religion as a dying mythos, persuading themselves, in Matthew Arnold's famous prophecy, that "what now passes with us for religion . . . will be replaced by poetry" (Trilling and Bloom 234). Emerson's transcendental apotheosis of the secular poet of nature in essays like "The American Scholar" anticipates later hybrids of the sacred and secular imaginations in Anglo-American literature and criticism. Such hybrids were to appear explicitly, as in Joyce's Thomist notion of artistic "epiphany" or Ginsberg's scatological vision of the "Holy" in *Howl*, as well as implicitly, in the negative Logoism of Stevens's "Supreme Fiction," to cite one example, or, for that matter, in the hierophantic overtones of a "verbal icon." But while poets and critics were only too happy to appropriate the numinous metaphysics of a supposedly moribund faith, they tended to leave religion's moral authority and prerogatives undisturbed.[6] They found little use for moralizing.

Mainline Protestant churches today have begun to follow the example of their modernist secular counterparts. In spite of preaching's long tradition of moralistic content, and in spite of religion's long-standing antipathy toward secular culture, including literature, current preaching practices in mainline Protestant denominations generally reflect the amoral secularism traditionally associated with modern literary studies. As Nathan Scott puts it, "The only norms by which our [religious] course is to be steered are those provided by the best secular wisdom of our age." The works of Bonhoeffer, Barth, Tillich, and Bultmann have combined, says Scott, to bring about "a revolution of nearly Copernican dimensions . . . in the evaluation of modern secularism by Christian Theology" (161). Sydney Ahlstrom agrees, arguing that our modern realization of the impotence of traditional American religion has led us to accept "naturalism or secularism as a way of interpreting life" (1087).

Contemporary American Protestant churches have been greatly influenced by trends toward individualism, the authority of psychotherapy, ideological relativism, and the reliance on rational procedures that mark our culture as a whole (Witten, *All* 5). One

---

[6] T. S. Eliot is probably the most famous exception to this general attitude among literary modernists.

case in point, a sermon chosen more or less randomly from a contemporary collection of Methodist sermons by James W. Moore, includes references to the actor Jack Klugman from "The Odd Couple," Tolstoy's *War and Peace*, Archie Bunker, Flip Wilson, and *The Exorcist* (13–21). Not only do sermons now range freely across the entire spectrum of popular secular culture, but ministers need pack no moral compass for the trip. Marsha Witten notes "a variety of softening rhetorical devices" by which preachers today "accommodate" the idea of wrongdoing to "secular sensibilities":

> The device of depersonalization, which renders notions of sinfulness vague and abstract; . . . the device of deflection, through which sin is projected off listeners and onto groups of outsiders; the device of mitigation, employed to modify the potential for audience identification with sinful characters; and the device of therapeutic tolerance, through which sin is translated as errant behavior, explanations for misdeeds are sought in the social context rather than in the individual, and the response of judgment is replaced by that of empathy. (*All* 101).

"It is no easy task to preach on sin," admits William R. White. "Scolding and moralizing . . . make people feel bad without leading them to repentance" (13).

In short, secular description and explanation have replaced sermonic moralizing. Consider this excerpt from William P. Tuck's "Exorcising Demons in the Modern World," a sermon in the Baptist tradition: "We are, in Carl Sandburg's words, a menagerie. Within the wilderness inside each of us is a wolf, a fox, a hog, a fish, a baboon, an eagle, and other creatures. We are indeed paradoxical creatures. We are loving and hateful, harmful and saving, educating and destroying, wise and foolish, visionary and shortsighted. Each of us is the 'Keeper of the Zoo'" (216). The replacement of admonition by description and of sin by psychology is clearly registered in a passage like this, where the soul's moral struggles are represented as a zoomorphic psychomachia. As "keeper of the zoo," one is expected to do little more than maintain peaceful relations among the totemic representatives of one's "pet" virtues and vices. All human emotions, even the "hateful," the "harmful," the "destroying," the "foolish," and the "shortsighted," seem to have a valid place in the Linnaean order of our mental "menagerie."

The importance of psychological explanation in contemporary mainline preaching has its origins, ironically, in the literary tradition that the religionists once distrusted. High Romanticism promoted the value of psychological understanding, close attention to the way we "associate ideas in a state of excitement" (Wordsworth 245), and empathy, even with murderers. Coleridge's intense analysis of Hamlet's personality and motivations in his Shakespeare lectures is one case in point; Blake's sympathy for the "devil's party" in *Paradise Lost*, another.[7] The idea of poetry as a form of subjective expression inviting empathic identification rather than moral judgment is a commonplace of Romantic theory and practice. For Keats, a "chameleon" response to character is warranted whether that character take the shape of an "Iago" or an "Imogen" (157). This empathic approach to literature was undermined as early as 1917, in "Tradition and the Individual Talent," when Eliot reduced the poet's role in the creative process to that of a "catalyst" in an impersonal chemical reaction (54). It was no doubt hastened in 1954 by Wimsatt's and Beardsley's attacks on the "intentional" and "affective" fallacies, and finished off once for all by deconstruction's "death of the author" and embrace of the "author function" (Eliot 54).[8] To judge from Tuck, however, the original Romantic emphasis on psychological explanation and moral amelioration is apparently alive and well in contemporary mainline Protestant preaching.

Another feature of Tuck's zoological analogy is noteworthy: it is derived from a secular poet, Carl Sandburg, rather than a sacred text. This is a subject we touched upon above, but it is worth reiterating. Traditionally an occasional practice at best, the incorporation of secular media in sermons and liturgical readings has become so commonplace among mainline denominations that on

---

[7] "The reason Milton wrote in fetters when he wrote of Angels & God, and at liberty when of Devils & Hell, is because he was a true Poet and of the devils party without knowing it" (Blake 35).

[8] "The progress of an artist is a continual self-sacrifice, a continual extinction of personality" (Eliot 53). On the intentional affective fallacies, see the two introductory essays by W. K. Wimsatt, Jr., and Monroe C. Beardsley in Wimsatt's *The Verbal Icon*. On the deconstructive "death" of the author, see Roland Barthes's "The Death of the Author," Paul De Man's "Autobiography as Defacement," and Michel Foucault's "What Is an Author?"

Sunday morning one is as likely to hear citations from Gail Sheehy or Robert Fulghum as from Matthew, Mark, Luke, or John. Ironically, Arnold's prediction of the fate of religion is coming true, but not in the way he anticipated. We will be lucky if most of what now passes for religion has in fact been replaced by poetry, and not pop wisdom.

The dwindling importance of moral leadership in mainstream Protestant preaching is reflected not only in an increasing preference for contemporary secular sources of homiletic and liturgical inspiration, but also in a growing emphasis on the aesthetics of worship. Once upon a time, Pope could earn applause for excoriating those who read poetry "as some to church repair, / Not for the doctrine, but for the music there." It was not until more than a century later that literary critics began to turn their attention away from the "doctrines" of their own sacred texts and to concentrate more on the "music." Today, liberal Protestant denominations are following suit.

Especially in large liberal congregations, where the theological views of worshippers are likely to be diverse and ill-defined, says the Reverend Clarke Wells, church services can provide a non-doctrinal source of group coherence by being more "imaginative, evocative, utilizing myth, symbol and the arts" (53). Such an emphasis on liturgical aesthetics may be helpful in building congregational solidarity, and there is nothing wrong with a desire for beauty in worship. But too exclusive an attention to aesthetics can distract from moral content, or even lead to the confusing of moral with aesthetic value, if it is not moderated by attention to the central meaning of worship. Thus, in a recent sermon urging her denomination to be less "self-conscious" about artistic innovation and expression in worship, Carolyn Owen-Toole, co-minister of the First Unitarian Universalist Church of San Diego, expressed dismay at the "restrained tones of sepia, of dead-leaf beige, or aging grays and browns" found in the typical liturgical objects and worship spaces of "our esteemed forebears," "the works of our heritage" (14).[9] She went on to state that such "disregard of taste and inattention to detail corrupt worship"(14). We doubt that Owen-Toole's forebears would have so closely identified "corruption" with bad taste. While the argument for beauty

---

[9] See also Jane's R. Rzepka's response, "Meditations."

in worship, as for the inclusion of imaginative literature, is not new,[10] what is new in Owen-Toole's sermon is the denigration of traditional liturgical symbols and objects because they lack aesthetic appeal, and the identification of the aesthetically unappealing with a traditionally negative moral category.

Beecher, Ware, and Moody drew on a standard Christian theology and apologetics, as well as a standard Christian symbolism, to make their moral points and to define their moral stance. But there is no reason why preachers in the most liberal and theologically diverse, even secularized and aesthetically sensitive, denominations should not be able to focus thoughtful attention on moral or ethical values. As members of the Unitarian Universalist Association—one of the most liberal, not to say radical, of mainline denominations—we do not believe that traditional notions of God or Christ or Satan or the soul or immortality or eternal reward and punishment are essential to the religious task of reminding people of their moral and ethical responsibilities. What alarms us is not the passing away of that "old time religion," a process that has been going on for centuries among the most liberal denominations, but the passing away of moral perspectives in preaching.

While mainline churches keep moving nearer to the point in their liturgical practice of embracing Pater's "love of art for art's

---

[10] The publication of the *Book of Common Prayer* in 1549 formally marked the beginning of the doctrinaire Anglo-American iconoclasm and anti-aesthetic bias that Owen-Toole and others are protesting. Its introduction reads, in part, as follows: "But these many yeares passed this Godly and decent order [of worship] of the auncient fathres, hath been so altered, broken, and neglected, by planting in uncertein stories, Legendes, Respondes, Verses, vaine repeticions, Commemoraciones, and Synodalles, that commonly when any boke of the Bible was begon: before three or foure Chapiters were read out, all the rest were unread. . . . For this cause be cut of Anthemes, Respondes, Inuitatories, and suche like thynges, as did breake the continuall course of the readyng of the scripture . . . and is ordeyned nothyng to be reade, but the very pure worde of God" (Whitchurch 3–4). It was not until 1925 that Willard Sperry, in *Reality in Worship*, would argue that the "priest must be an artist" (332) and that "the minister must keep his imagination alive by more or less constant reading of fiction, poetry, and drama" (331). Two years later, William Norman Guthrie, in *Offices of Mystical Religion*, would quote Keats's envoi to "Ode on a Grecian Urn"— "Beauty is Truth, Truth Beauty"—in support of the importance of aesthetics to the representation of doctrinal truth (xxv). Only recently, however, have aesthetic values in worship begun to be widely promoted by mainline denominations. (We are grateful to the Reverend Mark Belletini of the Starr King Unitarian Universalist Church of Hayward, California, for these references.)

sake" (320), literary criticism cannot seem to rid itself of the idea fast enough. Raymond Williams's statement in *Marxism and Literature* could stand as a motto for many in the present generation of literary scholars: "We have to reject 'the aesthetic' both as a separate abstract dimension and as a separate abstract function. We have to reject 'Aesthetics' to the large extent that it is posited on these abstractions" (156). Terry Eagleton puts the case more forcefully: "power in [the bourgeois social order] has become *aestheticized*. It is at one with the body's spontaneous impulses, entwined with sensibility and the affections . . . inscribed in the minutiae of subjective experience" (61). The "power" that Eagleton is talking about is political and economic, not aesthetic, but he locates it in precisely the spot—"subjective experience"— where Pater once tried to quarantine the aesthetic. It is time we recognized, says Barbara Herrnstein Smith, "the historical or cultural contingency of aesthetic value" and of the "aesthetic axiology" that has directed literary studies and established the baseline of legitimate criticism in the era of modernism and the new criticism (36). Acting on premises like these, and citing the example of Harriet Beecher Stowe's *Uncle Tom's Cabin*, Jane Tompkins has argued for "reconstituting the notion of value in literary works" by trying to determine whether the aims and achievements of an author "were good or bad" in a moral sense (xviii).

The history of this sea-change in critical orientation is, by now, familiar to most of us, and does not require extensive retelling here. Suffice it to say that, along with increased campus activism in the 1960s, there arose a changed understanding of the relationship between literature and society, and between literary criticism and literature itself. A wide array of social institutions—including the media and the academy—were now understood to participate in the dissemination of certain representations of society that served to perpetuate unjust distributions of political and economic power. The aesthetic realm was now recognized as a major player in shaping culture and, thereby, group consciousness or "ideology." The personal—including personal aesthetic response— could no longer be insulated from the realm of public policy. The personal was now political.

Soon afterward, formalism reached its ironically self-destructive apogee with the rise of structuralism and then deconstruction. The textual focus of formalism now shifted from the self-integrated work of art to "discourse" and "intertextuality," that is, to the work's intersection with an almost infinite web of linguistic conventions, precursor and contemporary texts, and cultural assumptions implicit in the ambiguous and arbitrary construction of meaning within language as a whole. The next step in this critical reorientation, inaugurated principally by Foucault, was to resituate the notion of "discourse" in a larger, historical context and social structure of "dominance" and "power." Soon, New Historicists were studying texts as sites for cultural reproduction and "self-fashioning," for the working out of societal contradictions, anxieties, and subject-positions, and for the discursive repression and sublimation of history.

The result of these developments has been an explosion of writing on the social, historical, and cultural determinants of individual literary works, forces that tend to align or disalign them, as well as their creators, with a "dominant" or "hegemonic" ideology. This ideology is assumed to be grounded in material culture and perpetuated in the multifarious domains of cultural representation that ultimately, and invariably, shape public policy. Currently, the most popular and prevalent modes of literary criticism within the academy—gender and feminist theory, cultural and material critique, the New Historicism and post-colonial theory—in one way or another take as axiomatic the assumption that literary forms of representation, like all other material artifacts of culture, in every period and at every level, must be understood as engaging with structures of "power" and "domination," and necessarily working in concert with or in opposition to the interests of a dominant or "hegemonic" class, gender, nation, or race. Almost invariably this dominant group is identified as middle- or upper-class, male, Western, and white, and its material interests are taken to be advanced by its "policing" of literary practice so as to maintain the unequal structural relationships that have long kept it dominant. Unlike preachers and ministers who assume that systemic social conditioning can extenuate personal moral responsibility, many contemporary literary critics barely hesitate before passing moral judgment on specific literary works or writers, depending on whether or not the work or writer in question can be said to have advanced or opposed the interests of the dominant ideology.

Ironically, such criticism has engendered its moralizing mirror-image, with appropriate left-right symmetry, in the backlash of right-wing cultural "fundamentalists," as David Bromwich calls them (xiii).[11] Like Matthew Arnold's advocacy of "culture" in the shaping of one's "best self," the arguments advanced by such self-appointed guardians of Western civilization and tradition as George Will, Dinesh D'Souza, William Bennett, Allan Bloom, Harold Bloom, and Roger Kimball are directed at preserving moral values and building individual character through the academic curriculum. With few exceptions, as Bromwich also points out, these "right-wing" literary moralists speak mostly to and for an extra-academic audience, leaving the intra-academic arena occupied, largely, by their "left-wing" counterparts (xiii).[12] Since it is to the latter arena that we are directing our attention, "left-wing" literary moralizing will, of necessity, dominate the discussion that follows.

The field of Jane Austen studies provides numerous examples of moral positions explicitly or implicitly assumed by participants in the current literary critical debates over culture and ideology.[13] Not long ago, first in an article, then in a chapter of his book *Culture and Imperialism*, Edward Said offered a reading of *Mansfield Park* intended to "set" Austen's "art in the global, earthly context" of her time (7).[14] Focusing on the novelist's passing references to the source of the Bertrams' wealth—namely, West Indies plantations worked by slaves—Said portrayed Austen as deeply

---

[11] Bromwich criticizes right-wing "fundamentalism" specifically in his second chapter, "Moral Education in the Age of Reagan" (55–97).

[12] He adds, "Both groups [left and right] show an enormous deference toward institutions: they believe in the power of institutions to shape the thoughts of an individual mind; they think this power is irresistible, and the great question therefore becomes how to give it the correct bias." We tend to agree, supporting Bromwich's judgment that "to one degree or another all these movements tend to be intolerant" (48).

[13] Consider, for instance, the long-standing disagreement between those, like Marilyn Butler in *Jane Austen and the War of Ideas*, who see Austen as a traditional upholder of Burkean and Evangelical conservatism, and those, like Margaret Kirkham in *Jane Austen, Feminism, and Fiction*, Alison Sulloway in *Jane Austen and the Province of Womanhood*, and Sandra Gilbert and Susan Gubar in *Madwoman in the Attic: The Woman Writer and the Nineteenth-Century Literary Imagination*, who situate her more squarely in an Enlightenment version of the feminist critique of patriarchy.

[14] Said wishes to "show the involvements" of Austen's domestic "culture with expanding empires" and "map its affiliations" with English imperial ambitions in the Napoleonic era (7).

implicated, along with nearly all the English novelists of the nineteenth century, in maintaining "the continuity of British imperial
policy" by not "rais[ing] more questions" about such exploitative
arrangements. In this way, Austen and her literary cohort helped
"to keep the empire more or less in place," perpetuating and
reinforcing an imperialistic "structure of attitude and reference"
(74, 76).[15]

Susan Fraiman's rebuttal in a recent issue of *Critical Inquiry* takes
Said to task on ideological and, we would argue, fundamentally
moral grounds, defending Austen on the basis of her assumed
feminism and criticizing "the gender politics underlying Said's
anti-imperialism" in *Culture and Imperialism* (819). Fraiman sees
Said's attack on Austen as motivated by masculinist bias, a delin-
quent sense of the extent to which his own anti-imperialist discourse is rooted in gender assumptions and sexual stereotypes.
Fraiman even sees Austen as very subtly criticizing imperialism
and patriarchy through her veiled attack on the hypocrisy, lying,
and bullying prevalent at the Bertrams' estate, Mansfield Park.

Clearly, Said and Fraiman are not arguing about aesthetics.
Both seem to believe that Austen is a compelling, complex, and
highly sophisticated novelist. What they are arguing about is the
social and historical *impact* of Austen's aesthetic genius, what she
uses it *for.* Her outstanding talent is precisely what makes her so
dangerous and indictable for Said, and so heroic and praiseworthy
for Fraiman.[16] In fact, the real question at issue between Said and
Fraiman is, as we said, a moral one: Did Austen help to advance
the cause of the oppressed, the marginal, the silenced, and the
exploited of Napoleonic Era England—black or female or
both—or was she complicitous in, thereby giving tacit approval

---

[15] Of Austen's uncritical references to Sir Bertram's slave plantations in Anti-
gua, Said writes: "More clearly than anywhere else in her fiction, Austin here
synchronizes domestic with international authority. . . . She sees clearly that to
hold and rule Mansfield Park is to hold and rule an imperial estate in close, not
to say inevitable, association with it" (87).

[16] There is, of course, an entirely different moral tone that often arises in evalu-
ative discussions of poetics and aesthetics. This kind of "disinterested" moralizing was exemplified in the period of High Modernism by Ezra Pound, when, in
"How to Read," he insisted that it was "as important for the purpose of thought
to keep language efficient as it is in surgery to keep tetanus bacilli out of one's
bandages" (22). There is, in other words, a form of aesthetic moralism that posits
a duty on the part of the author or critic to practice her or his skills seriously and
conscientiously.

to, the modes of domination and exploitation endemic to her society?

If questioned on such matters, both Said and Fraiman would probably object to our use of the word "moral" to describe the judgments they are making about Austen. Indeed, the notion of moral judgment we are invoking here has little if anything to do with the personal kind of moral decision-making that Austen is famous for having explored with such wit and ruthlessness in her novels. Nonetheless, there is a distinct tone of moral approbation or disapprobation informing the critical discussion between Said and Fraiman, and that tone, shading at times into more overt forms of denunciation, has become almost a standard feature of current scholarship in literary and cultural history.

Indeed, it is almost too easy to find moral judgments and moralistic attitudes in contemporary literary criticism. A random selection among works that adopt an ideological or culturally critical perspective yielded the following representative examples. In a study of slave narratives and female gothic fiction, Kari J. Winter states, "In this book I read both genres as sites of ideological struggle," adding that her "central concern is to examine how female gothic novels and slave narratives engaged the dominant classist, racist, patriarchal discourse and created possibilities for new, feminist ways of thinking" (13, 14). Questions of aesthetic form and function are subordinated to Winter's focus on the male/female gothic tradition as a "sexual/textual power struggle" (23). Characteristic of her method is her interpretation of a scene from Matthew G. Lewis's *The Monk*, where a "prioress has abused her power in the convent" and is beaten to death by an unruly mob: "Lewis suggests that the victim is to blame for her own suffering. . . . In a patriarchal society, women are blamed for everything from the fall of man onwards. M. G. Lewis reproduces this 'poisonous pedagogy' by blaming women for the violence inflicted on them by men" (27). "Reproduces" is a morally loaded term that transforms the otherwise value-neutral concept of literary representation into a process something like the replication of a devastating virus. According to Winter, *Monk*'s representation of the "poisonous pedagogy" of mysogynistic mob violence entails its "reproduction" or dissemination, an action tantamount to approving and promoting it. Clearly, Winter's book is intended not to examine or enhance our aesthetic appreciation of Lewis's work (little as that may be to begin with), but to identify the "poisonous" ideology disseminated under cover of the aesthetic. In the end, aesthetic pleasure is transformed into a source of guilt, redeemable only as an occasion for examining our unreconstructed consciences.

Gothic novels are not the only popular genre to have responded to a feminist critical methodology, or to have elicited moral judgments on novelists. On the very first page of her study of fictional women detectives, Kathleen Gregory Klein states, "The unacknowledged sabotage of these purported heroes is the focus of this book" (1). Klein will show that "the genre's inherent conservatism upholds power and privilege in the name of law and justice as it validates readers' visions of a safe and ordered world. In such a world view, criminals and women are put in their proper, secondary places" (1). Klein's "focus" is clearly ideological, not aesthetic, but her denunciatory tone seems best suited to the traditional religious genres of the moralizing and prophetic.

Kwame Anthony Appiah's protest against the West's ideological contamination of Africa's standards for evaluating its own indigenous literature reminds us of the cynicism toward aesthetic "disinterestedness" that informs much of the current cultural, social, and historical critique of literature: "This final challenge—to the assumption of Western cultural superiority—requires us, in the last analysis, to expose the ways in which the systematic character of literary (and, more broadly, aesthetic) judgments of value is the product of certain institutional practices and not something that exists independently of those practices and institutions." Not only does Appiah's critical terminology reflect the moralistic attitudes and standards of evaluation that are inherent in much of today's cultural critical discourse and that characterize that criticism's own "subject position," but it also poses a moral injunction: the Western "assumption of cultural superiority . . . *requires* us," Appiah says, "to *expose*" the hidden, and therefore suspect, dependence of aesthetic judgments on "institutional practice" (160; emphasis added).

"Power struggle," "dominance," "poisonous," "blaming," "violence," "sabotage," "put in their . . . places," "requires us," "expose": contemporary academic criticism bristles with prophetic anger and moral indignation. How could it be otherwise, given the belief that literature influences, for good or ill, the power-relationships between social groups, and that history is, therefore, best understood as a "struggle" between in-groups and out-groups, between "hegemonic" forces and "oppressed" communities or individuals? If critics are indeed implicated, regardless of intent, in the power-structures of their time and place, then they are morally obliged to choose sides when describing the history of such formations, and to make that choice clear. Not to choose is, necessarily, to side with the aesthetic establishment, with the academic hegemony that would represent literature and criticism as disinterested and universal in outlook, the better to defend its covert investments in the aestheticized forms of "power" deployed by "the bourgeois social order."[17]

Today, the wan light cast on individual morality from the mainline, liberal pulpits is as a candle in the wind compared to the high-wattage beam trained on writers and fellow critics by contemporary literary and cultural theorists. The moral orientation that prevails in much of the academy has even changed our standards for evaluating what is worthy of literary study, and why. This includes entire genres, as well as individual works and writers. We think it safe to say that these new objects of literary study, and many old objects considered in this new moral light, have not been singled out for attention "for their own sake." At least, no one to our knowledge has yet tried to make the case, either in print or in conversation, that Thomas De Quincey's racist diatribes against the abolition of slavery or Sarah Trimmer's insufferably condescending catechistic tracts for young readers (to take only two recent instances) make pleasurable reading "for their own sake."[18] Any pleasure the academic critic takes in such writings must depend on their susceptibility to a particular biographical, historical, or cultural analysis. When the ultimate object of such analysis becomes a "hegemony" or an "ideology," however, it seems all but impossible for the critic to refrain from portraying history as an epic "struggle" between the villains of "domination"

---

[17] In *Distinction: A Social Critique of the Judgment of Taste*, Pierre Bourdieu isolated the academic and cultural mechanisms by which such power, in the form of "cultural capital," is perpetuated so as to maintain the social supremacy of the middle class.

[18] Josephine McDonagh draws on De Quincey's essays on West Indian slavery in *De Quincey's Disciplines*, while Sarah Trimmer receives attention from Alan Richardson in *Literature, Education, and Romanticism: Reading as Social Practice*.

and "oppression" on the one hand and the heroes of "resistance" and "subversion" on the other. Shaped by the implicit millenarianism of their own discursive practices, such cultural critics often end up telling much the same tale as John of Patmos, with much the same (recurring) lesson: everlasting salvation for the children of light, everlasting damnation for the children of darkness.

While we are disturbed by such developments, our main purpose here is not to decide whether or not moral judgments belong in literary criticism, but to show how deeply such judgments are in fact implicated in the style, tone, and methodological assumptions of contemporary critics, even as the traditionally moralistic field of ecclesiastical homiletics reflects an ever decreasing interest in the passing of moral judgments.[19] Why such moral cross-dressing between liberal preaching and literary criticism should be occurring at the present time can only be a subject for speculation in a brief essay like this. Perhaps the secularizing of religion and the eschatologizing of criticism reflect larger social trends toward locating the moral basis of human action in social institutions and professional or communal affiliations, rather than in an original and conscientious relationship to an authority—whether a being or a principle—presumed to stand outside human history. Such trends would explain not only the disengagement of contemporary preachers from traditional religious sources of moral reflection, but also the contemporary critic's investment of the heretofore secular sphere of modernist literary culture with a moral dimension. Whatever the reasons for the transformations we have identified here, moral cross-dressing between literary critics and mainline ministers shows few signs of diminishing any time soon.

WORKS CITED

Abrams, Meyer H. *The Mirror and the Lamp: Romantic Theory and the Critical Tradition.* New York: Norton, 1953.

---

[19] The preaching half of this article's corporate authorship attests that, in seven years of teaching a preaching course at Harvard Divinity School, she has yet to hear a moralistic sermon from a single student studying for the ministry in a mainline Protestant denomination.

Ahlstrom, Sidney. *A Religious History of the American People*. New Haven: Yale UP, 1972.

Appiah, Kwame Anthony. "Out of Africa: Topologies of Nativism." *The Bounds of Race: Perspectives on Hegemony and Resistance*. Ed. Dominick La Capra. Ithaca: Cornell UP, 1991. 134–63.

Barthes, Roland. "The Death of the Author." *Image, Music, Text*. Trans. Stephen Heath. New York: Hill & Wang, 1977. 142–48.

Blake, William. "The Marriage of Heaven and Hell." *The Poetry and Prose of William Blake*. Ed. David V. Erdman. New York: Doubleday, 1982. 33–44.

Bosley, Harold. "The Role of Preaching in American History." *Preaching in American History*. Ed. Dewitte Holland. Nashville: Abingdon, 1969. 17–35.

Bourdieu, Pierre. *Distinction: A Social Critique of the Judgment of Taste*. Trans. Richard Nice. Cambridge, MA: Harvard UP, 1984.

Bromwich, David. *Politics by Other Means: Higher Education and Group Thinking*. New Haven: Yale UP, 1982.

Butler, Marilyn. *Jane Austen and the War of Ideas*. Oxford: Clarendon, 1975.

Coleridge, Samuel Taylor. *Biographia Literaria, or, Biographical Sketches of My Literary Life and Opinions*. Ed. George Watson. London: Dent, 1956.

Cox, James W., ed. *The Twentieth-Century Pulpit*. Vol. 2. Nashville: Abingdon, 1981.

De Man, Paul. "Autobiography as Defacement." *Modern Language Notes* 74 (1979): 919–30.

Eagleton, Terry. "Free Particulars: The Rise of the Aesthetic." *Contemporary Marxist Literary Criticism*. Ed. Francis Mulhern. London: Longman, 1992. 55–70.

Eliot, T. S. "Tradition and the Individual Talent." *The Sacred Wood: Essays on Poetry and Criticism*. London: Methuen, 1920. 47–59.

Emerson, Ralph Waldo. *Selections from Ralph Waldo Emerson: An Organic Anthology*. Ed. Stephen E. Whicher. Boston: Houghton Mifflin, 1957.

Foucault, Michel. "What Is an Author?" *Language, Counter-Memory, Practice: Selected Essays and Interviews*. Ed. Donald F. Bouchard. Trans. Donald F. Bouchard and Sherry Simon. Ithaca: Cornell UP, 1977. 113–39.

Fraiman, Susan. "Jane Austen and Edward Said: Gender, Culture, and Imperialism." *Critical Inquiry* 21 (Summer 1995): 805–21.

Frye, Northrop. *Words with Power: Being a Second Study of "The Bible and Literature."* New York: Harcourt Brace Jovanovich, 1990.

Gilbert, Sandra, and Susan Gubar. *Madwoman in the Attic: The Woman Writer and the Nineteenth-Century Literary Imagination*. New Haven: Yale UP, 1979.

Greenblatt, Stephen, and Giles Gunn, eds. "Introduction." *Redrawing the Boundaries: The Transformation of English and American Literary Studies*. New York: MLA 1992.

Guthrie, William Norman. *Offices of Mystical Religion*. New York: Century, 1927.

Keats, John. *Letters of John Keats: A New Selection*. Ed. Robert Gittings. Oxford: Oxford UP, 1970.

Kirkham, Margaret. *Jane Austen, Feminism, and Fiction*. Totowa, NJ: Barnes & Noble, 1983.

Klein, Gregory. *The Woman Detective: Gender and Genre*. Urbana: U of Illinois P, 1988.

McDonagh, Josephine. *De Quincey's Disciplines*. Oxford: Clarendon, 1994.

Moore, James W. *Yes, Lord, I Have Sinned But I Have Several Excellent Excuses*. Nashville: Abingdon Press, 1991.

Owen-Toole, Carolyn. "Beauty Crowds Me Til I Die." *World: Journal of the Unitarian Universalist Association* 8/6 (November/December 1994): 12–15.

Pater, Walter. "Conclusion" In Trilling and Bloom.

Peters, Ted. *Sin: Radical Evil in Soul and Society*. Grand Rapids, MI: Eerdmans, 1994.

Plantinga, Cornelius, Jr. *Not the Way It's Supposed to Be: A Breviary of Sin*. Grand Rapids, MI: Eerdmans, 1995.

Pound, Ezra. *Literary Essays of Ezra Pound*. Ed. T. S. Eliot. New York: New Directions, 1918. 15–40.

Richardson, Alan. *Literature, Education, and Romanticism: Reading as Social Practice*. Cambridge: Cambridge UP, 1994.

Rzepka, Jane R. "Meditations." *World: Journal of the Unitarian Universalist Association* 8/6 (November/December 1994): 72.

Said, Edward. *Culture and Imperialism*. New York: Knopf, 1993.

Scott, Nathan A., Jr. *The Broken Center: Studies in the Theological Horizon of Modern Literature*. New Haven: Yale UP, 1966.

Smith, Barbara Herrnstein. *Contingencies of Value: Alternative Perspectives for Critical Theory*. Cambridge, MA: Harvard University Press, 1988.

Sperry, Willard. *Reality in Worship*. New York: Macmillan, 1925.

Sulloway, Alison. *Jane Austen and the Province of Womanhood*. Philadelphia: U of Pennsylvania P, 1989.

Tompkins, Jane P. *Sensational Designs: The Cultural Work of American Fiction, 1790–1860*. New York: Oxford UP, 1985.

Trilling, Lionel, and Harold Bloom, eds. *Victorian Prose and Poetry*. New York: Oxford UP, 1973.

Wagenknecht, Edward. *Ambassadors for Christ*. Oxford: Oxford UP, 1972.

Ware, Henry, Jr. *On the Formation of the Christian Character: Addressed to Those Who Are Seeking to Lead a Religious Life*. *The Unitarian Conscience: Harvard Moral Philosophy, 1805–1861*. Ed. Daniel Walker Howe. Middletown, CT: Wesleyan UP, 1988. 106–108.

Wellek, René, and Austin Warren. *Theory of Literature*. 3rd ed. New York: Harcourt, Brace, 1956.

Wells, Clarke. *Worship Reader: Essays in Worship Theory*. Newport, RI: The Congregation of Abraxas, 1980.

Whitchurch, Edward. *The Booke of the Common Prayer and Administracion of the Sacramentes, and Other Rites and Ceremonies of the Churche after the Use of the Churche of England*. London, 1549.

White, William R. *Fatal Attractions: Sermons on the Seven Deadly Sins*. Nashville: Abingdon, 1992.

Williams, Raymond. *Marxism and Literature*. Oxford: Oxford UP, 1977.

Wimsatt, W. K., Jr. *The Verbal Icon: Studies in the Meaning of Poetry*. Lexington: U of Kentucky P, 1954.

Winter, Kari J. *Subjects of Slavery, Agents of Change: Woman and Power in Gothic Novels and Slave Narratives*. Athens: U of Georgia P, 1992.

Witten, Marsha. "Accommodation to Secular Norms in Preaching." *Homiletic* 19 (1994): 1–3.

———. *All Is Forgiven: The Secular Message of American Protestantism*. Princeton: Princeton UP, 1993.

Wordsworth, William. "Preface to *Lyrical Ballads*." *Lyrical Ballads*. Ed. R. L. Brett and A. R. Jones. London: Methuen, 1965. 241–72.

II

Some Practical Approaches

6

The Saint's Underwear: A Postmodern Reflection on *The Rule* and *Life* of St. Benedict with help from Gregory the Great and Hildegard of Bingen

Robert Kiely

SOMETIME IN THE LATE 1150s a monastic community of men wrote to the famous Abbess Hildegard of Bingen asking her to send them advice on the best way to interpret and follow "what is needful to us regarding the Rule of our blessed father Benedict" (Hildegard 16). Though the identity of the male community is uncertain, it is clear from the text of their letter that the monks had been criticized for being lax and that they looked to the great abbess to set them straight: "For we are called liars, perjurors and violators of that aforesaid Rule" (Hildegard 16). Hildegard's response is filled with practical advice, but what is surprising, given her reputation as a spiritual teacher, is that she has little to say about Benedict's theological and moral vision. Perhaps she took it for granted that Benedict's and her own theology was too orthodox and well known to need elaboration, even to an imperfect community. Or perhaps there was another communication with the monks, written or oral, now lost to us.

Whatever the reason, Hildegard's letter goes into most detail on matters pertaining to schedules, diet, sleeping arrangements, and clothing. One of her longest sections is devoted exclusively to underwear, which seems odd since underwear is hardly an issue in Benedict's *Rule* and, in fact, is mentioned only once in passing: "Brothers going on a journey should get underclothing from the

wardrobe. On their return, they are to wash it and give it back"
(Fry 263).

If monks were advised by Benedict to put on underwear when
traveling, it seemed evident to the abbess that while at home in
the cloister the holy men of Montecassino wore nothing under
their robes. Since most people in those days did not wear under-
garments, it is not surprising, Hildegard argues (nor, she implies,
should her contemporaries regard it as scandalous), that monks
followed the same custom. Hildegard's emphasis, however, is not
on historical fashion, but on modesty and the possibility of sexual
arousal at the sight and touch of bare flesh:

> One can understand that monks who lived under the teaching of
> this father did not use underclothing except when they were leav-
> ing their quarters. The majority of people did not use underclothes
> at that time. . . . But now in our times, because the customs of men
> indicate it, it is not displeasing to God if monks, because of the
> blasphemy of sacrilege which they might experience in naked flesh,
> wear underclothes so that they will not be naked and touch flesh
> with flesh, and thus be reminded of fleshly sins. (Hildegard 38)

Elsewhere in her letter, Hildegard again exposes her anxiety
about nudity when she interprets Benedict's dictate that the
brothers sleep in their habits girded with belts. According to Benedict, such an arrangement made it possible for the monks "always to be ready to arise without delay" for night and morning
prayer (Fry 219). For Hildegard, conscious of the fact that monks
slept in dormitories in beds close together, the rationale is different: "They sleep . . . so that the clothes they are wearing will not
fall off and so that they will not appear naked" (Hildegard 27).

In several ways, however different her intentions may have
been, Hildegard's letter and especially her interest in monks' underwear, illustrates, even epitomizes in "prophetic" fashion, postmodern preoccupations and habits of reading. First, Hildegard, as
a twelfth-century German woman interpreting a book written six
centuries earlier primarily for a small group of Italian men (and a
few Goths) living at Montecassino, reminds us that for any given
text, however limited its original audience, there is no such thing
as a single "stable" reader of one gender, nationality, or time.
Though Hildegard refers to herself as "a poor little female in

form," she confides to her correspondents, with a fine mixture of humility and self-confidence, that "the matters in the teaching of the Rule which are more difficult and obscure to human understanding might be revealed to me through the grace of God" (Hildegard 18). Though his monastic experience was male and mostly Italian, Benedict would have understood this since his sister Scolastica formed her own community based on his *Rule* and he knew before his death that his teaching was being disseminated beyond Italy. Compact and direct as the language of *The Rule* may be, it was inevitable that in time readers, including those most earnest in wishing to follow Benedict's guidance, would bring to his text their own experience, anxieties, and interests.

Secondly, in seizing a minor detail and following its implications at some length, Hildegard's letter, however respectful and edifying her intentions may have been, points the way to a deconstructive reading of *The Rule*. A "rule," by definition, attempts to regulate life and to arrange its own language in a measured, neatly woven pattern with every word and act in its "right" place. Hierarchy and proportion (or, in literary terms, sequence and measure) determine everything. The wisdom of *The Rule* flows from God through the scriptures (prophets and evangelists) through tradition through Benedict through the abbot to communities of monks. That order is never to be forgotten or disturbed, and no subject (word or person) is to be given a higher or lower place, more or less attention, than it merits.

While appearing to leave *The Rule* intact, Hildegard takes a stitch from an obscure corner of the fabric and lets the whole unravel, if only a little. She does not engage in the kind of punning (with underwear, nakedness, and unraveling) that a Derridean disciple would revel in; nor does she attempt to leave *The Rule* in disarray. She does demonstrate, however, the way language can quite easily (some would say, inevitably) be made to deviate from the normative structures in which it is found. The Hildegardian "deconstruction" does not demolish the text, but, in selecting a marginal or "hidden" entry point of ambiguity, sensitivity, or seeming triviality, it shows the whole to be less fixed and transparent than it may first have appeared.

Thirdly, Hildegard's section on underwear could well be the beginning of a New Historicist approach to understanding Benedict and his *Rule*. While traditional historians have studied Benedict in relation to the development of Christian ascetism and monasticism in the line of Cassian, Pachomius, Basil, and Augustine or in the context of the barbarian invasions of the Italian peninsula, a New Historian might, like Hildegard, reflect on an "insignificant" detail of daily life—personal hygiene, diet, bedding, fashion, monastic economy, the scarcity of linen—and, through it, attempt to piece together an historical picture hitherto overlooked. For the New Historian and for Hildegard, a monastery was not simply a link in a chain of political and religious institutional developments to be viewed over long stretches of time, but a living community of individuals with a complex network of relationships, customs, and modes of defining goals and dealing with perceived threats to those goals.

Fourthly, in being so much more explicit about the dangers of naked flesh than Benedict, Hildegard opens a door to the postmodern scholarly fascination with sexuality (of interest especially if found in places where sexual activity is not supposed to take place or be mentioned). In referring to the touching of "flesh with flesh" (in the absence of underwear), Hildegard, with refreshing directness, assumes that auto-stimulation (feeling pleasure in one's own naked flesh) and homosexual delight in seeing or touching the flesh of a fellow monk are likely eventualities in communities of men or women. Hildegard refers to such feelings as "blasphemies" and "sacrilege," and would almost certainly have labeled them an indication of humanity's fallen state, yet her matter-of-fact assumption that they are a common aspect of human behavior brings her close to some ever-broadening postmodern definitions of what constitutes the "natural." The fact that Hildegard takes same-sex attraction for granted (since the "experience," sight and touch of "flesh with flesh," is all imagined within the cloistered walls) gives her letter a surprisingly contemporary feeling. While Benedict's *Rule* shows, according to Georges Duby, "an unarticulated but obsessive fear of homosexuality," Hildegard comes right out with what, in her opinion, determines many of *The Rule*'s working, dressing, and sleeping arrangements (Aries 56).[1]

Finally, with virtual if not actual clairvoyance, Hildegard almost

---

[1] For further discussion of this subject, see James Boswell, *Christianity, Social Tolerance, and Homosexuality* 137–166.

seemed to know that some day postmodern critics would be on the lookout for untraveled territory. In the debate about canon, few scholars are truly ready to say that Dante and Shakespeare are finished or should be neglected or even that the last word has been said about them. But in the study of literature, until "theory" disturbed the tranquil scene, much scholarship and criticism was becoming redundant. Too many books and essays were being written about the same writers and even about the same passages from the same works by the same writers. Postmodern methods are not immune to this tendency, but they have frequently led critics to explore subjects that previously had been considered (and still are considered by some readers) to be "unliterary" or, worse, beneath the dignity of the "serious" scholar. To contemplate Benedict's views about underwear may indeed be a trivial pursuit or a desperate effort to find something new to write about. But with the help and inspiration of Hildegard of Bingen, it may serve as a clue to some of the productive ways a postmodern reader can revisit a classic religious text.

Hildegard acknowledges, without apology, that parts of *The Rule* are "out of date," but her proto–deconstructive unraveling of bits of the text is clearly intended not to leave it in tatters, but to rescue it from antiquated legalism and oblivion. She is not out to "trash" *The Rule*, but to salvage it for monastics of her own time. What she unravels, she reknits. In the past few years, much postmodern "theory" has itself begun to seem "dated"— somewhat more rapidly than was the case with *The Rule*! Increasing numbers of students and scholars have come to feel that theoretical orthodoxies have rigidified into unreadable and irrelevant discourses and that a persistent anti–metaphysical bias has hardened into a predictable "rule of thumb" that is unnecessarily and unpersuasively limiting.

There is no doubt that all writing, both sacred and secular, eventually goes "out of date." The danger is not that old books will be reread or even misread according to the preoccupations of later generations, but that they will be forgotten altogether. Thus, wrestling with an old text, even when the exercise includes rude and irreverent moves, has a Midrashic element, a desire, pious despite itself, to bring the words back to life. Hildegard's example, whether or not one wishes to press the deconstructive analogies, shows yet again an ancient tradition within Christianity of reverent irreverence and, albeit unintentionally, provides some clues about how certain postmodern critical instruments can be released from their negative anti-metaphysical bondage and employed for purposes of revival and reconstruction. The objective of this essay, therefore, is not to consign religious classics to "history," but to renew and reread them for the present.

Much better known than Hildegard's twelfth-century "Explanation" of *The Rule* is the narration of the "Life and Miracles of Saint Benedict" that occupies the second book of the four-part *Dialogues* of Pope Gregory the Great, first published in 594, fifty years after Benedict's death. Though the legend can stand alone, it makes sense to read it, like Hildegard's "Explanation," as a commentary on Benedict's *Rule*. While it is no longer assumed that Gregory lived by *The Rule* in his years as a monk before becoming pope, scholars agree that by the time of the writing of *The Dialogues*, Gregory not only knew *The Rule*, but, in a way typical of his pontificate, saw it as a powerful, balanced, and practical instrument for spreading the faith.

Gregory's stated intention in writing *The Dialogues* was to recall and celebrate the virtues and miraculous deeds of the Italian saints, and most especially Benedict, for the edification of a people depressed and devastated by barbarian invasions, plague, and famine. One commentator has observed that "the pedagogical purpose is so apparent . . . that one may wonder at the reality of the events" (Fry 75). But while readers (even before the nineteenth century) questioned the authenticity of many of the wonders attributed to Benedict and the other saints, a postmodern critic is more likely to raise different questions and doubts. Allowing Gregory his stated intention, we want to know what else was going on of a less "apparent" and pious kind in his text. Can we, like Hildegard, both admire and deconstruct Gregory's legend and, in doing so, find in his reading of *The Rule* any signs of "irregularity" or "deregulation"?

The general outline of Benedict's life—his birth in Nursia, his schooling in Rome, his three years alone in the wilderness of Subiaco, his move to Montecassino, the establishment of many small communities, and the writing of *The Rule*—was already in Gregory's time supported by several sources of evidence and is accepted still as historically accurate (Fry 73–79). The wonders and miracles attributed to the saint came to Gregory from four monks who had known Benedict and claimed either to have witnessed them or to have heard them described by eyewitnesses. Gregory did not invent Benedict's life, but, like all storytellers, he had the freedom to arrange events, place emphasis, intrepret with his own comments, and structure the narrative as he pleased. The move from monastic rule to saint's life is both an act of piety and a genre shift from a hierarchical and legalistic code to a relatively fluid narrative form with potentially radical destabilizing consequences.

Central to Gregory's fiction is an imaginary conversation between himself, as pope and teacher, and a young disciple, Peter, who asks him "innocent" questions and makes flattering comments, such as "I like the way you interpreted that passage" and "I find this discussion very enjoyable" (Gregory 9, 69). While the form resembles a Platonic dialogue, Gregory was more likely imitating the dialogues of Boethius whose works were extremely influential in his time. Yet the choice remains intriguing, especially as a "companion" to a *Rule* which is strikingly univocal and which begins, "Listen carefully, my son, to the master's instructions" (Fry 157). The "son" addressed in Benedict's *Rule* does not ask questions or make comments, flattering or otherwise, and, indeed, though perfectly silent (absent) throughout the text, is admonished more than once to "control his tongue and remain silent, not speaking unless asked a question" (Fry 201).

Innocent and conventional as it may seem, Gregory's decision to relate the saint's life in dialogue form disturbs two fundamental components of *The Rule*, the unquestioned authority (and uninterrupted voice) of the master and the obedient silence of the disciple. By introducing dialogue, between himself and young Peter, but also within the narrated episodes of the saint's life, Gregory sets in motion a dialectical continuum with infinite possibilities. The story begins with legendary simplicity: "Some years ago there lived a man who was revered for the holiness of his life. Blessed Benedict was his name" (Gregory 1). In Latin, "blessed Benedict" is a redundancy, *benedictus Benedictus*, which seems to be setting the tone and establishing the structure of the narration as pious, repetitious, and uncomplicated, a litany of praise without interruption or contradiction. But, in fact, Gregory invents dialogue for the saint in which he is "heard" instructing and preaching, but also in which he is challenged and opposed.

Midway through the legend when Benedict has moved his community to Montecassino, he is pursued by "the ancient enemy of mankind" who would not be silent. A loud voice shatters the quiet of the monastery and the monotony of the narrative by shouting at the saint "so that all the brethren could hear him: . . . 'Benedict, Benedict, blessed Benedict! . . . Cursed Benedict! Cursed, not blessed!' " (Gregory 28–29). *Benedictus Benedictus* becomes, in a startling moment, *Maladictus Benedictus!* Benedict, of course, triumphs over his enemy, but the silence of *The Rule* and the simplicity of the narrative have been temporarily broken, not by an argument or even a particular crime, but by a taunt, a refusal to keep quiet, and, most threatening of all, by a play on words that questions the conformity of adjective with noun, the saint's reputation with his name. Overcoming adversity and silencing the devil are, of course, essential to all hagiography. What is noteworthy about Gregory's "Life" is that talking back to the saint is not exclusively the devil's business.

Gregory is not, as Blake said of Milton, "of the Devil's party," but there is no doubt that he takes advantage of the dialogue form to express his own views when they are not consistent with *The Rule* and especially when he thinks *The Rule* is too severe and legalistic. One of the tactics of a deconstructionist reading of any text is to look for "breaks" in the continuity, interruptions, ruptures that may expose contradictions or weaknesses in the constructed framework. On the surface, Peter's naïve questions give Gregory the opportunity to defend and justify Benedict's life (and, by implication, *The Rule*). Peter, like most of the friends and pupils of Socrates, is a convenient dunce. The truly interesting dialogue is the one that takes place, as it were, in the margins, between Gregory and Benedict. Since the only document that is directly attributed to Benedict is *The Rule*, Gregory's patient and paternal answers to unsophisticated Peter are, in fact, the comments, questions, and challenges of the highly sophisticated and learned disciple Gregory to the patriarch Benedict. It may be true, as is often said, that Gregory's "Life" complements Benedict's *Rule*; it is no less true that the "Life" talks back to and, in its own fashion, deconstructs certain elements of the revered text.

Since we began with Hildegard and her preoccupation with underwear and the temptations of the flesh, it is worth looking at the way *The Rule* addresses sexual desire and then at Gregory's narration and commentary on the same subject. In chapter seven on humility, Benedict gives a characteristically economical and scripturally supported warning: "As for the desires of the body, we must believe that God is always with us, for *All my desires are known to you* (Ps 37). . . . We must then be on guard against any base desire, because death is stationed near the gateway of pleasure. For this reason, Scripture warns us, *Pursue not your lusts* (Sir 18:30)" (Fry 195). The most effective aid to self-control, according to this passage, is fear of being seen and punished. Benedict warns his monks that even if they are able to hide their behavior from superiors, God never sleeps. The teachings of *The Rule* are nearly always supported by quotations from Scripture, but since Jesus refused to condemn the woman taken in adultery and befriended Mary Magdalene, Benedict resorts here to passages from the Hebrew Bible less forgiving than the gospels.

In chapter two of his "Life of Saint Benedict," Gregory tells of the holy youth living alone in a cave above Subiaco when one day he remembers a woman he had once seen "and before he realized it his emotions were carrying him away." Just as he is about to abandon his hermitage (presumably to go in search of the woman), he sees a patch of nettles and briars, throws off his clothes, and flings himself naked onto the thorns until "his whole body had put out the fires of evil in his heart" (Gregory 7–8). After this, according to the legend, Benedict was permanently free from temptations of the flesh and therefore "ready to instruct others in the practice of virtue." Since the episode parallels that of Saint Anthony of the Desert, the great model of all Christian hermits, it functions as a symbolic moment that places Benedict in an heroic tradition of asceticism.

Gregory comments on the story rather surprisingly by referring to a passage in the Book of Numbers: "That is why Moses commanded the Levites to begin their service when they were twenty-five years old and to become guardians of the sacred vessels only at the age of fifty" (Gregory 8). Predictably, young Peter does not understand the quote or its relevance until Gregory explains that "the temptations of the flesh are violent during youth, whereas after the age of fifty, concupiscence dies down" (Gregory 9). Whether or not we agree with Gregory's account of the biological clock, it is clear that, in marked contrast with the legend of self-laceration (mutilation?) and the threat of punishment in

The Rule, Gregory uses Scripture to establish what Hildegard too had seen as the ordinariness of sexual desire, especially in youth, and the expectation or hope that it will be modified in time. Without threat or alarm, he places sexual desire in both a biblical and a natural context. Like the preacher in Ecclesiastes, he thinks that there is a time for everything and, while he does not advocate license, his advice to his (possibly lusty) young listener removes all but the symbolic thorns from the briar patch. He acknowledges (with the authority of Moses) that "boys will be boys" (Hildegard would undoubtedly have added, "and girls will be girls"), suggests that time and patience are great healers, and thereby discounts the menace and humanizes the severity of *The Rule*. Reference to the proximity of death and the "gateway of pleasure" is replaced or at least modified by another biblical reference which acknowledges that the service of God must be accommodated to the age, maturity, and self-discipline of the individual. What in *The Rule* is an abrupt warning becomes in the narrative a slowing down of time, a graduated and charitable reassurance.

As Hildegard's example shows, a typical deconstructive gesture is to take an apparently minor portion of a text and treat it as major, deliberately making a mountain out of a molehill. One of Gregory's most profound philosophical disputes with *The Rule* appears in the next break in the narrative just after Benedict has abandoned a corrupt community of monks who begged him to be their superior and then tried to poison his wine. According to Gregory, Benedict then "went back to the wilderness he loved, to live alone with himself in the presence of his heavenly Father" ("Tuncque ad locum dilectae solitudinis rediit et solus in superni spectatoris oculis habitavit secum") (Gregory 11).[2] Peter conveniently does not "quite understand what you mean by saying 'to live with himself' " ("habitavit secum"), which allows Gregory to indulge in one of his longest digressions on this brief and seemingly unimportant phrase. Gregory defends Benedict's leaving the wicked monks by pointing out that to have remained with them would have forced him to concentrate his attention on their problems until "he would have been in danger of losing sight of

---

[2] The Latin text is taken from *Alle Fonti della Spiritualità Silvestrine. I. Regola e Vita di S. Benedetto*, a cura di Lorenzo Sena e Vincenzo Fattorini (Fabriano, Monastero San Silvestro Abate, 1990) 364.

himself" ("et se forsitan relinqueret"). Gregory goes on to give other examples of being "carried out of ourselves," through sin, as in the parable of the Prodigal Son, or through contemplation, as in St. Peter in ecstasy. Gregory is not opposed to contemplation, but the balanced, middle way that he advocates in this discussion involves an almost Platonic self-knowledge, finding one's true and better self, as Benedict did "out in that lonely wilderness by always keeping his thoughts recollected" (Gregory 13).

Since Christ spent forty days alone in the desert and frequently went off by himself, there is nothing unorthodox in Gregory's discussion unless one compares it with references to the self in *The Rule*. It would appear that, according to the master of *The Rule*, the "true" self is never a "better" self, but is always debased and without merit: "The monk . . . regards himself as poor and worthless [*malum se iudicet et indignum*] . . . saying to himself with the Prophet, *I am insignificant and ignorant, no better than a beast*"; "A man not only admits with his tongue but is also convinced in his heart that he is inferior to all . . . saying with the Prophet, *I am truly a worm, not a man* [*ego autem sum vermis et non homo*]"; Monks "no longer live by their own judgment, giving into their whims and appetites; rather they walk according to another's decisions and directions" (Fry 189, 199).[3]

Even allowing for metaphorical hyperbole, the "self" alluded to in these passages would hardly be worth "living with" in the way so admired by Gregory. Without directly challenging *The Rule*, Gregory assumes an important distinction between humility before God and what in contemporary terms might be called a "healthy" sense of one's rational and moral worth. It was not lost on him that many of the saints, including Benedict, who advocated "self-denial," possessed extremely powerful egos and often exerted their influence by refusing to bend to the authorities of their times. One of the patterns that Gregory traces in Benedict's life is insubordination. He leaves home at an early age, drops out of his school in Rome, runs away from his nurse to go off alone to the wilderness, walks out of the first monastery where he serves as abbot, abandons Subiaco when harassed by an envious priest, refuses to be intimidated by Totila the Gothic king, and so on.

The Benedict portrayed by Gregory and certainly the author of

---

[3] Latin text from *Regola e Vita*, 86.

The Rule appears, by all accounts, to have been a man who knew and trusted his own mind and pursued with incredible perseverance and determination his own path. According to the language of *The Rule*, synthesized from earlier monastic codes, especially the *Regula Magistri*, as well as based on Benedict's wilderness experience, it is not one's own inclinations, intelligence, or judgment that should be followed, but the will of God, as interpreted by superiors and the customs and traditions of the community. Gregory's lyrical and loving repetition of the phrase "to live with himself" (*an illum secum fuisse; hunc ergo venerabilem virum secum habitasse*), with its almost Protestant, even Thoreauvian, foreshadowings, places Benedict's example in contradiction to his *Rule*. Gregory's "self" is neither a worthless "worm" nor an anarchical "free spirit," but an entity shaped by the institutions and culture of its time yet confident of the value of reason, individual conscience, and free will. Far from accentuating "inferiority" and therefore hierarchy, Gregory, in his papal writings, continually stressed the value and equality of all: "All possess distinct and separate gifts"; "Nature begets all men as equals" (Mayvaert "Gregory" V, 12 and "Diversity" VI, 157). For Gregory, living with and knowing oneself, being true to oneself, and recollecting one's own thoughts are not only consistent with the love of God but essential to it and to the love and respect of other human beings.

One of the last and longest stories in the narrative of Benedict's life involves a visit to his sister Scolastica in a house outside the monastery gates. It is a parable of the triumph of love over rules. When the time comes for Benedict to leave, his sister begs him to spend the night visiting with her, but he reminds her with some indignation—"What are you saying, sister?"—that it is against *The Rule* for him to stay away from the monastery. At this, Scolastica, in good Italian fashion, makes a scene, praying and weeping until a violent thunderstorm crashes around them preventing Benedict from departing until morning.

Gregory's comment on the episode and the sequence of events following it give a particular spin to his reading of *The Rule* and the examples to be drawn from Benedict's life.

If we consider his point of view, we can readily see that he wanted the sky to remain clear. . . . But this wish of his was thwarted by a miracle almighty God performed in answer to a woman's prayer.

We need not be surprised that in this instance she proved mightier than her brother; she had been looking forward so long to this visit. Do we not read in St. John that God is love? Surely it is no more than right that her influence was greater than his, since hers was the greater love. (Gregory 69)

To a postmodern and feminist reader, to say nothing of Hildegard of Bingen and the Jesus of the gospels, Gregory's comment would seem not only just but obvious. Yet in the context of a pope's life of a male saint, a patriarch, and in relation to a *Rule* that established the right conduct for a holy life, it is breathtakingly radical. Not only does the sister prove to be "mightier" than the brother, even when he has overcome trials and temptations and become a revered master, but "his point of view," determined by the dictates of *The Rule*, is shown to be petty and insensitive in contrast with her love. That Gregory quotes the gospel of John, the gospel of love, to support his reading of the event is particularly telling as a response to Benedict's habit of quoting the Hebrew prophets whenever he wishes to be be legalistic and threatening.

Three days after the visit, Benedict sees Scolastica's soul leave her body and depart for heaven. If any question remained, her righteousness and foresight are vindicated by this coda to the episode. We do not know what the sequence of events was in the oral tradition with which Gregory was working, but it suits his own theological and moral disposition that immediately after the visit and his sister's death, Benedict has another extraordinary vision:

In the dead of night he suddenly beheld a flood of light shining down from above more brilliant than the sun, and with it every trace of darkness cleared away. . . . According to his own description, the whole world was gathered up before his eyes in what appeared to be a single ray of light. (Gregory 70)

Of course, this epiphanic vision can be explained as the result of Benedict's lifetime of prayer and self-discipline. Yet in Gregory's telling, Benedict "sees the light" only after his sister's lesson of love and her death. His earlier "point of view," wishing for clear skies so that he could obey his own *Rule*, seems peculiarly narrow and limited in contrast with the clarity of a mystical perspective in which the whole world, including rules and regulations and anxieties about them, is "gathered up . . . in a single ray of light."

That Gregory should have written the only life of Benedict is at once appropriate and ironic. It is appropriate because Gregory had lived as a monk and clearly had a profound respect for Benedict and dedication to the spirit of communal living. Yet, as one of the most brilliantly innovative popes in Christian history, he earned a reputation for being unusually tolerant about the application of what he regarded as minor rules and regulations involving church practices and customs. In a famous letter to Augustine of Canterbury he wrote:

> You, Brother, know the usage of the Roman Church in which you were brought up: hold it very much in affection. But as far as I am concerned, if you have found something more pleasing to almighty God, either in the Roman or the Frankish or in any other Church, make a careful choice and institute in the Church of the English . . . the best usages which you have gathered. . . . For we should love things not because of the places where they are found, but places because of the good things they contain. (Mayvaert, "Diversity" VI, 144)

Because of this and similar liberalities, one eighteenth-century author referred to Gregory as the "Lutheran Pope" (Mayvaert, "Gregory" V, 4). And a nineteenth-century French monsignor declared that Gregory could not have written so un-Roman a letter: "Cette lettre est certainement inauthentique. . . . Ce n'est pas un Romain ni surtout un pape, qui eut pu écrire la phrase: 'Non enim pro locis res sed pro rebus loca nobis amanda sunt'" (Mayvaert, "Diversity" VI, 145). ("This letter is certainly inauthentic. . . . It is not a Roman and above all not a pope who could write the sentence: 'We should love things not because of the places where they are found, etc.'")

And what might Benedict have said to Gregory? Would he have been scandalized like the French monsignor by liberal and deconstructive tendencies in one of his disciples? Probably not. In chapter three of *The Rule* Benedict qualifies his imposition of silence by requiring every abbot to listen carefully and regularly to the advice and opinions of all members of the community at chapter meetings. "The reason why we said all should be called for counsel is that the Lord often reveals what is better to the younger" (Fry 179).

Gregory, like Hildegard, was obviously not attempting to discredit *The Rule* which he saw, on the whole, as a moderate and sensible code of conduct for monastic communities, couched in the language and sensibilities of an earlier time. His appeal to the postmodern reader—like Hildegard's—is in his demonstrating that the best way for a student to show respect for a teacher (or a reader for an author) is not to remain silent, but to keep the text alive, to ask hard questions, raise objections, and make the lessons his or her own. And to keep the dialogue going. In a particularly postmodern move, Gregory resists closure by telling Peter at the conclusion of the legend that what looks like an end is merely a pause: "Let us interrupt our discussion for a while. If we are going to take up the miracles of other holy men, we shall need a short period of silence to rest our voices" (Gregory 78).

WORKS CITED

Aries, Philippe, and Georges Duby, eds. *A History of Private Life.* Vol II. Trans. Arthur Goldhammer. Cambridge, MA: Harvard UP, 1988.

Boswell, James. *Christianity, Social Tolerance, and Homosexuality.* U of Chicago P, 1980.

Fry, Timothy, o.s.b., ed. *RB 1980: The Rule of Saint Benedict in Latin and English with Notes.* Collegeville, MN: Liturgical Press, 1981.

Gregory the Great. *Life and Miracles of Saint Benedict.* Trans. Odo J. Zimmermann, o.s.b. Westport, CT: Greenwood, 1980.

Hildegard of Bingen. *Explanation of the Rule of Saint Benedict.* Trans. Hugh Feiss, o.s.b. Toronto: Peregrina, 1990.

Meyvaert, Paul. "Diversity Within Unity, a Gregorian Theme." *Benedict, Gregory, Bede, and Others.* London: Variorum, 1977. Chapter 5.

——."Gregory the Great and Authority." *Benedict, Gregory, Bede, and Others.* London: Variorum, 1977. Chapter 5.

Sena, Lorenzo, and Vincenzo Fattorini, eds. *Alle Fonti della spiritualità silvestrine.* I. *Regola e vita di S. Benedetto.* Fabriano: Monastero San Silvestro Abate, 1990.

7

Prayer, Poetry, and *Paradise Lost:* Samuel Johnson as Reader of Milton's Christian Epic

Stephen Fix

THIS ESSAY AIMS TO TELL THE STORY of the encounter between the English tradition's most influential critic and the most important poem ever written in his language on a religious subject. Samuel Johnson's whole critique of *Paradise Lost*, and in particular his commentary on the way readers respond to the poem, has been generally misunderstood—in large part, I believe, because we have underappreciated the unusual degree to which the poem's religious subject matter and rhetorical strategies shaped Johnson's critical response to it.[1]

An earlier version of this essay, titled "Johnson and the 'Duty' of Reading *Paradise Lost*," appeared in substantially similar form in *ELH*, 52 (1985): 649–71. I am grateful to the editors of *ELH* for permission to reuse material from that essay in the present volume.

[1] A brief word about Johnson's religion may be useful as background to this essay. Maurice J. Quinlan writes: "Although Johnson occasionally gave a special emphasis or an unusual interpretation to certain doctrines, on the whole he was an orthodox member of the Church of England. What most struck his contemporaries was not the nature of his convictions but rather his deep religious fervor" (ix). In his essay "The Conflict of Faith and Fear in Johnson's Moral Writing," Charles E. Pierce, Jr., writes that "Johnson was a deeply religious man who accepted without question the existence of God, who affirmed his faith in the principal truths of Christianity, who was an ardent Church-of-England man, and who sought throughout his life to render himself worthy of salvation" (317). Among the most significant modern studies of Johnson's religion, in addition to those cited above, are: Arieh Sachs, "Reason and Unreason in Johnson's Religion"; Chester F. Chapin, *The Religious Thought of Samuel Johnson*; W. Jackson Bate, *Samuel Johnson*, especially 448–60; and Charles E. Pierce, Jr., *The Religious Life of Samuel Johnson*. See also recent studies by Nicholas Hudson and J. C. D. Clark that locate Johnson's religious views in the philosophical, theological, and political controversies of his day. Johnson's prayers are collected

Johnson wrote about or alluded to *Paradise Lost* frequently throughout his career, but his most sustained commentary on the poem appeared in 1779 in his *Life of Milton* (one of the series of critical biographies that eventually came to be called *The Lives of the Poets*). From the moment of its publication to the present day, the *Life of Milton* has been controversial—a source, even for some committed Johnsonians, of at least mild embarrassment. Johnson's distaste for Milton's personal character and political allegiances is palpable, and his dismissive contempt for such poems as "Lycidas" is regarded by many as wrong-headed and infuriating—a sure sign of Johnson's prejudicial desire to minimize Milton's achievement.

Against the backdrop of his apparent hostility toward Milton, critics have tried to understand Johnson's famous (or infamous) remarks about the reader's response to *Paradise Lost*. He calls it a book "the reader admires and lays down, and forgets to take up again. None ever wished it longer than it is. Its perusal is a duty rather than a pleasure."[2] This seems a surprising conclusion, for Johnson's commentary on the poem begins with the extraordinary claim that *Paradise Lost*, "considered with respect to design, may claim the first place, and with respect to performance the second, among the productions of the human mind" (170). Some critics, trying to reconcile these apparently conflicting views, have been led to argue that Johnson found the experience of reading *Paradise Lost* tedious, and that he regarded the poem as the object of scholarly "duty," or as a monument on a tour of literary history that no one is allowed to miss seeing, however laborious a journey it requires.[3] Other critics have argued that although Johnson admired the genius of *Paradise Lost*, he held the poem at such distance from himself that he was able only to appreciate its skill, but not feel its power.

---

in Volume 1 of *The Yale Edition of the Works of Samuel Johnson*. Johnson's sermons are collected in Volume 14 of *Yale Works*.

[2] Samuel Johnson, *Lives of the English Poets*, 1:183. Subsequent references to the *Lives* will be cited parenthetically in the text of the essay by volume and page number. References to the *Life of Milton* are from Volume 1, and will be cited by page number only.

[3] George Watson, for instance, comments: "Johnson writes of *Paradise Lost* as if the poem were a visit to the dentist, or a regrettable aspect of Sunday observance, like compulsory church-attendance. His analysis is an act of self-persuasion, and one unconvincing and unconvinced reason after another is advanced why the epic has to be praised." See *The Literary Critics: A Study of English Descriptive Criticism*, 91–92.

I wish to propose a quite different interpretation of these controversial remarks by arguing that there is a subtle causal link between Johnson's claim for the poem's literary preeminence, his vision of its religious and moral purposes, and his sense of our extreme difficulty in reading it. By exploring these connections, we can understand in a new way the consistency of Johnson's complicated argument about *Paradise Lost*, grasp the logic of his claim that reading Milton's Christian epic is a "duty," and penetrate the critical psychology of Johnson's response to a poem whose moral and spiritual effects he finds "awful," terrifying, and intimidating.[4]

I

Several aspects of Johnson's critique provide preliminary but significant clues about the stance he wishes to adopt toward *Paradise Lost*. He writes about it in an exceptionally respectful way, and is unusually eager to set it apart from other poems. While most authors, Johnson says, write for fame and money, Milton's purpose—"to adorn his native country by some great performance" (134)—is unaffected by such self-interest. Johnson dwells in almost obsessive detail on the poem's publication and financial history, noting that booksellers paid only a few pounds for each edition of the poem, and stressing that they, not Milton, later enjoyed the profit the poem produced (144–47). Johnson says in wonder that "the greatest benefaction that *Paradise Lost* ever procured the author's descendents" (160) came not from the poem itself, but from a 1750 benefit performance of *Comus* (for which Johnson wrote a prologue). The likely intent of these sorts

---

[4] Most earlier commentaries on Johnson's remarks about the reader's response to *Paradise Lost* have appeared in studies whose purpose was to explore his views on a variety of general critical issues, rather than his specific views on Milton's unique achievement. I believe this has limited and distorted our understanding of Johnson's point, which must be understood in the context of his overall argument about the poem. Jean Hagstrum's comments, however, in the chapter titled "The Beautiful, The Pathetic, and The Sublime," in *Samuel Johnson's Literary Criticism*, are helpful in any effort to contextualize and interpret Johnson's remarks about *Paradise Lost*. For general commentary on Johnson's larger goals and strategies in the *Life of Milton*, see my essays "Distant Genius: Johnson and the Art of Milton's Life," and "The Contexts and Motives of Johnson's *Life of Milton*."

of remarks—whose length and detail are highly unusual in Johnson's criticism—is to isolate the composition of *Paradise Lost* from such common authorial motives as greed and self-aggrandizement. Johnson keeps Milton well away from Grub Street, for *Paradise Lost* is not a poem for the marketplace.

It is also noteworthy that, when he writes about *Paradise Lost*, Johnson studiously avoids the mocking, parodic tone he often adopts in commentaries on Milton's other poems—such as "Lycidas," where he ridicules the rhetorical questions asked by the shepherds, or *Comus*, where he belittles the brothers for making clever speeches while their sister is imperiled. Johnson is careful never to appear flippant or clever about either the composition of *Paradise Lost* or about the poem itself. His treatment of Milton's belief that the climates and seasons could influence a poet's powers of composition (135–38), and his dismissal of romantic theories of inspiration (138–39), are the closest Johnson comes to parody or flippancy in discussing *Paradise Lost*, and these arguments never touch the poem itself. Johnson's restraint seems all the more significant since the opportunity to secure his point at Milton's expense was readily at hand: how, he might have asked, could the author of a great poem about the freedom of human will trivialize his sophisticated understanding of this subject by submitting his own will to the vagaries of climate? Johnson never allows this potential question to surface, or to compromise the poem's exemplary instructive value.

A third example also involves what Johnson chooses *not* to say about the poem. The issue of "decorum" was much on Johnson's mind when criticizing Milton's work, and the greatest challenge Milton faced in this regard was how, in Johnson's words, "to make Satan speak as a rebel, without any such expressions as might taint the reader's imagination" (173). Since what seems to Johnson most to distinguish *Paradise Lost* from Milton's other poems ("Lycidas," most notably) is the suitability of its language and sentiments to its speakers and occasions, Johnson might have suggested that Satan's insolence, his language of insubordination and rebellion, could have been the creative product only of a man well acquainted with such qualities. But here again Johnson declines the opportunity to score an easy *ad hominem* point in the guise of a legitimate critical remark. Although he detests Milton's political views and activities, Johnson does not draw the connection the Romantics later would draw between Milton, the political rebel, and Milton, the creator of Satan. In fact, Johnson slides right past this equation, carefully restricting his discussion to literary exigencies: "The language of rebellion," he concludes simply, "cannot be the same with that of obedience" (173).[5]

Such choices on Johnson's part suggest, at the very least, that his purpose as a critic of *Paradise Lost* was not to disparage the poem or discredit its author (as is alleged almost routinely). If anything, Johnson seems exceptionally eager to avoid any remark that might make *Paradise Lost* seem to be a common or tainted poem. He writes in the conviction that *Paradise Lost* requires of its readers and critics more than ordinary carefulness and circumspection, and that the poem has a purity and integrity which the critic must respect. So when, in the *Life*, Johnson dismisses Milton's "little pieces" to turn to the study of *Paradise Lost*, his comment that "a greater work calls for greater care" (170) does more than predict the scope and length of the inquiry to follow; it hints at the posture Johnson believes he must assume before a poem of a "greater" kind.

II

We can gather a more detailed sense of what responsibilities Johnson thinks he has toward *Paradise Lost* by examining the role that literary criteria play—and fail to play—in his commentary. Johnson's critique of *Paradise Lost*, comprising nearly one-fourth of the *Life of Milton*, is the most extensive one he wrote of any single literary work, yet perhaps its most remarkable characteristic is the eagerness Johnson shows throughout to abandon his specifically *literary* analysis of the poem. Though he dutifully mentions many of the topics and categories traditionally deployed in epic criticism, they function only long enough for him to describe their

---

[5] This feature is also related to Johnson's effort earlier in the *Life* to assure readers of Milton's theological purity. Milton, says Johnson, was "untainted by any heretical peculiarity of opinion," and "had full conviction of the truth of Christianity" (155). Moreover, Johnson refuses to echo the charge, made by Joseph Addison and other critics, that Milton alluded to heathen fables too often in *Paradise Lost*—a charge that Johnson himself was quick to make about "Lycidas."

inadequacy in discussing *Paradise Lost*. "Of the probable and the marvellous," Johnson writes, "*Paradise Lost* requires little to be said" (174). "Of the machinery," he continues, "another fertile topic of critical remarks, here is no room to speak" (175). Many categories that might be useful in judging other epics seem to Johnson pedantic when applied to *Paradise Lost*. "The questions," he asserts in summary, "whether the action of the poem be strictly one, whether the poem can be properly termed heroick, and who is the hero, are raised by such readers as draw their principles of judgement rather from books than from reason" (175–76).[6]

Johnson's impatience here with slavish applications of generic categories will come as no surprise to readers of his criticism; he was equally dismissive, for instance, about arguments objecting to Shakespeare's violation of the dramatic unities. But it is significant that, throughout the *Life of Milton*, Johnson seems remarkably eager to suggest the inappropriateness not just of a specific set of critical criteria, but of the whole effort to judge *Paradise Lost* primarily on literary grounds. He goes out of his way to undercut the significance even of his own objections to the poem's literary technique, quickly minimizing, for example, the importance of the several reservations he records about occasional improprieties in Milton's imagery, diction, and use of allegory (184–88). When he spots problems in the poem, he introduces them mostly as "inconveniences" rather than as defects or faults. When describing these inconveniences, he interrupts himself to defend *Paradise Lost* against his own mildly stated objections (187f.). And when he can make no such defense, his language becomes tentative, unassertive, almost embarrassed: "To find sentiments for the state of innocence was very difficult," he says, "and something of anticipation perhaps is now and then discovered. . . . I know not whether his answer to the angel's reproof for curiosity does not want something of propriety . . ." (186–87). It seems that *Paradise Lost* is a poem of such integrity, and represents an achievement so absolute, so extraordinary, that it coerces Johnson into sacrificing even his most cherished critical values: "But whatever be the advantage of rhyme I cannot prevail on myself to wish that Milton had been a rhymer, for I cannot wish his work to be other than it is . . ." (194).

---

[6] For background on Johnson's place in eighteenth-century criticism of epic, see H. T. Swedenberg, Jr., *The Theory of the Epic in England, 1650–1800*.

The reasons for Johnson's gingerly deference toward the poem, and for his self-conscious attempt to downplay the importance of his critical objections, are best explained by quoting the conclusion of a *Rambler* essay in which he excuses Milton's apparent lack of interest in accommodating sound to sense in *Paradise Lost*:

> He had, indeed, a greater and a nobler work to perform; a single sentiment of moral or religious truth, a single image of life or nature, would have been cheaply lost for a thousand echoes of the cadence to the sense; and he who had undertaken to "vindicate the ways of God to man," might have been accused of neglecting his cause, had he lavished much of his attention upon syllables and sounds. (*Yale Works* 4:142–43)

The priorities ascribed here to Milton are mirrored in Johnson's own critique of *Paradise Lost*: though Johnson is attentive to literary issues, his cause as a critic, like Milton's as a writer, is to focus primarily on the poem's moral and religious aspirations. Johnson is unwilling to press very aggressively any complaints about the technique of a poem which, as he says in the *Life of Milton*, "contains the history of a miracle" (174) and whose purpose is "to shew the reasonableness of religion" (171). In short, *Paradise Lost*, uniquely among the works of literature he discusses, assumes for Johnson a religious importance that helps the poem transcend any discussion of its literary merits or defects.

It is Johnson's sense of the religious purposes of *Paradise Lost*, then, that makes him eager to distinguish the poem from the "vulgar epick" (174) and thus from the norms we use to judge such poems. Though many earlier critics had recognized that Milton's ambition to write what might be called "the Christian epic" altered the poet's opportunities and, to some extent, the critic's responsibilities, Johnson was the first major critic of *Paradise Lost*, I believe, who allowed religious ideas profoundly to shape his critical response to the poem.

We may see more clearly the distinctive nature of Johnson's stance in this regard by noting some of the differences between his commentary and that of Joseph Addison, whose influence in the eighteenth century as a critic of Milton equals or surpasses Johnson's. Addison sets out to show that *Paradise Lost* has "all the beauties of the highest kind of poetry" (*Spectator* 2:539), and to that end he quotes large portions of Milton's text throughout his eighteen essays on the poem. His purpose is to show the greatness of *Paradise Lost* as *poetry*, and quite literally to "set [*Paradise Lost*] before an English reader in its full beauty" (3:169). Johnson, on the other hand, quotes the poem only once in his unusually long critique, implicitly suggesting that the analysis of technique or a display of "beauties" is not his principal purpose.

Johnson understands that Addison emphasizes the literary aspects of *Paradise Lost* in an effort to make Milton accessible to common readers, an effort that Johnson in his *Rambler* essays on Milton's versification not only praises, but cites as the forerunner and inspiration of his own work on the subject. But apparently he thinks this narrow literary context is the only one in which Addison's work on Milton can be praised enthusiastically, for in his *Life of Addison* Johnson suggests that his predecessor had as many limitations as virtues:

> An instructor like Addison was now wanting, whose remarks being superficial, might be easily understood, and being just might prepare the mind for more attainments. Had he presented *Paradise Lost* to the publick with all the pomp of system and severity of science, the criticism would perhaps have been admired, and the poem still have been neglected. . . . (2:146–47)

Addison's criticism was popular and useful because it made what is on the surface of the poem, what is "superficial" and "easily understood," available to general readers. But in doing so, Johnson stresses, Addison only *prepared* "the mind for more attainments," and cleared away obstacles to a more profound understanding of the poem. What is really worth knowing about *Paradise Lost*, Johnson suggests, is deeper and more challenging.

For Johnson, a truly sophisticated treatment of the poem would take its religious purposes and effects more fully into account. This becomes evident when we compare the different emphasis Johnson and Addison give when treating similar subjects. When Addison writes about Books XI and XII, he praises them for completing the epic design, and for conveniently solving the old problem of finding a happy ending. He does not care much for Book XI, but concedes its importance—along with that of Book XII—in making *Paradise Lost* conform to the epic tradition:

> I have hinted, in my sixth paper on Milton, that an heroic poem,
> according to the opinion of the best cricks, ought to end happily.
> . . . Accordingly [Milton] leaves the adversary of mankind, in the
> last view which he gives us of him, under the lowest state of morti-
> fication and disappointment . . . and Adam triumphant in the
> height of misery. (3:388)

But when Johnson writes about Books XI and XII, he praises
them for representing the completion of the cycle of life, death,
and rebirth that Christian history comprehends; they complete
the Christian epic as it must be completed. For Johnson, the "integrity" of the poem is spiritual as well as literary; *Paradise Lost* is
complete because it imitates Christian history, not because it
meets Aristotle's requirements or duplicates the Homeric pattern.
Addison had stressed a different kind of integrity, and had portrayed Milton's tasks and choices in the last two books as straightforwardly literary. But Johnson is more interested in discussing
the significance of what he calls man's "restoration to hope and
peace" in the closing books (172).[7]

A second instance reflects a similar difference in sensitivity to
what is really valuable and interesting in *Paradise Lost*. In his *Spectator* essay on Book IX, Addison introduces the section on the fall
in this way:

> When Dido in the Fourth *Aeneid* yielded to that fatal temptation
> which ruin'd her, Virgil tells us, the Earth trembled, the Heavens
> were filled with flashes of lightning, and the Nymphs howl'd upon
> the mountain tops. Milton, in the same poetical spirit, has describ'd
> all Nature as disturbed upon Eve's eating the forbidden fruit.

After quoting some of Milton's narrative about the fall, and calling this section of the poem wonderfully imaginative, Addison
then adds:

> Adam's converse with Eve, after having eaten the forbidden fruit,
> is an exact copy of that between Jupiter and Juno, in the fourteenth
> *Iliad*. Juno there approaches Jupiter with the girdle which she had
> receiv'd from Venus, upon which he tells her, that she appeared

---

[7] For another example of Johnson's spiritual appreciation of Books XI and
XII, see *Yale Works* 4:47.

more charming and desirable than she had ever done before. . . .
(3:311)

Here, as elsewhere, Addison's impulse is to show the sources and
analogues of Milton's literary success.

But Johnson's is to show that the poem succeeds because it
properly and movingly represents the rupture of those corre-
sponding relationships that link man with woman, and both with
God. About Milton's handling of the fall and its aftermath, Johnson writes:

> But with guilt enter distrust and discord, mutual accusation, and
> stubborn self-defence; [Adam and Eve] regard each other with
> alienated minds, and dread their Creator as the avenger of their
> transgression. At last they seek shelter in his mercy, soften to repen-
> tance, and melt in supplication. (174)

In focusing on the loss of mutual trust and sympathy, Johnson—
who seems here remarkably attuned to the energy and argument
of Milton's poem—bypasses formal questions about how to end
the epic and emphasizes instead its spiritual theme. He understands that this sudden perception of the distance from Eve to
Adam, Adam to Eve, and both to God, is what defines our fallen
nature, and he praises Milton for his ability to convey the power
and terror of this rupture.

Johnson knew Addison himself had argued that Christianity re-
vived the possibility of writing an epic, and that in *Paradise Lost*
Milton had seized the opportunity of doing so. "I think we may
say," Johnson had read in *The Spectator*, ". . . that there is an
indisputable and unquestioned magnificence in every part of *Paradise Lost*, and indeed a much greater than could have been formed
upon any pagan system" (2:542). But apparently Johnson also
thought that Addison had failed to explore the consequences of
this perception, and had not sufficiently allowed the explicitly
Christian nature of Milton's epic to shape the emphasis and argument of his commentary on *Paradise Lost*.[8]

---

[8] I therefore disagree with critics like Leopold Damrosch who argue that Johnson's critique of *Paradise Lost*, "at least in its positive half, is essentially a restate-
ment of Addison's" (*The Uses of Johnson's Criticism* 94). Though there are indeed
many points of agreement between Johnson and Addison, the two critics ultimately value and emphasize quite different things.

III

If Johnson found Addison's ideas and approach "superficial," what then informs Johnson's understanding of *Paradise Lost*? I wish to suggest that, beneath the literal level of Johnson's critique of the poem, there is always at work a set of silent analogies— analogies which lead Johnson to link the poem to holy texts, such as Scripture, and to holy acts, such as prayer, and which help him locate the uniqueness of Milton's religious and poetic aspirations in *Paradise Lost*.

Elsewhere in his criticism, Johnson defines and rejects two kinds of religious poetry: "devotional" or "pious" poetry, in which speakers pray to God in verse; and "sacred" poetry, or, more literally, scriptural poetry, which essentially is a direct re- writing of Scripture in the voice of the bardic and prophetic his- torian.[9] Since figurative language is jarringly inconsistent with the voice of sincere prayer, Johnson thinks, devotional poetry will always fail, because its "ideas . . . are too simple for eloquence, too sacred for fiction, and too majestick for ornament" (1:292). Similarly, he rejects sacred poetry because the literary reformula- tion of scriptural truths is not only needless but arrogant, perhaps even sacrilegious. Attacking Cowley's *Davideis*, for instance, Johnson writes: "All amplification is frivolous and vain: all addi- tion to that which is already sufficient for the purposes of religion seems not only useless, but in some degree profane" (1:49–50).

Johnson, then, is keenly aware of the difficulties Milton faced in writing a poem like *Paradise Lost*. Confronted with the narrow- ness of the Genesis account, Milton could have done what other poets did: either turn the poem into a devotional meditation on the fall, thereby avoiding the need to elaborate on the scriptural account; or else, as Cowley and others had done, merely repeat a scriptural story in different words. But Johnson thinks Milton does neither one of these things. He praises Milton's poem as one which achieves the goals of sacred and devotional poetry, but which assumes the form and voice of neither one directly. John- son's claim, in effect, is that in writing *Paradise Lost* Milton per-

---

[9] For some of Johnson's most important comments on sacred and devotional poetry in the *Lives*, see 1:48f.; 1:291–93; and 3:310. For an interesting commen- tary, see David R. Anderson, "Johnson and the Problem of Religious Verse."

formed a remarkable balancing act: the poem resembles the scriptural text without becoming sacred poetry, and resembles prayer without becoming devotional poetry.

Johnson's account of how Milton accomplishes this is cast in the most admiring and fervent terms. When describing Milton's relation to Genesis, Johnson praises his extraordinary combination of faithfulness and inventiveness:

> Known truths however may take a different appearance, and be conveyed to the mind by a new train of intermediate images. This Milton has undertaken, and performed with pregnancy and vigour of mind peculiar to himself. Whoever considers the few radical positions which the Scriptures afforded him will wonder by what energetick operations he expanded them to such extent and ramified them to so much variety, restrained as he was by religious reverence from licentiousness of fiction. (182–83)

Milton elaborates the story of Genesis by extending Scripture's truth, not by writing a substitute version of it. Thus Johnson's language carefully keeps Milton in close touch with his scriptural source, as he praises Milton for having "expanded" and "ramified" the Genesis story, but still for having avoided the "licentiousness of fiction." Milton does so by means of what Johnson calls "a new train of intermediate images"—images, that is, which mediate the familiar truths known from a sacred source, and the new truths guessed by Milton's imagination. Johnson's quiet claim here is a significant one: in *Paradise Lost*, he seems to say, one finds a text that is—like Scripture itself—the meeting point of divine revelation and human talent.

Paradise Lost is not sacred poetry, but is closely linked with the source sacred poetry imitates. Similarly, *Paradise Lost* is not devotional poetry, but is closely linked with the action that genre imitates: prayer. Johnson may think that the different arts of praying and of making poems approach each other more nearly and more successfully in *Paradise Lost* than in any other poem he knew. Johnson's own prayers and sermons reflect his belief that proper prayer is both an act of praise and a formal acknowledgment of our subservience and dependence before God; it is an instrument whose rhetorical form and content remind us that we are creatures obliged to observe the creator's laws.[10] That, for Johnson, is the purpose of prayer; and here is Johnson's full statement of the purposes of *Paradise Lost*: " 'To vindicate the ways of God to man'; to shew the reasonableness of religion, and the necessity of obedience to the Divine Law" (171). Like prayer itself, Johnson thinks, *Paradise Lost* is a linguistic construct whose purpose is to remind human beings of their status before God. The poem shows that it is reasonable to act and think as a creature, and it teaches, he says, "the sentiments and worship proper to a fallen and offending being . . ." (180).[11]

Perhaps the most beautiful and suggestive evidence that Johnson linked *Paradise Lost* with prayer appears in that section of the *Life* where he dismisses the popular belief that little or no time was devoted to formal prayer in Milton's household. Johnson responds: "Prayer certainly was not thought superfluous by him, who represents our first parents as praying acceptably in the state

---

[10] See, for example, Johnson's vow "to consider the act of prayer as a reposal of myself upon God and a resignation of all into his holy hand" (*Yale Works*, 1:97). In a sermon he composed on John Taylor's behalf, Johnson wrote: "The great efficient of union between the soul and its Creator, is prayer; of which the necessity is such, that St. Paul directs us, to pray without ceasing; that is, to preserve in the mind such a constant dependence upon God, and such a constant desire of his assistance, as may be equivalent to constant prayer. No man can pray, with ardour of devotion, but he must excite in himself a reverential idea of that Power, to whom he addresses his petitions; nor can he suddenly reconcile himself to an action, by which he shall displease him, to whom he has been returning thanks for his creation and preservation, and by whom he hopes to be still preserved" (*Yale Works* 14:34).

[11] Johnson himself seems to have used the text of *Paradise Lost* at moments when he thought about his distance from God and his need for reconciliation. Arthur Murphy reports that whenever Johnson was brooding over the prospect of death, "whosoever sat near his chair, might hear him repeating" these lines from *Paradise Lost*: "Who would lose / For fear of pain, this intellectual being" (*Johnsonian Miscellanies*, 1:439). To conclude one of the few *Rambler* essays on religion (#110, a sermon-like essay on repentance and reformation), Johnson chooses these lines from *Paradise Lost*, and by presenting them without introduction or attribution, has them function as a kind of benediction:

> What better can we do, than prostrate fall
> Before him reverent; and there confess
> Humbly our faults, and pardon beg, with tears
> Wat'ring the ground, with our sighs the air
> Frequenting, sent from hearts contrite, in sign
> Of sorrow unfeign'd, and humiliation meek?

The quotation is from Book X, lines 1086, 1087–92. Johnson combines lines 1086 and 1087. See *Yale Works*, 4:225–26.

of innocence, and efficaciously after their fall. That he lived without prayer can hardly be affirmed; his studies and meditations
were an habitual prayer" (156).[12] As the *Life* makes clear, Johnson
believes the greatest product of these "studies and meditations" is
Paradise Lost, a work that itself gives evidence of a poetic consciousness prayerfully submissive to the creator in a fallen world.

In Johnson's view, then, Milton found a voice for poetry that
escapes the limitations of sacred and devotional verse, yet still
achieves the religious effects such poetry seeks to produce. And
though Johnson's analogies to Scripture and to prayer are developed neither fully nor explicitly in the *Life of Milton*, they deeply
affect, I believe, his view of the poem's value. They help us understand his conclusion that the poem's "every line breathes sanctity of thought" (179), and his desire to treat those lines with such
deferential care. To conceive of *Paradise Lost*, either in its purposes
or in its effects, chiefly in literary terms, is to respond to it in a
"superficial" way. And as we now shall see, this poem has a religious impact on Johnson, and, he thinks, on all readers, that is
anything but superficial.

IV

Johnson's understanding of *Paradise Lost*'s religious purposes
greatly influences his description of the poem's rhetorical strategy—of the means, that is, by which Milton approaches and influences his readers.[13] As David Morris and others have shown,
religion and sublimity were often related subjects in eighteenth-
century criticism, so it is hardly surprising that when a critic like
Johnson writes about a poem whose aspirations are primarily religious, he should dwell on its sublime effects.[14] "Sublimity," John-

---

[12] Robert Folkenflik calls this the most dramatic and definitive of the rare
instances in the *Lives* when Johnson invokes literary evidence to argue against
reported biographical facts. See *Samuel Johnson, Biographer*, 145.

[13] My understanding of Johnson's commentary on Milton's rhetorical strategies has been influenced by Stanley Fish's work, especially *Surprised by Sin: The
Reader in "Paradise Lost."* While he does not treat Johnson directly, the portrait
Fish draws of *Paradise Lost*'s intimidated and broken reader is similar in important
ways to the one I wish to draw of Johnson.

[14] See David Morris, *The Religious Sublime: Christian Poetry and Critical Tradition
in Eighteeth-Century England*, especially 209–21, for his discussion of Johnson's

son says, "is the general and prevailing quality" of *Paradise Lost* (180). This implies for Johnson the presence of certain qualities, and the relative absence of others, in Milton's poem:

> The characteristick quality of his poem is sublimity. He sometimes descends to the elegant, but his element is the great. He can occasionally invest himself with grace; but his natural port is gigantick loftiness. He can please when pleasure is required; but it is his peculiar power to astonish. (177)

"To astonish" is an important phrase in Johnson's critique; he uses it explicitly to describe the poem's effect on the reader. In his *Dictionary* Johnson defines "to astonish" as "to confound; to amaze; to surprise; to stun." Johnson says *Paradise Lost* contains many "awful" scenes; the term is defined as "that which strikes with awe." "To strike," another term he often uses to describe the poem's effect on readers, means "to stamp, to impress."

All such terms are well suited to Johnson's purpose as a critic of *Paradise Lost* because they help him define an aggressiveness in Milton that leaves the ravished reader at the poet's mercy. This sublime poem, Johnson suggests, overpowers readers, disorients them, harasses them with visions of things greater than themselves. It puts uncomfortably strong pressure on the reader's mind, as many of Johnson's other phrases make still clearer. Johnson finds Milton "enforcing the awful, darkening the gloomy, and aggravating the dreadful" (177). He says that "the anguish arising from the consciousness of transgression and the horrours attending the sense of the Divine Displeasure, are very . . . forcibly impressed" (180). From *Paradise Lost* the reader must "retire harassed and overburdened" (183–84). In short, Johnson finds *Paradise Lost* an imposition on the reader, an assault on his or her equilibrium.

That this is Johnson's constant view of the poem is made most dramatically clear on those many occasions when Johnson, thinking that he is quoting *Paradise Lost*, says that Milton's purpose is to "vindicate the ways of God to man." "Vindicate" is Pope's word (*Essay on Man*, I:16); "justify" is Milton's (I:26). Johnson

---

commentary on *Paradise Lost*. Hagstrum, in his discussion of Johnson's views on the sublime and the beautiful, says that Johnson's "most important use of the sublime as a critical concept" is in the *Life of Milton* (147).

makes this mistake every time he quotes the line, even when he uses it to illustrate the word "vindicate" in the *Dictionary*. When thinking about Milton's purposes, Johnson's memory selects the more strident word, the word with the more aggressive sound and meaning. "Justify" would suggest that the poem seeks to explain and persuade; "vindicate" implies that the poem seeks to announce and overwhelm.

Johnson's view of the poem's rhetoric and purpose significantly affects the images he selects to represent both *Paradise Lost*'s author and its readers. Johnson conjures an image of readers as Milton's prisoners. We are hemmed in by the poem: "Of the machinery . . . here is no room to speak" (175). Or we are burdened with more than we can control: Milton's poem "crowds the imagination" (179).[15] Milton's sublime poetry so overpowers its readers that, like prisoners, our only option is to submit: "Such is the power of his poetry," Johnson writes of Milton, "that his call is obeyed without resistance, the reader feels himself in captivity to a higher and a nobler mind, and criticism sinks in admiration" (190). Johnson sustains but reverses this imagery when he describes the author of *Paradise Lost* as "our master" (184)—one who, unlike the prisoners, is free of all constraints. Milton, says Johnson, has an "unlimited curiosity" and an "unrestrained" imagination, and he rejects reality as "a scene too narrow for his mind" (177–78).[16] Johnson pictures Milton as having the almost god-like power "to sport in the wide regions of possibility" (177–78).

The implication of Johnson's argument here is that readers of *Paradise Lost* are mastered by Milton in much the same way as all men and women are mastered by God. For the creator of *Paradise Lost*, as for the creator of the world, Johnson claims special powers: Milton, like God, can make creatures of his readers. The implicit analogy for Johnson is not profane because he believes Milton uses his powers for pious ends. Indeed, the point of Mil-

---

[15] In an interesting commentary on this remark, Angus Fletcher analogizes the position of a critic like Johnson before the poetry of Milton to the position of Augustine before the Bible. See *Allegory: The Theory of a Symbolic Mode*, 240–42.

[16] Johnson occasionally uses similar terms when describing the "genius" of other writers, as in the *Life of Pope* (see especially 3:217). But only in the *Life of Milton* do such phrases and concepts function as a part of Johnson's broader effort to define the aggressive nature of the writer's power over readers.

tonic sublimity, in Johnson's view, is so to overpower and control his readers that we are maneuvered, like it or not, into a consciousness of our powerlessness and creaturehood—a consciousness which is prayer's most fertile ground. The method and message of *Paradise Lost* thus closely mirror each other: as our vision is directed upward, we are made aware of a master whose power profoundly surpasses our own; so that in reading *Paradise Lost*, as in praying, we are made acutely conscious of our dependence and subservience.[17]

Such a process of instruction is particularly well suited to Milton's task, Johnson thinks, for *Paradise Lost* can "teach" morality only in a particular way: it can make us ripe for moral action, but it cannot teach us specific courses of action. *Paradise Lost* is not the kind of didactic poem that helps solve specific moral problems, partly because its moral cannot be easily reduced or separated from the narrative:

> Bossu is of [the] opinion that the poet's first work is to find a moral, which his fable is afterwards to illustrate and establish. This seems to have been the process only of Milton: the moral of other poems is incidental and consequent; in Milton's only it is essential and intrinsick. (171)

In Milton's poem the moral is not appended as an incidental consequence of the story; nor is its determination left to the chance interpretations of readers or critics. The narrative of *Paradise Lost* is not a vehicle to truth, but the "substance" of truth (174). This perfect integrity does not permit readers to minimize the poem's effect by reducing its moral to some easily neglected aphorism. Indeed, the subject of the poem precludes the opportunity of doing so:

> Splendid passages containing *lessons* of morality or *precepts* of prudence occur seldom. Such is the original formation of this poem

---

[17] My argument here is at odds with F. R. Leavis's influential assertion that "Johnson cannot understand that works of art *enact* their moral valuations. . . . For Johnson a moral judgment that isn't *stated* isn't there" ("Johnson and Augustanism," 110–11). Damrosch, 120–21, expresses a similar view. My argument is that Johnson's criticism of *Paradise Lost* shows that he is capable of the kind of understanding these critics would deny him, and that for Johnson the poem does indeed "enact" its "moral valuations."

that as it admits no human manners till the Fall, it can give little assistance to human conduct. (176–77; emphasis added)

The moral goal of *Paradise Lost*, which Johnson thinks is achieved through the sublime, can only be something greater, more general, and finally more important: "Its end is to raise the thoughts above sublunary cares or pleasures" (177). Here again the language of morality is also the language of the sublime. *Paradise Lost* can give "assistance to human conduct" only by making us aware that we are creatures under the control of a higher power.

There is, then, a deep connection between the two things that, according to Johnson, are "essential" (the moral) and "characteristic" (the sublime) in *Paradise Lost*. The sublime is what defines Milton's distance from and power over us; it is the means by which he affects us, often at the expense of our comfort; and it is the means by which the poem teaches—by directing our vision upward. And both of them are linked, I believe, with Johnson's inclination to think of the poem as he thinks of prayer: *Paradise Lost* imposes on us the consciousness of subservience we wish to avoid having, and shows us that "to obey is best."[18]

V

Having shown how *Paradise Lost* achieves its purposes, Johnson turns to the subject of the reader's "interest" in *Paradise Lost*. My purpose now is to explain—in the context of my previous argument—Johnson's controversial assertions that Milton's epic is a poem "the reader admires and lays down," and that no reader "ever wished it longer than it is."

In the remark quoted earlier, Johnson distinguished sublimity from its opposite, elegance or grace—to which, he adds, Milton only occasionally "descends." He is deploying here a version of the usual eighteenth-century distinction between the beautiful and the sublime. Johnson's *Dictionary* defines "elegance" as "beauty rather soothing than striking." The beautiful, the *Dictionary* says elsewhere, requires an "assemblage of graces"; but epic poetry, says Johnson when introducing his critique of *Paradise*

---

[18] I disagree, then, with Morris's conclusion that "for Johnson, Milton was sublime in spite of, not because of, his religious subject . . ." (221).

Lost, "requires an assemblage of . . . *powers*" (170; emphasis added).

Johnson's commentary on *Paradise Lost* is, at its core, the story of how Milton gains power over his readers for the purpose of moral or religious instruction. The logic of Johnson's argument leads him to claim that *Paradise Lost* cannot very often please or be "soothing" without compromising its rhetorical purpose. He says that though Milton "can please when pleasure is required," he does so only to relieve momentarily the constructive tension he builds to achieve his moral effect. When beautiful passages do appear in *Paradise Lost,* readers—Johnson included—grasp eagerly at them, but such passages are for Johnson in every way at the edge of the poem. Of the autobiographical introductions Milton wrote for several books of *Paradise Lost,* Johnson says: "The short *digressions* . . . might doubtless be spared; but *superfluities* so *beautiful* who would take away? . . . Perhaps no passages are more frequently or more attentively read than those *extrinsick* paragraphs" (175; emphasis added). Yet however much we may love such passages, Johnson suggests, we must recognize that they are incidental, as everything "beautiful" is incidental, to the purposes of *Paradise Lost.*

On a related point, Johnson argues that since "human passions did not enter the world before the Fall, there is in the *Paradise Lost* little opportunity for the pathetick" (180). So, one by one, his critique eliminates those qualities which would make reading *Paradise Lost* both alluring and comfortable. The human passions are what engage the attention of readers; beauty is what soothes and pleases them. If as readers we find so little of either in *Paradise Lost,* why should we submit to the domination that Milton's mastery of the sublime permits him? Why, in short, should we bother to read *Paradise Lost*?

A glimpse of the answer, and of its consequences, may be found in Johnson's description of how readers respond to the poem's most religiously significant scenes:

> Of the ideas suggested by these awful scenes, from some we recede with reverence, except when stated hours require their association; and from others we shrink with horrour, or admit them only as salutary inflictions, as counterpoises to our interests and passions. Such images rather obstruct the career of fancy than incite it. (182)

The sublimity of such moments in *Paradise Lost* is so striking, so awful, that readers are startled away from any wish for extended or renewed acquaintance with them. We do not seek out or revel in the religious sublime, but confront its images and ideas only under pressure; we "admit them only," says Johnson, "when stated hours require their association." These "stated hours," it would seem, are the hours when we are praying and the hours when we are reading *Paradise Lost*, for such ideas are the substance both of our prayers and meditations, and of our encounter with Milton's Christian epic. Johnson—and, he thinks, all men and women—find such moments painful, for their purpose is to make us conscious again of our fallen nature, and aware of our need for those "salutary inflictions" and "counterpoises to . . . interests and passions" that help keep us justified before God. From these "inflictions," however "salutary," and from these "counter-poises" to our fallen inclinations, we seek, of course, the earliest possible escape. None ever wished such sternly corrective moments to last longer than they must.

In this light we may now reconsider, in its entirety, Johnson's summary claim about the reader's reaction to the poem:

> The want of human interest is always felt. *Paradise Lost* is one of the books which the reader admires and lays down, and forgets to take up again. None ever wished it longer than it is. Its perusal is a duty rather than a pleasure. We read Milton for instruction, retire harassed and overburdened, and look elsewhere for recreation; we desert our master, and seek for companions. (183–84)

Since Johnson explicitly praises *Paradise Lost* as "artfully constructed so as to excite curiosity and surprise expectation" (171), clearly his point here is not that the poem is uninteresting, or that it fails to engage our attention. Nor can he be claiming that it is needlessly and laboriously lengthy, since Johnson twice goes out of his way to emphasize that *Paradise Lost* could not reasonably be expected to be shorter than it is:

> . . . [Milton] has interwoven the whole system of theology with such propriety that every part appears to be necessary, and scarcely any recital is wished shorter for the sake of quickening the progress of the main action. (171)

> To the compleatness or integrity of the design nothing can be ob-
> jected. . . . There is perhaps no poem of the same length from
> which so little can be taken without apparent mutilation. (175)

Johnson's point, rather, is that "none ever wished it longer than it is" because *Paradise Lost* assaults us so forcefully that every moment of attention we give it is emotionally and psychically taxing. The pressure is relentless. As we read *Paradise Lost*, Johnson argues, we find no reassuringly familiar figures, no friends or companions, inhabiting the poem's world. The absence of such familiar figures "is always felt," is always vexing, because their humanizing presence would have made this sublime and imposing world easier for us to bear, and thus interfered with the poem's purpose.[19] Even Adam and Eve, Johnson says, "act and suffer . . . in a state which no other man or woman can ever know" (181).[20] Whereas for Addison—as very probably for most modern readers—*Paradise Lost* is a poem which is "wonderfully contrived to influence the reader with pity and compassion" toward Adam and Eve, and to raise in readers "the most melting passions of humanity and commiseration,"[21] for Johnson the pos-

---

[19] I therefore do not share the view, expressed by Damrosch and held by many other critics, that Johnson regards "the want of human interest" as *Paradise Lost's* "crucial *flaw*" (103; emphasis added).

[20] Commenting on *Davideis* in the *Life of Cowley* (1:48–51), Johnson makes a similar remark about the difficulty we have identifying with characters who live and act in "sacred" time. But whereas the distance we feel from such characters is fatal to Cowley's poem, it is central to Milton's successful strategy—as Johnson defines it—to make his reader feel isolated, lonely, and disoriented.

[21] Here is Addison's full remark: "The representation he gives of them [Adam and Eve], without falsifying the story, is wonderfully contrived to influence the reader with pity and compassion towards them. Tho' Adam involves the whole species in misery, his crime proceeds from a weakness which every man is inclin'd to pardon and commiserate, as it seems rather the frailty of humane nature, than of the person who offended. Every one is apt to excuse a fault which he himself might have fallen into. It was the excess of love for Eve that ruined Adam and his posterity. . . . Adam and Eve, in the book we are now considering, are likewise drawn with such sentiments as do not only interest the reader in their afflictions; but raise in him the most melting passions of humanity and commiseration" (3:333). Addison claims it is possible for readers to project themselves into the places of Adam and Eve—in short, to identify with them. Addison's homely implication is that any man who, against his better judgment and from "excess of love," sometimes succumbs to his wife's suggestions, is familiar on at least a basic level with the kind of weakness Adam shows, and therefore can see his "interests" represented in the poem. On this issue, see also T. S. Eliot, "Milton II," 177.

sibility that we actually identify with our first parents and feel some tender, filial sympathy for them is blocked out by his deep perception of the poem's stern moral purpose and sublime religious rhetoric, is blocked out by the booming voice of "vindication" in *Paradise Lost*. Johnson cannot and will not allow himself—or us—any refuge in the beautiful and pathetic sentiments Addison describes.

Johnson is summarizing his whole analysis, then, rather than glibly brushing off *Paradise Lost*, when he calls it a poem one "admires and lays down, and forgets to take up again." The relentless logic of Johnson's argument will hardly allow him to imagine any other response. To a beautiful poem, as to those beautiful but "extrinsick" introductions in *Paradise Lost*, Johnson might return again and again for pleasure; but finally he regards *Paradise Lost* as a poem of such sublime power that the act of reading it is uncomfortable, and the prospect of re-reading it is threatening.

To those who hear and feel the poem's softer voice and gentler argument, Johnson's may seem an extreme or overly specialized view of *Paradise Lost*. But if we are to fault his critique, it might be for his generous belief that all readers are as competent as he, and as profoundly moved by religious experience. By a reader of Johnson's competence, the power of *Paradise Lost*—which he calls "a book of universal knowledge" that "crowds" and "fills the imagination"—is indeed felt immediately, fully, and exhaustingly. The reader Johnson imagines is as capable as he himself is of being driven to emotional extremes by great literature, and of being forcibly reminded in religious moments of humankind's fundamental sinfulness and powerlessness. Because it brings together in a single text the literary techniques and religious visions that affect him most, *Paradise Lost* pushes Johnson to the extremes of psychic and emotional experience.[22]

In such a context it is easier to understand what it means to "forget" to take up *Paradise Lost* again. Johnson celebrates its end

---

[22] I therefore depart from the explanation of Johnson's views provided by Irene Samuel and other critics. Samuel, who begins from the premise that Johnson found *Paradise Lost* "tedious," readily ascribes what she regards as his inability to appreciate the poem's softer sentiments to his own emotional deficiencies, and perhaps to his marital difficulties. See "*Paradise Lost* as Mimesis,"16 and 21–22.

not because the poem affects him too little, but because it affects him too much. Since he finds that the process of reading the poem is a turbulent one, he can only view its conclusion as an escape, a welcome liberation into a safer, more familiar world. The old and eminent Samuel Johnson, reader of *Paradise Lost*, is not unlike the young and callow Sam Johnson, reader of *Hamlet*: he must finish reading his text in all possible haste, and then—transformed but trembling—run for the reassuring calm of the everyday world around him.[23] Johnson deserts his master, and seeks for companions. And once in that everyday world again, Johnson must think, readers who have truly felt the power of *Paradise Lost* do not accidentally forget to read it again; we choose to forget, and by doing so, acknowledge the poem's profound power.

It should now be clear why no reader "ever wished" *Paradise Lost* to be "longer than it is," but another question remains: Why is the perusal of *Paradise Lost* a duty? In all his criticism Johnson consistently rejects the view that men and women have an intellectual duty to be familiar with great literary works. So it only makes sense for Johnson to speak of reading *Paradise Lost* as a "duty" if he thinks the experience of reading the poem has more than intellectual or literary significance. What that significance is, and what analogy has stood behind the logic of Johnson's entire argument, can best be made evident by quoting together the two passages from the *Life of Milton* where Johnson speaks of reading as a "duty":

> As the best preservative against Popery [Milton] recommends the diligent perusal of the Scriptures; a duty, from which he warns the busy part of mankind not to think themselves excused. (148–49)

And later, of *Paradise Lost*:

> Its perusal is a duty rather than a pleasure. We read Milton for instruction, retire harassed and overburdened, and look elsewhere for recreation. . . . (183–84)[24]

---

[23] James Clifford writes: "One day when he was reading *Hamlet* in the kitchen, he was so powerfully moved by the ghost scene that he suddenly rushed upstairs to the street door in order to see people about him" (63). See also James Boswell, *Life of Johnson*, 1:70. It is also worth recalling that Johnson willingly "forgot" to re-read *King Lear* for many years because he was so "shocked" and moved by it.

[24] It should be noted here that two of Johnson's definitions of "duty" in the *Dictionary* are "Acts or forbearances required by religion or morality" and "Act

It is possible, of course, that men and women will take some pride and pleasure in fulfilling their duty; but reading *Paradise Lost*, like praying and reading Scripture, remains for Johnson first and foremost a duty. Pleasure, like beauty, is incidental to the experience. Johnson comes to *Paradise Lost*, as he would to a holy text, "for instruction." He thinks that we are chastened, over-powered by the sublimity we find there—a sublimity undimin-ished by the presence of familiar characters who might have reassured us at a time when the poem, to achieve its goals, most needs to unsettle us. Addison, who had sought and found "com-panions" in the poem, wrote only a "superficial" critique of it. He stayed with friends to avoid confronting the poem's sublime truth. But for Johnson, reading *Paradise Lost*, like praying, is a solitary activity. When reading the poem, as when praying, he feels the loneliness and disorientation the Fall itself introduced. Readers of *Paradise Lost*, as Johnson imagines us through the prism of his own experience, are held captive by Milton's sublime great-ness; we are forced to confront the story of our lost innocence; and, finally, we break down. We need not just "recreation," but re-creation. We need—and know we need—something more than literature alone can give us.

VI

Johnson does not forsake his responsibilities as a literary commen-tator or forget that *Paradise Lost* is liable to critical evaluation; but his emphasis suggests that whatever critical response we have to *Paradise Lost* is subordinate to—and is, in fact, a consequence of—our religious response to the poem. In its most vital, compelling, and controversial moments, then, Johnson's critique of *Paradise Lost* becomes the record of his struggle with a text that demands a more inclusive and complicated response than the vocabulary of literary criticism alone can hope to provide. It is Johnson's testi-mony to, and exemplification of, his belief that "there are laws of

---

of reverence or respect." To illustrate the former definition, Johnson selected this passage from *Taylor's Devotion*: "All our duty is set down in our prayers, because in all our duty we beg the Divine Assistance; and remember that you are bound to do all those duties, for the doing of which you have prayed for the divine assistance."

higher authority than those of criticism" (*Yale Works* 7:339). Only by recognizing this, and by acknowledging how firmly this commentary is rooted in Johnson's religious faith and fears, can we appreciate the logic and subtlety of his argument about *Paradise Lost*.

Though he brought every aspect of his mind and personality to bear on all his literary judgements, *Paradise Lost* was perhaps the most likely poem of all to engage Johnson so deeply and affect him so profoundly. Its story is the central story of Johnson's own writing: in *Paradise Lost*, the author of "The Vanity of Human Wishes," *The Rambler*, and *Rasselas* finds his culture's most forceful poetic exploration of the sources of good and evil, of the human desire to know more, of the justice of suffering, and of the possibilities of renewal.[25] And the counsel Milton's poem gives, both through its form and through its argument, is at the heart of Johnson's spirituality: to be prayerful, to "be lowly wise," to be reverential.

In a sermon he wrote on John Taylor's behalf, Johnson declared: "The great purpose of revealed religion is to afford man a clear representation of his dependance on the Supreme Being, by teaching him to consider God as his Creator, and Governour, his Father and his Judge" (*Yale Works* 14:29). Of all the poetic texts he knew, *Paradise Lost* was, for Johnson, the one most closely and powerfully aligned with that purpose.

WORKS CITED

Addison, Joseph. *The Spectator*. Ed. Donald F. Bond. 5 vols. Oxford: Clarendon, 1965.

Bate, W. Jackson. *Samuel Johnson*. New York: Harcourt Brace Jovanovich, 1977.

Boswell, James. *Life of Johnson*. Ed. G. B. Hill. Rev. L. F. Powell. 6 vols. Oxford: Clarendon, 1934, 1950.

Budick, Sanford. *Poetry of Civilization: Mythopoeic Displacement in the Verse of Milton, Dryden, Pope, and Johnson*. New Haven: Yale UP, 1974.

Chapin, Chester F. *The Religious Thought of Samuel Johnson*. Ann Arbor: U of Michigan P, 1968.

---

[25] For a persuasive discussion of similarities between *Paradise Lost* and "The Vanity of Human Wishes," see Sanford Budick, *Poetry of Civilization: Mythopoeic Displacement in the Verse of Milton, Dryden, Pope, and Johnson*, 156–72.

Clark, J. C. D. *Samuel Johnson: Literature, Religion, and English Cultural Politics from the Restoration to Romanticism.* Cambridge: Cambridge UP, 1994.

Clifford, James. *Young Sam Johnson.* New York: Oxford UP, 1961.

Eliot, T. S. "Milton II." *On Poetry and Poets.* New York: Farrar, Straus, 1957.

Fish, Stanley. *Surprised by Sin: The Reader in "Paradise Lost."* London: Macmillan; New York: St. Martin's, 1967.

Fix, Stephen. "The Contexts and Motives of Johnson's *Life of Milton.*" *Domestick Privacies: Samuel Johnson and the Art of Biography.* Ed. David Wheller. Lexington: U of Kentucky P, 1987. 107–32.

———. "Distant Genius: Johnson and the Art of Milton's Life." *Modern Philology* 81 (1984): 244–64.

Fletcher, Angus. *Allegory: The Theory of a Symbolic Mode.* Ithaca: Cornell UP, 1964.

Folkenflik, Robert. *Samuel Johnson, Biographer.* Ithaca: Cornell UP, 1978.

Hagstrum, Jean. "The Beautiful, The Pathetic, and The Sublime." *Samuel Johnson's Literary Criticism.* Minneapolis: U of Minnesota P, 1952.

Hudson, Nicholas. *Samuel Johnson and Eighteenth-Century Thought.* Oxford: Clarendon, 1988.

Johnson, Samuel. *Lives of the English Poets.* Ed. G. B. Hill. 3 vols. Oxford: Clarendon, 1905.

———. *The Yale Edition of the Works of Samuel Johnson.* Ed. Allen T. Hazen et al. New Haven: Yale UP, 1958—.

Leavis, F. R. "Johnson and Augustanism." *The Common Pursuit.* London: Chatto and Windus, 1952.

Morris, David. *The Religious Sublime: Christian Poetry and Critical Tradition in Eighteenth-Century England.* Lexington: U of Kentucky P, 1972.

Pierce, Charles E., Jr. "The Conflict of Faith and Fear in Johnson's Moral Writing." *Eighteenth-Century Studies* 15 (1982): 317–38.

———. *The Religious Life of Samuel Johnson.* London: Athlone; Hamden, CT: Archon, 1983.

Quinlan, Maurice J. *Samuel Johnson: A Layman's Religion.* Madison: U of Wisconsin P, 1964.

Sachs, Areih. "Reason and Unreason in Johnson's Religion." *Modern Language Review* 59 (1964): 519–26.

Samuel, Irene. "*Paradise Lost* as Mimesis." *Approaches to "Paradise Lost": The York Tercentenary Lectures.* Ed. C. A. Patrides. Toronto: U of Toronto P, 1968.

Swedenberg, H. T., Jr. *The Theory of the Epic in England, 1650–1800.* University of California Publications in English 15. Berkeley: U of California P, 1944.

Watson, George. *The Literary Critics: A Study of English Descriptive Criticism.* London: Chatto and Windus, 1964.

8

Reading Transcendentalist Texts Religiously: Emerson, Thoreau, and the Myth of Secularization

Kevin Van Anglen

FOR A LONG TIME, there have been two currents in American Transcendentalist studies. One has sought to give a largely secular account of the movement, either by allying it with the freethinking tendencies of its own age or by treating it as the forerunner of later, explicitly nonreligious, intellectual developments. Many distinguished studies thus link Emerson, Thoreau, and the rest to such forces as international romanticism, German philosophy, and radical reform (all to a greater or lesser degree deprived of their religious dimension); while many others argue that the Transcendentalists were either literary modernists or postmodernists, philosophical Heideggerians or Nietzcheans, born out of time.[1] By

---

[1] Distinguished examples of scholarship placing Transcendentalism in an early nineteenth-century secular context include: Weisbuch, *Atlantic Double-Cross: American Literature and British Influence in the Age of Emerson*, which focuses on transatlantic literary relations in the antebellum period; Wellek, *Confrontations: Studies in the Intellectual and Literary Relationship Between Germany, England, and the United States During the Nineteenth Century* (153ff.), which relates New England Transcendentalism to contemporary German Idealism; and Rose, *Transcendentalism as a Social Movement, 1830–1850*, which considers its political and social thought in light of the theory and praxis of early nineteenth-century socialism and reform. Examples of scholarship treating Transcendentalism as a harbinger of later secular intellectual trends include: Cavell, *The Senses of Walden: Expanded Edition*, and Kuklick, *The Rise of American Philosophy: Cambridge, Mass. 1860–1930*, both of which admirably place Emerson and Thoreau at the head of the Pragmatist tradition and its twentieth-century philosophical heirs; Garber, *Thoreau's Fable of Inscribing*, which reads Thoreau in terms of Heidegger and the phenomenological school; Ellison, *Emerson's Romantic Style*, which does the same with regard to virtually every postmodernist literary critical and philosophical movement; and Poirier, *The Renewal of Literature: Emersonian Reflections*, which interprets Emerson vis-à-vis Anglo-American literary modernism.

contrast, the opposing critical school maintains (as its most famous exponent, Perry Miller, put it) that "Transcendentalism was not primarily a literary phenomenon . . . fed by . . . mere aesthetics." Rather, it "is most accurately to be defined as a religious demonstration," aimed at the reformation of Church and State—the last attempt in New England's history at achieving that quintessentially Protestant *desideratum*: an unmediated relationship with the Spirit, even in a civilization of machines (Miller 8–9). From its inception on down to its late nineteenth- and early twentieth-century canonization, therefore, Transcendentalism, in this view, was principally a theology, a spirituality, and a religious reform (one typically Yankee in its idiosyncratic originality, but one nevertheless with traceable roots in such diverse sources as New England Calvinism, contemporary Boston Unitarianism, the Asian religions, neoplatonism, Swedenborgianism, and nineteenth-century American religious, social, and political thought.[2]

The stronger by far of these two schools has been the one that places Transcendentalism in a mostly secular light. This should not be surprising, since as Jenny Franchot has recently reminded us, despite the fact that America is a profoundly religious nation (one which even today, "at least outside the academy," frames its public debates "to varying degrees, within religious discourses"), the great majority of "Americanist literary and cultural critics have [had] little to say" about religion during the last generation, other than to denounce it as reactionary ("Invisible Domain" 833–834). In part, Franchot argues, this is because of the predominance of "literary theory" within university literature departments, which "has further tended to marginalize interest in institutionalized religion and the more private regions of the 'interior life' as naïve unless those regions are subordinated to the domain of linguistic representation or the critiques of Marx, Nietzsche, Freud, and Foucault." Whatever the cause, however, the result has been that American academics have tended to deem belief either "deviant" (and so, unworthy of intellectual inquiry), or epiphenomenal (something "which inhibits, transmutes, or enables political change but is hardly ever an achievement whose

---

[2] Many examples of scholarship treating Transcendentalism as a primarily religious phenomenon are discussed below. One classic example is Hutchison, *The Transcendentalist Ministers: Church Reform in the New England Renaissance*.

priorities take precedence over the social") ("Invisible Domain" 834–836). We have as a consequence what Franchot characterizes as an often "singularly biased scholarship," which refuses "to engage intensively with . . . religious questions . . . as religious questions ("Invisible Domain" 839)[3] (rather than as manifestations of something else), at best placing religion (in McGreevy's words) "at the bottom of a list of variables presumed to shape individual identity, as an ethical afterthought to presumably more serious matters of class, gender, and ethnicity" (4).[4]

So dominant is this intellectual mindset that even studies attentive to Transcendentalism's religious element have often been influenced by it, albeit usually unintentionally. This is why, for example, so many historians and critics of the movement have tended to mediate between the two opposing views of the movement, either by dividing its adherents into primarily "secular" figures (like Margaret Fuller) and "religious" ones (like Jones Very), or by segmenting the careers of individual Transcendentalists (like Emerson and Thoreau) into earlier ("more religious") and later ("more secular") periods. For by doing so, they can affirm the religious dimension of Transcendentalism while still paying heed to the prevailing tendency in the academy to view literary history in overwhelmingly secular terms. Ironically, however, even when it involves putatively "religious" authors or biographical periods, this meliorist approach all too frequently ends up privileging "secular" interpretations of the evidence at hand, thereby problematizing the explicitly religious element in Transcendentalist art and experience.

Yet, the truth is that Transcendentalist lives and texts are resistant to partial or complete secularization, whatever form it takes. For one thing, they defy all categorizations into the "religious" and the "secular." Thus, while it is true, for example, that the Transcendentalist poet and mystic Jones Very did write his most famous poems believing *literally* in their divine inspiration, he was

---

[3] Franchot herself admits that her condemnation of the academy is a bit overdone: "we can all think of fine studies that include among their pages treatments of religion." Some of these are particularly prominent in the scholarship of American Puritanism and Transcendentalism. Yet she is surely correct with regard to the general drift of American Studies in the last thirty years or so.

[4] For a provocative account of the rise of secularism in the academic subculture, see Marsden, *The Soul of the American University: From Protestant Establishment to Established Non-Belief.*

also in many respects (in his Emersonian Idealism, his interest in the sonnet form, and his belief in poetic sincerity) a *self-consciously* romantic poet of a more familiar ("secular") sort. Individual Very poems bespeak this eclecticism, as do his three important essays on Shakespeare and epic poetry (which illustrate as well the particular difficulty of separating traditional Protestant belief structures from the secular traditions of English and German romantic literary criticism). In much the same way, Very's life story itself demonstrates the danger of reading Transcendentalist lives in a radically secularized way that transposes categories of religious experience into modern secular terms. For while his biography (like every other) is legitimately open to inspection from a modern psychological perspective, Very lived in a culture in which spiritist beliefs were widespread, one in which (as Walt Whitman proves) even among the educated a belief in divine poetic inspiration had not yet been reduced to mere literary conceit. Consequently, it is only by accepting the fundamentally religious character of his experience for analysis' sake that we can fully understand what his "affective years" of claimed divine possession represent. Howevermuch they may have proceeded from psychological difficulties, they also represent a personal religious struggle (for which there was much precedence in New England history) to escape the defective spirituality of mainline Yankee Protestantism.[5] Simi-

---

[5] Evidence for the conflicting secular and religious aspects of Very's life and work abounds in the standard biography of the poet, Gittleman's *Jones Very: The Effective Years, 1833–1840*. However, Gittleman also illustrates the tendency among contemporary scholars to reconcile these opposing strands in a largely secularist direction. For instance, while he goes out of his way biographically to credit the religious dimension to Very's life, in the end he fails to take his subject's beliefs (or those of Emerson) seriously enough. This leads him in particular to interpret the events of Very's "affective" years psychoanalytically, without sufficient reference to the spiritual issues that so typically concerned nineteenth-century New Englanders. Had he done so, he might have concluded that Very's millenial beliefs, charismatic theology, emotional religiosity, and search for a contemplative spirituality were well within the cultural bounds of normality in his day—something one must take into account in assessing his admitted psychological difficulties. Indeed, Gittleman's subject was only the latest in a long line of New Englanders to react along these lines against the inability of moderate puritanism and its theological descendants (whether "Old Light" congregationalist or Unitarian) to entertain eschatological hopes or commend forms of spirituality and conversion other than the cognitive or ethical. (A theological and spiritual set of issues that in the end is arguably as explanatory of the events of this period in Very's life as are the insights of contemporary psychology.) Two recent treatments of the origins of these interrelated patterns of dissent in New

larly, from the opposite direction, while Margaret Fuller might appropriately be regarded as a mostly "secular" author (one who stands at the head of any number of later nineteenth- and twentieth-century currents of thought), to regard her (as most of her biographers do) solely in this light would be to ignore the strongly religious dimension of such aspects of her life as her intense interest in neoplatonism, her early adherence to Emersonian Transcendentalism, and even her later, typically nineteenth-century Protestant ambivalence toward Italy and Catholicism.[6]

The same is true of Emerson and Thoreau, neither of whose biographies can be neatly divided into "religious" or "secular" periods. To be sure, in both cases there was a decided drift toward "the secular." Yet throughout their lives strong counter-currents existed in both directions. Thus, the Thoreau who before 1850 is supposed to have been a philosophical follower of Emerson imbued with a strongly spiritual attitude toward nature and an interest in Eastern religions was also a thinker who from his earliest years had a sturdily skeptical, even Lockean side—something which made him capable of writing texts in the same genre that betray very different attitudes toward religion and science (e.g., "Natural History of Massachusetts" and "A Walk to Wachusett"). Likewise, the Thoreau who after 1850 is commonly supposed to have adopted a more empirical, philosophically materialist stance

England culture demonstrate that they centered on matters of eschatological expectation and spirituality as much as class: Gura, *A Glimpse of Sion's Glory: Puritan Radicalism in New England, 1620–1660*, and Cohen, *God's Caress: The Psychology of Puritan Religious Experience*. Both Hatch and Butler (cited below) show how they then played out historically in New England and elsewhere into the nineteenth century. For a relevant theoretical model of the relationship between psychology and spirituality, one which draws upon the ideas of Bernard Lonergan, s.j., and Karl Rahner, s.j., see Conn, *Christian Conversion: A Developmental Interpretation of Autonomy and Surrender.*

[6] Although, in contrast to some earlier biographies, Von Mehren's recent *Minerva and the Muse: A Life of Margaret Fuller* and the first volume of Capper's ongoing *Margaret Fuller: An American Life* touch at times upon the religious element in Fuller's thought and life, a more balanced study of this issue is still needed—particularly in light of Richardson's suggestive account of the deeply spiritual roots of her fascination with Emerson and his idealist philosophy in *Emerson: The Mind on Fire* (see especially 235–41). Similarly Franchot, *Roads to Rome: The Antebellum Protestant Encounter with Catholicism* and Vance's magisterial two-volume *America's Rome* (especially 2: 3–76) describe early nineteenth-century American reactions to Italy and the Roman Catholic Church in ways which suggest that there is a religious grounding to Fuller's appreciation of her Roman experiences.

toward nature was the same Thoreau whose political writings (e.g., in defense of John Brown or in denunciation of slavery) were simultaneously veering toward more intensely traditional—indeed, puritanic—religious language and feeling.[7] Similarly, the Emerson who founded New England Transcendentalism was (we now know from his *Journals* and *Miscellaneous Notebooks*) a man who even in his periods of greatest *efflatus* was still struggling with questions of belief; and even when, after the late 1840s, he began to be less the former clergyman and more the Victorian sage, he was nonetheless still a thinker profoundly influenced by New England Protestantism and its habits of the mind and heart.[8]

Difficulties of a parallel sort emerge too in the case of those

---

[7] Studies supporting the notion that Thoreau's shifting interests in the last decade or so of his life had their roots in his scientific and philosophical evolution toward materialism (especially after 1850), include Stoller, *After Walden*; Porte, *Emerson and Thoreau: Transcendentalists in Conflict*; Howarth, *The Book of Concord: Thoreau's Life as a Writer*; Richardson's companion to his just-cited biography of Emerson, *Henry David Thoreau: A Life of the Mind* (especially 321ff.); and Peck, *Thoreau's Morning Work* (especially 39–114). However, Porte also provides ample evidence that the groundwork for these developments had been laid even in Thoreau's college years. As a result, even in the early 1840s, he could swing from writing excursions (like "Natural History of Massachusetts") that are highly Transcendentalist and somewhat skeptical toward empiricism to writing ones (like "A Walk to Wachusett") that take the opposite position in matters of religion and philosophy (see Van Anglen, "True Pulpit Power: 'Natural History of Massachusetts' and the Problem of Cultural Authority"; Adams and Ross, *Revising Mythologies: The Composition of Thoreau's Major Works* 29; and Milder, *Reimagining Thoreau* 26–28. For a brief comment upon his counter-balancing return to political and religious patriarchalism in the *Reform Papers* of his later period, see Van Anglen, *The New England Milton: Literary Reception and Cultural Authority in the Early Republic* 223–24.

[8] The professional and intellectual changes in Emerson's career have been variously discussed and dated since Whicher's *Freedom and Fate: An Inner Life of Ralph Waldo Emerson*, which was the first study to explore the complications of thought and feeling evident in his *Journals and Miscellaneous Notebooks*. Sattelmeyer, "When He Became My Enemy: Emerson and Thoreau, 1848–1849" is a short but persuasive account which dates his metamorphosis from heterodox Transcendentalist preacher to Victorian sage just after his return from his second trip to Europe, claiming as well that it precipitated the final deterioration in his relationship with Thoreau). However, whenever it finally occurred, most commentators view this transition as only one episode in Emerson's more general process of "secularization." See, for example, Bishop, *Emerson on the Soul*, and Robinson, *Emerson and the Conduct of Life: Pragmatism and Ethical Purpose*. Once again, however, the relevant portions of Richardson's *Emerson* (e.g., 500–503) suggest the persistence of both strongly Protestant and more generally religious concerns in Emerson's life, even as he turned toward a more "secular" world-view; in this connection, see also Packer, *Emerson's Fall*.

who view Transcendentalism as a movement with a religious dimension, but then circumscribe that insight by their perhaps unconscious acceptance of "the myth of secularization": the belief
(now seriously challenged by sociologists of religion) that like the
academy, American culture shifted decisively away from religious
faith in the middle of the nineteenth century, and is on that trajectory still.[9] Perhaps the best example is the distinguished (and justly
influential) work of Professor Lawrence Buell. Far better than any
scholar of his generation, Buell has demonstrated how Transcendentalist discourse drew upon the thought and literary forms of
Protestant New England. Likewise, his work is equally renowned
for its sensitivity to the fact that the Transcendentalists were also
denizens of the early nineteenth-century intellectual world (not
least on account of their upbringing in Unitarian Boston), and so
were exposed as well to such secularizing influences as the Higher
Criticism of the Bible and the skeptical thought of the Enlightenment. Significantly, however, although Buell admits that the
world-view and attitudes toward religion that resulted from these
polarizing influences were unrepresentative of the beliefs and religious practices of nineteenth-century America in general, at strategic points he resolves the tension in Transcendentalist thought
and feeling caused by these contradictory forces by assuming the
truth of the so-called "secularization model" of American religious development, and then making the Transcendentalists com-
plicit with it.

   Thus, he concedes that on the whole "American thought before 1865 was markedly religiocentric." This "was especially true
of New England, owing to the Puritan imprint, which Enlighten-

---

[9] Prominent examples of the sociological and historical scholarship currently
challenging "the myth of secularization" include Wuthnow, *The Restructuring of
American Religion: Society and Faith since World War II*; Roof and McKinney,
American Mainline Religion; and Greeley, *Religious Change in America*. This scholarship is in part inspired by such factors as the recent rise of the charismatic,
pentecostal, and evangelical churches and the decline in popularity of mainstream Protestantism and liberal Catholicism; the rapid growth in America of
Islam and various other traditional faiths, as well as of Asian and New Age spiritualities; the development of hard statistical evidence challenging the notion that
(in America, at least) increased education leads to increased secularization; and,
above all, the recognition that because American religious bodies operate differently in cultural and political terms than do the state churches of northwestern
Europe, Marxist and other models developed in an Old World context often
lack relevance to the American situation.

ment rationalism did not erase." Yet in his view this religiosity did not hold the Transcendentalists in check for long, for two reasons. In the first place, "the Bible's privileged status" in America had become so eroded by the Higher Criticism that:

> during the Romantic period especially, the distinction between sacred and secular writing was not just blurred but sometimes even inverted by such claims as the argument that Scripture is only a form of poesis, hence dependent for its authority on inspired vision, which artists have in greatest measure. Consequently, a number of Anglo-American writers, starting with Blake in England and Emerson in America, took the position that the poet has the right, indeed the duty, to reconstruct mythology for himself and his era. In the second place, the decline of scriptural authority was symptomatic of a general softening of dogmatic structures, particularly in mainline Protestant sects, that had the effect of pushing homiletics and apologetics themselves in a more literary direction, away from the systematic presentation of doctrine and toward impressionistic appeals to intuition and experience. (*New England Literary Culture* 166–67)

As a result, whatever misgivings they had at the "relativity of all doctrinal truth" and secularization of metaphor (Buell, *New England Literary Culture* 115, 121) caused by these secular intellectual influences, the Transcendentalists responded to them by reacting negatively to their largely evangelical culture. In the process, furthermore, Buell argues that they became the harbingers of an imminent transition in American society toward twentieth-century theological modernism and unbelief. Indeed, in some ways this is for him implicitly the broader cultural significance of Emerson, Thoreau, and the rest. For at a number of points he advances the view that the chief by-product of the doctrinal relativism and metaphoric secularization they absorbed in their reading was the insertion into American culture of that enhanced sense of negative liberty and the empowerment of a self freed from the claims of tradition and community which characterize secular modernity. Thus, proximately, the Higher Criticism might threaten "to reduce holy scriptures to myth in the bad sense—to quaint superstitious fabrication. Concomitantly, however, a less parochial and more creative understanding of the religious imagination now became possible, an affirmative reading of myth as the expression of spiritual archetypes informing not only the Bible but the scrip-

tures of all cultures, and not only ancient texts but—at least potentially—the literature of one's own day as well." And so, for
Boston and Concord, as later for America at large, "at least partially offsetting the disillusioning sense that prophets were no
more than poets was the exciting dream that poets might be
prophets" (*"Moby-Dick"* 55–56).[10]

Leaving aside some of its more general unstated assumptions
about religion (e.g., the post-Enlightenment belief that freedom
from a particular tradition is necessarily "less parochial and more
creative" than being rooted *in* a tradition), for all its strengths,
the problem with Buell's argument is that it too neatly enlists
Transcendentalism in aid of the myth of secularization: the view,
now rejected even by some of its original proponents (like Harvey
Cox), that American culture (like the American academy or certain parts of northwestern Europe) has been journeying predictably toward becoming a "secular city."[11] As a result, there is a
tendency in his writings to regard religion as a receding rather
than as a persisting or emergent cultural force—and so, too, unconsciously, to privilege the "secular" side of Transcendentalist
thought and feeling, at times even reducing religion to the secondary role complained of by Franchot and McGreevy.

Yet as recent studies of antebellum American religion have
shown, even granting the peculiarity in these matters of "the
neighborhood of Boston," the cultural context in which Transcendentalism existed was hardly that of a local or regional culture
undergoing development in an overwhelmingly secularist direction. Even in eastern Massachusetts, the response to industrializa-
tion and modernity was as often a return to religion (especially of
an evangelical or orthodox sort) as a move to embrace skepti-

---

[10] Interestingly, in *The Environmental Imagination: Thoreau, Nature Writing, and
the Formation of American Culture* (especially 311ff.), Buell likewise assumes the
truth of the secularization model when he argues that Thoreau's posthumous
reception and canonization were the result of a combination of the triumph of
liberal religion among the reading public and raw market forces within the publishing industry.

[11] Something of the impact upon students of American religion of the newer
scholarship challenging the myth of secularization can be seen by comparing
Cox's once influential *The Secular City* with his *Fire from Heaven: The Rise of
Pentecostal Spirituality and the Reshaping of Religion in the Twenty-First Century*,
written a quarter-century later (in which he substantially modified his earlier
views).

cism.[12] Moreover, as David S. Reynolds has shown, the mass audience to which the Transcendentalists hoped to appeal was one deeply influenced by the strongly evangelical cast of contemporary popular culture.[13] Buell acknowledges all this, of course (especially in his magisterial *New England Literary Culture*).[14] Yet in treating what is admittedly one of the most "secularized" groups before the Civil War, his unstated assumption about the long-term fate of traditional religious belief in America sometimes leads him to overlook the ways in which the Transcendentalists were prone to confusion, contradiction, and the persistence of older beliefs, spiritual habits, and concerns.

Abandonment of the paradigm of inexorable secularization and adoption of a more complex view of the place of religion in antebellum New England (seeing it as being culturally persistent, even

---

[12] Recent research into the complex general situation of early nineteenth-century American Christianity belies the old belief in an eventual, uniform transit toward modernity and theological liberalism assumed by Buell and many of the historians of a previous generation upon whom he relies (e.g., Ahlstrom, *A Religious History of the American People* 385–509). For instance, despite real differences in approach both Butler's *Awash in a Sea of Faith: Christianizing the American People* and Hatch's *The Democraticization of American Christianity* have conclusively demonstrated that this is not true. Similarly, the standard history of New England Unitarianism, Howe's *The Unitarian Conscience: Harvard Moral Philosophy, 1805–1861* (especially 7–12), also admits the existence of competing sectarian strands in antebellum Boston (where Unitarians of the aestheticizing, semirationalist strain privileged by Buell were an ever smaller—albeit culturally and institutionally influential—minority).

[13] See Reynolds, *Beneath the American Renaissance: The Subversive Imagination in the Age of Emerson and Melville* (especially 13–112), which discusses the specific interaction between Emerson and Thoreau and the highly religious element in the popular culture and literature of the day.

[14] Buell acknowledges that in religion as in so many other matters, Transcendentalists were part of a tiny, unrepresentative elite. Elsewhere, "on the level of popular culture, religious behavior arguably moved in a direction precisely opposite to that of the secularization process that I have charted. Historians of American religion have shown, for example, that evangelicalism and church membership dramatically increased during the early nineteenth century, at the very time when the higher criticism was taking hold in elite circles" (*New England Literary Culture* 188). Yet like many of the historians he cites, he is so committed to the secularization model that he firmly believes that the antebellum religious liberals and skeptics represented the party of the future and that antebellum evangelicals (however powerful in their day) were the party of the past. As a result, he privileges the more secular side of Trnscendentalism, and does not see the degree to which Emerson, Thoreau, and the rest also resisted secularization in ways that are significant (thus making them more complex figures than he allows).

in intellectual circles, and emergent at times elsewhere) helps explain, for instance, the enormous lifelong influence on Emerson
of the faith of his Trinitarian Congregationalist aunt, Mary
Moody Emerson (something Buell rather dismisses). Likewise, it
helps explain why his search as an adult for an affective and contemplative spirituality was so important to him. For the persistent
emotional hold both of Calvinist patterns of belief and of radical
puritanism's spiritist objections—bordering at times on gnosti-
cism—to moderate puritanism's (and later Unitarianism's) psy-
chologically defective spirituality had as strong an appeal for the
otherwise freethinking Emerson as it did for Hawthorne or Melville. Similarly, his moral individualism and suspicion of commu-
nitarian social and political reform also had firm intellectual and
emotional roots in New England's antinomian past, with its radical Protestant antihierarchicalism and affirmation of justification
by faith alone. Indeed, on these and many other counts, throughout his life Emerson moved *toward* the religious beliefs and feelings of his ancestors, even as he moved simultaneously toward
those of his secular European and American contemporaries. No
less than William Blake, in fact, was he as much a radical Protestant *manqué* as a confirmed theological liberal or secularist.[15]

Paradoxically, this is why even in his most "forward-looking"
works, the ones most influenced by the Higher Criticism and the
secularist thought of his age, Emerson was as much engaged in
continuing the traditions of New England Protestantism as in
pulling that particular temple down around him. For instance,
much though he might look at the end of *The Divinity School
Address* for "the new Teacher" whose insight could bring all the
"fragmentary" scriptures of the past "full circle" in his compre-

---

[15] Few would, for instance, now denigrate and dismiss the deep influence (particularly in a traditional religious direction) of the remarkable Mary Moody Emerson on her nephew, as Buell does in *New England Literary Culture* 268. For
more balanced views, see Richardson, *Emerson* (especially 23–28); Barish, *Emerson: The Roots of Prophecy* (especially 36–53 and 132–44); and Simmons, *The
Selected Letters of Mary Moody Emerson*, which also underscores her strongly affective and contemplative spirituality. Emerson's spiritual and political affinity with
the New England puritan past has been much commented upon, perhaps most
famously by Miller in his essay "From Edwards to Emerson." Given Buell's
invocation of him as a parallel "secularizer," it is significant that William Blake
too has recently been viewed in his Protestant religious (rather than a modern
secular) context—by no less than the late E. P. Thompson in *William Blake:
Witness Against the Beast (William Blake and the Moral Law)*.

hensive soul (Emerson 1:92–93), Emerson nonetheless self-consciously did so—*really* did so, in all seriousness, not just in the
hope of thereby rhetorically currying favor with his original audience—as a descendant of the Hutchinsonians and Gortonites and
Edwardseans of the previous centuries: as a radical puritan born
out of time to protest the fact that the pulpit of his native village
had been "usurped by a formalist" (Emerson 1:85) as lifeless as
any Laudian;[16] as one commissioned to call for a new, truly re-
formed religion of the heart and the contemplative will made one
with God. Consequently, therefore, in passages like the following,
he is in dead earnest in deploying the antinomian language of
the religious affections alongside words and phrases drawn from
Coleridge and other more recent sources; for it is a tradition to
which he is loyal still, after his fashion:

> The question returns, What shall we do? I confess, all attempts to
> project and establish a Cultus with new rites and forms, seem to
> me vain. Faith makes us, and not we it, and faith makes its own
> forms. All attempts to contrive a system, are as cold as the new
> worship introduced by the French to the goddess of Reason,—to-

---

[16] This famous passage referring to the service on a winter Sunday morning
in the Unitarian meeting house in Concord deserves quoting in its entirety:
"Whenever the pulpit is usurped by a formalist, then is the worshipper de-
frauded and disconsolate. We shrink as soon as the prayers begin, which do not
uplift, but smite and offend us. We are fain to wrap our cloaks about us, and
secure, as best we can, a solitude that hears not. I once heard a preacher who
sorely tempted me to say, I would go to church no more. Men go, thought I,
where they are wont to go, else had no soul entered the temple in the afternoon.
A snowstorm was falling around us. The snowstorm was real; the preacher
merely spectral; and the eye felt the sad contrast in looking at him, and then out
of the window behind him, into the beautiful meteor of the snow. He had lived
in vain. He had no one word intimating that he had laughed or wept, was
married or in love, had been commended, or cheated, or chagrined. If he had
ever lived and acted, we were none the wiser for it. The capital secret of his
profession, namely to convert life into truth, he had not learned. Not one fact
in all his experience, had he yet imported into his doctrine. This man had
ploughed, and planted, and talked, and bought, and sold; he had read books; he
had eated and drunken; his head aches; his heart throbs; he smiles and suffers;
yet there was not a surmise, a hint, in all the discourse, that he had ever lived at
all. Not a line did he draw out of real history. The true preacher can always be
known by this, that he deals out to the people his life,—life passed through the
fire of thought. But of the bad preacher, it could not be told from his sermon,
what age of the world he fell in; whether he had a father or a child; whether he
was a freeholder or a pauper; whether he was a citizen or a countryman; or any
other fact of his biography" (Emerson 1: 85–86).

day, pasteboard and filigree, and ending to-morrow in madness and murder. Rather let the breath of new life be breathed by you through the forms already existing. For, if once you are alive, you shall find they shall become plastic and new. The remedy to their deformity is, first, soul, and second, soul, and evermore, soul. A whole popedom of forms, one pulsation of virtue can uplift and vivify. . . . What hinders that now, everywhere, in pulpits, in lecture-rooms, in houses, in fields, wherever the invitation of men or your occasions lead you, you speak the very truth, as your life and conscience teach it, and cheer the waiting, fainting hearts of men with new hope and new revelation. (Emerson 1: 92)

The same is true of Henry Thoreau. His keen interest in Asian religions was, for example, arguably as much the product of native New England traditions of spiritual discontent as of his exposure to the internationalism of the Enlightenment or the Higher Criticism—as much due to the same need for an affectionate religion that had impelled Mistress Hutchinson to remonstrate against formalism and "legal preachers," or to the need for a contemplative spirituality that caused Edward Taylor to look beyond his Puritanism to Anglican and Catholic meditational sources, as to his readings in Herder or Sir William Jones, or his desire to overthrow traditional Christianity. Likewise, Thoreau's propheticism and jeremiad-like rhetoric, as well as his theological and political patriarchalism during the run-up to the Civil War (acknowledged by Buell and others more as an exception to his freethinking ways or a rhetorical strategy than anything else), take on a new literalness when we abandon the notion that he was mainly developing in a secularist direction. Rather, if we acknowledge the persistent hold of older belief patterns on the Transcendentalists, his plea for Captain Brown as Christ reborn and crucified upon the Cross becomes something more than a metaphor meant to ring the persuasive rhetorical changes for his less "enlightened" audience:

I am here to plead his cause with you. I plead not for his life, but for his character—his immortal life; and so it becomes your cause wholly, and is not his in the least. Some eighteen hundred years ago Christ was crucified; this morning, perchance, Captain Brown was hung. These are the two ends of a chain which is not without its links. He is not Old Brown any longer; he is an Angel of Light. (Thoreau 137)[17]

For this is, in fact, the statement of a contemporary of George Eliot and Emily Dickinson, of one for whom (like them) "the disappearance of God" had not yet (at least in an affective level) quite occurred. Indeed, if we recognize Thoreau as having been as genuinely Janus-faced in matters of faith as he was in those of civilization and nature, then this epimethean turn toward the world of Cromwell and Hutchinson and Milton seems as "natural" (as fully and appropriately a part of his eclectic nineteenth-century life) as his promethean explorations in the same directions as Darwin or twentieth-century philosophy.[18]

---

[17] The two standard works on Thoreau and Asia are Christy, *The Orient in American Transcendentalism: A Study of Emerson, Thoreau, and Alcott* (especially 185–233); and Versulis, *American Transcendentalism and Asian Religions* (especially 79–99). They advance the view that Thoreau's interest in the spiritual writings and techniques of the East (like that of the other Transcendentalists) bespeaks both his partial liberation from the narrowness of the New England religious past, and his status as a forerunner of the region's later religious diversity and alleged secularization. Yet both books fail to recognize this interest as marking the persistence as well of older New England religious concerns: ones specifically illustrated by the similar spiritual issues at stake in the case of Ann Hutchinson (see Gura 237–75), and the spiritual journey of Edward Taylor (a moderate Puritan who in the absence of a native contemplative spirituality had to turn—via Richard Baxter—to the meditational techniques of George Herbert and Saint Francis de Sales). See also Martz's foreword to Stanford's edition of *The Poems of Edward Taylor*, or either of two more "Protestant" readings of Taylor's poems, though ones that do not wholly contradict the essential point that he was seeking a more contemplative spirituality: Scheick, *The Will and the Word: The Poetry of Edward Taylor* and Keller, *The Example of Edward Taylor*.

Similarly, Buell sees Thoreau's use of the jeremiad form in "A Plea for Captain John Brown" and elsewhere during the debates over slavery as marking a genuine exception to the general process of religiocentric secularization found elsewhere in his career (a return to the religious seriousness as well as the religious rhetoric of the seventeenth-century); see *Literary Transcendentalism* 122–23. I wish to argue, however, that if we abandon the Whiggish belief that the trajectory of Thoreau's career (and that of other Transcendentalists) was solely in the secular or religiously modernist direction of the modern university, we can begin to see such outbreaks of traditional religious sentiment as being more typical of (and frequent in) the authors of this period. Certainly, from a political perspective, Thoreau's use of the jeremiad is an instance of such cultural persistence with strong religious roots. See Bercovitch, *The American Jeremiad* 132ff.

[18] The term "the disappearance of God," is, of course, taken from J. Hillis Miller's study of the same name concerning the literary impact of the rise of unbelief in Victorian England.

As this implies, a more open approach to the question of secularization *vs.* the persistence of traditional religious faith helps us
to read individual Transcendentalist texts with a greater sensitivity
to their complexity and capacity for embodying contradictions in
matters of belief and unbelief. It alerts us, too, to the danger of
imposing a late twentieth-century academic world-view on these
early nineteenth-century writings, thereby either ignoring their
religious dimension or vitiating its seriousness by transposing religious concerns into currently more amenable psychological or
intellectual historical ones—something that is common enough
today in light of the current tendency of "secular" thinkers to lose
a sense of cultural difference when reading the Transcendentalists,
making them their intellectual ancestors or colleagues rather than
letting them be themselves: which, after all, even at their most
"secularized" and "freethinking," only makes them (like Melville
or Dickinson) *nineteenth-century* skeptics still haunted by God, not
postmodern ones.

Similarly, we need to avoid imposing the secularization model
upon American cultural history in ways that rob Transcendentalist
poetry and prose of their complexity as documents indicating the
ebb and flow of religious belief. For while, under the influence
of the Higher Criticism, what Buell calls "literature and scripture" may have tended to "become interchangeable categories"
among some members of the Boston and Concord elite (*"Moby-
Dick"* 57), this does not lead to the conclusion that Transcendentalist texts uniformly take the form of "literary scriptures"[19] (i.e.,
texts that preserve something of the sentiment of belief and repli-
cate the preacher's voice, while eclectically merging "piety . . .
with aestheticism" and transferring "faith in the authority of the
original text [the Bible] . . . to faith in the literary process" (*New
England Literary Culture* 185). For such a reading makes *Walden*
and *The Divinity School Address* into works which ultimately take
religious belief and the spiritual life seriously only insofar as they
allowed their authors mythopoetically to do something else. It is
a way of reading Transcendentalist texts religiously, in other
words, that ever so subtly renders religion marginal or epiphenomenal; and makes Transcendentalist authors *just* men-of-letters

---

[19] I take this term from the title of Chapter 7 in Buell, *New England Literary
Culture.*

orientated toward such modern ambitions as creative empowerment and autonomy, not men of faith too (however heterodox),
seeking "to front a FACT" along a different line: one that drew
them toward the puritan seventeenth-century even as they looked
East as much as toward (what some still persist in believing is) the
secular twentieth century.

WORKS CITED

Adams, Stephen, and Donald Ross, Jr. *Revising Mythologies: The Composition of Thoreau's Major Works.* Charlottesville: UP of Virginia, 1988.

Ahlstrom, Sydney E. *A Religious History of the American People.* New
Haven: Yale UP, 1972.

Barish, Evelyn. *Emerson: The Roots of Prophecy.* Princeton: Princeton UP,
1989.

Bercovitch, Sacvan. *The American Jeremiad.* Madison: U of Wisconsin P,
1978.

Bishop, Jonathan. *Emerson on the Soul.* Cambridge, Mass.: Harvard UP,
1964.

Buell, Lawrence. *The Environmental Imagination: Thoreau, Nature Writing,
and the Formation of American Culture.* Cambridge, Mass. Harvard UP,
1995.

———. *Literary Transcendentalism: Style and Vision in the American Renaissance.* Ithaca: Cornell UP, 1973.

———. *"Moby-Dick* as Sacred Text." *New Essays on "Moby-Dick."* Ed.
Richard H. Brodhead. Cambridge: Cambridge UP, 1986. 53–72.

———. *New England Literary Culture: From Revolution Through Renaissance.* Cambridge: Cambridge UP, 1986.

Butler, Jon. *Awash in a Sea of Faith: Christianizing the American People.*
Cambridge, Mass.: Harvard UP, 1990.

Capper, Charles. *Margaret Fuller: An American Life.* New York: Oxford
UP, 1992.

Cavell, Stanley. *The Senses of Walden: Expanded Edition.* San Francisco:
North Point P, 1981.

Christy, Arthur. *The Orient in American Transcendentalism: A Study of Emerson, Thoreau, and Alcott.* New York: Columbia UP, 1932.

Cohen, Charles L. *God's Caress: The Psychology of Puritan Religious Experience.* New York: Oxford UP, 1986.

Conn, Walter. *Christian Conversion: A Developmental Interpretation of Autonomy and Surrender.* New York and Mahwah: Paulist, 1986.

Cox, Harvey G. *Fire from Heaven: The Rise of Pentecostal Spirituality and* the Reshaping of Religion in the Twenty-First Century. Reading: Addison-Wesley, 1995.

————. *The Secular City. New York: Macmillan, 1971.*

Ellison, Julie. *Emerson's Romantic Style.* Princeton: Princeton UP, 1984.

Emerson, Ralph Waldo. "The Divinity School Address." *The Collected Works of Ralph Waldo Emerson.* Vol. 1. Ed. Alfred R. Ferguson, et al. Cambridge, Mass.: Harvard UP, 1971—. 71–93.

Franchot, Jenny. "Invisible domain: Religion and American Literary Studies." *American Literature* 67 (1995): 833–42.

————. *Roads to Rome: The Antebellum Protestant Encounter with Catholicism.* Berkeley: U of California P, 1994.

Garber, Frederick. *Thoreau's Fable of Inscribing.* Princeton: Princeton UP, 1991.

Gittleman, Edwin. *Jones Very: The Effective Years, 1833–1840.* New York: Columbia UP, 1967.

Greeley, Andrew M. *Religious Change in America.* Cambridge, Mass.: Harvard UP, 1989.

Gura, Philip F. *A Glimpse of Sion's Glory: Puritan Radicalism in New England, 1620–1660.* Middletown: Wesleyan UP, 1984.

Hatch, Nathan O. *The Democraticization of American Christianity.* New Haven: Yale UP, 1989.

Howarth, William L. *The Book of Concord: Thoreau's Life as a Writer.* New York: Viking, 1982.

Howe, Daniel Walker. *The Unitarian Conscience: Harvard Moral Philosophy, 1805–1861.* Cambridge, Mass.: Harvard UP, 1970.

Hutchison, William R. *The Transcendentalist Ministers: Church Reform in the New England Renaissance.* New Haven: Yale UP, 1959.

Keller, Karl. *The Example of Edward Taylor.* Amherst: U of Massachusetts P, 1975.

Kuklick, Bruce. *The Rise of American Philosophy: Cambridge, Mass., 1860–1930.* New Haven: Yale UP, 1977.

Marsden, George M. *The Soul of the American University: From Protestant Establishment to Established Non-Belief.* New York: Oxford UP, 1994.

Martz, Louis L. Foreword. *The Poems of Edward Taylor.* Ed. Donald E. Stanford. New Haven: Yale UP, 1960. xiii–xxxvii.

McGreevy, John T. *Parish Boundaries: The Catholic Encounter with Race in the Twentieth-Century Urban North.* Chicago: U of Chicago P, 1996.

Milder, Robert. *Reimagining Thoreau.* Cambridge, Eng.: Cambridge UP, 1995.

Miller, J. Hillis. *The Disappearance of God: Five Nineteenth-Century Writers.* Cambridge, MA: The Belknap P of Harvard UP, 1963.

Miller, Perry. "From Edwards to Emerson." *Errand into the Wilderness.* Cambridge, Mass.: Harvard UP, 1956. 184–203.

————. *The Transcendentalists: An Anthology*. Cambridge, MA: Harvard UP, 1950.

Packer, Barbara. *Emerson's Fall*. New York: Continuum, 1982.

Peck, H. Daniel. *Thoreau's Morning Work*. New Haven: Yale UP, 1990.

Poirier, Richard. *The Renewal of Literature: Emersonian Reflections*. New Haven: Yale UP, 1987.

Porte, Joel. *Emerson and Thoreau: Transcendentalists in Conflict*. Middletown: Wesleyan UP, 1965.

Reynolds, David S. *Beneath the American Renaissance: The Subversive Imagination in the Age of Emerson and Melville*. New York: Knopf, 1988.

Richardson, Robert D., Jr. *Emerson: The Mind on Fire*. Berkeley: U of California P, 1995.

————. *Henry David Thoreau: A Life of the Mind*. Berkeley: U of California P, 1986.

Robinson, David M. *Emerson and the Conduct of Life: Pragmatism and Ethical Purpose*. Cambridge, Eng.: Cambridge UP, 1993.

Roof, Wade Clark, and William McKinney. *American Mainline Religion: Its Changing Shape and Future*. New Brunswick, NJ: Rutgers UP, 1987.

Rose, Ann C. *Transcendentalism as a Social Movement, 1830–1850*. New Haven: Yale UP, 1981.

Sattelmeyer, Robert. "When He Became My Enemy: Emerson and Thoreau, 1848–1849." *New England Quarterly* 62 (1989): 187–204.

Scheick, William J. *The Will and the Word: The Poetry of Edward Taylor*. Athens: U of Georgia P, 1974.

Simmons, Nancy Craig, ed. *The Selected Letters of Mary Moody Emerson*. Athens: U of Georgia P, 1993.

Stoller, Leo. *After Walden*. Stanford: Stanford UP, 1957.

Thompson, E. P. *William Blake: Witness Against the Beast (William Blake and the Moral Law)*. Cambridge: Cambridge UP, 1993.

Thoreau, Henry David. "A Plea for Captain John Brown." *The Writings of Henry D. Thoreau*. Ed. Wendell Glick. Princeton: Princeton UP, 1973. 111–38.

Van Anglen, Kevin P. "True Pulpit Power: 'Natural History of Massachusetts' and the Problem of Cultural Authority." *Studies in the American Renaissance: 1993*. Ed. Joel Myerson. Charlottesville: UP of Virginia, 1993. 119–47.

————. *The New England Milton: Literary Reception and Cultural Authority in the Early Republic*. University Park: Pennsylvania State UP, 1993.

Vance, William L. *America's Rome*. New Haven: Yale UP, 1989.

Versulis, Arthur. *American Transcendentalism and Asian Religions*. New York: Oxford UP, 1993.

Von Mehren, Joan. *Minerva and the Muse: A Life of Margaret Fuller*. Amherst: U of Massachusetts P, 1994.

Weisbuch, Robert. *Atlantic Double-Cross: American Literature and British Influence in the Age of Emerson.* Chicago: U of Chicago P, 1986.

Wellek, René. *Confrontations: Studies in the Intellectual and Literary Relationship Between Germany, England, and the United States During the Nineteenth Century.* Princeton: Princeton UP, 1965.

Whicher, Stephen E. *Freedom and Fate: An Inner Life of Ralph Waldo Emerson.* Philadelphia: U of Pennsylvania P, 1953.

Wuthnow, Robert. *The Restructuring of American Religion: Society and Faith since World War II.* Princeton: Princeton UP, 1988.

9

Gender and the Religious Vision: Katharine Lee Bates and Poetic Elegy

Melinda Ponder

KATHARINE LEE BATES (1859–1929), widely published author of fiction, poetry, literary reviews, and college texts of the classics, is best known today for writing the words of "America the Beautiful." In it she gave utterance to her own prayer for the future of a United States badly torn apart in 1893 by labor unrest, economic depression, and growing class and race hostilities. Her patriotic poem shows her lifelong interest in how a poet can use her voice and poetic form to articulate devotional ideas and petition for divine intervention and blessing. The daughter of a Congregational minister, Bates saw her vocation as a poet closely tied to that of a minister whose words could inspire and heal. Though she was barred by her gender from preaching from an ordained pulpit, her most famous poem has become our national hymn, with its images of spacious skies, amber waves of grain, purple mountains' majesty, its patriotic but maternal and familial images of fertility and peace, and its hope for brotherhood which could unite all parts of the country "from sea to shining sea." While Bates had written "America the Beautiful" at a time of national spiritual crisis, thirty years later, while experiencing her own crisis of faith, she memorialized her dearest friend, Katharine Coman, in *Yellow Clover*, a collection of poems crowned with an extraordinary sonnet sequence, "In Bohemia." Her literary and religious questions and their poetic answer, revisionary in its themes, drama, form, and gender politics, testified in its structural innovations and narrative of spiritual transformation to the ongoing feminist influence and presence of the departed woman Bates thought she had lost to death. Her prayers for relief were answered by visions of Coman as a female savior, the only possible redeemer of Bates from spiritual despair.

Like other women of her era, Bates thought and wrote about spiritual and religious ideas without ever joining a church (Palmieri 74–75; Jenkins), partly because, as Ruth Y. Jenkins points out, "patriarchal cultures eliminate women's active and authoritative place within sacred myth and the resulting institutions" (22). However, Bates was familiar with Christianity and the Bible throughout her life. The daughter of a Congregational minister who was born a month before her father's death, Bates was raised in an orthodox New England religion but was an independent searcher for truth who tried to practice Christianity as an individual. As a young professor at her alma mater of Wellesley College in 1890, she refused to join a church to keep her job or to conform to the rigorous orthodox requirements of the college's evangelical founder (Burgess 84–88). However, as a poet who published prolifically in such periodicals as *The Congregationalist* and *The Christian Union*, Bates frequently wrote devotional poetry which focused on the individual's responsibility to others in a Christian context and quoted Horace's idea that a poet had a divine calling: " 'The poet is the gods' anointed priest' " ("Musarum Sacerdos"). Her interest was in the practical application of religious precepts to daily life and the ways in which our goals and values should come from God and result in healing and noble deeds. Her niece and first biographer wrote:

> She was profoundly troubled and sometimes felt that there must be some weakness within her that prevented her from saying, with her friends, "I believe." She loved the symbolism of the great cathedrals and the intimate wayside crosses. . . . From her soul-searchings emerged [her] individual Trinity: "Christ," "Love," and "God." She found her assurance . . . in the love of her friends, and in her instinct for worship of "Him on Whom my longings wait." (Burgess 66–67)

Bates had published prayers for children, for Easter and Christmas, often creating her own description of a biblical passage and using natural images to present a fairly simplistic theology (e.g., a rainbow is a path to heaven). But while she was able to write from an early age almost glibly of her own desire for spiritual peace, it was not until she wrote *Yellow Clover*, and particularly "In Bohemia," that she put her spiritual crisis at the center of her poetry. Nevertheless, while honest about her own moral short-comings and doctrinal doubts, she had been drawn to lyric devotional poetry for her entire life as a writer, English literature professor, and critic, unconsciously training herself for what would be her most painful but most virtuosic poetic creation at Coman's death.

One of the devotional poets most important as a model for Bates was Christina Rossetti, a woman whose female perspective, interest in women's lives (Smulders), and religious intensity were also loved by Katharine Coman. Bates knew "more than fifty of her poems by heart," and she was the poet the two women read together most often (Burgess 166–67). Moments before she died, Coman uttered, "Yea, Lord," the final lines from a Rossetti poem:

> Shall not the Judge of all the earth do right?
> Yea, Lord, altho' Thou say me nay!
> Shall not His Will be to me life and light?
> Yea, Lord, altho' Thou slay. (Scudder 22)

Rossetti had been important to Bates long before Coman's death in 1914. In 1894, Bates had written to Rossetti before the poet's death, and in Rossetti's memory Bates delivered a talk on her poetry and published both an elegiac sonnet and a literary discussion of her work.[1] As she worked on developing her own poetic voice, Bates particularly praised Rossetti's voice in her devotional poetry which uttered ". . . the Godward yearnings of her soul, the strain that outsoared that intellectual narrowness . . . and became at once pure religion and pure song,—a thrilling rich expression of that divine thirst which . . . is the strongest force in man" ("Rossetti" 15–16). Her words, Bates felt, gave "a language to that homeless faith so rife in our day and generation,—the faith that may not 'fix itself to form' " (19–20).

---

[1] Appropriately, Bates gave this talk at Denison House, a settlement house in Boston which Coman and Bates had helped create and for whose committee Coman served as chairman; Coman later served as the president of its parent organization, the College Settlement Association, begun by graduates of women's colleges in 1890.

Years after she described Rossetti's power to voice both doubt and faith as well as expressions of "divine thirst" and the "God-ward yearnings of her soul," Bates herself found and developed such a voice in her 1922 limited- edition *Yellow Clover,* a collection of poetry written for, about, and in memorial to her dearest companion, mentor, and Wellesley College colleague, Katharine Coman, who had died of cancer in 1914.

Bates had become friends with Katharine Coman soon after Coman's arrival in 1880 at Wellesley College. A professor first of history and then of political economy and sociology, Coman was born in 1857, two years before Bates, and raised on a farm in Ohio. Coman's pastoral background, picturesque but unmonied, was similar to Bates's childhood home in the Cape Cod village of Falmouth. When Bates met Coman, Bates was still Wellesley's most promising graduate, a poet who wanted to spend all her energies and time on her writing, a financial impossibility. Although she joined Wellesley's faculty in 1885, she saw her teaching and scholarship only as a means of supporting her poetry writing. But Coman offered Bates a new and useful way of seeing her career as a woman professor and scholar, pulling her up several levels, modeling serious vocational and professional commitment to her teaching, and introducing her to the wider world of social, economic, cultural, gender, and spiritual issues.

Coman's religious faith, in contrast to Bates's questioning, was deep and abiding. Emily Greene Balch, Coman's student and later the winner of the Nobel Peace Prize, recalled that Coman's ". . . trust in God was like a part of the texture of her nature. It was a clear, serene conviction, strengthening as the body grew weaker, till it seemed as if the screen between the material and [the] real became almost transparent before our eyes" (7). Another student remembered her ". . . absolute faith in a Power not ourselves that makes for righteousness, that in that Power she lived and moved and had her being. God was in her, and she was in God" (Blauvelt). Coman inspired spiritual interest in those around her and ". . . laid her own experience under contribution to the needy spiritual lives around her . . ." (Scudder 21), helping ". . . a devout group of girls . . . study with her the social teachings of Jesus, while a group of youthful heretics discussed religious and philosophical problems under her guidance. The impress of her spiritual power [was] a vital power with these questioning souls . . ." (Halsey). Vida Scudder, another Wellesley College professor of English and religious activist in the Anglo-Catholic church movement, praised Coman's tolerance and sympathy with anyone searching for God, regardless of creed, but stressed that Coman's ". . . own belief was distinctly Christian, Christocentric. Close, devout intimacy with the Gospels was the basis of her teaching and her social activities; in the living Christ she found her strength" (21–22).

Coman put her religious beliefs to work in all she did. As Vida Scudder pointed out, Coman's ". . . whole outlook on social and industrial life was determined by her firm belief in the principles revealed in the Gospels . . ." (22). Her personal warmth and presence enabled her to reach and change many around her. As one student wrote about Coman after her death, "I don't think she was a philosopher. . . . Ideas were so much less important to her than people. I think she was a saint" (qtd. in Balch 3). As an economic historian, Coman pioneered serious academic work on such humanitarian issues as immigrant working conditions, child labor, and social insurance, and lived an activist's life, organizing women in the garment industry, helping Jane Addams at Hull House in Chicago, and organizing the College Women's Settlement Association, which established settlement houses staffed mainly by women's college graduates in New York, Philadelphia, and Baltimore. In Boston, she served as the chairman of Denison House, a settlement house where many Wellesley College faculty, graduates, and students created and ran a community center mainly for working women. She was also an active member of the Consumers' League and advocated for the protesting women in the Chicago Garment-Workers Strike of 1910–11.

Bates saw in Coman a tall, handsome woman of great energy, a serious intellectual who did original scholarship as a means of improving the world around her, a feminist who believed in the unlimited abilities of and possibilities for women, and her most intimate friend.[2] For Bates, Coman became a mentor and role model, a determined woman who took her work seriously and saw the entire globe as her research site. She shared her great love

---

[2] For discussions of such relationships as "Wellesley" or "Boston" marriages, see Palmieri, 137–42; Horowitz, 188–91; Faderman, 147–230. For a discussion of *Yellow Clover* in the context of a romantic lesbian relationship, see Schwarz.

of the open spaces of the Midwest and West with Bates, traveling
with her to Colorado to teach summer school in the fateful summer of Bates's trip up to the top of Pike's Peak where she wrote
"America the Beautiful." Coman also traveled many times with
Bates to England, introducing her to pioneering women who
wore bloomers and rode bicycles in Oxford, and educating Bates
on the less poetic side of England's history and industry. They
collaborated on *English History as Told by English Poets*, with its
emphasis on social utopias, a clear reflection of Coman's political
and intellectual influence. Their relationship was deep and broad,
growing out of their shared professional lives and their place as
lifetime companions in the Wellesley College community.
Coman was an extraordinary woman whose warmth and "free
and ample nature" attracted people of all ages and backgrounds
to her (Balch 7). With her death, Bates had lost the person most
dear to her and the joy of her life, and because Coman's own
religious faith was so strong and central to her, Bates felt that her
dear friend had left her behind, both humanly and spiritually.

Bates eventually memorialized and drew close to this woman
who had pioneered her profession and relished all adventures in
her life—intellectual, emotional, and spiritual—by herself pioneering a book whose poems dramatize the religious salvation of
one woman by another, an event appropriately revolutionary to
memorialize a woman never limited by gender conventions.
Seven years after Coman's death Bates collected her various lyric
poems for Coman into a beautiful limited edition volume entitled
Yellow Clover, whose appearance and revisionary poetry represented their continuing union. Its ivory-and-sage–colored cover
with gold lettering and special decorative band of block-printed
yellow clover designs reflected the beauty in their life together as
women, their love of all the elements in a natural landscape, their
values of simplicity and the pastoral life, and their joint investment
in handcrafted art. In their many trips to England, they had pursued their interest in the Arts and Crafts Movement at the turn of
the century, an interest evident in their love for the Pre-Raphaelite art movement, for Christina Rossetti's poetry, for the handcrafted editions of William Morris and the Kelmscott Press, and
for John Ruskin's and William Morris's eventual role in the so-

cialistic and communal ideas put into practice in the settlement house movement in East London.[3]

Bates conceived *Yellow Clover* as a unique addition to the centuries-long male poetic tradition of memorializing elegy. Her collection of poems for a departed female beloved opens with a beautiful burnished vignette, a vintage photograph of the youthful Katharine Coman as Bates first saw her, her identity represented by her signature. Then, on the frontispiece under her dedication to Katharine Coman, Bates announces her revisionary project by means of her bold epigraph, a quotation from the opening line of Horace's twenty-fourth ode in Book I of his *Carmina*: "Quis desiderio sit pudor aut modus / Tam cari capitis?" This question, "What shame or limit should there be to grief for one so dear?" are the words Horace addressed to Vergil on the death of their mutual friend Quintilius Varus.[4] These lines suggest Bates's poignant themes of irreplaceable loss, depth of grief, and the extraordinary heartbreak at the death of a person so dearly loved. In addition, by beginning her memorial to Coman with these famous words spoken by Horace, the premier Roman lyric poet, to Vergil, the great epic poet, Bates places her poetry in the most important classical line of elegy. She is also reminding her readers of the long tradition honored in classical literature of deep and strong single-sex friendships, which she now joins with her poems for Coman. Appropriately, in poems that honor a woman who pioneered new professional traditions herself, Bates follows Coman's example and places her work in the company of the ancestral fathers who began the traditions she will enlarge.

Using thematic strands from their shared interests and lives as women teachers, writers, scholars, travelers, and Christians which she links together, Bates uses her poetry to create a visible sign of her life with Coman, a relationship she did not want to believe had ended. She was like the speaker in Wordsworth's final sonnet,

---

[3] Two authors begin to account for Bates's and Coman's interest in this movement, Marsh and Pearce, who give an excellent feminist perspective on this period. For an essay on feminist elements in William Morris, see Boos. For a fascinating overview of these interests as antimodernism, see Lears, particularly chapter two, "The Figure of the Artisan: Arts and Crafts Ideology," and chapter five, "The Religion of Beauty: Catholic Forms and American Consciousness."

[4] I am grateful to John L. Mahoney and his acute intellectual curiosity for this information.

a sonnet she had marked in her own copy of Wordsworth from his sonnet series, "The River Duddon."[5] Wordsworth writes that the only real memorial we can leave behind for future generations is "something from our hands" which has "power / To live, and act, and serve the future hour" (601). Like Wordsworth, Bates knew that it was what she could craft with her pen that would eternalize her bonds with her subject.

Since there were no models for such a poetic memorial, Bates designed her own arrangement of poems in *Yellow Clover*. She opened her book with the title poem, "Yellow Clover," a five-page, loosely structured lyrical poem which sets the tone of the entire volume by describing the tender nature of the love of the two Katharines for each other and the tiny flower that symbolized their ubiquitous love. In this title poem Bates asks if Coman remembers the "yellow clover, / Which once in parting for a time / that then seemed long, . . . How suddenly we halted in our climb, / Lingering, reluctant, up that farthest hill, / Stooped for the blossoms closest to our feet, / And gave them as a token / Each to each, / In lieu of speech, / In lieu of words too grievous to be spoken, / Those little, gypsy, wondering blossoms wet / With a strange dew of tears." Yellow clover thus became "their tenderest language," as they surprised each other with it, plucking, taming, and even mailing it to each other on separate continents "that so our hearts might reach / And touch within the yellow clover. . . ."

The poem ends with Bates's denial of the existence of the possibility that such a symbol can still unite them:

> My sorrow asks no healing; it is love;
> Let love then make me brave
> To bear the keen hurts of
> This careless summertide,
> Ay, of our own poor flower,
> Changed with our fatal hour,
> For all its sunshine vanished when you died.
> Only white clover blossoms on your grave.

This opening poem of sorrow and loneliness, symbolized by the absence of the symbol of their love, is answered at the end of

---

[5] Bates's marked copy of Wordsworth is in the Special Collections of the Wellesley College Library.

the book with a sonnet corona of seven sets of seven interlocking sonnets entitled "In Bohemia," the name of Katharine Coman's attic rooms in Bates's home. The form Bates chose and then enlarged beyond any previously published such corona suggests the poet's traditional crown of "bayes" or laurel, especially appropriate in the elegy tradition and referred to by John Donne in his own "corona" poems. It also suggests the crown of thorns worn by Jesus Christ during his crucifixion. In addition, it has a special significance to Bates and Coman, as a kind of literary chain of poems, a reminder of the clover chain made of the yellow clover they wound together, intricately woven of single images of their love tied together.

In the first four sections Bates depicts Coman's spiritual growth from her physical suffering to her death and life beyond earth, a growth made possible by Coman's strong religious faith which seemed only to grow the more she suffered from cancer. Bates knows the importance of Jesus to Coman, and because of the association in her mind between Coman and Jesus, an association which grew, in part, from Coman's own identification with Jesus's suffering, begins to suggest that Coman takes on many of his roles for Bates—of shower of the way, teacher, minister, and savior.

In "Felices" Bates uses an image from the New Testament to describe the transmutation through suffering Coman experienced:

> Crown of Thorns, Way of the Cross,
> Consuming Fire that burns the spirit pure.
> By luster of the gold set free from dross,
> By light of heaven seen best through earth's obscure,
> By the exceeding gain that waits on loss—
> Behold, we count them happy who endure. (23)

These lines suggest that those who suffer shed their gross material "dross," enabling them to reflect the light of heaven more than those who have no pain to endure. The poem in its context refers to Coman's battle with cancer which seemed to Bates to bring her even closer to the pain and suffering of Jesus. The subsequent poem, "The Tryst," recounts Bates's realization, after Coman's first operation for cancer, that Bates's own tryst was not with

Grief but with "God's will," a realization that enabled her to feel joy at the possibility of growth in her own relationship with a divine power. The two poems taken together suggest Coman's role for Bates: she is a sufferer, a kind of female Christ-figure, whose transformation and spiritual growth during her illness inspired and taught Bates to feel that she too must listen to and grow from acknowledging God's will.

Bates further emphasizes this link that she sees between Coman and Jesus in the poem "Good Friday in Paris":

> There at the pale feet of the Crucified,
>> With not a sob breaking your quiet breath,
> You knelt and offered up your body's pride
> And beauty to a creeping, torturing death.

Coman's own faith enabled her to teach Bates that God was a God of Love, "Life, Death, / The word is God's, whose every word is Love" ("How Oft With Thee," 29). That a loving God would will the death of her dear friend was impossible for Bates to accept unless she could see a positive transformation occurring in Coman, a question she would develop further in "In Bohemia."

In the poem "Holy Spirit Gone Free," written soon after Coman's passing, Bates wonders where Heaven is for her, again emphasizing her friend's close relationship with Christ:

> Art thou adoring the Throne,
>> Kissing the Wounded Feet?
> Art thou greeting thine own,
>> Souls home-sweet?

Bates then begins to connect her own suffering to that of Jesus; writing of "The Broken-Hearted," those who are grieving for the loss of a loved one, she sees that ". . . on their foreheads is the dew / Anointed eyes may see / Of dark Gethsemane" (46).

In the later poems, Coman becomes linked even more strongly in Bates's mind with a religious teacher. Bates addresses her with the hope that Coman's faith will enable her to minister to those she left behind: "Christ is thy Jerusalem, Wheresoe'er His service calls. . . . May thy ministering bless / Till remember what we miss" ("Westering Heart" 59). This use of the word "minister" is especially poignant in light of the Wellesley College motto prominently displayed on the walls of the Chapel and frequently repeated and emphasized in college events, "Non Ministrari sed Ministrare," not to be ministered unto but to minister, a verse from Matthew 20:28 and Mark 10:45 in which Jesus describes his conception of his mission, "Even as the Son of man came not to be ministered unto, but to minister, and to give his life as ransom for many" (Matt. 20:28). Although she has passed beyond human existence, Coman can still teach and serve Bates as a kind of minister, perhaps more potent in her womanly love than any other minister could be to her, a theme Bates intensifies and develops in detail in the climactic sonnet corona "In Bohemia."[6]

For the poetic structure of "In Bohemia," the striking conclusion to her poetic memorial, Bates works with two forms more modern than the lyric ode of Horace, combining a corona form with a sonnet series of seven sets of seven sonnets linked by the first and last lines. Its title associates Bates with Coman's place of death and beginning of immortal life. Likewise Bates's poems link her with Coman as they intertwine with each other in their lines which end one sonnet and begin the next. The seven sets of seven sonnets conclude with the final line as a repetition or slight revision of the opening line of the seven sonnets which circle back to form seven circles. They are the larger links in a circle which is made by the repetition of the first and last lines and thus a conjunction of the entire set. Their drama comes from the formal completion of the circle which coincides with Bates's own psychological and spiritual closure on grief and religious growth, which enables her to both give the crown of poems shining with love and to wear it as the only person who could have created such a gift.

Its form embodies precisely the elements of pioneering new experiences for women that Bates wanted to memorialize in Coman. Though based on a traditional male form, the elegy as written by Horace, it builds on both male and female models, suggesting the rich androgyny Bates saw in Coman. Appropriately, it is a narrative about spiritual growth, a concept central to

---

[6] For descriptions of other nineteenth-century women who thought in terms of a female Christ, see Jenkins's discussion of Florence Nightingale, 51–58, and Elizabeth Gaskell, 105. Jenkins notes that "saviour" can mean one who saves from error (51).

Coman's life; and Bates's poetic voice, as well as her sonnet sequence form, shows that she, like their favorite writer, Christina Rossetti, can write out of her own "divine thirst" for a female Jesus who will save her ("Christina Rossetti").

As Celeste M. Schenck has noted, several contemporary women poets have reworked the central symbolisms and procedures of elegy, because it has traditionally been a patriarchal genre "modeled on archaic initiation rituals" of "sons succeeding their poetic father . . . a ritual hymn . . . [in] which a new poet presents himself as heir to the tradition" (13). Schenck sees the masculine elegy as a "rite of separation . . . that depends upon rupture," a form not used by female elegists who instead "seem to achieve poetic identity in relation to ancestresses, in connection to the dead," a pattern Schenck explains with reference to Nancy Chodorow's explanations of the continuity in female relationships. Schenck emphasizes the contrast between the male elegists' linear progression toward elegiac compensatory consolation and transcendence with the female poets who critique such a pattern by using patterns of form which suggest continuous mourning. Like such female poets as Anne Sexton, Amy Clampitt, and Aphra Behn, Katharine Lee Bates uses nonlinear structure to stress several types of continuity. But, as the creator of a beautifully crafted circle, a crown or "coronal" of poems, she seeks to bring closure to her mourning through the recuperative act of voicing and writing her memorial, and thus, like the male elegiac poet, presents herself "as heir to the tradition" (Schenck 13), a tradition that now includes a woman poet mourning the loss of her beloved female companion who herself becomes the answer to spiritual despair.

As Department Chair of the Wellesley College English Department for thirty years and its resident poet, Bates had frequently been called upon to write memorials for members of the college community. Familiar with the long tradition of elegiac poetry, as a critic, poet, and former teacher of Latin and Greek, Bates created her corona of forty-nine linked poems by drawing on the dramatic situations, themes, and voices of the poetry of John Donne, Alfred Lord Tennyson, and Christina Rossetti, and weaving them into a new and original creation.

Bates's "In Bohemia" is woven together in the interlocking pattern of John Donne's seven-poem "La Corona" of the Divine

Poems. Each sonnet begins with the final line of the preceding sonnet, and the final line of the seventh sonnet restates the first line of the first sonnet. Donne explains his conceit of weaving a "crown of prayer and praise / Weav'd in my low devout melancholie," which he hopes will gain him "A crowne of Glory, which doth flower alwayes; / The ends crowne our workes, but thou crown'st our ends." Because his soul is thirsty for salvation, Donne's speaker retells the story of the life of Jesus, using the circle form to encompass "the speaker and the subjects of his praise" (Walker 42). Margaret Maurer notes the paradox of using such a form:

> The circle as shape and as motion is an emblem of the paradoxes of Christianity. God is beginning and end; and the story of the Redemption is replete with incidents in which the God-man is raised by being cast down. The circle as shape without beginning or end and the virtual and self-sustaining motion of rotation in which every fall at one point is a rise at another are thus especially appropriate to the story on which "La Corona" is based. . . . In human terms, however, these paradoxes encompass deep ambivalence. The circle not only symbolizes perfection; it stands in mathematics for nothing. (54)

The drama of the sonnet sequence centers in the struggle of the speaker who feels cut off from God, unworthy to be rescued. He prays to Jesus Christ, "Now thou art lifted up, draw mee to thee, / And at thy death giving such liberall dole, / Moyst, with one drop of thy blood, my dry soule." His poetic retelling of the story of Christ's ascension awakens his own faith, and he feels redeemed: "O strong Ramme, which hast batter'd heaven for mee, / Mild lambe, which with thy blood, hast mark'd the path; / Bright torch, which shin'st that I the way may see." He asks that Christ accept his crown of prayer and praise, his poems, if his holy spirit was raised by the poet's Muse. Donne thus suggests the power of his language and conceit to help him reach the Holy Spirit and overcome his "melancholie," a struggle Bates dramatizes rather astoundingly by magnifying Donne's seven sonnets into seven times seven sonnets, an even more complex corona, with a surprising parallel to Jesus's role of giving salvation.

Where Donne's corona of sonnets gave her a structural model

for an inquiry into the struggle for the religious faith she needed in order to reach Coman in her immortality, Bates turned to Tennyson's "In Memoriam" for a model of elegiac poetry. She took a leaf from Tennyson's book by naming her poems to Coman "In Bohemia," suggesting both Coman's former room as well as Bates's own literal and psychological movement to Coman in the space, both geographical and literary, where Bates could feel closest to Coman for all the years she outlived her.

Bates's title suggests her awareness that she was treading on traditionally male elegiac territory. Although Tennyson's "In Memoriam" examines the subject of immortality symbolized by Jesus (Shatto 10), its real subject, according to Christopher Craft, is the unfulfilled "same gender desire" of the mourner, "the medial space of unclosed longing" crafted into "a desiring machine whose first motive is the reproduction of lost Hallam . . . " (66, 75, 78), a subject replicated by Bates in her longings for spiritual union with Coman. Both Tennyson and Bates follow traditional elegies in their classical structure—the "propemptikon (farewell to the departed traveler), followed by a reminiscence (genethliakon) and the epicedia (funeral lament)" (Shatto 27–29)—with its stock themes and conventions: "all men must die; it is better to have been happy for a short time than never to have been happy at all; it is better to control sorrow than to indulge it; time will ease the sorrow, but reason should do so first; it is vain to grieve on our own account or on that of the dead, who cannot be recalled to life; the dead are happy, indeed, they are probably happier than the living; and the dead would not wish us to grieve for them" (30). Tennyson and Bates alike make significant use of the mourner's desire to communicate with the deceased and the comforting apparition of the deceased to the mourner in a dream or waking vision (Shatto 30). Tennyson's form is circular in its way also; as Linda M. Shires notes, "the advance and retreat of the elegy means that the desire expressed is finally more persuasive than the narrative transformation of Ha[l]lam into God or the final notes of optimism in the Epilogue" (58). But where Tennyson made the consolatory moment of his poem the heterosexual marriage which indirectly united him to Hallam, Bates instead celebrates the joys of her years with Coman, and finds consolation in her own spiritual growth which enables her to feel union with Coman herself, not with a male substitute for her.

The third poet whose work Bates appropriately drew on was
Christina Rossetti. Fittingly, because of Coman's admiration for
her poetry and spirituality, a dedicatory sonnet written by Rossetti
to her mother may have given Bates the inspiration for her crown
of poems for Coman. Rossetti wrote: "And so because you love
me, and because / I love you, Mother, I have woven a wreath /
Of rhymes wherewith to crown your honored name" (Dedication to *A Pageant and Other Poems*). In another poem Rossetti
names the "crown of life" alluded to in Revelations (qtd. in
Smulders 580 from "Margery") the prize of eternal life given for
patient endurance, like the crown Bates describes Coman as
wearing.

Rossetti may also have inspired Bates with two long sonnet
sequences: "Monna Innominata," fourteen sonnets "on the conventional sonnet subject, love" (Whitla 116), and "Later Life: A
Double Sonnet of Sonnets" (twenty-eight sonnets), an extended
consideration of the speaker's lifelong desire to understand and
praise God, as she contemplates the death of those she loved who
may still be "exceeding near . . . watching us . . . Brimful of
words which cannot yet be said," a theme Bates will develop
further. In these sonnets Rossetti also uses the crown image: al-
pine flowers weave a crown for the Alps and the crown of eternal
life comes close to slipping through the hands of the unsaintly
speaker on her deathbed.

In Bates's "In Bohemia," the seven sets of sonnets focus on the
spiritual crisis of the survivor who feels abandoned by the beloved
who has gone on to a higher level of existence. In Bates's case,
the distance was especially great because, as the earlier poems in
the book show, she felt that her companion had always been living in a more spiritual realm than she had and had been preparing
herself to be a bride of Christ, something from which Bates felt
very distant.

Bates asks Coman for largesse so that she might also prize death
and share Coman's faith. Bates's pain nearly overwhelms her as
she recalls Coman's suffering from cancer and the loss she now
suffers as the survivor. She notes the irony in the fact that Coman
still lives, because of her great faith in God, while it is Bates who
is dead: "My life has vanished, life of joy I led / folded in yours."
But her greatest fear is that Coman has vanished, "quenched in
darkness, like a shooting star." The drama of the sonnet cycle is

Bates's movement toward a greater understanding of Coman's immortal life.

The speaker's voice in these sonnets of longing and despair directly addresses the beloved. Her words are spoken to maintain the contact she wants with Coman, paralleling the direct address of the speaker in Donne's "La Corona" and Rossetti's "Monna Innominata." It is a personal voice beseeching a beloved listener to respond. Significantly, Bates's use of such a speaker combines both the subject of Rossetti's poem—human and divine love—with that of Donne's more traditional devotional plea to God, Mary, Joseph, and Christ (Walker 41). Bates is like a mourner addressing Christ, suggesting that Coman is both the object of Bates's human love as well as a Christ figure who serves, teaches, heals, intercedes, and blesses, a role sketched out in the earlier four sections of *Yellow Clover*. Like Rossetti, who demonstrates that the "same old" love story is "transcended by its incorporation into the 'new' story of Christian scripture" (Rosenblum, *Poetry* 204), Bates combines the traditional imagery of romantic love poetry with that of religious devotional poetry.

Each of the seven sets of seven sonnets emphasizes this characterization of Coman, and dramatizes the dawning of this healing idea in Bates's consciousness. In the seven sets, the speaker (to whom I am referring as Bates the woman and poet) journeys from grieving over Coman's human life which ended in death to understanding the eternal nature of her spiritual life, a life which Bates can join with enough spiritual growth and help from Coman. The fourteen-line sonnets are bifurcated into octets and sestets for the entire forty-nine sonnets, a form which easily enables Bates to posit her questions or doubts in the octet and develop or reply to them in the sestet. She varies the rhyme scheme within the octets and sestets, particularly at dramatic moments in the overall narrative. Her rhyme schemes, ABBAABBACCD-CCD, ABBAABBACDECDE, etc., emphasize linked enclosures, with the end rhymes of lines connecting them to each other. They dramatize how one person can construct links that become a chain by a language of love and devotion which connects two lives and two spirits.

The first set of sonnets and the corona as a whole begin with the line, "I give you joy, my Dearest. Death is done," a line which is repeated at the conclusion of the corona with an enlarged meaning. When Bates first makes the statement in the opening sonnet, she means the line literally, in that she will give Coman the joy of knowing that her difficult human suffering and death from cancer are finished. Coman's "Crown / Of sainthood, woven of such pains as drown / Remembering eyes in tears," is a crown woven of human pain, visibly obvious to her human friends. Although she died as a text for her friends to read about religious faith (her face is "where we yet may trace / A holy script") and her last words "'Bless the Lord, my soul'" point her mourners to a holy experience, Bates instead can only "pore upon" her human face, although she knows that Coman is listening to something other than human voices. When Coman prayed, as she lay dying, " 'And all that is within me, bless His name!' " Bates thought only of the literal meaning of that phrase, that her offering was only what was within her, cancer's "bitter woe." She sees Coman's death materially in images of physical release when the "Angel of the Lord" smote the chains of the "iron gates of pain." At this point in the sonnets Bates can conceive of her dear friend as existing only in a human body which has been destroyed by a gruesome cancer, has died, and is gone from Bates's human view. She remembers the physical manifestations of her death, her withering "bright hair," her bending shoulders, her "numb, forgetful hand," her "hard gasps," her wan, worn face. Bates recalls the morning of Coman's death, her body's appearance, and the object she gave her to hold, an olive cross from Bethlehem Coman had loved.

The seventh and concluding sonnet of the first set presents Bates as reconciled to Coman's death only because death was the way she could escape physical pain. Bates tries to feel joy for her friend because her physical suffering is over and she has joined her human memories of her in "In Bohemia" by physically moving into Coman's room after her death:

> But in your upper chamber, in your own
> Bohemia, wide-windowed to the sun,
> We are together, all our suffering through,
> Our long suspense and dread a shadow flown.
> I give you joy, my Dearest. Death is done.

Bates's reference to Coman's "upper chamber" is literally appropriate since her room was on the top floor of Bates's house, but it suggests the upper room of Jesus's last supper (Mark 14:15, Luke 22:12). As the next six sections progress, Bates will need to learn to see that the many levels of existence she and Coman have are beyond the human if she is to truly feel the "joy" described in the last line of the sonnet, which ties up the end of the section by connecting it to the identical first line. The circular-link shape of the sonnet set symbolizes completeness and eternity, but it cannot be a crown without the subsequent links which show Bates's progress.

Bates's theme in the second set of sonnets continues to be joy, but still the joy of a human love, now remembered in detail "to employ / My aching thoughts, lest lurking grief decoy / My spirit from its vow." In the third section of sonnets Bates begins to move forward in the healing process, realizing that it is Coman who lives while Bates is dead, "Bewildered past all pain, past all desire." She knows that she will never again use her human senses to delight in Coman's physical presence, welcoming her back on the station platform after a long journey. Intellectually, Bates knows that she should not be sorrowful now again that the "crown of thorns" has been lifted from Coman's brow (again, an image associating Coman with Jesus), but her sorrow isolates her from any other expressions of love. Only "One heart is home. . . . Your life was of my life the warp and woof / Whereon most precious friendships, disciplines, / Passions embroidered rich designs." Bates cannot find a substitute for her: "No Rainbow Weaver in my heaven's calm blue."

The fourth set of sonnets opens with Bates, fearful that they are becoming more separate from each other, reminding Coman of the beauties of her "dear-loved earth," especially of their adventurous travels to Heidelberg, the Sphinx, Hawaii, Norway, England, Switzerland, Florence, Rome, and France. However, when Bates repeats the question that has opened this section—"Do you remember still your dear-loved earth?"—we feel she is still too focused on human life to reach her friend.

The fifth section, in some ways the most poignant, develops Bates's sad question which underscores the distance she feels on earth from Coman: "Do saints go gypsying in Paradise?" Almost angry with Coman for moving to a new place, Bates asks if she has anything in heaven to rival what she has left on earth— wildwood, a bungalow by "water's edge" where she can take a "sunrise bath," laughing children, and their adored collie. But then Bates finally begins to picture the spirits Coman will have around her—her departed family members, their friends and colleagues from Wellesley College, and more famous people, Lincoln, St. Francis, Christina Rossetti, "who while still on earth knew well, / Even as the psalmist king of Israel, / Heaven's joy of harping." And then, recalling that the last words of Coman's were Rossetti's addressed to Jesus ("Yea, Lord"), Bates understands that once Coman has passed from human life, Jesus may choose to come to her, "His follower, His saint." While Bates rejoices in her vision of Coman wiping Jesus's feet with "Ointment from your alabaster box / Of precious faith" (Matt 26:7), straightaway "doubt strikes chilly" as she wonders, "How may the earth-blind bulb behold the lily?" "Thought reels before the metamorphosis / Of mortal to immortal," and Bates slips back into thinking of Coman as a human being who has simply moved to a new address:

> Have they no need of us who need them so?
> Do they never, of eternity grown weary,
> Long for the river-song of Time's onflow?
> Can one tree, even the Tree of Life, suffice?
> Do saints go gypsying in Paradise?

In the sixth section Bates asks if their quarter-century of joy can be all, afraid that Coman has finally disappeared from her human view, "Too pure a light for my enshadowed eyes," or if Coman's "vanished spirit, beautiful as brief, / Be quenched in darkness, like a shooting star." At this point Bates realizes that her "mortal vision" is insufficient, that she must discard her senses and journey past "all space / And pealing rhythm of time" before she can be "Spirit to apprehend your spirit face." Bates fears, however, that Coman may have "merged in some transcendent grace," a fear that she finally overcomes by rousing her shaky faith in God. Bates compares herself to a "shipwrecked mariner, whose frail / Boat lurches while he leaps to caulk and bail, / Make fast his water-keg with shred of rope, / Still searching, searching, dizzy eyes a-grope, / The blank of ocean for a saving sail" in a sea of incertitude, like Jesus's disciples who needed Jesus to calm the seas and their doubts for them (Matt. 14). Bates, like Donne, wonders how she can still worship God if she still doubts Him. However, her love for Coman encourages her to pray directly for enough faith to reach Coman, with Coman as her "interpreter" who can "pray / The prayer" Bates cannot.

Bates's thought of Coman as her intercessor links her solidly in her mind with Jesus, and, at the beginning of the final seventh section of sonnets, she associates Coman in her despair at her doctors' prognosis with "the forsaken Christ. . . . But straight you turned, so gallantly that God / Was proud of you." Bates recalls that while Coman's "mortal beauty dimmed, the glow / Of spirit brightened, till the soul had flown." She asks if for her, left behind in her spiritual despair, there cannot be "a Way, a Truth, a Life" by which she can reach Coman, again echoing the words Jesus used to describe himself (John 14:6). In the turning point of the poem, Bates realizes that there have been moments when she feels Coman's presence, but in realizing this is a spiritual rather than a physical presence, Bates begins to cease her grieving over Coman's loss and turns her attention to the kind of spiritual experience which will unite her with Coman:

> Have I not sometimes felt your presence nigh?
> You said: "I will not leave you comfortless."

Bates's memory of Coman's promise, one echoing Jesus's words (John 14:18), suggests Bates's new ability to apprehend Coman's discussions with her of eternal life as a gift of divine love. Jesus had followed his promise with another: that he would come to those who believed in God (John 14:19). Thus, Bates begins to pray for the first time to Coman for continued comfort and connection:

> Oh, still shed blessing on me from those wings
> Of whose soft tarriance I would be aware,
> Light intimations, fleet evanishings,
> Speech finer than all syllables, a rare
> Shining with my soul, a thrill intense
> That breaketh not Death's law of reticence.

Bates feels that Coman, a Christ-figure, has responded, that she can still hear Bates, intercede for her, teach her, and save her so that she can join Coman in her faith in eternal life. The seven

years since Coman's death, symbolized by the seven sets of seven
sonnets, have given Bates time to see Coman as her savior and
spiritual exemplar:

> By seven springs has your far grave been grassed,
> And in my depth of sorrow are astir
> New powers, perceptions, joys, against my earth
> Up-pressing, secret agonies of birth,
> At bidding of their angel gardener:
> "The Life Eternal! Let us hold it fast!"

As she did in life, so in death, Coman continues to transform
Bates, enabling her to finally understand that she can join Coman
only by transforming her vision of Coman and herself as living
spiritual rather than human existences. Although motivated more
by her love of Coman than by her own religious beliefs, Bates
can finally understand Coman's words to her as she lay waiting
for surgery: " 'Oh, have no fear, Dear Heart, for life and death /
Are one,' you smiled, 'and God is All in All.' " Bates at last sees
Coman clearly as a risen Christ from whom she is not separated
because they both are surrounded by God:

> In His eternal radiance you dwell,
> Fulfilling His High Word as sunbeams quell
> These earthly shadows. In your dying, gall
> You tasted, felt the spear your flesh appal,
> Were crucified with Christ, but it is well
> With you at last in that bright citadel
> Pain cannot storm, beyond the shining wall
> Grief may not scale.

It is Bates's understanding of this which brings her peace. In
the concluding line of the sonnet, the section and the corona
which echoes its opening line, she has moved from giving Coman
"joy" on her deathbed to giving her "joy" because she realizes
Coman's spiritual life is ongoing and that, as a Christ-figure,
Coman can continue to guide and lead Bates. Now, when Bates
says, "Death is done," she means that she now sees Coman's
human death as the beginning of eternal life and that her own
death of the spirit is "done" because she feels Coman's constant
ministering presence in her spiritual life.

Bates's sense of union with Coman, arriving seven years after her death, and here dramatized in the seventh set of seven sonnets, suggests that she was able to bring closure to her grief, in tying up the chain of poems in art and publishing them. The formal perfection of this crown, celebrating the vitality, adventurous spirit and abiding spiritual presence of their love, becomes a celebration of Coman's exploration and conquering of traditional male territory. Like Horace, Bates shows why no amount of grief was too much for an extraordinary person. Like Donne, Bates moves through despair at her religious doubts to a sense of reconciliation with Christian theology, but in the context of an intimate human love which helps her embrace a Christian one. Like Tennyson, Bates feels a sense of peace and the presence of her beloved at her poem's conclusion, but where Tennyson feels this only intermittently, Bates makes a lasting change in her life by recognizing Coman's life in God which Bates has begun to enter through her own spiritual growth. Like Rossetti, Bates's sonnet sequence depicts a human love story in devotional imagery, but moving beyond Rossetti, "to whom breath was prayer" (Bates "Passing"), Bates's single-sex love brought her into relation with the divine. Instead of becoming a bride of Christ, like Rossetti (Harrison 97), Bates could be saved by her beloved, herself a female Christ. Her literary memorial was a woman's crown, a corona.[7] It symbolized the crown of eternal life (1 Cor. 9:25, 2 Tim. 2:5), an "unfading crown of glory" (1 Pet. 5:4), which Coman had shown Bates how to discover.

NOTE

I am grateful to Elizabeth Olmstead, niece of Katharine Lee Bates, for her special gift of *Yellow Clover*, and to Joy Hennig and Judith Jaffe, Pine Manor College librarians, for their help.

---

[7] Its drama is one that Bates herself had described in 1908 in a review of Sophie Jewett's translation of "The Pearl," when a man's daughter in Heaven appears to him in a dream and "teaches him the mysteries of faith, and guides him to a hilltop whence he catches glimpses of the New Jerusalem. The essential content of the threnody—its anguish of loss, its wistful look into Paradise—is of universal appeal" (Review).

WORKS CITED

Balch, Emily Green. "Katharine Coman: Biographical Sketch." *The Wellesley College News* (April 1915): 2–7.

Bates, Katharine Lee. "Christina Rossetti." Unpublished manuscript. 3P Katharine Lee Bates Papers. Manuscripts of various writings. Manuscripts of Prose: Undated, 1877.

———. "Musarum Sacerdos." *The College Beautiful and Other Poems.* Boston: Houghton, 1887. 20.

———. "The Passing of Christina Rossetti." *The Dial.* (March 1, 1895): 135.

———. Review of "The Pearl." *The Dial.* (Dec. 16, 1908): 450–52.

———. *Yellow Clover.* New York: Dutton, 1922.

Blauvelt, Mary Taylor. "Memories." *The Wellesley College News.* (April 1915): 13.

Boos, Florence S. "An (Almost) Egalitarian Sage: William Morris and Nineteenth-Century Socialist-Feminism." *Victorian Sages and Cultural Discourse.* Ed. Thais Morgan. New Brunswick: Rutgers UP, 1990. 187–206.

Burgess, Dorothy. *Dream and Deed: The Story of Katharine Lee Bates.* Norman: U of Oklahoma P, 1952.

Craft, Christopher. " 'Descend, and Touch, and Enter': Tennyson's Strange Manner of Address." *Homosexual Themes in Literary Studies.* Ed. Wayne R. Dynes and Stephen Donaldson. New York: Garland, 1992.

Donne. The Laurel Poetry Series. New York: Dell, 1962.

Faderman, Lillian. *Surpassing the Love of Men.* New York: Morrow, 1981.

Flowers, Betty. " 'Had Such a Lady Spoken For Herself': Christina Rossetti's 'Monna Innominata.' " *Rossetti to Sexton: Six Women Poets at Texas.* Ed. Dave Oliphant. Austin, Texas: The Harry Ransom Humanities Research Center, 1992. 13–29.

Halsey, Olga S. Letter quoted in "Memories." *The Wellesley College News.* (April 1915): 15. Originally published in "The Survey." (Jan. 23, 1915).

Harrison, Antony H. "Christina Rossetti and the Sage Discourse of Feminist High Anglicanism." *Victorian Sages and Cultural Discourse: Renegotiating Gender and Power.* Ed. Thais E. Morgan. New Brunswick: Rutgers UP, 1990. 87–104.

The Holy Bible. King James Version.

Horowitz, Helen. *Alma Mater.* 2nd ed. Amherst: U of Massachusetts P, 1993.

Jenkins, Ruth Y. *Reclaiming Myths of Power: Women Writers and the Victorian Spiritual Crisis.* Lewisburg: Bucknell UP, 1995.

Lears, Jackson. *No Place of Grace: Antimodernism and the Transformation of American Culture, 1880–1920*. New York: Pantheon, 1981.

LeVay, John. "Christina Rossetti's 'Monna Innominata #10.' " *The Explicator* 46.2 (Winter 1988): 17–19.

Marsh, Jan. *Pre-Raphaelite Women*. London: Weidenfeld and Nicholson, 1987.

Maurer, Margaret. "The Circular Argument of Donne's 'La Corona.' " *Studies in English Literature* 22.1 (Winter 1982): 51–68.

Palmieri, Patricia Ann. *In Adamless Eden: The Community of Women Faculty at Wellesley*. New Haven: Yale UP, 1995.

Pearce, Lynne. *Woman/Image/Text: Readings in Pre-Raphaelite Art and Literature*. Toronto: U of Toronto P, 1991.

Pinnington, Adrian. "Prayer and Praise in John Donne's 'La Corona.' " *Poetry and Faith in the English Renaissance*. Ed. Peter Milward. Tokyo: The Renaissance Institute, 1987. 133–42.

Rosenblum, Dolores. *Christina Rossetti: The Poetry of Endurance*. Carbondale: Southern Illinois UP, 1986.

Rossetti, Christina G. *Poems*. Boston: Little, Brown, 1898.

Rothblum, Ester D., and Kathleen A. Brehony, eds. *Boston Marriages*. Amherst: U of Massachusetts P, 1993.

Schenck, Celeste M. "Feminism and Deconstruction: Re-Constructing the Elegy." *Tulsa Studies in Women's Literature* 5.1 (Spring 1986): 13–27.

Schwarz, Judith. "*Yellow Clover*: Katharine Lee Bates and Katharine Coman." *Frontiers* 4.1 (1986): 59–67.

Scudder, Vida. "Religious Life." *The Wellesley College News* (April 1915): 21–22.

Shatto, Susan, and Marion Shaw. *Tennyson: In Memoriam*. Oxford: Clarendon, 1982.

Shires, Linda M. "Rereading Tennyson's Gender Politics." *Victorian Sages and Cultural Discourse: Renegotiating Gender and Power*. Ed. Thais E. Morgan. New Brunswick: Rutgers UP, 1990. 46–65.

Smulders, Sharon. "Women's Enfranchisement in Christina Rossetti's Poetry." *Texas Studies in Literature and Language* 34.4 (Winter 1992): 568–88.

Walker, Julia. "The Religious Lyric as a Genre." *English Language Notes* 25.1 (Sept. 1987): 39–45.

Weathers, Winston. "Christina Rossetti: The Sisterhood of Self." *Victorian Poetry* 3 (Spring, 1965): 81–89.

Whitla, William. "Questioning the Convention: Christina Rossetti's Sonnet Sequence 'Monna Innominata.' " *The Achievement of Christina Rossetti*. Ed. David A. Kent. Ithaca: Cornell UP, 1987. 82–131.

Wordsworth, William. *The Poetical Works of William Wordsworth*. Cambridge Edition. Boston: Houghton Mifflin Company, 1982.

10

In the Churchyard, Outside the Church: Personal Mysticism and Ecclesiastical Politics in Two Poems by Charlotte Smith

John M. Anderson

MUCH OF WHAT WE CALL GREAT POETRY, the poetry that stands most securely at the center of the canons of literature however much change may occur on its fringes, owes its stability to the fact that it is grounded in a foundation of shared narratives, genres, and tropes acquired in the course of a classical education. Writers who have been denied access to such an education (for reasons, most usually, of race, class, or gender) have often grounded their work in another, more broadly accessible tradition—that of the scriptures and of religious experience in general.[1] This tradition is, however, a hazardous source of raw materials because it partakes of revealed Truth; the very qualities which may make religious subjects attractive to "minor" poets— the certainty of its seriousness, the familiarity and at the same time the mystery of its imagery, and the strictly dogmatic conventions of religious expression (as opposed to the profound individuality which often characterizes individual religious experience)—may

[1] Donna Landry characterizes the poems of one such group, eighteenth-century working-class women, as "a discourse elaborately coded and formalized: the same genres, modes, tropes, and preoccupations occur again and again, apparently without mutual recognition. . . . We can characterize this verse by the predominance of class-conscious georgic and pastoral poems, verse epistles to women, poems critical of marriage and of women's condition in general, poems in response to much-admired (usually male) poets, and versified narratives from the Scriptures" (13).

lead sophisticated readers to shy away from this poetry.[2] Such readers may give religious poetry superficial attention, may judge according to prejudice and thus never distinguish the valuable from the worthless. Thus, little magazines in *The Poets' Market* that receive floods of unsolicited submissions often seek to reduce the numbers by including in their advice to contributors the phrase "No Religious Poetry, Please." In the end, a canonical bias against religious poetry has necessarily contributed to the historical exclusion of important underprivileged poets, including women poets. The immense critical effort at present to restore to the canon important women poets of the past will necessarily involve re-reading, reconsidering, and perhaps appreciating for the first time much notable religious poetry.

A fine example is Charlotte Smith (1749–1806), who—besides being the author of a series of popular (often political) novels—often wrote poetry about religion. She never paraphrased the scriptures, as many of her contemporaries did, but the religious questions she addresses range from the social role of the church to psychological portraits of a woman's struggle between faith and despair. These are, of course, two quite different aspects of religion, and Smith addresses them in very different poetic forms—the one in an epic of powerful rhetoric and subtle political ideas, and the other in sonnets of psychological insight. We have remained too long unaware of the important social concerns, the complex ambiguities, the epic strength and lyrical passion of Charlotte Smith, who, as a religious poet, looks forward to George Eliot and Emily Dickinson.

These writers were not given to sweeping summary rejections like Shelley's "The Necessity of Atheism" or Keats's "Written in Disgust of Vulgar Superstition"; still less did they invent alternative mythologies in the manner of Blake. Their associations with established religion, as a social fact and as a source of language and imagery, went far too deep for such a response. Like Eliot and Dickinson, Smith underwent a complex struggle with the established church and defined a position for herself outside orthodoxy. Like Shelley's, Smith's reasons were certainly political,

---

[2] Roger Lonsdale writes, "The misrepresentation of the verse written by women in the eighteenth century of which I am most conscious is the limited space I have devoted to their efforts in the more ambitious or morally earnest genres, their pindaric odes, paraphrases of Scriptures, hymns" (xliv).

shaped by her support of the ideals of the French Revolution. Yet she places the most prominent explicit statement of her position—the ending of her epic *The Emigrants*—in the strongly apolitical imagery of an isolated soul finding completely sufficient communion with her God in nature.

The passage in question consists of only thirty-three lines, in a poem of nearly nine hundred. But the contemporary cultural significance of these lines is clear from the overwhelming critical response they received. Though other passages were more often quoted by critics—especially the action sequences which eventually made up the "fragment" that Smith later excerpted from her most ambitious poem—none received more critical comment. The reviewer for the *British Critic*, for example, expressed strong displeasure at considerable length:

> we lament that the gifted powers of imagination should be so grossly perverted, and we cannot but suspect that vanity (which absorbs all other considerations) predominates in the mind of a writer, who can court applause by the affectation of a criminal singularity. . . . This writer makes it her boast, that for her part she needs no exhortation to piety, since the works of creation serve her for that purpose. And, let us ask, what good heart do they *not* influence in the same manner? . . . Yet the genuine philosopher will not be content with silent meditation among hills and rocks: living, as he does, in social intercourse, he will join in social worship. (406)

This critic suggests ironically that Smith is affecting to avoid the crowd precisely in order to "court [its] applause." While the whole context of *The Emigrants* makes it clear that this "apolitical" passage does have political reverberations—that Smith has perhaps set herself apart from the crowd partly in order to address the crowd—the purpose is not to "court applause" but to commune with God. A rather more careful reading of the passage is clearly called for.

Though, like Wordsworth's nuns, she never fretted at working within the narrow room of the sonnet,[3] Smith, in her poetry, is rarely comfortable indoors. Like Dickinson, she rejoices in a free and solitary thought beyond the strictures and the censure of con-

---

[3] Wordsworth acknowledged that he read Smith's sonnets before composing his own.

ventional society. But Dickinson would find this freedom and solitude in the confines of her room; Smith repeatedly finds it outdoors.[4] The church inspires in her a kind of moral claustrophobia.

Smith concludes her long poem with a kind of verse Last Will and Testament, and she thus reflects upon her own death, upon the reputation which will outlive her. She expects to be blamed, among other things, for her church attendance.

> And if, where regulated sanctity
> Pours her long orisons to Heaven, my voice
> Was seldom heard, . . . yet '*my prayer*' was made
> To him who hears even silence; not in domes
> Of human architecture, fill'd with crowds,
> But on these hills. (*Emigrants*, II.387–92)

Smith's conventional, female personification of "sanctity" here allows her to contrast this cool abstraction and her passionate self. The abstract regularity of "sanctity" is apparent in the structure of its "domes," so geometrical in comparison to the unpredictable, natural shapes of "these hills." *The Emigrants* is a political poem, and it is appropriately the church's exterior, political aspect that Smith objects to in these lines. She considers its interior, spiritual claims to mystical efficacy only by implication; these seem distorted by the oppressively regular forms that contain them.

She proceeds adroitly to a landscape imagery that is intricately designed to demonstrate that nothing essential is lost in moving beyond these forms.

> I made my prayer
> In unison with murmuring waves that now
> Swell with dark tempests, now are mild and blue,
> As the bright arch above; for all to me
> Declare omniscient goodness. (II.401–405)

The sea is the manifestation of God in these lines. Its atmospheric extremes are reconciled in the single concept of "omniscient

---

[4] Dickinson was never confined in her imagination, of course, and her poem "Some keep the Sabbath going to Church—," though it speaks of "staying at home," is similar to Smith's in its outdoor setting, among other things.

goodness." Smith emphasizes that her escape to the wilderness has not, in the end, removed her so far from the "crowds," or from the conventions of church service. Like a preacher, she seems to have chosen a text, here from Psalm 65:7, which speaks of God stilling "the noise of the seas, the noise of their waves, and the tumult of the people." As the Psalmist's words point out, the fickle and "murmuring waves" are not much different from the crowds Smith has tried to leave behind. And Smith, exercising what her critic called "a criminal singularity" by praying outside the community, presents herself praying in quite orthodox "unison" with this crowd, away from any "dome," perhaps, but nevertheless beneath a church-like "arch."

The "bright arch above" to which Smith refers is a uniform blue and thus seems here to indicate the vault of the sky, though in architectural terms. The word "arch" is more appropriate to the rainbow—certainly an apt image, scriptural, in this context. But the rainbow, a prismatic analysis of pure white light, is an image fundamentally at odds with the "unison" upon which Smith insists.

The ironic contradictions of language and of the speaker's positioning of herself in relation to the community become more pronounced in the lines that follow:

> nor need I
> Declamatory essays to incite
> My wonder or my praise, when every leaf
> That Spring unfolds, and every simple bud,
> More forcibly impresses on my heart
> His power and wisdom. (II.405–10)

Pursuing a familiar argument against the corrupting intervention of language in favor of a pure direct experience of the Creation (an argument which has, despite its antiquity, come to sound so "Wordsworthian"), Smith continues to reject the community that shares the language in common, to champion instead the unspoken "impressions" made by Nature.

But like any such argument expressed in the very language it aspires to reject, this one cannot stand up to analysis. And Smith's speaker herself is less naïve than she may seem; she certainly chooses her examples shrewdly. Like the pure blue of the "bright

arch," the single green that suffuses a natural "leaf" surely presents a clearer message than the artificial leaves of books with their
eternally striving blacks and whites; yet the one like the other
requires reading, though being "forcibly impresse[d]" sounds like
a more passive process. And buds do come across as "simple"
though each contains within it the potential for both fruit and
seed—and for all the forked twigs of future trees. Still more suspi-
ciously ingenuous is Smith's selection of "Spring" for her examples. It is stacking the deck in Nature's favor, surely, to make no
mention of Winter.

But this manipulated imagery serves a rhetorical purpose of
demonstrating the poet's generous willingness to give Providence
the benefit of the doubt. She must establish that she has the best
intentions, for she is about to venture into still more explosive
territory. Still writing in a sympathetic, unimpassioned tone,
Smith seeks to distinguish between the praiseworthy moral and
emotional essence of religion and the destructiveness that occurs
when this essence is corrupted.

> Saint-like Piety,
> Misled by Superstition, has destroy'd
> More than Ambition. (II.415–17)

The simplicity which finds its strength in purity, Smith suggests
in an aphorism so filled with allegorical figures that it seems orac-
ular, can easily become the simplicity of naïveté. This is an argument which seems unexceptionable when it is applied to any sect
other than one's own, and Smith allows her readers to think here
of the misled Catholics, rather than to apply the observation
closer to home. Yet this depiction of over-zealous true-believers
can be applied to excuse, or at least explain, the excesses of one's
own community, religious or political. Smith erases the distinction:

> the sacred flame
> Of Liberty becomes a raging fire,
> When License and Confusion bid it blaze. (II.417–19)

With these lines, Smith returns to the explicitly political focus of
The Emigrants, and indeed the remainder of the poem is wholly
political, though it takes the form of a prayer.

Having examined the adroit political positioning which Charlotte Smith the epic poet achieves in an explicitly religious passage, it is the more enlightening to examine the subtle metaphysical explorations pursued by Charlotte Smith the writer of sonnets. Immediately before the passage I have quoted from *The Emigrants*, Smith gives a brief demonstration of the orthodox piety which she is about to bring into question; she paraphrases Thomas Gray's famous "Elegy Written in a Country Churchyard": "'I gave to misery all I had, my tears'" (II.386). One of her Elegiac Sonnets again recalls the Gray poem, but from the heightened remove of an almost Gothic context.

In comparison to *The Emigrants*, which remained out of print from its first publication in 1793 until Smith's collected poetry was published two hundred years later, Elegiac Sonnet XLIV, "Written in the church-yard at Middleton in Sussex" (which I shall refer to for the sake of brevity as the "Middleton" sonnet) has been reprinted rather often. It is one of the most prominent poems in recent anthologized selections of Charlotte Smith's work. Though it is not among the eight Smith poems selected by Dale Spender and Janet Todd for their 1989 anthology, it is one of the seven in Roger Lonsdale's landmark anthology of the same year, and Jennifer Breen includes it among the four Smith poems in her 1992 anthology.[5] Here is the text of the poem, including Smith's footnote.

> Press'd by the Moon, mute arbitress of tides,
>   While the loud equinox its power combines,
>   The sea no more its swelling surge confines,
> But o'er the shrinking land sublimely rides.
> The wild blast, rising from the Western cave,
>   Drives the huge billows from their heaving bed;
>   Tears from their grassy tombs the village dead,★
> And breaks the silent sabbath of the grave!
> With shells and sea-weed mingled, on the shore
>   Lo! their bones whiten in the frequent wave;
>   But vain to them the winds and waters rave;
> *They* hear the warring elements no more:
> While I am doom'd—by life's long storm opprest,
> To gaze with envy on their gloomy rest.

---

[5] See Spender 294–99; Lonsdale 367–68; Breen 39–42.

*Middleton is a village on the margin of the sea, in Sussex, con-
taining only two or three houses. There were formerly several acres
of ground between its small church and the sea, which now, by its
continual encroachments, approaches within a few feet of this half-
ruined and humble edifice. The wall, which once surrounded the
church-yard, is entirely swept away, many of the graves broken up,
and the remains of bodies interred washed into the sea; whence
human bones are found among the sand and shingles on the shore.[6]

A superficial reading of these lines might tempt us to dismiss
them lightly as sentimental. They create perhaps a melancholy
mood, a *frisson* of horror even—but little more than the fireworks
of a minor poem. More considered rereadings lead to the recognition of something more profound. This is a considerable religious
sonnet, worthy of the tradition of John Donne. The "Middleton"
sonnet is a small masterpiece of compression, in which the poet
has underscored her meanings with every resource available to
her: the ambiguities and allusive reverberations of her language,
the sound patterns created by that language, and the imagery it
evokes. Ezra Pound would someday call these aspects of a poem
logopoeia, *melopoeia*, and *phanopoeia*, respectively, but in favor of a
simpler—though less precise—terminology, I will call them sense,
sound effects, and imagery. Though these characteristics of the
poet's art all function simultaneously, I will artificially untwist the
strands in order to examine them each thoroughly.

The poem's most immediate impressions are probably visual.
Smith has chosen a visually striking scene—the scattered bones of
the churchyard, laid bare by the raging sea, lying white in the
moonlight—made more striking by the juxtaposition of antitheti-
cal images. The "warring elements" of wind and water rage in
stark contrast with the serenity of the moon above and the "grassy
tombs" below. And the vastness of the sea and sky emphasizes the
vulnerability of the little churchyard and its "village dead." This
scene, which might have served as a subject for any number of
Romantic painters—a Delacroix, say, or a Turner—is made still
more Romantic by the addition of the melancholy figure of the
speaker in the final couplet, whose whole life is epitomized as a
"long storm." If this depiction of sublime nature has a religious

---

[6] Lonsdale excludes the footnote, Breen restores it.

significance, it is surely one of despair, a dark night of the soul.
Yet this speaker is contemplative. A final striking contrast made
visible by the picture Smith paints here is that between the insistent, intrusive physical world and the brooding, self-aware, interpreting mind that gazes "with envy on [the bones'] gloomy rest."

The imagery of this sonnet presents a moody study of contrasts,
then, emphasizing the irreconcilable elements of the scene. The
despair that these images convey arises from their striving, contradictory polarity. But this polarity is on the surface of the poem.
Its sound effects, which work on a profounder and perhaps less
conscious level, produce exactly the opposite effect. They weave
these disparate elements together in intricate patterns which emphasize their unexpected similarities. Much of the religious power
of the "Middleton" sonnet is the result of the subliminal workings
of its unifying musical quality; to understand its religious depth,
therefore, it is important first to examine in detail the sound effects by which Smith implies a divine order underlying and per-
vading the chaos of her visible world.

There is far more rhyming, far more sound effects of every
kind, in the "Middleton" sonnet than the sonnet form requires.
The poem begins, for instance, with a kind of ABBA form within
the first line: *Press'd, Moon, mute, arbitress*. The painstaking brick-
work of such patterning establishes a firm, resisting foundation—a
consoling foundation of sounds which has little to do with ration-
ality—within and upon which the poem's violent action and argument swirl. This patterning pervades the poem, from its first
word, "Press'd," which rhymes with its last word, "rest." It must
be noticed that these boundary-marking words rhyme, furthermore, in a particular way. The sound of *rest* is simply *Press'd* without its opening letter—an effect familiar from those "echo"
poems in which the rhyming words diminish.[7] And the meanings
of these two words are as nearly opposite as are their positions at
the beginning and the end. The moon's pressing provides all the
motion in the poem; the "rest" (a word which incidentally recalls
the "remains"—all that is left—which Smith mentions in her
footnote as well as "Rest in Peace") brings that motion to an

---

[7] A more famous religious poet than Smith—George Herbert—is perhaps the
most remarkable practitioner of this technique. In his "Paradise," a poem in
which the guiding metaphor is that of pruning, the rhyme words are themselves
pruned: Grow, Row, Ow; Charm, Harm, Arm; and so on.

end. It is a kind of musical "rest" as well, a silence. The moon is characterized as "mute"—an adjective which reflects audibly back on the noun with both alliteration and assonance. This silence characteristic of the governing moon is important in a poem of sound effects, where silence is a sign of both death and resurrection.

But before it reaches this final "rest," the poem is full of music. Smith employs both alliteration and assonance to great effect throughout. Consider the abundance of v's in lines 5–11. The rhyming nouns *cave* and *grave* (5, 8)—which "rhyme" in their sense as well as their sound—are rhymed again with *wave* and *rave* (10, 11)—and to this overflow is added *Drives, heaving, village,* and *vain.* And this v-sound returns in the final line—where it is used for the first time to describe an internal state, *envy.* This unusual, evocative, reverberating consonant provides a unifying note that vibrates quietly but insistently beneath the poem (and beneath the surface hiss of the equally insistent alliteration on the letter s). This musical constant softens the modulation when the sonnet shifts from the wide range and the wild noise of the octave to the hushed, reflective focus of the sestet.

Note the long-*i* sounds in the first five lines–all four of the rhyme words for the first quatrain—*tides, combines, confines, rides; while* and *sublimely, wild* and *rising.* With the first word of line 6, *Drives,* this sound suddenly ceases, to reappear only twice, as highlighting in the Rembrandt-gloom of lines 6–12: *silent* and *whiten.* In stark contrast, the sound appears three times in the penultimate line: *While, I,* and *life's.* Moreover, each of these words is essential. *While* marks the shift of meaning at the beginning of the couplet; *I* introduces the speaker for the first time; and *life's* explicitly expands the poem's specific imagery to a general application. A similar echo, again providing a darker contrast for the bright long-*i,* occurs when the interior rhyme of *doomed* and *gloomy* in the final couplet picks up the sound of the "moon, mute" in the opening.

The sounds and sights that the sonnet presents are emphatic, perhaps even verging on the melodramatic, but Smith creates all these effects in a nearly conversational tone which argues at last for an aesthetic of realism.[8] None of the images or sound effects

---

[8] This aesthetic distinguishes the "Middleton" sonnet from such hypnotically

seems unnatural or calls attention to itself in the manner of Smith's Della-Cruscan contemporaries. The same understated realism applies to the sense of the "Middleton" sonnet. Especially in her footnote Smith insists upon the "two or three houses" of the village, and its "small," "humble" church. This subdued presentation of the subject does nothing to diminish the poem's symbolic aspirations. It is appropriately set in a place called Middleton, beside a "half-ruined church," for it pivots quite thoroughly between a literal, materialistic, empirical expression of a melancholy longing for death on one hand, and on the other a metaphorical, allusive expression of hope in transformative resurrection.

Such ambiguities go to the heart of the poem. This sonnet is about the equinox, described as a powerful time of year—though an event of the solar, not the lunar calendar—but nowhere does it indicate which equinox is meant. The same word describes two quite different moments. Do we have here to do with the autumnal equinox, when all nature turns from light into darkness? Read with the right intonation, it is a spooky poem, and the traditional Christian holidays around the autumnal equinox, especially Halloween and All Souls' Day, fit it well. Or the vernal equinox, which marks the turning point from the death of winter's cold darkness toward the warm light of spring and life? The poem does not declare—it thus invites us to try each possibility. This equinox is not only powerful but "loud"—an odd adjective for the noun in any other poem than this.

Throughout the "Middleton" sonnet, the language revels in an almost Dickinsonian ambiguity. Let us take a single line (one which might have been written by Dickinson) as an example: "O'er the shrinking land sublimely rides." The word *shrinking* is both a literal description of the land which is being reduced in size by the action of the waves and also a personification of the land as a sentient creature which can draw back in fear. The word *sublimely* is a precise term for the kind of aesthetic effect the sea is producing, erasing boundaries, defying comprehension—but it is a deeply ambivalent effect, one which fascinates by horrifying.

"sounding" religious works as Gerard Manley Hopkins's "The Leaden Echo and the Golden Echo" which use very similar devices more extremely to achieve much the same effect of religious unity.

Finally, *rides* is very curiously employed here. Perhaps the word is used according to this OED definition: "(8) To float or move upon the water"—though Smith's line reverses the imagery and lets the water "move upon" the land. But other definitions may tell us at least as much: (9b), for instance, is "Of heavenly bodies: to appear to float in space," a definition which has much to recommend it, in a poem with such an explicitly sublunar setting (and the OED supports this definition with two citations from Milton about the moon). And the whole structure of the poem encourages support for (10) "To rest or turn *on* or *upon* something of the nature of a pivot." The pivoting that is the central motion of Smith's sonnet is made possible by such verbal ambiguities.

But she avails herself of ambiguities of structure as well. Take the opening image of the moon, for example. Seen only glancingly and never mentioned again, it is the only gendered figure in the poem; like "sanctity" in the *Emigrants* passage above, the moon is female (this is, in any case, a traditional Western conceit, from Artemis onward). We have seen already that this moon's pressing brings about all the action in the poem. She resembles the poet, and her abrupt disappearance is mirrored by the abrupt appearance of the speaker in the final couplet. In many of Smith's sonnets the moon plays an important role.[9] And here the moon causes the sea to rave, like the "lunatic" of another important Smith sonnet, LXX, "On being cautioned against walking on an headland overlooking the sea, because it was frequented by a lunatic" (Smith 61). That poem ends with Smith's speaker feeling the same "envy" for the lunatic as she feels here for the dead.

The *Elegiac Sonnets* as a whole provide one literary context for reading the "Middleton" sonnet—a context which emphasizes the tensions of its ambiguities. But for a religious understanding of the poem, there is clearly a still more important source, and not an unexpected one in a poem about a churchyard: the Bible. The Biblical story this poem most conspicuously recalls is a famous passage from Ezekiel, the allegory of the dry bones. "So I prophesied as I was commanded: and as I prophesied there was a noise, and behold a shaking, and the bones came together, bone to his bone" (37:7). It is a hopeful, resurrectional passage, in

---

[9] Beginning with Elegiac Sonnet IV, "To the moon"(Smith 15) and continuing through LXX, "To the invisible moon" (Smith 69).

which God proceeds to promise "I will open your graves, and cause you to come up out of your graves, and bring you into the land of Israel" (37:12). But if Smith recalls this passage, she complicates her allusion by reversing important details: the bones Ezekiel is shown are most emphatically very dry; those that lie beneath Smith's gaze are very wet; Ezekiel speaks of a noise, Smith of silence. And most remarkably, Ezekiel presents his parable as a triumphant erasing of ambiguity, of difference, "And I will make them one nation in the land upon the mountains of Israel; and one king shall be king to them all; and they shall be no more two nations, neither shall they be divided into two kingdoms any more at all" (37:22). Smith seems to find a definitive explanation as well, but it is despair. The only hope available in the "Middleton" sonnet is the possibility of ambiguity. The "grassy" tombs of line 7 evoke a proverbial image of the brevity of human life—but it is clearly at the same time evidence of the triumph of life over death, as poets from King David to Whitman have implied.

There are a number of apocalyptic images in the poem—the sea rages beyond its limits, contrary to the promise God makes to Noah in Genesis 9:11. The dead leave their places of rest (see Matthew 27:52–53: "And the graves were opened; and many bodies of the saints which slept arose, And came out of the graves after his resurrection"), breaking the "silent sabbath of the grave!" The moon, which we learn in Genesis exists largely to mark holy days, is necessarily closely connected to the Sabbath. "Thus saith the Lord God: The gate of the inner court that looketh toward the east shall be shut the six working days; but on the sabbath it shall be opened, and in the day of the new moon it shall be opened" (Ezekiel 46:1). The Sabbath marks a boundary like the sea. "Or who shut up the sea with doors, when it brake forth, as if it had issued out of the womb. . . . And said, Hitherto shalt thou come, but no further: and here shall thy proud waves be stayed?" (Job 38:8, 11).

But of course Christ breaks the Sabbath repeatedly. And he justifies this behavior by referring to a higher reality, in much the same terms as Smith will use in *The Emigrants*. "Or have ye not read in the law how that on the sabbath days the priests in the temple profane the sabbath, and are blameless? But I say unto you, That in this place is one greater than the temple" (Matt. 12:5–6).

The Resurrection itself is presented in the Gospels not as a break-ing of the Sabbath, but as superseding it. "In the end of the sab-bath as it began to dawn toward the first day of the week" (Matthew 28:1). A number of places in the Gospels which deal with this issue seem particularly relevant to the poem. Christ him-self used the question of the Sabbath to explore polarities very like those in which Smith has positioned her poem. "Then said Jesus unto them, I will ask you one thing: Is it lawful on the sabbath day to do good, or to do evil? to save life, or to destroy it?" (Luke 6:9). These dichotomies are very much in accordance with the prophets; Ezekiel presents God bemoaning priests who "have put no difference between the holy and profane, neither have they shewed difference between the unclean and the clean, and have hid their eyes from my sabbaths, and I am profaned among them" (Ezek. 22:26). But the difficulty is the very ambi-guity of the proof text. According to one interpretation it might be used to justify Christ's labors on the Sabbath; according to another it is the very passage to condemn them. In a fundamen-tally similar way, the same words which express the speaker's de-spair in the "Middleton" sonnet express her hope as well.

Charlotte Smith's religious opinions are impressively difficult to pin down in either of these poems. The subtly shifting rhetoric of her consideration of the church as a political entity is as ambiv-alent as the Negative Capability apparent in her psychological portrayal of religious experience. Her view from the inside out is as volatile and provocative as her view from the outside in. She never reaches the complacent or conventional stasis which we are too ready to expect of religious poetry. It is certainly time to expose the vivid bones of poetry long buried beneath such expec-tations; they may clatter unexpectedly together and take on new life.

WORKS CITED

Breen, Jennifer, ed. *Women Romantic Poets: 1785–1832: An Anthology.* London: Dent, 1992.

British Critic. 1 (1793): 406.

Landry, Donna. *The Muses of Resistance: Laboring-Class Women's Poetry in Britain, 1793–1796.* Cambridge: Cambridge UP, 1990.

Lonsdale, Roger, ed. *Eighteenth-Century Women Poets*. Oxford: Oxford UP, 1989.

Smith, Charlotte. *The Poems of Charlotte Smith*. Ed. Stuart Curran. Oxford: Oxford UP, 1993.

Spender, Dale, and Janet Todd, eds. *British Women Writers: An Anthology from the Fourteenth-Century to the Present*. New York: Bendrick, 1989.

11

The Sacramental Vision of Gerard Manley Hopkins

J. Robert Barth, S.J.

FOR MANY YEARS after his poetry first came to public notice, Gerard Manley Hopkins was naturally thought of and discussed as a Modern poet. He was, after all, first published in 1918 and was influential for such undeniably twentieth-century poets as Dylan Thomas, Robert Graves, and C. Day Lewis. Then in the 1960s, Hopkins was rediscovered as a Victorian poet. He was, we are reminded, a contemporary of Tennyson and Arnold, a student of Pater, a disciple of Newman. Now, I suggest, it is time for us to see Hopkins as being also in the tradition of the great Romantics: Keatsian in his sensuous imagery; Shelleyan in his remarkable ability to capture in words the swiftness of movement; Wordsworthian in his eye for the details and nuances of the natural world; Coleridgean—and indeed Wordsworthian—in his awareness of the relationship between the created world and the world of transcendent reality. It is this last characteristic—Hopkins's sacramental sense—that is the object of the following reflections.

We can perhaps best approach the "sacramental vision" of Gerard Manley Hopkins by savoring it first in his own words, by feeling the "stress" of it in our own hearts. Thus I begin with the opening stanzas of that great poem, "The Wreck of the Deutschland":

1

Thou mastering me
God! giver of breath and bread;
World's strand, sway of the sea;
Lord of living and dead;
Thou hast bound bones and veins in me, fastened me flesh,
And after it almost unmade, what with dread,
Thy doing: and dost thou touch me afresh?
Over again I feel thy finger and find thee.

2

I did say yes
O at lightning and lashed rod;
Thou heardst me truer than tongue confess
Thy terror, O Christ, O God;
Thou knowest the walls, altar and hour and night:
The swoon of a heart that the sweep and the hurl of thee trod
Hard down with a horror of height:
And the midriff astrain with leaning of, laced with fire of stress.

3

The frown of his face
Before me, the hurtle of hell
Behind, where, where was a, where was a place?
I whirled out wings that spell
And fled with a fling of the heart to the heart of the Host.
My heart, but you were dovewinged, I can tell,
Carrier-witted, I am bold to boast,
To flash from the flame to the flame then, tower from the grace
to the grace.

4

I am soft sift
In an hourglass—at the wall
Fast, but mined with a motion, a drift,
And it crowds and it combs to the fall;
I steady as a water in a well, to a poise, to a pane,
But roped with, always, all the way down from the tall
Fells or flanks of the voel, a vein
Of the gospel proffer, a pressure, a principle, Christ's gift.

5

I kiss my hand
To the stars, lovely-asunder
Starlight, wafting him out of it; and
Glow, glory in thunder;
Kiss my hand to the dappled-with-damson west;
Since, tho' he is under the world's splendour and wonder,
His mystery must be instressed, stressed;
For I greet him the days I meet him, and bless when I understand.

There is a whole theology of sacrament implicit in these remarkable lines. First, there is the centrality of that sacrament so
dear to Hopkins's heart, the Eucharist—as, alone before the altar,
he "fled with a fling of the heart to the heart of the Host." It is
what the Christian sacrament must be, a personal encounter between the Christian and God, mediated through the person of
Christ in the sharing of the sacrificial meal. It is an encounter in
love, here mediated through suffering but transforming suffering
into light: "To flash from the flame to the flame then, tower from
the grace to the grace."

But beyond this "great sacrament" from among the seven can-
onized by the Church, the poet himself is clearly sacrament, a
sensible sign mediating God's presence: "Thou hast bound bones
and veins in me, fastened me flesh." He is "stressed" with the life
of God himself, sustained by grace as underground streams feed a
well:

> I steady as a water in a well, to a poise, to a pane,
> But roped with, always, all the way down from the tall
>   Fells or flanks of the voel, a vein
> Of the gospel proffer, a pressure, a principle, Christ's gift.

The poet himself, like every Christian who shares in the life of
Christ, is himself a sign, whether in suffering or in joy, of the
presence of God in the world, because he lives with the very life
of God.

In a November 7, 1883, letter, Hopkins wrote of his special use
of the term "stress" that it is "the making a thing more, or making
it markedly, what it already is; it is the bringing out its nature"
(*Letters* 179). For Hopkins the life of humankind is "stressed" with
the energy of God himself. Humankind is by its very nature not
only human but Godlike; that "stress" from God makes mankind
"markedly" what he or she already is—both human and a sharer
in the divine nature: "Acts in God's eye what in God's eye he
is— / Christ" ("As kingfishers catch fire"). The poet, like every
sharer in human nature, is a sacrament of God's presence to the
world.

Even beyond this, the world itself is sacrament for Hopkins.
God is in the starlight and the thunder, and the poet—kissing his
hand to the stars—can waft him out of it. God is "under the

world's splendour and wonder," but as mystery—to be pondered and plumbed. This divine presence is not the mystery of ultimate incomprehensibility, but the mystery that is (in I. A. Richards's memorable phrase) "inexhaustible to meditation" (Richards 171). "His mystery must be instressed, stressed": it must be impressed on us ("stressed") that his "stress," his life and energy, is everywhere. Then this divine energy must be kept at stress *within* us, so that we shall be ready to meet him—so that we too can "flash from the flame to the flame, tower from the grace to the grace"—so that we can "greet him the days we meet him, and bless when we understand."

Very clearly, the foundation for this sacramental vision is the Incarnation of Christ. As the world itself might be said to be, by virtue of the Creation, the *primal* sacrament—the first sensible sign of God's presence outside himself—in the new dispensation Christ is the *prime* sacrament. In the memorable phrase of the Dutch theologian Edward Schillebeeckx, Christ is "the sacrament of the encounter with God." It is Christ who, for the Christian, mediates the life, the energy, the "stress," of the Godhead to humankind and to the world. To the world: "This piece-bright paling shuts the spouse Christ home" ("The Starlight Night"); and to humankind: "Christ plays in ten thousand places, / Lovely in limbs and lovely in eyes not his" ("As kingfishers catch fire").

But for Hopkins the Incarnation is focused through a very special prism, the *Spiritual Exercises* of St. Ignatius Loyola. This remarkable little book was deeply formative for Hopkins, as it is for every follower of St. Ignatius in the Society of Jesus. It is neither a book of devotion nor a rule of life; it is not even a blueprint for a retreat. It is, rather, a set of guideposts for a journey, but a journey whose guideposts are often markers at crossroads—where personal decisions must be made and ultimately one must trust God to point the way.

Because the *Spiritual Exercises* are so deeply rooted in the Incarnation of Christ, they are filled with Ignatian particularities. This is fostered by the belief, as Walter Ong writes, that "each and every one of the specific actions in Jesus' life were, individually, infinitely salvific" (74). A familiar passage in the *Autobiography* of St. Ignatius records how in the Holy Land he bribed a watchman so that he could return to the supposed site of the Ascension and verify the direction in which Jesus's feet were pointing at the moment he ascended into Heaven (Ong 75). In the *Spiritual Exercises*, Ignatius is insistent that the exercitant, contemplating a mystery of the life of Christ, imagine as vividly as possible the details of the scene: the cave of the Nativity, where it is situated, what is looks like; the Garden of Gethsemane, its shape, its size; how Jesus conducts himself with his disciples, with his mother, with those who oppose him—how he speaks and walks and gestures. And this insistence on specificity in the life of Jesus is matched by Ignatius's concern for the details of the exercitant's own life, whether during the retreat or outside it: the position of the body in prayer, the forms of address one uses, what one eats and drinks, how one works and plays.

But these particularities—whether in the life of Christ or in one's own life—are not for their own sake. As Walter Ong says, Ignatius uses detail—and wants his exercitants to use detail—"as a means of implementing or recalling or extending a personal relationship" (75). Throughout the four so-called "weeks" of the *Spiritual Exercises*—the foundational week of the encounter with God through one's own sinfulness, the second week of the encounter with Christ in his ministry, the third week of sharing in the Passion of Christ, the climactic week of the Risen Life—the emphasis is on personal encounter between the individual and God. It is significant that each exercise, whether on one's own sinfulness or on some touching moment in the life of Christ, moves through the details into a "colloquy"—a conversation in which one finds one self alone with God, praising, sharing, listening. And it is precisely through the particularities—of Christ's life and ours—that God reveals himself.

To see this in Hopkins's poetry one can look almost at random, for the central concept of "inscape" that informs all his mature poetry expresses precisely this love of and attention to the particularities of things. Inscape is, after all, that which makes any created thing to be what it is: inscape is its innate principle of individuality, its "inner landscape." We see such tender attention to the specificities of creation in the "bright boroughs" and "circle-citadels" of "The Starlight Night"; in "the glassy peartree leaves and blooms" that "brush the descending blue" in the poem "Spring"; and in the "silk-sack clouds" and "azurous hung hills" of "Hurrahing in Harvest." Such loving records of inscape are everywhere in Hopkins.

But the theological principles that undergird this view are also frequently enunciated. In "God's Grandeur," it is both the power of God and the loving presence of his Holy Spirit that continue to quicken things with life.

> The world is charged with the grandeur of God.
>   It will flame out, like shining from shook foil;
>   It gathers to a greatness, like the ooze of oil
> Crushed. Why do men then now not reck his rod?
> Generations have trod, have trod, have trod;
>   And all is seared with trade; bleared, smeared with toil;
>   And wears man's smudge and shares man's smell: the soil
> Is bare now, nor can foot feel, being shod.
>
> And for all this, nature is never spent;
>   There lives the dearest freshness deep down things;
> And though the last lights off the black West went
>   Oh, morning, at the brown brink eastward, springs—
> Because the Holy Ghost over the bent
>   World broods with warm breast and with ah! bright wings.

There is no created thing—not the dirt that smudges our face, not the smell of our body, not the earth beneath our feet—that is not instressed by God's presence: "There lives the dearest freshness deep down things"—all things. For over our "bent world" the Holy Ghost broods and abides.

"No wonder of it," either. For the source of all the quirks and particularities of our world is the Maker of it, who fathers it forth out of his own boundless being, as we see in "Pied Beauty":

> Glory be to God for dappled things—
>   For skies of couple-colour as a brinded cow;
>   For rose-moles all in stipple upon trout that swim;
> Fresh-firecoal chestnut-falls; finches' wings;
>   Landscape plotted and pieced—fold, fallow, and plough;
>   And all trades, their gear and tackle and trim.
>
> All things counter, original, spare, strange;
>   Whatever is fickle, freckled (who knows how?)
>   With swift, slow; sweet, sour; adazzle, dim;
> He fathers-forth whose beauty is past change:
>   Praise him.

But it is perhaps in his "kingfisher" poem that Hopkins expresses most explicitly the incarnational principle that is implicit
throughout: that each created being has a God-given "inner
shape"—an inscape—that it must express outwardly, and that for
humankind that inner shape is Christ himself.

> As kingfishers catch fire, dragonflies draw flame;
>   As tumbled over rim in roundy wells
>   Stones ring; like each tucked string tells, each hung bell's
> Bow swung finds tongue to fling out broad its name;
> Each mortal thing does one thing and the same:
>   Deals out that being indoors each one dwells;
>   Selves—goes itself; *myself* it speaks and spells,
> Crying *What I do is me: for that I came.*
>
> I say more: the just man justices;
>   Keeps grace: that keeps all his goings graces;
> Acts in God's eye what in God's eye he is—
>   Christ. For Christ plays in ten thousand places,
> Lovely in limbs, and lovely in eyes not his
>   To the Father through the features of men's faces.

As in the *Spiritual Exercises*, so in all of human experience of the
world, it is in the particularities—the moment the kingfisher
catches fire (catching both the silver fish and the light of the sun
as he strikes the water), the harp string at the moment it is
plucked, the bell echoing with its own sound—that inner being
is revealed. "Each mortal thing does one thing and the same: /
Deals out that being indoors each one dwells." And as we hear
each one "Crying *What I do is me: for that I came,*" we may hear
an echo of Jesus's words to Pilate, "for this was I born, for this
came I into the world" (John 18:37), and reflect that it is not only
Christ—the "firstborn of all Creation"— but all created things,
that glorify God by acting out a destiny, an inscape. Clearly, Hopkins learned well the lesson of Ignatius, which is the lesson of the
Incarnation itself: that it is in the specificities of creation and of
our own experience that we most deeply encounter both the
world and God. The Incarnation of Christ has touched the whole
creation into new life.

We have seen that the *Spiritual Exercises* involve a journey, and
I suggest that this journey is toward the culminating vision of the

Exercises, the "Contemplatio ad Amorem" (Ignatius 103–104). Just as each Exercise moves toward a "Colloquy," the whole of the *Exercises* moves toward a great crowning colloquy, the "Contemplatio"—the "Contemplation for Obtaining Divine Love." The "Contemplatio" is a privileged source for Hopkins's sacramental view of self and the world, for here we can see how his sacramental view is truly symbolic.

The "Contemplatio" begins with the reminder that love is shown in deeds more than in words, and above all in a mutual sharing of self and all one has between lover and beloved. The four points of the Exercise then proceed to demonstrate how God shares with humankind: first, by the gifts he gives, such as Creation itself, Redemption by Christ, and the particular gifts of one's own life; then, how God not only gives to us but even dwells in his creatures—in the elements of the earth, in plants, in animals, above all in mankind, his image; next, how God acts, even labors, within all created things, charging them as it were with the energy of their being; finally and climactically, the exercitant is asked to imagine all these gifts—filled with God's presence and energy—descending from heaven, like the rays of light from the sun or water from a fountain. Clearly the movement is into deeper and deeper union between ourselves and God, a deeper intensity of relationship.

Equally important, however, is the response the exercitant is asked to make at the end of each of these four reflections: a personal colloquy of self-offering—a loving response to the love one experiences from God—which Ignatius expresses as follows:

> Take, Lord, and receive all my liberty; accept my memory, my understanding, and my entire will. All that I have and possess you have given to me; I return it all to you, O Lord. All is yours; dispose of it according to your will. Give me only your love and your grace, and I am rich enough and ask for nothing more.

With each of these exchanges of love, one enters more deeply into loving union with God.

The imagery of the closing section of the "Contemplatio ad Amorem" is particularly significant: the rays of light descending from the sun, the water flowing down from the fountain. Such an intensity of union has been reached that one can no longer

separate the beloved from the lover: the rays of light, the down-
flowing water, are not separate from their source—distinct, yes,
but not separate. Such a phenomenon is what Samuel Taylor
Coleridge has called the "translucence" of symbol. In his great
essay *The Statesman's Manual* (in which he explores the imagination at work in sacred Scripture), Coleridge writes of symbol:

> a Symbol . . . is characterized by a translucence of the Special in
> the Individual or of the General in the Especial or of the Universal
> in the General. Above all by the translucence of the Eternal
> through and in the Temporal. It always partakes of the Reality
> which it renders intelligible; and while it enunciates the whole,
> abides itself as a living part in that Unity, of which it is the represen-
> tative. (30)

We now turn aside for a moment to explore this Coleridgean
notion of the translucence of symbol, which will be brought to
bear shortly on the *Spiritual Exercises* and on Hopkins.

When Coleridge speaks of a symbol "abiding itself as a living
part in that Unity, of which it is the representative," the Unity he
is speaking of is God, imaged here (implicitly) as light. As I have
expressed it elsewhere, "if a symbol of the Eternal is 'translucent,'
then God is the light that passes through it—the Eternal revealing
itself 'through and in the Temporal' " (Barth, "Scriptural" 137).
Throughout the Bible (Coleridge's privileged example of symbolic expression), God—the Eternal—is constantly revealing
himself in and through the Temporal, whether it be in a person
like Abraham or David, an action like the crossing of the Red
Sea, or through the very rich profusion of the creation itself. "In
the Bible," Coleridge says, "every agent appears and acts as a self-
subsisting individual: each has a life of its own, and yet all are one
life" (*Statesman's Manual* 31). God is distinct from Abraham, from
the Red Sea, from his creation—but he is not separate from them;
he remains abidingly present in his power and in his love.

The image of a stained-glass window may serve to explain this
conception. The colored window and the light of the sun are
quite distinct, but in an act of vision they are not separate; the sun
and the stained-glass are "translucent" to each other. We perceive
them, not separately, but in a single act of vision. This is "symbolic" vision: not merely metaphor, in which one reality "points

to" another that remains separate from it; but symbol, in which two realities—distinct but not separate—have become so intimately united that we cannot perceive one without the other. The same light at once reveals both; they are "translucent" to each other.[1]

This is what takes place, I suggest, as one reaches the climax of the "Contemplatio ad Amorem": the lover and the beloved, God and man, become so intimately united in love that they are perceived together, in a single act of seeing—as the rays that emanate from the sun remain one with it, as the water from the fountain is one with its source. I suggest that this is what happens, too, in the most intense of Hopkins's poetry: his experience of the "Contemplatio ad Amorem" flows over into his poetic experience, so that his vision of created reality is at the same time a vision of the Creator.

Something of this poetic is implicit in Hopkins's view of Mary in his remarkable poem, "The Blessed Virgin compared to the Air we Breathe." Mary's role is, in effect, analogous to that of all creation: "who / This one work has to do— / Let all God's glory through." Through her, as through creation itself, God and humankind are united, so that humankind becomes at the same time more Godlike and, with lovely irony, more itself.

> Men here may draw like breath
> More Christ and baffle death;
> Who, born so, comes to be
> New self and nobler me. (lines 66–69)

Like the stained-glass window, Mary—and by implication, I think, all creation—allows God to be present to the world in a way that we can grasp. In the poem, a hand lifted up as a shield from the sun becomes, like the stained-glass, a means of mediating God's glory:

> Again, look overhead
> How air is azurèd;
> O how! Nay do but stand
> Where you can lift your hand

---

[1] This image and Coleridge's notion of translucence are discussed in "Coleridge's Scriptual Imagination," 137–38. See also Barth's "Theological Implications of Coleridge's Theory of Imagination."

> Skywards: rich, rich it laps
> Round the four fingergaps.
> Yet such a sapphire-shot,
> Charged, steepèd sky will not
> Stain light. Yea, mark you this:
> It does no prejudice.
> The glass-blue days are those
> When every colour glows,
> Each shape and shadow shows.
> Blue be it: this blue heaven
> The seven or seven times seven
> Hued sunbeam will transmit
> Perfect, not alter it.
> Or if there does some soft,
> On things aloof, aloft,
> Bloom breathe, that one breath more
> Earth is the fairer for. (lines 73–93)

Were it not for Mary, for human flesh, for creation—which makes God visible to us—we could not know him as we do:

> A mother came to mould
> Those limbs like ours which are
> What must make our daystar
> Much dearer to mankind;
> Whose glory bare would blind. . . .
> Through her we may see him
> Made sweeter, not made dim,
> And her hand leaves his light
> Sifted to suit our sight. (lines 104–13)

We can distinguish this softer light of creation from its source, "whose glory bare would blind," but we cannot separate them; they are one light, one glory. We can distinguish God and his creation, but we cannot separate them; they are bound together, one in life, one in love. To know and love creation is to know and love God, the Author of creation.

In order to achieve this perception—of God and his creation in a single act of vision—one must have what Hopkins calls a "single eye." The phrase is from "The Wreck of the Deutschland," where it is attributed to the tall nun, the leader of the five Franciscan nuns who went to their death on the fateful night of

December 7, 1875. In the midst of terror and suffering, of darkness and confusion, she found Christ, calling out to him: "O
Christ, Christ, come quickly"— "The cross to her she calls Christ
to her, christens her wild worst Best." To the poet, only she read
the true meaning of the shipwreck:

29

Ah! there was a heart right!
There was single eye!
Read the unshapeable shock night
And knew the who and the why:
Wording it how but by him that present and past,
Heaven and earth are word of, worded by?—
The Simon Peter of a soul! to the blast
Tarpeian-fast, but a blown beacon of light.

But if this is true of the nun in the midst of the storm, it is also
true of the poet, who is called to the same vision—as are all who
read him. He and all of us are meant to aspire to the "heart right"
and the "single eye." As she read "the unshapeable shock-night"
and "knew the who and the why"—knowing God in the
storm—the poet too can do so. For him, as for her, the storm can
be "translucent," revealing God even as it hides him. He is truly
"under the world's splendour and wonder."

   We turn finally to two sonnets which express perhaps most
completely Hopkins's ideal of the "single eye," by which his symbolic, translucent vision of a sacramental world is perceived and
articulated.

   The first is "Hurrahing in Harvest," in which the poet dramatizes precisely the coming together—in the experience of the
poet's "single eye"—of the beauty of creation, the glory of the
Savior, and the heart of the beholder.

Summer ends now; now, barbarous in beauty, the stooks rise
Around; up above, what wind-walks! what lovely behaviour
Of silk-sack clouds! has wilder, wilful-wavier
Meal-drift moulded ever and melted across skies?

I walk, I lift up, I lift up heart, eyes,
Down all that glory in the heavens to glean our Saviour;
And, eyes, heart, what looks, what lips yet gave you a
Rapturous love's greeting of realer, of rounder replies?

And the azurous hung hills are his world-wielding shoulder
Majestic—as a stallion stalwart, very-violet-sweet!—
These things, these things were here and but the beholder
Wanting; which two when they once meet,
The heart rears wings bold and bolder
And hurls for him, O half hurls earth for him off under his feet.

In the opening quatrain, we see earth and sky already moving toward unity: the fields forced upward, as "the stooks" (the shocks of grain) "rise around"; the sky in turn taking on characteristics of earth and its harvest—the "wind-walks," the "silk-sack clouds" ready to hold the grain, the "meal-drift" look of yet other clouds. In the second quatrain, the poet "gleans" from this harvest of sky the Saviour he longs to see. Clearly, the Creator has been deeply present in his creation. Indeed the very hills are, as the sestet begins, "his world-wielding shoulder." The movement toward unity continues, as the beholder of all this beauty at last becomes explicitly part of the sum: "which two when they once meet." The result is the ecstatic vision we feel at the close of the poem, as the poet is drawn outside himself, possessed in loving union by the Saviour and all the beauty of his creation. The earth has turned almost upside down for him, because he has experienced God and the world in a new and exciting way.

But note that his heart only "*half*-hurls earth for him off under his feet," because the Saviour is present in the world as well as outside it, is both immanent and transcendent. Just as in the opening lines earth and sky become one yet without losing their identity—distinct but inseparable—so at the close the poet and the Saviour he has gleaned, the earth and its Creator, remain themselves even as they are bound together in an ecstatic union of love.

The earth and its harvest are for the poet sacraments—indeed transcendent symbols—mediating the presence of God in "rapturous love's greeting." The earth and sky, the harvest, the poet himself, all partake of the being of God: in Coleridge's words, a symbol "always partakes of the reality which it renders intelligible." Clearly, for Hopkins these fields were indeed "white for the harvest," and the harvest —for him as for us—is the Saviour who instresses them with his life and energy.

In "The Windhover," on the other hand, the Saviour does not appear; there is no explicit transcendent dimension. There is only the beautiful bird—and the poet in hiding.

THE WINDHOVER:
To Christ our Lord

I caught this morning morning's minion, king-
　　dom of daylight's dauphin, dapple-dawn-drawn Falcon, in
　　　his riding
　　Of the rolling level underneath him steady air, and striding
High there, how he rung upon the rein of a wimpling wing
In his ecstasy! then off, off forth on swing,
　　As a skate's heel sweeps smooth on a bow-bend: the hurl and
　　　gliding
　　Rebuffed the big wind. My heart in hiding
Stirred for a bird,—the achieve of, the mastery of the thing!

Brute beauty and valour and act, oh, air, pride, plume, here
　　Buckle! AND the fire that breaks from thee then, a billion
Times told lovelier, more dangerous, O my chevalier!

　　No wonder of it; shéer plód makes plough down sillion
Shine, and blue-bleak embers, ah my dear,
　　Fall, gall themselves, and gash gold-vermilion.

The kestrel, "dapple-dawn-drawn"—sketched out against the beauty of the dawn as if by an artist's hand—dominates the morning sky with the authority of a regal figure, and its movements have the beauty and energy of a great horse or of its royal rider. This bird is the first-born of the kingdom of daylight and it is clearly master of the elements.

The poet, in hiding from this masterful bird of prey, is awestruck by a power and grandeur almost beyond his ken. But as he watches—as he admires the union (the "buckling" together) of "brute beauty and valour and act, oh, air, pride, plume"—suddenly all this beauty "buckles" (now taking the verb in quite another sense): the bird draws in its wings to dive toward its prey, the poet in his hiding place on earth. In this moment, as the predatory bird becomes its truest self—as the kingfisher does in the moment it strikes the water—it reveals its inscape, its destiny.

Diving to earth it reveals itself to be both beautiful and dangerous.
Nor should one be surprised at this duality, for many things contain their opposites: the plow in the earth shines from use and the
seemingly dead embers of a fire burst forth into flame, like the
flash of fire the plummeting bird becomes as it dives toward the
earth and its poet-prey.

A poem about a bird? Yes, clearly and triumphantly so—about
a bird and a poet. And yet, lest our reading stop at this, in his last
revision Hopkins added the dedication: To Christ our Lord. It is
as if he would draw our attention beyond the beauty of a stained-
glass window, asking us to be aware of the light it mediates. But
the window and the light cannot be perceived separately; they
have so "interpenetrated" that they must be seen together. So too
with the windhover and Christ, in the poet's vision of them:
Christ and creation have so interpenetrated that they cannot be
separated; as in the "Contemplatio ad Amorem," God and his
creation are distinct but not separate. "Ah! There was a heart
right! / There was single eye!"

The poet's problem was, of course, that we do not all have
—or at least do not yet have—that "single eye." We cannot all
yet "read the unshapeable shock night / And know the who and
the why." Thus he must give us the clue we need: "To Christ
our Lord." Given that single key, we need no further referent
within the poem. We can see, as the poet saw, not a metaphor
and its referent outside itself, but the referent *in* the symbol—the
sunlight interpenetrating the stained-glass window—the Lord
Christ *in* the lordly falcon, the Creator *in* his creation.

Through Hopkins's poetry, we draw close not only to creation
but to the Creator, not only to beauty but to "beauty's self and
beauty's giver." For the Holy Ghost does indeed "over the bent /
World brood with warm breast and with ah! bright wings."

WORKS CITED

Barth, J. Robert, s.j. "Coleridge's Scriptural Imagination." *Coleridge,
    Keats, and the Imagination: Romanticism and Adam's Dream—Essays in
    Honor of Walter Jackson Bate.* Ed. J. Robert Barth, s.j., and John L.
    Mahoney. Columbia: U of Missouri P, 1989. 135–42.

————. "Theological Implications of Coleridge's Theory of Imagination." *Studies in the Literary Imagination* 19 (1986): 23–33.

Coleridge, Samuel Taylor. *The Statesman's Manual. Lay Sermons.* Ed. R. J. White. Vol. 6 of *The Collected Works of Samuel Taylor Coleridge.* Ed. Kathleen Coburn. Bollingen Series 75. Princeton: Princeton UP, 1972.

Hopkins, Gerard Manley. *The Poems of Gerard Manley Hopkins.* Ed. W. H. Gardner and N. H. MacKenzie. 4th ed. London: Oxford UP, 1967.

————. *Further Letters of Gerard Manley Hopkins.* Ed. Claude Colleer Abbott. 2nd ed. London: Oxford UP, 1956.

Ignatius of Loyola. *The Spiritual Exercises of St. Ignatius.* Trans Anthony Mottola. New York: Image-Doubleday, 1964.

Ong, Walter J. *Hopkins, the Self, and God.* Toronto: U of Toronto P, 1986.

Richards, I. A. *Coleridge on Imagination.* Bloomington: Indiana UP, 1960.

Schillebeeckx, Edward, O.P. *Christ the Sacrament of the Encounter with God.* New York: Sheed & Ward, 1963.

12

Reading Modern Religious Autobiographies: Multidimensional and Multicultural Approaches

David Leigh, S.J.

TWENTIETH-CENTURY RELIGIOUS AUTOBIOGRAPHY calls for a new method of reading. Because modern life, as Yeats said, "seems to be a preparation for something that never happens," modern spiritual autobiographers have struggled to find meaning that is not easily provided by religious, social, or philosophical traditions. Often separated from the mediation of a religious community, alone as faceless individuals in a pluralistic society, and living without a definite sense of a self or a master story, recent autobiographers have had to become authors of themselves by using many of the methods of prose fiction to construct a plausible story of their search for ultimate meaning. The modern Augustine or Teresa must also be a Faulkner or Woolf.

As autobiographies, according to Roy Pascal, these stories discover and create a unified movement from a coherent standpoint of their entire lives in which the external events symbolize their inner journeys. As religious autobiographies, these stories involve a spiritual search for Mystery, a search which is seen, from the standpoint of a later conversion, to be a pattern of orientation, wandering, and return to a relationship with an ultimate source of meaning. Among the hundreds of such spiritual autobiographies of this century, readers seem to have acclaimed a handful of classics. I would suggest the following ten to be close to canonization: Mohandas Gandhi's *An Autobiography: The Story of My Experiments with Truth* (1929), Black Elk's *Black Elk Speaks* (1932),

Thomas Merton's *Seven Storey Mountain* (1949), Dorothy Day's *The Long Loneliness* (1954), C. S. Lewis's *Surprised by Joy* (1955), Nikos Kazantzakis's *Report to Greco* (1961), Malcolm X's *The Autobiography of Malcolm X* (1965), Paul Cowan's *An Orphan in History* (1982), Rigoberta Menchu's *I, Rigoberta Menchu* (1983), and Nelson Mandela's *Long Walk to Freedom* (1994). In this essay, we will explore how readers might use modern literary methods—textual, contextual, and intertextual—to understand and critique these classics of modern religious autobiography.

READING AN AUTOBIOGRAPHY AS A NOVEL

To read an autobiography as if it were a novel calls for close analysis of the structural patterns of the text—narrative point of view, plot outline, character roles and development, image patterns, use of metaphor, symbol, and language, and, finally, the use of silence. First, bringing to the reading a formalist, structuralist, and deconstructivist eye, the reader learns to discern the religious standpoint from which the story is told. For many of these ten classics, the final viewpoint is that of the fully converted believer—the Catholic monk Merton, the Anglican layman Lewis, the orthodox Muslim Malcolm X, the conservative Jewish Cowan, or the liberation activist Menchu with her synthesis of Catholic and native ways. For some, the horizon shifts from an earlier religious viewpoint to a later secular and political one (Mandela), or to a later "transubstantiated horror" of looking at an ultimate "abyss" with a "Cretan Glance" (Kazantzakis 486). These points of view are often given in the preface, as when Gandhi describes his story as of a man striving for "self-realization, to see God face to face" through a series of "experiments" in the "political field" and the "spiritual field" (xii–xiii). Even when he disclaims any final or absolute truth, Gandhi claims to have reached a standpoint that seems as close to Truth as he can be at that time. Only Kazantzakis explicitly denies that he has reached a stable viewpoint, affirming in its place that, after ascending four steps (Christ, Buddha, Lenin, and Odysseus) of religious, political, and aesthetic experience, he has reached a summit that is only a "Cretan Glance" at the life force. The final horizon of the autobiographer also expresses itself in most of these stories through Bakhtinian multiple voices in

each of the episodes of the plot, one voice describing the immediate experience of a temporary viewpoint, the other voice critiqu-
ing the inadequacy of that viewpoint. For instance, Malcolm X
repeatedly expatiates on events or beliefs as a member of the Nation of Islam, only to end the section by telling the reader that
the event would be "prophetic" (265) or that "in years to come,
I was going to have to face a psychological or spiritual crisis" of
his excessive faith in Elijah Muhammed (210).

The plot outline of most modern religious autobiographies is
that of the spiral pilgrimage. In this pattern, the author maps out
the life story in a three-stage narrative: first, the childhood orientation in which the seeds of later transformations are sown
through questions, experiences, and influences; second, the adolescent and young adult wanderings in a downward spiral toward
objects that are the opposite of the earlier seeds; third, a final
upward stage in which the questions are answered and the seeds
of transformation harvested. In each of the stages, parallel persons,
events, or symbols often appear, as in the unfeeling father of Day's
lonely youth, the false father-lovers of her wanderings, and the
transforming father in Peter Maurin at the Catholic Worker.
Within the third stage of spiritual transformation, the narrator
may undergo several further conversions, as when Malcolm X
becomes first a Black Muslim and later an orthodox Moslem, or
when Merton seeks first to be a Franciscan friar and later a Cistercian monk, or when Lewis thinks his way to becoming first a
theist and later a Christian. Kazantzakis, of course, does not follow
this pattern, presenting instead his life as a steady ascent through
Greek Christianity, Eastern Buddhism, Russian communism, and
finally an Odyssean aesthetic view of the abyss.

Among the "characters" of modern autobiographical plots, the
reader will discover the "hero" to be the narrator/author, but not
as a simple source of action and reflection. As a modern person
without a commonly accepted definition of the "self," the narrator will play a series of roles or experiments with his or her identity. Merton becomes the precocious boy, the adolescent aesthete,
the Cambridge dissipate, the Big Man on Campus at Columbia,
the aspiring novelist, the Franciscan postulant, and only finally the
Trappist novice. Malcolm X changes his clothes and appearance
as he moves from being a neglected child, a youthful "mascot,"
an adolescent hipster, a young adult hustler, a captured prisoner, a

Black Muslim devotee, a national spokesman for the Nation of Islam, and finally a universalist Moslem. Menchu grows from being a naïve village girl to become a catechist, a witness to martyrdom, a native feminist, and a practitioner of liberation theology. Surrounding the "hero" on the spiral pilgrimage are a series of "mediators," either false, temporary helpers, or true, permanent guides to a final conversion. Black Elk speaks of his father and mother, his shaman, and his cousin Crazy Horse as his most important guides on his journey to spiritual leadership among the Lakota Sioux. C. S. Lewis describes his mediators as either friends (Owen Barfield, J. R. R. Tolkien) or books (George MacDonald's fantasies, Samuel Alexander's philosophy). Nelson Mandela speaks mostly of his political mentors, some of whom, like Oliver Tambo, were also spiritual guides in his youth. False or temporary mediators can be found in Gandhi's teenage bad companion, in Merton's worldly godparents in London, in Malcolm X's Elijah Muhammed, or Dorothy Day's friend Rayne Proehme.

In all these classic conversion stories, the reader will uncover a pattern of "directional images," usually derived from childhood experience or notions, and then followed throughout the three-level plot. For example, one finds Merton shaping his self-image as that of a "captive traveler" seeking a permanent home to replace the unstable houses of his childhood. One reads Day's story as a search for "communion," expressed in imagery of family meals, which will overcome the "long loneliness" of her youth and wandering. C. S. Lewis's childhood fascination with a toy garden produced a lifelong image of Paradise. Gandhi's fascination with the Truthfulness of his father led to the very subtitle of his books and to his image of God as Truth. Black Elk has a vision at the age of nine of a circular ideal of harmony for which he searches and leads his people during his adult years. Paul Cowan's exiled orthodox grandfather, Malcolm X's nightmare of racial conflicts, Kazantzakis's Cretan grandfather challenging him to "reach what you cannot," Nelson Mandela's early tribal picture of harmony amid diversity—all these are instances of directional images, from which the metaphoric patterns of the autobiographies emerge. Thus, Merton's "captive traveler" will summarize his life in the final paragraph of his story as a God-driven journey "from Prades to Bermuda to St. Antonin to Oakham to London to Cambridge to Rome to New York to Columbia to Corpus

Christi to St. Bonaventure to the Cistercian Abbey of the poor men who labor in Gethsemani" (423–24).

Along with an awareness of these image patterns, the reader of modern autobiography must be sensitive to language—both the language which expresses the self and the silence which obscures the self. Because many of these modern spiritual writers are journalists, or their story is told with the help of a journalistic ghost writer, the style of their stories is relatively unpoetic. But most authors weave together a factual account of external events with reflective comments and analyses, as in the opening paragraph of Merton's *Seven Storey Mountain* or the first chapter of Dorothy Day's *The Long Loneliness* on her ancestors. Here Merton and Day describe their birth or family in journalistic style of place, date, and circumstances, and then reflect on the event with a theological commentary drawn from their later religious experience. Merton, the narrator who "came into the world" on "the last day of January 1915 . . . in the year of a great war," becomes in the next sentence "the prisoner of my own violence and my own selfishness, in the image of the world into which I was born" (3). Day, the teller of her family history, becomes at the end of the first chapter the adult who "wonders if those stories of our ancestors took away the fear of death that comes to us all, or whether it mitigated it" (15). Analogously, Black Elk and Rigoberta Menchu as oral narrators show the influence of their ghost writers by the sudden appearance of poetic patches in *Black Elk Speaks* or of anthropological vignettes in *I, Rigoberta Menchu*. Although many of the details in these ten autobiographies are for the sake of verisimilitude, nearly all the stories contain symbolic events or use repeated metaphors which give the story a larger dimension. Thus, readers must be alert to the power of organic imagery in Gandhi, of train journeys in Merton, of books in Malcolm X, Day, or Lewis, of rituals in Black Elk, and of home visits to his tribal village in Mandela. These image patterns can, at times, become the primary method of coherence within the plot, serving as both a literary and a theological device. The primary example of this use of symbolic events is Lewis's predominant experience of "joy," which also becomes his theological way into a series of conversions. The childhood experiences of "longing" in response to his brother's toy garden or to the Castlereagh Hills are transformed into similar youthful experiences of unsatisfied Joy in reading Beatrice Potter or Longfellow's *Saga of King Olaf,* all of which reappear in adolescent reading of Norse legends or hearing Wagnerian music. These experiences provide the imaginative basis for his later intellectual and religious conversions.

The gaps or silences, as deconstructionists have taught the reader, can be at times as significant as what the narrator reveals in the plot or symbolic pattern. This is especially true of autobiography, but is not readily evident without contextual information from a competent biography. In the vagueness of Merton's account of his expulsion from England by his godparent, in the unanswered questions raised by Day's story of her brief marriage and European travels, or in the unclear circumstances of the very writing of Gandhi's autobiography during a mid-life crisis—in all these cases, biographers have uncovered some painful facts which make the silences speak loudly to the reader (Mott; Miller; Erikson). Other gaps may occur because the author is telling the story as exclusively an autobiography of the spirit. Thus, C. S. Lewis explicitly leaves out details of his years as a teacher or scholar, or Paul Cowan omits the grind of his life as a reporter for *The Village Voice.* Other gaps occur because of tensions between the outer and the inner journey, as when Kazantzakis "attempts to aestheticize all these elements [of his personality] by giving the entire life an outward coherence it never possessed . . ." (Bien 43). In all these cases, the reader must be alert for puzzling omissions, silences, euphemisms, idealizations, or disguises.

Through a close study of the point of view, plot, characters, image patterns, language, and gaps of these classic modern autobiographies, there emerge several major themes. One common motif is the ultimate significance of early experiences of loss or death, which usually lead to crises, despair, and eventually a search for faith. It is not insignificant that six of these ten classic writers lost a parent in childhood or adolescence: Gandhi's father, Merton's mother and then father, Lewis's mother, Malcolm X's father, Menchu's father and mother, and Mandela's father. Among the others, the child Black Elk experiences his father's getting wounded; young Kazantzakis spends a chapter describing the loss of his grandfather; Day is effectively disowned by her father when she is eighteen; and Paul Cowan begins to write his autobiography in mid-life following upon the painful death of both his parents in an apartment fire. A second motif in these stories is that of the power of writing (or speech, in the oral narratives) as a method of meeting spiritual crises or resolving inner conflicts. Several of these authors—Gandhi, Merton, Day, Lewis, Kazantzakis, Cowan, Mandela—told parts of their life stories in novels or articles before writing their full spiritual autobiographies. A third common motif is that of *place*, the journey from one to another place constituting both the structure of the plot and the thematic of the inner life pattern. Gandhi travels physically and spiritually from Porbandar to London to South Africa and then throughout India in his experiments with Truth; Merton travels from France to Long Island to Bermuda to France again, then to England and New York and finally to Kentucky in his search for a true home; Kazantzakis leaps from Crete to Greece to Italy to Jerusalem to Paris to Vienna to Berlin to Russia, before returning full-circle to the land of Odysseus and Zorba; Mandela's long walk takes him to all parts of South Africa (as well as Africa) in his pursuit of freedom. Another motif is that of various experiences of God—from Merton's *aseitas*, to Day's "communion," to Lewis's sense of Joy or longing, to Kazantzakis's mixture of the abyss and *élan vital*. For all of them, their journey is a purifying or transforming of both their notion of God and their response to the divine presence or absence. Thus Gandhi announces in his introduction to his autobiography that "I worship God as Truth only. I have not yet found Him, but I am seeking after Him" (xiv). His story consists of his "experiments" with relative human truth in order to bring it closer to Absolute Truth. Finally, as we shall see in a later section of this essay, most autobiographers in this century pattern their lives on the theme of conversion, radical transformation of their deepest selves on all levels. This thematic pattern, however, is more adequately discussed in relation to the next major section of this essay, that of the context of modern spiritual autobiographies.

READING RELIGIOUS AUTOBIOGRAPHIES IN CONTEXT

Although each autobiographer tells a story of a unique self, the reader of the texts finds, as we have suggested, a number of common patterns through a formal analysis of the stories as variety of prose fiction. But these common patterns vary greatly in their contexts—whether psychological or familial situations, social or cultural environments, philosophical or religious backgrounds, and even the methods of writing or producing the autobiographies. Let us examine the significance of these four contexts for the ten classic religious autobiographies.

Psychological and Family Situations

Recent developmental psychologists have described patterns of human growth that can assist the reader of autobiographies to better understand the psychic and family contexts of the authors. For Erik Erikson, each stage from infancy through adulthood is seen as a struggle of the self for a particular virtue which overcomes the tensions between two challenges (e.g., love overcoming the tensions between intimacy and isolation in Stage 6 of his system). For Lawrence Kohlberg, each stage is a mental and moral process of differentiation brought about by moral conflicts. For Carol Gilligan, adding a dimension from her study of female development, all stages lead toward an ethic of care and responsibility, rather than merely an ethic of rights and principles.

A combination of these three frameworks, as Walter Conn has shown in his study of Merton, or even the extended application of one framework, as Erik Erikson has shown in his study of Gandhi, can be very helpful in understanding these ten spiritual journeys. For instance, the identity crisis as anatomized by Erikson for most teenagers (and especially if modified by Kegan's modification of the crisis by the addition of a stage of adolescent struggle for affiliation in the face of abandonment) can make greater psychological sense out of Merton's youthful enthusiasms, Day's college experiments, or Gandhi's London wanderings. The importance of the identity crisis also helps the reader understand the role-playing of the hustler years of Malcolm X or the growth of Menchu through her roles as catechist, organizer, village leader, and political witness. The stage of intimacy and the struggle for love speaks to the silences of Lewis about his ambiguous relationship with Mrs. Moore, the emotional vulnerability and crushes of Merton, or the conflicted views of women in the stories by Gandhi and Malcolm X. The moral conflicts in the youth of Black Elk, Nelson Mandela, or Rigoberta Menchu also clarify the relative lack of difficulty each of them had in finding an identity and their early entrance into what Erikson calls generativity. These same conflicts perhaps also explain to some extent their silences about their emotional lives.

In all these spiritual autobiographies, the psychological struggle is also part of a family drama. In most instances, the narrator struggles to integrate the conflicting values associated with either parent. Thus Malcolm X strives to synthesize the power values of the black, separatist preacher who is his father, and the contemplative values of the mixed-race, reconciliatory, educated woman who is his mother. Gandhi struggles to integrate the fierce adherence to Truth of his father with the religious vows of Fidelity of his mother. Day fights the inner conflicts coming from tension between her authoritarian, individualist, Victorian father and her sensitive, community-minded mother. Kazantzakis speaks of his "struggle to make a synthesis" of the "twin currents of blood" from his Greek mother and his Arab father (36).

Social and Cultural Contexts

Beyond the psychic and familial context lies the social and cultural territory of each of these spiritual travelers. In most of their autobiographies, the forces of modernity confront the latent resistance of tradition: the former's individualism, technological pragmatism, and secular assumptions are in tension with the latter's communalism, its ultimate concerns, its sacred ontology, and its sense of the sacramental. For Black Elk, Mohandas Gandhi, or Rigoberta Menchu, the cultural imperialism of modern Western society creates the underlying conflict into which the autobiographer is born. Black Elk feels a call to become a shaman for his people and to lead them in resisting the manifest destiny of American economic and military domination of the Black Hills and the native way of life. Gandhi experiments with a variety of practical truths—nonviolence, ashrams, religious education—to resist the British Empire with its modernization of India. Menchu risks her life to protect her traditional native Catholic village life in the highlands of Guatemala. Mandela's autobiography loses its opening spiritual dimension by becoming almost entirely a story of political and cultural resistance to the apartheid regime of the Nationalist Party in South Africa. In less obviously political stories, the autobiographies of Merton, Day, and Cowan express the

struggle of the individual in a secular First World society to recover a religious identity and to work for social transformation
out of religious motives. Other social contexts that permeate these
ten life stories are the rise of racial and feminist movements,
which emerge in Merton's and Day's lives and then become central in Malcolm X's, Menchu's, and Mandela's. The crises of socialism and capitalism, which also deeply influenced Merton, Day,
Kazantzakis, Malcolm X, Menchu, and Mandela, constitute essential elements in their personal and social conversions.

Religious Contexts

The religious contexts of these modern classics of autobiography
provide an overview of the spectrum of twentieth-century faiths.
Lewis, Day, and Merton embody traditional Christian conversions within their Protestant or Catholic communities. Gandhi's
experiments with truth include dialogue with Christians but remain ultimately an expression of his Hinduism. Malcolm X's life
story moves him into two forms of Muslim religion, the marginal
American form in the Nation of Islam and then the worldwide
form of orthodox Islam. Paul Cowan's *An Orphan in History* tells
the story of his recovery of Judaism, first through his encounter
with orthodox rabbis and later through his adoption of a conservative synagogue in New York City. Both Black Elk and Rigoberta Menchu combine in their life stories their traditional native
religions and Catholicism, but in Black Elk's story, the latter phase
is left out by the translator, John Neihardt, whereas in Menchu's
narrative, the speaker clearly shows her ability to synthesize
Christian "liberation theology" beliefs and practices with her native way of life. Mandela's childhood reception of his family's
animist traditions with his mother's practice of Methodist Christianity seems to remain with him throughout the narrative, the
native religion expressed in his recurrent dream of returning to
his village and the Protestantism quietly present in comments on
prison religious services. Kazantzakis's *Report to Greco* reads like a
tour of various ideological islands—Greek Orthodox Christianity,
psychoanalysis, communism, Nietzscheism—all by an Odysseus
without a firm cultural story or spiritual homecoming.

Within this wide context of world religions, the reader also
might gain light from the context of recent theories of conver-

sion. If one accepts the work of Walter Conn on this subject, one finds in these stories instances of at least five types of personal and social transformation. As a "conversion," these transformations involve a leap from one level to the next of human consciousness, a leap that changes the entire self and its horizon along with restructuring its content of beliefs. The five types of conversion include (*a*) affective conversion of one's feelings from self-centeredness to concern for others' feelings; (*b*) imaginative conversion of one's directional imagery to lead one beyond oneself toward a lifelong search for ultimate meaning; (*c*) intellectual conversion of one's mind from naïve awareness of a given world to reflective self-awareness and the beginning of an authentic sense of truth and value; (*d*) moral conversion of one's values from preconventional concern for simple pleasure and pain to postconventional care for the common good; (*e*) religious conversion of a partial or secular world-view into a commitment to total cosmic meaning in a life story centered on ultimate Mystery.

The clarity and distinctiveness of this five-level conversion theory provides an ideal context for, but does not substitute for, a close reading of spiritual classics. Thus, the reader finds that these ten autobiographies exhibit a variety of patterns of these conversions. For instance, Merton goes through discernible imaginative and intellectual conversions at Cambridge and Columbia, but intermingles his moral and religious conversions, and never gives evidence of a satisfactory affective conversion. Day follows a fairly predictable sequence of development from imaginative conversion in high school to intellectual conversion in college to affective conversion in her working years. Yet her religious and moral transformations merge together as she faces a religious predicament in having to choose between her common-law marriage and her Catholic faith. For Gandhi, moral conflicts in his youth lead to many of his later conversions. Malcolm X seems alone in that his intellectual and religious conversion to the Nation of Islam underpins all his later transformations. Cowan follows the more predictable pattern of five levels, but speaks little of any intellectual transformation in his years at Harvard. What marks almost all these ten autobiographies as modern is that they explicitly include a societal or political transformation as part of their moral or religious conversions. As modern converts in a century of social consciousness and radical change, the final twist on their spiral pilgrimage is toward political commitment. For several of the autobiographers, in fact, this turn to social concern precedes and precipitates their religious transformation (Day, Gandhi, Cowan, Menchu). For Merton, what he entitles a "step to moral conversion" occurs at Columbia University when he becomes a Communist for three months. Later in his search, he finds a more satisfying way to live out his Catholic conversion in his work for Catherine de Hueck's Friendship House in Harlem. For Malcolm X, entry into the Black Muslims means that he has to work on projects for black education and economic change. For Menchu, the call to social change and the call to be a Catholic catechist come together in her work as a liberation teacher in her villages.

The final context of these autobiographies to which the reader should attend is their method of writing and publication. Six of them are composed by the author as narrator of the written text, thereby allowing for direct control of the text by the author, with a few exceptions, such as Merton's addition of a theory of grace and nature in response to his editor's requirement. The other four autobiographies are the combined work of the autobiographer and another person. In *Black Elk Speaks*, the "other" is the white Nebraskan poet John Neihardt, who created a fatalistic framework for the story into which he rearranged the episodes described to him by Black Elk. In Malcolm X's autobiography, Alex Haley, a fellow African-American and journalist, helped the speaker interpolate commentary from his final orthodox Islamic perspective into the text dictated during his earlier Black Muslim years. In *I, Rigoberta Menchu*, the reconstruction of the oral narrative by Elisabeth Burgos-Debray fractured the personal life story with interspersed cultural explanations which make it difficult to evaluate the status of Menchu's liberation theology perspective. Even Gandhi's narrative, written in prison in the form of newspaper columns to respond to a personal and political crisis, loosens its narrative thread because of its method of production.

READING RELIGIOUS AUTOBIOGRAPHIES INTERTEXTUALLY

Just as a reader has to be aware of the complex contexts from which these autobiographies emerge, so too must he or she search for the "master stories" behind these modern stories. There are at least four such intertextual narratives. The central and founding autobiography of the West is Augustine's *Confessions*, which is explicitly mentioned in the autobiographies of Merton and Day, and is certainly influential in Gandhi as well as in the Western writers. Augustine's use of symbolic personal experiences, of biblical and classical allusions, of stages of development, of theological interpretations within the narrative, and his self-consciousness as a rhetorician and writer—all these traits are picked up by these modern autobiographers. The second historical influence comes from the master "success story" of American literature, Ben Franklin's *Autobiography*. Several critics have shown the parallels between Franklin's success story of his self and the far different stories of Malcolm X, Thomas Merton, and Paul Cowan. In Gandhi, we find a sort of inverted Franklin autobiography in that the narrator continuously mixes success stories with failure stories. The third influence comes from oral tradition narratives, such as Native American legends behind *Black Elk Speaks* or Guatemalan witness stories behind *I, Rigoberta Menchu*. These oral traditions help account for the loose structure and colloquial language of these dictated autobiographies. Finally, behind many of these stories of the self lies the tradition of Christian "conversion narratives" begun in the seventeenth century and expressed in such classics as John Bunyan's *Grace Abounding* and Frederick Douglass's *Autobiography*.

To read these contemporary non-traditional autobiographies within the context of twentieth-century individualism and the intertext of previous spiritual autobiographies may lead to the conclusion that these modern stories create a new sort of tradition. To undergo a religious transformation today is to be called to join a tradition of spiritual stories of the self-in-transition. Such stories are not told just for the sake of the teller or the edification of converts. Rather they are told for the readers, who may be at any stage of their own life journeys. As John S. Dunne has shown, the modern story is the failure of the story of the "self" and the search for what Dunne calls the "soul" (or what Merton calls the "deep self"). One step in this modern story is to pass over sympathetically to others' life stories and then to come back to one's own story (Dunne, *Search* chs. 1 and 6). This passing over and coming back with new insight is, for Dunne and many contemporary readers, "the spiritual adventure of our time." Summing up his method, Dunne says, "What one does in passing over is to try to enter sympathetically into the feelings of another person, become receptive to the images which give expression to his feelings, attain insight into those images, and then come back enriched by this insight to an understanding of one's own life which can guide one into the future" (*Way* 53). Thus, the ten classics themselves become new mediators for contemporary readers in their effort to create a life worthy of becoming a spiritual autobiography for future readers.

Works Cited and Consulted

Selected Twentieth-Century Spiritual Autobiographies

Black Elk. *Black Elk Speaks*. As told through John G. Neihardt. 1932. New York: Pocketbooks, 1972.

Burrows, Ruth. *Before the Living God*. Denville, NJ: Dimension, 1981.

Cowan, Paul. *An Orphan in History*. New York: Doubleday, 1982.

Day, Dorothy. *The Long Loneliness*. New York: Harper & Row, 1952.

Gandhi, Mohandas. *An Autobiography: The Story of My Experiments with Truth*. 1929. Boston: Beacon, 1957.

Jung, C. G. *Memories, Dreams, Reflections*. Rev. ed. Aniela Jaffe. Trans. Richard Winston and Clara Winston. New York: Vintage-Random, 1965.

Kazantzakis, Nikos. *Report to Greco*. Trans. P. S. Bien. New York: Simon & Schuster, 1965.

Lewis, C. S. *Surprised by Joy*. New York: Harcourt, 1955.

Mandela, Nelson. *Long Walk to Freedom*. New York: Little, Brown, 1994.

Menchu, Rigoberta. *I, Rigoberta Menchu*. Ed. Elisabeth Burgos-Debray. Trans. Ann Wright. London: Verso, 1984.

Merton, Thomas. *The Seven Storey Mountain*. New York: Harcourt, 1948.

Nolan, Christopher. *Under the Eye of the Clock*. New York: St. Martin's, 1987.

Schweitzer, Albert. *Out of My Life and Thought*. 1933. Trans. C. T. Campion. New York: NAL, 1949.

Vanauken, Sheldon. *A Severe Mercy*. New York: Harper & Row, 1977.

Wakefield, Dan. *Returning: A Spiritual Journey*. New York: Doubleday, 1988.

Weil, Simone. *Waiting for God*. Trans. E. Craufurd. New York: Putnam, 1951.

Selected Criticism of Modern Religious Autobiography

Barbour, J. D. *The Conscience of the Autobiographer*. New York: St. Martin's, 1992.

Bien, Peter. *Nikos Kazantzakis*. New York: Columbia UP, 1972.

Brereton, Virginia Lieson. *From Sin to Salvation: Stories of Women's Conversions, 1800 to the Present*. Bloomington: Indiana UP, 1991.

Conn, Walter. *Christian Conversion*. New York: Paulist, 1982.

Cooper, David D. *Thomas Merton and the Art of Denial*. Athens: U of Georgia P, 1989.

Couser, G. Thomas. *American Autobiography: The Prophetic Mode*. Amherst: U of Mass P, 1979.

Culley, Margo, ed. *American Women's Autobiography*. Madison: U of Wisconsin P, 1992.

Dorsey, Peter A. *Sacred Estrangement: The Rhetoric of Conversion in Modern American Autobiography*. University Park: Pennsylvania State UP, 1993.

Dunne, John S. *The Search for God in Time and Memory*. New York: Macmillan, 1969.

———. *The Way of All the Earth*. New York: Macmillan, 1972.

Eakins, Paul John. *Fictions in Autobiography*. Princeton: Princeton UP, 1985.

Egan, Suzanne. *Patterns of Experience in Autobiography*. Chapel Hill: U of North Carolina P, 1984.

Elbacz, Robert. *The Changing Nature of the Self: A Critical Study of Autobiographical Discourse*. Iowa City: U of Iowa Press, 1987.

Erikson, Erik. *Gandhi's Truth*. New York: Norton, 1970.

———. *The Life Cycle Completed*. New York: Norton, 1984.

Fichtelberg, Joseph. *The Complex Image: Faith and Method in American Autobiography*. Philadelphia: U of Pennsylvania P, 1989.

Fleishman, Avron. *Figures of Autobiography*. Berkeley: U of California P, 1983.

Gilligan, Carol. *In a Different Voice: Psychological Theory and Women's Development*. Cambridge, MA: Harvard UP, 1982.

Griffin, Émile. *Turning: Reflections on the Experience of Conversion*. New York: Doubleday, 1980.

Hawkins, Anne. *Archetypes of Conversion*. Lewisburg, PA: Bucknell UP, 1985.

Jelinek, Estelle C., ed. *Women's Autobiographies: Essays in Criticism*. Bloomington: Indiana UP, 1980.

Kegan, Robert. *The Evolving Self: Problem and Process in Human Development.* Cambridge, MA: Harvard UP, 1982.

Kohlberg, Lawrence. *The Psychology of Moral Development.* San Francisco: Harper & Row, 1984.

Lejeune, Philippe. *On Autobiography.* Ed. Paul John Eakin. Trans. Katherine Leary. Minneapolis: U of Minnesota P, 1989.

Miller, William. *Dorothy Day: A Biography.* San Francisco: Harper & Row, 1982.

Mott, Michael. *The Seven Mountains of Thomas Merton.* Boston: Houghton, 1984.

Olney, James, ed. *Autobiography: Essays Theoretical and Critical.* Princeton: Princeton UP, 1980.

———. *Studies in Autobiography.* New York: Oxford UP, 1988.

Pascal, Roy. *Design and Truth in Autobiography.* Cambridge, MA: Harvard UP, 1960.

Spengemann, W. C. *The Forms of Autobiography.* New Haven: Yale UP, 1980.

Stone, Albert E. *Autobiographical Occasions and Original Acts.* Philadelphia: U of Pennsylvania P, 1982.

Weintraub, Karl J. *The Value of the Individual: Self and Circumstance in Autobiography.* Chicago: U of Chicago P, 1978.

13

"Large and Startling Figures": The Grotesque and the Sublime in the Short Stories of Flannery O'Connor

Michael Raiger

> The world is charged with the grandeur of God.
> It will flame out, like shining from shook foil;
> It gathers to a greatness, like the ooze of oil
> Crushed. Why do men then now not reck his rod?
>
> —GERARD MANLEY HOPKINS, "God's Grandeur"

THE AUTHOR OF "God's Grandeur" raises the central problem that would confront Flannery O'Connor in her fictional work: how to point out to an unapprehending soul the obvious fact that God is everywhere present to creation? However, unlike the great Jesuit poet of Romantic sensibility, hers was a language which did not call forth the beautiful as the image of God's grandeur. Rather, grace for Flannery O'Connor appears in the midst of an absence—a space cleared away by a subtracting imagination and by the compulsion to sin, which nevertheless cannot wholly obliterate God's perduring presence in creation. The example of Hopkins is instructive for understanding Flannery O'Connor, for it points, by way of similitude, to a difference of imaginative preoccupation which is largely determined by historical and cultural circumstances. We recall that Hopkins wrote his "terrible sonnets" in which the absence of God is also drawn in the grief-torn darkness of a soul tormented by searing reflection. But like the Psalms, Hopkins's poetry is divided into two forms of address to God: one in lamentation and suffering in the experience of absence; the other from an abundance of joy in the presence of

God. In contrast, O'Connor's work is clearly monotone; the enjoyment of the natural as the sign of God's presence is completely foreign to her fictional writing.

The source of this difference lies with the audience of each, in regard to which O'Connor stated: "St. Augustine wrote that the things of the world pour forth from God in a double way: intellectually into the minds of the angels and physically into the world of things. To the person who believes this—as the Western world did up until a few centuries ago—this physical, sensible world is good because it proceeds from a divine source" (*Mystery* 157). The metaphysical principle of the analogy of being—that the Creator and created are bound through participation in the act of being, despite the chasm which separates them—serves as the conducting thread to which metaphor connects itself in charging the things of nature with the moving principle of God. With the rise of empiricism and the reign of the literal, this tenuous thread is severed. The poetry of Hopkins stands as a challenge, a strenuous effort to reclaim analogy on the dying embers of the Romantic symbol. Hopkins writes for an age in which the residue of the analogy of being still resonates with some readers just enough so that a poetics of the transcendent is possible.[1] For the modern milieu in which Flannery O'Connor writes, this residue has been entirely covered over by the shimmering surface of the literal, and occluded by the arresting figure of scientism.[2]

---

[1] The idea of the eclipse of analogy by the rhetoric of the literal was first suggested to me in discussions with Blanford Parker on Augustan culture and its philosophical and religious preoccupations. The phrase "the eclipse of analogy," an especially felicitous phrase that describes the ascendancy of the literal over the metaphorical, is from a study that Parker has recently completed on Augustan poetry. See Blanford Parker, *The Triumph of Augustan Poetics: English Poetry from Butler to Johnson.*

[2] My argument that Flannery O'Connor's negative method of representing God's grace is wholly determined by the presuppositions of her readership has been vigorously opposed by various critics. See, e.g., Martha Stevens, *The Question of Flannery O'Connor,* for the argument that O'Connor's religious sensibility is of an entirely otherworldly nature, issuing in a "constant injunction to renunciation of the world" (4), in effect arguing that O'Connor denies the efficacy of Christ's Incarnation. While I disagree with this position, there is evidence that O'Connor did not share with Hopkins a Romantic religious sensibility, as a passage from her letters attests: "In some pious writers there is a lot about the Church being the bride of Christ. This kind of metaphor may have helped that age to get a picture of a certain reality; it fails to help most of us. The metaphor can be dispensed with." See Flannery O'Connor, *The Habit of Being,* 369. On the other hand, O'Connor also sensed the limits of her own approach: "I have

Hopkins's "God's Grandeur" is illustrative of a further concern shared by O'Connor—of marking the paradox that although the world has been made barren by human sin, "for all this, nature is never spent." In a letter written a year before she died, Flannery O'Connor lamented that Catholic critics, in seeking an "ideal intention" in her writing, failed to grasp "its sort of 'inscape' as Hopkins would have had it" (*Habit* 517). The peculiar form of O'Connor's "inscape" is shaped by a double difficulty, owing to the disjunction between her central preoccupation and the predisposition of her readers. O'Connor is concerned with revealing the moment of grace, the location of the "crossroads where time and place and eternity somehow meet" (*Mystery* 59). This amounts to representing the operation of grace, issuing from outside of nature, upon a soul deformed by sin, which is a privation, an absence of good. From the perspective of Thomistic epistemology in which knowledge begins in the senses,[3] the crossroads at which grace and sin must be represented in figures of the sensible—a task of evoking a dual invisibility. It is a difficulty that,

---

got to the point now where I keep thinking more and more about the presentation of love and charity, or better call it grace, as love suggests tenderness, whereas grace can be violent or would have to be to compete with the kind of evil I can make concrete. At the same time, I keep seeing Elias in that cave, waiting to hear the voice of the Lord in the thunder and lightning and wind, and only hearing it finally in the gentle breeze, and I feel I'll have to be able to do that sooner or later, or anyway keep trying. . . ." See *Habit* 373. These two passages, written three weeks apart, suggest that although Flannery O'Connor tended to see the operation of grace as violent rather than comforting, it did not completely obscure her aesthetic vision from the possibility of seeing the natural as a positive sign of God's grace. If the shape of her art was bent into the grotesque, it was due to the dictates of a mimetic art concerned with representing the modern age, rather than issuing from the form of her faith or the shape of her mind and heart. And it is a further loss to us that she did not live to attempt such a representation.

[3] For a brief summary of how Thomistic epistemology informs Flannery O'Connor's understanding of the dynamic between the senses and the understanding with special emphasis on the relation between reason and faith, see Sura P. Rath, "Ruby Turpin's Redemption: Thomistic Resolution in Flannery O'Connor's 'Revelation.'" My essay might be seen, by way of a tropological analysis employing the literary form of analogy as a mode of knowledge, to suggest a resolution to the problems that Rath imputes to Flannery O'Connor's dramatic presentation of the operations of grace. The idea of metaphor as a form of knowledge is explored with great insight in Edward Kessler, *Flannery O'Connor and the Language of Apocalypse*, where argument is made that O'Connor's violent use of "metaphors constitute verbal strategies for engaging the unknown, for making what Eliot called 'raids on the inarticulate.' "

as O'Connor herself recognized, was made more difficult by the spirit of modernism, which is dead to both God and sin: "In any age this would be a problem, but in our own, it is a well-nigh insurmountable one" (*Mystery* 161). To the modern mind, both the "terrible sonnets" and the nature sonnets of Hopkins must be read as a form of psychological projection rather than address—both are unintelligible in their original intention as prayers of supplication and praise. This is the world in which Flannery O'Connor wrote.

The strategy O'Connor employed in confronting this difficulty is one of distortion: "to the hard of hearing you shout, and for the almost-blind you draw large and startling figures." Lacking the ability to assume, as the cognitive equipment shared by her readers (both Catholic and non-Catholic), an awareness of beauty as a sign of God's impress upon creation, and the recognition of the deformity of sin as the turning from God's grace, Flannery O'Connor opted for the language of extremity in summoning the forces of the supernatural to bear upon her literary creations.[4] This essay is an attempt to trace the contours of her created figures, blasted by sin beyond the recognition of God's image, but nevertheless held in the superabundance of God's gift of being.

The concessions made to her readers do not of course entail an embrace of modernism. It is clear from Flannery O'Connor's prose writing that she was heavily influenced by Thomistic thought (most especially by the twentieth-century philosopher Jacques Maritain), both in her aesthetics and in her metaphysics. Despite the cultural rift that separates her from the aesthetic sensibility of a Hopkins, Flannery O'Connor remains in the tradition of an Aristotelian mimetic theory and an orthodox Christian hermeneutics. Her realism, founded upon a concern for the universal in human existence, is one in which art mirrors nature not as a mere copy, but in its essence. According to such a theory of imitation, the essential is disclosed in human action, thought, and in-

---

[4] Frederick Asals first employed the word "extremity" as a term suggesting that the grotesque in O'Connor's work was employed in a prophetic vision of distortion that maintained an indissoluble tension between the comic and the terrifying. See Frederick Asals, *Flannery O'Connor: The Imagination of Extremity.* For a discussion that places O'Connor in a tradition of employing the grotesque as an exaggerated attempt to reveal the horror of sin, see Linda Schlafer, "Pilgrims of the Absolute: Léon Bloy and Flannery O'Connor."

tention, wherein character is revealed according to its nature. In this openness to human reality is found the key to self-knowledge: "It is to measure oneself against Truth, and not the other way around" (O'Connor, *Mystery* 35). And in her adherence to a traditional approach to reading Scripture, and by extension to other texts as well, O'Connor finds herself drinking from that same well of Thomistic thought.

> The medieval commentators on Scripture found three kinds of meaning in the literal level of the sacred text: one they called allegorical, in which one fact pointed to another; one they called tropological, or moral, which had to do with what should be done; and one they called anagogical, which had to do with the Divine life and our participation in it. Although this was a method applied to biblical exegesis, it was also an attitude toward all of creation, and a way of reading nature which included most possibilities. . . . (O'Connor, *Mystery* 72–73)[5]

The reading of Flannery O'Connor's short stories that I want to suggest is grounded upon a mingling of the traditional and the modern in which the mimetic form is employed to expose the deep spiritual fissures in modern life. The originality of Flannery O'Connor lies in her use of modern forms of poetic sensibility— the grotesque and the sublime—for ends that smash the modern idols of the empirical, the material, and the literal.

The short stories of Flannery O'Connor can be read according to the tropology of medieval biblical exegesis; as in Scripture, however, the significance of a given story is not always readily apparent. What impresses the reader immediately is the literal, and it is through attending to the literal that the tropological makes its appearance. The nature of the literal—the matter at hand—in the stories of Flannery O'Connor is the medium through which a further significance is evoked.[6] The two dominant aspects under which the literal in O'Connor's short stories have been consid-

---

[5] For a discussion of how a biblical interpretation of history, and the Thomistic metaphysical principle of analogy, inform Flannery O'Connor's work, see John F. Desmond, *Risen Sons: Flannery O'Connor's Vision of History*.

[6] "In fact, O'Connor had little quarrel with allegory. She disliked it only when it reduced characters to abstractions because she believed that good fiction is scrupulously attentive to particular characters in specific settings." See J. Robert Baker, "Flannery O'Connor's Four-Fold Method of Allegory."

ered are that of (Southern) manners and the grotesque, with the latter receiving the far greater treatment. According to a tropological analysis, the grotesque as literal description opens upon the figurative—the grotesque in Flannery O'Connor's stories is both a literal rendering and a figural drawing.[7]

Flannery O'Connor's use of the grotesque has been interpreted in various ways, from reading the grotesque in the medieval tradition of Gothic aesthetics,[8] to seeing the grotesque as a form of the Romantic Gothic,[9] to a Bakhtinian analysis that considers the grotesque as a device of subversion,[10] to a reading that sees O'Connor succumbing to a poetics of despair in an extreme misanthropic vision,[11] to an interpretation that allies the grotesque with the devil's camp, with O'Connor herself as the chief archenemy.[12] In my own view, Flannery O'Connor's use of the grotesque is original, falling into none of the more traditional uses of the grotesque. It is not a form of medieval aesthetics, or of Bakhtinian subversion, for the world-view in which both operated is not available for O'Connor—both assume among their readers a Christian idea of nature and its attending metaphors in order to carry out their aesthetic functions. Flannery O'Connor's is an art that lacks the sentimentality and sensibility of the Romantic Gothic—her grotesque is one not of feeling but of thought, not of fantasy but of reality. And the claims that O'Connor's realism merely holds the mirror to a surreal world, or, further, testifies to a Manichæan philosophy in which evil is a positive force coequal with the good, must take into account a tropological analysis that expands the horizon of the literal to meet with the figures that trace the outlines of metaphorical signification. It is the (in)stress that is placed upon the figure of the grotesque that marks it as bearing the form of spiritual signification.

---

[7] Perhaps the first proponent of this type of tropological reading can be found in David Eggenschwiler, *The Christian Humanism of Flannery O'Connor.*

[8] See Gilbert H. Muller, *Nightmares and Visions: Flannery O'Connor and the Catholic Grotesque.*

[9] See Ronald Schleifer, "Rural Gothic: The Stories of Flannery O'Connor,".

[10] See Marshall Bruce Gentry, *Flannery O'Connor's Religion of the Grotesque*; Anthony DiRenzo, *American Gargoyles: Flannery O'Connor and the Medieval Grotesque.*

[11] See André Bleikasten, "The Heresy of Flannery O'Connor"; Irving Malin, "Flannery O'Connor and the Grotesque."

[12] See John Hawkes, "Flannery O'Connor's Devil"; Claire Katz, "Flannery O'Connor's Rage of Vision."

The extreme situation is the location in which the grotesque encounters grace in O'Connor's short stories. The reason is stated by O'Connor in *Mystery and Manners*, by way of introduction to a public reading of "A Good Man Is Hard to Find": "Violence is a force which can be used for good or evil, and among other things taken by it is the kingdom of heaven. But regardless of what can be taken by it, the man in the violent situation reveals those qualities least dispensable in his personality, those qualities which are all he will have to take into eternity with him . . ." (133–34). In O'Connor's short stories, the grotesque is the shape of a soul in pursuit of an idol of its own making; the human will, obsessed with a limited good as an absolute value, is thereby revealed in the grotesque gesture. The grotesque, revelatory of the inner motions of the soul, is the shape of action formed by habit, and set in a cast of mind. As such, the grotesque marks out the space occupied by sin. The encounter with grace is represented through a vision of the sublime which suspends thought and action. The grotesque traces the contours of a soul made crooked by a will bent in all-consuming appetite; the vision of the sublime arrests this movement of the will, indicating the action of grace which is revelatory of both the limits of created nature and the immensity of the ultimate object of human desire. The grotesque as an allegorical figure fleshes out the image of the human soul in a state of sin; the sublime as a symbol of vast emptiness reveals created nature as an alien territory, in need of reclamation and renewal. These two literary figures together reveal the state of a reprobate spirit, a state that Coleridge defines as "God present without the manifestation of his presence" (235). The tropes of allegory and symbol draw a distorted icon through which a soul broken on the wreck of its own desires makes transparent the need of God.

The grotesque is made a remarkably powerful image in O'Connor's work, being the action of the story bearing a literal meaning, while at the same time performing the tropological function of allegory: the characters in her stories live on the literal plane, while functioning on the figurative. In this way, Hopkins's notion of "inscape" as an act of being merges with Aristotelian mimetic theory, disclosing an action with universal and essential significance. Out of the grotesque gesture arises the vision of the sublime, which in O'Connor's short stories functions according to the Burkean idea in which the feelings of awe, terror, and fear are caused by objects immense, powerful, and incomprehensible.[13] The remarkable feat of O'Connor's craft lies in juxtaposing these two figures in such a way that the secret of their collaboration is disclosed, while maintaining the fundamental difference which separates the two.[14] For the grotesque and the sublime alike find their ultimate significance in the spiritual realm: through a dialectical movement the sublime as the apprehension of the infinite marks the limit of the grotesque, which through a distortion of the natural shape aspires to break free from the limitations of created form.

The grotesque as the figure of a movement of the will issues in a sublime vision in the stories of Flannery O'Connor. There is a logic that determines the course of this movement—it is the logic of mercy. As we shall see, the character deformed by the grotesque is compelled by an internal logic to confront its own significance, and to arrive at the destination marked out by the spiritual course that has been followed. In the course of this movement, the soul is brought to the precipice of an emptiness of its own making, where its own self-fashioning is revealed as a destructive bent that carries a privation, a lack, spilling into the

---

[13] Flannery O'Connor's use of the sublime follows Burke's formula of locating the source of the sublime in the terrible, inducing a fear "which effectually robs the mind of all its powers of acting and reasoning. . . ." See Edmund Burke, *A Philosophical Enquiry into the Origin of Our Ideas of the Sublime and the Beautiful* 57. The sublime for O'Connor is a modern form of catharsis which reduces her characters to their essential natures in the confrontation with an overwhelming power. In the spiritual negation which is the milieu of modernity, terrifying emptiness replaces spiritual damnation: "the world loses altogether its spiritual contour, nothing is worth doing, the fear is of a terrifying emptiness, a kind of vertigo, or even a fracturing of our world and body-space." See Charles Taylor, *Sources of the Self: The Making of Modern Identity* 18.

[14] "The reader is always to keep in mind that if the objects of horror in which the terrible grotesque finds its materials, were contemplated in their true light, and with the entire energy of the soul, they would cease to be grotesque, and become altogether sublime; and that therefore it is some shortening of the power, or the will, of contemplation, and some consequent distortion of the terrible image in which the grotesqueness consists." See John Ruskin, *The Stones of Venice* 150. My analysis of the grotesque owes a great debt to Ruskin's morally informed aesthetics; readers acquainted with Ruskin will recognize in my arguments a defense of O'Connor's use of the grotesque as falling under the categories of the true and noble grotesque. The element of mercy, so central to Ruskin's understanding of the true and noble grotesque, is a crucial aspect of O'Connor's employment of that tropological figure.

heart of being and clearing a space for the sublime vision. The vision of the sublime that is given marks the point at which nature and grace coalesce, marking a point of emptiness hollowed out by the movement of soul, but also disclosed as the nothingness that it has made itself. The response to this revelation marks the space in which free will operates, either continuing on its way into spiritual death, or away from its course toward spiritual life. Flannery O'Connor's short stories either find their end with a character suspended, like a figure in a cartoon, at the moment in which a free-fall into the abyss is apprehended, or dialectically pass over into the contemplation of a symbol that bridges the gap of the empty space disclosed. In both cases, the emptiness un-veiled is marked by a mercy stern and severe, revelatory of the nothingness meaning death that was the fate of the soul distorted by sin.[15] In what follows I will illustrate this dynamic movement through a reading of five stories that will serve to represent O'Connor's work as a whole.

The short story "Greenleaf" describes the shattering of a world dominated by a controlling will, which is the central mode of manifestation of the sublime in O'Connor's work. The story is-sues in the violent death of Mrs. May, a strong, domineering woman who runs her own farm; it plots the course of a will gro-tesquely distorted by rage—a rage bent on the destruction of its enemy, ironically succeeding only in an act of self-destruction. Mrs. May's fated death is brought about by a trespasser, a neigh-bor's bull, that is immediately seen as destructive, but also engen-dered with a strange positive sexual power. The paradoxical significance of the bull, and the various relations with men that complicate the plot of this story, deserves a closer reading than this essay permits, but the figure of the bull as a source of the sublime is throughout the story a controlling image.[16] The bull is

---

[15] This is the sublime under the aspect of sin. It is a premodern exploitation of the thoroughly modern notion of the sublime, a symbol of barren emptiness, an "object 'wanting in form or figure' " issuing in the idea of 'anti-nature,' " as Lyotard puts it in his work on the modernity of Kant's idea of the sublime in the *Critique of Judgment*. See Jean-François Lyotard, *Lessons on the Analytic of the Sublime* 183.

[16] "A bull is strong too; but his strength is of another kind [from the ox]; often very destructive, seldom (at least amongst us) of any use in our business; the idea of a bull is therefore great, and it has frequently a place in sublime descriptions, and elevating comparisons." See Burke, *Enquiry* 65. The source of conflict in

first apprehended by Mrs. May in a dream, but introduced to the reader by a gorgeously lush description of the bull's intruding presence: "Mrs. May's bedroom window was low and faced on the east and the bull, silvered in the moonlight, stood under it, his head raised as if he listened—like some patient god come down to woo her—for a stir inside the room" (O'Connor, *CS* 311). The understated beauty of the entire opening scene is drawn in fragile hues that are surrounded by an impending dark, the contrast heightening the sense of both. This spare description in stark contrasts stands almost like a dream vision, interrupted, paradoxically, by the dream of Mrs. May which gives shape to an underlying fear while also ushering the reader into the literal world of the care and concerns of Mrs. May's everyday life:

> She had been conscious in her sleep of a steady rhythmic chewing as if something were eating one wall of the house. She had been aware that whatever it was had been eating as long as she had had the place and had eaten everything from the beginning of her fence line up to the house and now was eating the house and calmly with the same steady rhythm would continue through the house, eating her and the boys, and then on, eating everything but the Greenleafs, on and on, eating everything until nothing was left but the Greenleafs on a little island all their own in the middle of what had been her place. (*CS* 311–12)

The bull, revealed later in the story to belong to these same Greenleafs, is a symbol of the destructive force of Mrs. May's own mind—the two Greenleaf boys' success underscores her deep dissatisfaction with her own two boys, and the comparison between the pairs is a constant source of misery that, like the bull, tears constantly at the edges of her mind. Thus, the moral contours of the story are disclosed in the subliminal fears of Mrs. May, which issue in a fear that is unknown, destructive—another key source of the sublime.

"Greenleaf," as I have suggested, is a complicated story rich in its exploration of familial ties, issues of gender, and sexual rela-

---

this story arises from the scrub bull's presence on her farm, symbolizing what Mrs. May sees as a destructive capacity for engendering life by insemination of her cows, while at the same time being a reminder of her own boys' manly impotence and failure relative to the Greenleafs.

tions. But the broad contours of O'Connor's concern in this story can be discerned in the maniacal pursuit of the bull by Mrs. May, disclosed finally as a demand for controlling superiority issuing in a gory and destructive end. The grotesque is not this final end, but the blind rage that grips Mrs. May as she seeks a man who is willing and able to satisfy her desire of removing the bull from her premises. The erotic is a theme that at all times lies just below the surface of the narrative, a source for Mrs. May of both attraction and fear: "The sun, moving over the black and white grazing cows, was just a little brighter than the rest of the sky. Looking down, she saw a darker shape that might have been its shadow cast at an angle, moving among them. She uttered a sharp cry and turned and marched out of the house" (O'Connor, *CS* 322). The presence of the bull serves to sublimate these repressed desires and fears in a struggle for the superiority of her sons over the Greenleaf boys, as the literal passes over into the metaphorical, disclosing the contorted shape of Mrs. May's love—for her sons, and for men in general. Though she is twisted by contempt for the failings of men, but with a need for a capable man who can bring her satisfaction, the trespass of the bull violates her own sense of superiority (which she secretly desires), and serves also as a glaring reminder of her sons' lack of manhood.

The final paragraph of this story is remarkable in its understated description that evokes the power of the sublime in its capacity to astonish. The view of Mr. Greenleaf—the father of the Greenleaf boys and her own hired hand—running to shoot the bull is seen through the eyes of Mrs. May, whose final vision appears to be burned on her retina and there viewed by the horrified reader:

> She saw him approaching on the outside of some invisible circle, the tree line gaping behind him and nothing under his feet. He shot the bull four times through the eye. She did not hear the shots but she felt the quake in the huge body as it sank, pulling her forward on its head, so that she seemed, when Mr. Greenleaf reached her, to be bending over whispering some last discovery into the animal's ear. (O'Connor, *CS* 333–34)

The gesture of a lover whispering in the ear of a beloved consummates and completes the image introduced in the opening paragraph of the story, as the grotesque passes over into the sublime

in the emptying-out of a love that is seared through with contempt and hatred.

The moment of grace, perceived at the moment in which Mrs.
May (willingly) receives the thrust of the bull's horn into her
body, lies on the horizon of vision in which the opacity of the
bull's corporal existence is made transparent in the symbol of an
empty landscape: "She continued to stare straight ahead but the
entire scene in front of her had changed—the tree line was a dark
wound in a world that was nothing but sky—and she had the
look of a person whose sight has been suddenly restored but who
finds the light unbearable" (O'Connor, *CS* 333). The empty
landscape, under the aspect of the sublime, mirrors the paradox
of Mrs. May's grotesque passion: that her raging love has been
satisfied in that which she had hated, and that the destruction of
this hated object marks the emptying-out of her own love.
Whether this marks a purification of her love, or its final consum-
mation in self-destruction, is a question that is forever sealed in
the ambiguous vision of a landscape emptied of literal significance, pointing to the invisible realm of the eternal. This final
vision, the natural result of Mrs. May's own frenzied pursuit, is
equally one of revelation that issues from outside—the light of
self-knowledge seen on the backdrop of the eternal.

The strange eroticism of "Greenleaf" traces the outline of a
desire contorted into the grotesque figure, leading to a vision of
landscape which is emptied into the nothingness of space. The
movement which leads to this line of vision of the eternal is the
inverse of an erotic of the beautiful (which finds its roots in Plato's
Phaedrus) that follows a path of love from the sensible to the spiritual, thereby revealing a continuity between the human and the
divine through sublimation of the physical. Flannery O'Connor's
sublime eroticism issues not in a vision of beauty in consort with
the good, but of the grotesque in league with the privation of
good. Whereas the desire of the beautiful is the sign of a plenitude
of being, the sublime signifies the emptiness of a desire for nothingness. This privation erupts from within nature as a space emptied by the movement of the human soul, making way for the
advent of grace, and revealing the deformity of the soul in need
of being made whole. The dialectic of the beautiful and the good
in an inverted form, this movement of the grotesque through the
sublime culminates in a vision that subtracts from the natural and

goes beyond it to the supernatural, through a sublimation that is
a condescension of mercy rather than an upward movement of
virtue. The great paradox of this spiritual terrain is that the destination arrived at is the same; the mystery of grace is that both
paths can lead to God, through sanctification, or purgation.[17]

The path of amorous fantasy leads to God in the short story "A
Good Man Is Hard to Find." This amorous passion, wishing to
be recaptured in memory and relived again by the grandmother,
is the engine that drives this story to its violent conclusion. All
roads, it would seem, lead to the meeting with "The Misfit,"
whose face is seen in the newspaper by the grandmother and her
son, where they read that he is headed to Florida, the destination
of the family's vacation. Warning her son of the irresponsibility of
taking the family where they might meet with the escaped killer,
the grandmother attempts to coax her son into visiting Tennessee
and the place of her youth. It is this desire, ironically, that leads
the family to their fateful encounter with the Misfit. The symbols
of the landscape in this story are the key to understanding the
movement through the sensibility of romance—an amorous self-
love—to the final moment of grace which issues in the pouring
forth of unselfish love.

On the road to Florida, just "[o]utside of Toombsboro," the
grandmother in regret and wishful longing chatters about

> an old plantation that she had visited in this neighborhood once
> when she was a young lady. She said the house had six white col-
> umns across the front and that there was an avenue of oaks leading
> up to it and two little wooden trellis arbors on either side in front
> where you sat down with your suitor after a stroll in the garden.
> She recalled exactly which road to turn off to get to it. She knew
> that Bailey would not be willing to lose any time looking at an old
> house, but the more she talked about it, the more she wanted to
> see it once again and find out if the little twin arbors were still
> standing. (O'Connor, CS 123)

---

[17] "The dynamics of guilt, with its need to repent and repay for sin, describe
the problem of love in negative terms." See Richard Giannone, Flannery O'Connor and the Mystery of Love 5. Giannone's study is a powerfully persuasive reclamation of Flannery O'Connor's artistic vision from the criticism which sees her
work as the product of a misanthropic and venomous hate, restoring it to its
proper place in the tradition of a prophetic calling, moved by the extreme unc-
tion of charity to show "the overwhelming boldness of divine love invading
human life" (6).

The significance of this passage lies in its pastoral delicacy framed around the harsh and hardened relations of the family. This reminiscence is full and clear despite its idyllic outline, whereas the silence of her son Bailey and his wife point out the vacuity of the normal everyday life of this family, whose relationships are drawn with an underlying tension throughout. The lack of love stands as the norm, evoked in a realism of negativity, whereas the ideal as escape is a romantic remembrance waiting to be repossessed.

The images of "an avenue of oaks" and the "two little wooden trellis arbors" line the route of romantic fantasy, symbols of a love unrealized in the grandmother's life. After convincing her son, through a ruse which sends the children into wild demands to see the plantation, to make the turn down a dirt path for a visit, the landscape of trees begins to take on an ominous aspect as the road becomes dangerous: "All at once they would be on a hill, looking down over the blue tops of trees for miles around, then the next minute, they would be in a red depression with the dust-coated trees looking down on them" (O'Connor, *CS* 124). It is, literally and figuratively, a road to nowhere, a road to death. The grandmother's spastic response when she realizes that the house that she remembered was not in Georgia but in Tennessee sends her cat (hidden in her basket against her son's wishes) into a panic, leaping upon Bailey's shoulders and precipitating a terrible accident. The car turns over once and lands right side up, and the dust clears with no one critically injured. The view from where they stand, however, is fraught with meaning: "Behind the ditch they were sitting in there were more woods, tall and dark and deep" (O'Connor, *CS* 125). The next sentence unfolds the impending doom in measured cadence: "In a few minutes they saw a car some distance away on top of a hill, coming slowly as if the occupants were watching them" (O'Connor, *CS* 125). The occupants of the car will shortly become the family's murderers; the woods, the location of their murder. In this brief moment, an error, trivial in itself, is disclosed as a judgment of life and death. As the twin arbors which symbolized a longed-for love become the dark woods of death, the path the grandmother has chosen is revealed in its moral contours, as the distorted image of a love which should have been found, but was lacking, in the family.

The extremity of the family's situation, in which they begin to realize that they are to be murdered by The Misfit and his crew, is in actuality a grace-given one. The sudden nobility of the wife, entirely absent as a human person up to this moment, the tenderness displayed by Bailey toward his mother and his son, and the small but clear signs of concern for each other are in sharp contrast to their everyday relations. But it is in the line of vision of the grandmother that the symbol of this grace is revealed. The conversation which takes place between The Misfit and the grandmother as the family is executed one by one in the woods cannot be paraphrased or reduced to a statement, with its discussion of Christology and redemption, sin and punishment, at intervals interrupted by the sound of pistol shots. But if The Misfit is a figure of the grotesque, then so are the contorted moral absolutions of The Misfit by the grandmother as she pleads vainly for her life. And this is consistent with the way the grandmother has acted up to this point—selfish even in her attentions to others, and interested in her own narrow concerns and gratifications. But it is the one act of love shown toward the Misfit that seals her own death—"She saw the man's face twisted close to her own as if he were going to cry and she murmured, 'Why you're one of my babies. You're one of my own children!' She reached out and touched him on the shoulder. The Misfit sprang back as if a snake had bitten him and shot her three times through the chest" (O'Connor, *CS* 132).

The preparation for this gratuitous act was the grandmother's isolation, seen in a vision that subtracts everything from the landscape of her surroundings but the trees, transformed from the idyllic arbor into a wood emptied of all human significance: "Alone with The Misfit, the grandmother found that she had lost her voice. There was not a cloud in the sky nor any sun. There was nothing around her but woods" (O'Connor, *CS* 131). The sublime subverts the tree metaphors which line the route to this final end in death, revealing the emptiness of amorous love, and disclosing the nature of genuine love as a gratuitous gift called forth out of the inner resources of the self. The moment of grace in this story, astonishing because it is an act which makes a break from the former self in being completely neglectful of self, is reached by a subtraction that leaves the soul alone in a landscape emptied of human ties, in which death to the self is seen and embraced in an act of merciful charity.[18] The scene in which the grandmother lies dead describes a true return to her youth, where pure love in a self-emptying gesture, rather than the illusory love of ideal romance, is attained in all its innocence: "Hiram and Bobby Lee returned from the woods and stood over the ditch, looking down at the grandmother who half sat and half lay in a puddle of blood with her legs crossed under her like a child's and her face smiling up at the cloudless sky" (O'Connor, *CS* 132). The smile on the face of the grandmother marks a victory over the grotesque in which the sublime is passed through to the reception of grace in a gratuitous act of love.

"A Good Man Is Hard to Find" stands at the transitional phase of my study, marking the point where the sublime passes over into a positive symbol in which grace coheres. The image of the grandmother in the final scene is an icon of Flannery O'Connor's idea of grace through the sublime, an icon which through its sheer force of violence smashes the idols of self-love and sentimental longing. The iconic image here is still of an empty sky in the eyes of dead women—a vision, indicated but not presented to the reader, of grace received but not fully manifested. The icon remains in the ambit of the sublime, suspended in an opaque negativity and emptiness, rather than attaining the transparency of the symbol that is the window through to the spiritual. The masterful short story "The Artificial Nigger" presents this line of movement through the grotesque to the sublime, but passes through it to a positive image given in a symbol of grace.

The story is one of moral discovery and enlightenment which shatters the idol of pride. A trip to the city is planned in which Mr. Head proposes to show his grandson Nelson "everything there is to see in the city so that he would be content to stay at home for the rest of his life" (O'Connor, *CS* 251). In Mr. Head's attempt to provide Nelson with a moral lesson, he is revealed as a man content in his own knowledge, thinking that "only with

---

[18] "When the Grandmother of the story touches the Misfit, she replicates Paul's laying on of the hands at the very moment she loses her artificiality and realizes that she and the Misfit are spiritual kin. . . . Those critics who argue for a 'realistic' interpretation of the story must ultimately acknowledge and account for O'Connor's biblical allusions." See Michael Clark "Flannery O'Connor's 'A Good Man Is Hard to Find': The Moment of Grace."

years does a man enter into that calm understanding of life that makes him a suitable guide for the young" (O'Connor, CS 249). Mr. Head's attitude is one that is rooted in tremendous pride: "his physical reactions, like his moral ones, were guided by his will and strong character, and these could be seen plainly in his features" (O'Connor, CS 249). Mr. Head's moral superiority is not one of reflection upon his strengths and weaknesses, but upon an assurance of self-reliance, an instinct of action completely unquestioned. The trip to the city for Nelson holds the promise of asserting his own independence, thereby establishing the line of conflict between Mr. Head and Nelson as a battle of wills.

Like Vergil for Dante, Mr. Head is leading Nelson into hell. The question that O'Connor raises with this comparison is whether, like Vergil, Mr. Head is capable of leading his charge into hell and out again. But Mr. Head considers himself without fault, and, as such, his conception of the evil of the city is seen through a narrow vision of sin, judged in accord with his own conception of himself as upright. In Mr. Head's view, the city is one of empty vanity, of sinful temptation, which must be seen and then rejected.[19] Mr. Head's strategy of acquainting Nelson with evil reveals his ignorance of the city (a sign of his own rigid and narrow moral knowledge), guarded like a secret to be kept from Nelson: "He thought that if he could keep the dome always in sight, he would be able to get back in the afternoon to catch the train again" (O'Connor, CS 258). Mr. Head's attempt to hide his ignorance from Nelson contrasts with the stately aura that surrounds Mr. Head at his home in the country, where the light of the moon "cast a dignifying light on everything" (O'Connor, CS 249). Mr. Head's figure is only partially disclosed in this surreal setting: "His eyes were alert but quiet, and in the miraculous moonlight they had a look of composure and of ancient wisdom as if they belonged to one of the great guides of men" (O'Connor, CS 249–50). At home alone Mr. Head exudes a quiet confi-

---

[19] Richard Giannone, rightly I think, argues that Mr. Head's bigotry is the emblem of his enormous pride. See Richard Giannone, "Flannery O'Connor Tells Her Desert Story." Giannone's approach is one that employs the writings of the desert fathers to show the evil of the city as the situation of Satan's victory of temptation over the human will, with the urban setting seen as a place of pride, in contrast to the aridity of the desert which engenders humility in self-renunciation and intense self-reflection.

dence; under the stress of city life which places him in proximity with others—under conditions which call for moral action—Mr. Head's narrow moral vision is disclosed. Mr. Head's reliance upon an external landmark, rather than his own (limited) experience, is an emblem for the unreliability of his own moral compass—an empty shell of vain pride rather than genuine moral fortitude.

The symbol of evil for Mr. Head is the city's sewer system, shown to Nelson in an unforgettable scene of both high comedy and high seriousness. Nelson, enamored of the novelty and excitement of the city, announces his pleasure in it by identifying it as his birthplace. Mr. Head, appalled by this claim, sticks Nelson's head down into the dark sewer—"an endless pitchblack tunnel" (O'Connor, CS 250)—and explains its inner workings and its secret designs: "At any minute any man in the city might be sucked into the sewer and never heard from again. He described it so well that Nelson was for some seconds shaken" (O'Connor, CS 259). The sewer, an image of sublimity in its dark and destructive aspect, is a metaphor for the mechanics of sin in Mr. Head's mind, where once a man falls, he is taken into the depths of hell without light, never to return. Nelson's claim to the possibility of avoiding this fate—"'Yes, but you can stay away from the holes'" (O'Connor, CS 259)—defines both Nelson's and Mr. Head's attitude of self-confidence, in that they both think themselves exempt from the possibility of falling. Thus, the sin of pride is a badge of honor that each wears in a sign of superiority; it is what blinds them both to the true nature of sin's origin, which lies not in the weakness of the will in overcoming temptation but in the false pride that masquerades as strength and self-reliance.

The dome of the train station is the compass on Mr. Head's map of the city, and when it disappears from sight, so do Mr. Head's bearings—it is a loss of moral orientation that will lead Mr. Head himself into the terrain of evil. Although now lost, Mr. Head maintains an appearance of self-assurance, while Nelson, tacitly admitting his disorientation, asks for directions from a voluptuous black woman—a symbol for Nelson of sexual awakening and longing for the maternal, emerging as a confrontation of his own fears in which "He felt as if he were reeling down through a pitchblack tunnel" (O'Connor, CS 262). Tired, hungry, and becoming more aware of his dependence on his grandfather, Nelson collapses on the sidewalk in sleep. At this point, the abominable shape of Mr. Head's pride manifests itself as he hides from Nelson; Mr. Head, under the false pretense of teaching the boy a lesson, assumes complete ascendancy by humiliating the boy, placing Nelson in a position of utter abjection. Waking to find himself abandoned, the boy is thrown into a panic in which he bolts down a crowded street, and runs into a woman who threatens to sue Nelson's guardian for the injury caused her. As Nelson turns to Mr. Head for support and protection—the position in which Mr. Head hoped to force Nelson—Mr. Head denies him. The scene is one of great pathos, ironically leading Mr. Head not into the exultation of victory he had imagined, but into bitter shame. His monstrous pride is herein revealed in its grotesque form, as those who witness the scene recoil from Mr. Head. "The women dropped back, staring at him with horror, as if they were so repulsed by a man who would deny his own image and likeness that they could not bear to lay hands on him. Mr. Head walked on, through a space they silently cleared, and left Nelson behind. Ahead of him he saw nothing but a hollow tunnel that had once been the street" (O'Connor, *CS* 265).

Revealed in his deformity, Mr. Head feels the shame of sin as an abdication of the responsibility which he bore in pride, but failed to bear in humility out of love for his grandson. Although they wander now out of the squalor of the inner city and into the affluent suburbs, the hell that Mr. Head has made is carried within him. The emptiness that opens around him is the genuine hell of the soul consumed by pride unable to find forgiveness. It is the emptiness of despair: "The old man felt that if he saw a sewer entrance he would drop down into it and let himself be carried away; and he could imagine the boy standing by, watching with only slight interest, while he disappeared" (O'Connor, *CS* 267). The sewer as a symbol of sin is now seen to be one that is entered by choice, rather than through moral failing: it is the deliberate choosing of the darkness to cover one's shame. Mr. Head's victory has been an ironic one: his own superiority over Nelson affirmed at the moment when he renounces his kinship with his own grandson. His victory of pride has been the loss of the boy as his sole love in the world.[20] Superiority and shame are here portrayed

---

[20] "Pride not only replaces God with the self but also undoes the closest human ties." See Giannone 56.

as the two faces of pride bent upon total isolation: it is the will to remain aloof and alone at all costs, the former disclosed in false exaltation by degrading others, the latter in the avoidance of all human contact from fear of being judged as guilty.

However, the seeds of transformation come with the realization that if left in the city overnight they will be beaten and robbed, bringing on humility through a genuine concern for the boy's safety, not his own. "The speed of God's justice was only what he expected for himself, but he could not stand to think that his sins would be visited upon Nelson, and that even now, he was leading the boy to his doom" (O'Connor, *CS* 266). For Nelson's sake, Mr. Head admits his own ignorance by pleading for directions (thus reversing the roles each played when lost in the inner city), his plaintive cry an admission of guilt before humans and God: " 'I'm lost and can't find my way and me and this boy have got to catch this train and I can't find the station. Oh Gawd I'm lost! Oh hep me Gawd I'm lost!' " (O'Connor, *CS* 267). Mr. Head's admission of ignorance and moral failure is at bottom a loving attempt to reclaim Nelson, whose "mind had frozen around his grandfather's treachery as if he were trying to preserve it intact to present at the final judgment" (O'Connor, *CS* 267). Having rejected the temptation to cover his shame in the darkness of the sewer, Mr. Head emerges on the path of humility, in the hopeful turning from despair by the clear admission of guilt; it is the sole act of courage and moral integrity performed by Mr. Head in this story.

The providential meeting of Mr. Head and Nelson with the "artificial Negro"— a statue that adorns the lawns of the wealthy all over the South in a grotesque gesture of vicarious bigotry— signals a passageway through the emptiness of despair and into forgiveness. The statue, symbolizing the deformity of pride masked in veiled condescension together with a sense of base abjectness, coalesces for Mr. Head and Nelson as a representation of their own sin: "It was not possible to tell if the artificial Negro were meant to be young or old; he looked too miserable to be either. He was meant to look happy because his mouth was stretched up at the corners but the chipped eye and the angle he was cocked at gave him a wild look of misery instead" (O'Connor, *CS* 268). The contradiction of the supposed happiness and the actual misery inscribed upon the statue reveals the paradox of grace as it attends upon the suffering of sin. "They stood gazing at the artificial Negro as if they were faced with some great mystery, some monument to another's victory that brought them both together in their common defeat. They could both feel it dissolving their differences like an action of mercy" (O'Connor, *CS* 269). The way out of the hell of despair is thus revealed in the forgiveness of sins, a truth that Mr. Head in his pride had failed before to grasp. Mr. Head's comment, one which Nelson looks to his grandfather to supply, is one of deep insight into the profoundly destructive effects of his own sin: " 'They ain't got enough real ones here. They got to have an artificial one.' " The comment is not, as some have argued, the perpetuation of a bigoted attitude in Mr. Head,[21] but its renunciation: he realizes in the blighted statue (a substitute slave for a post-abolitionist South) the effect of racism as the effacement of personality, both for the perpetrator and for the sufferer of racist hatred. Mr. Head finally speaks wisely, from the depths of a moral wisdom gained through suffering the effects of his own sin. It is through placing himself under its judgment that Mr. Head comes to see himself represented in the statue as the perpetrator of its misery, thereby admitting his complicity.

As Mr. Head's moral map is adjusted now to conform to the true lay of the moral landscape, his moral compass leads the two back home by the direction of humility rather than pride. Following the parallel ascent of *The Divine Comedy* suggested at the outset of this story, we see the outline of the moral terrain figured in the grotesque and the sublime, both symbols first of spiritual death then transformed into symbols of mercy. The prideful will of Mr. Head marks the lines of the grotesque, leading to a descent into hell, a dark vortex of sublime power and depth. In the suffering aspect of the statue in which pride effaces humanity, the mirror is held to the deformity of hatred. In the accepting of this representation as true the springs of mercy are on display; in the embrace of humility, divine mercy is released. The sublime as the descent into the harrowing hell of despair is revealed as a purgation in which pride is burned away in the self-knowledge of Mr. Head's

---

[21] "Despite the knowledge of his own unworthiness, Mr. Head persists in acting the wise man (or wise-cracker)." See Strickland 458. See also Kenneth Scouten, " 'The Artificial Nigger': Mr. Head's Ironic Salvation."

own sin. The sublime image of the sewer as the prison of sin is hereby transformed from a perpetual hell into a purgatorial passageway, as humility replaces pride, and mercy liberates the soul, allowing for a vision of suffering as a way out of the darkness of despair. The statue of "the artificial Negro," seen as a symbol of God's regenerative grace, restores all to a common humanity—all fallen, but all capable of forgiveness.

The general movement through the grotesque to the sublime has been charted in this study as an arc toward a vision of God's grace through the purgative action of mercy. This ascending arc has traced the lines of an iconoclastic iconography that shatters the flattened and opaque texture of human existence, revealing behind it a world of spirit in the space cleared by the human will. In "The Artificial Nigger" we find a positive symbol of the grace that, in the stories previously considered, has been intimated as a condescension coming to meet the soul. In the short story "Revelation" we follow this arc to a vision of the glory of God revealed in the ascent of souls into heaven. As such, "Revelation" concludes my study of Flannery O'Connor's short stories, for it contains in miniature the movement to a given representation of God's grace through the subtraction of all that is of a creaturely nature, thereby revealing in microcosm the entire scope of her literary project. "Revelation" fills the empty space that in other O'Connor stories can be seen as a window to the eternal, not yet given as an object in visual representation.

Like other O'Connor characters, Mrs. Turpin, the main subject of the story, is an allegory in flesh of the sin of pride, the root of all sin. Her thoughts are frequently directed to the classification of human beings into a hierarchical scheme. The complexity of her classification system is problematized in her mind by the impossibility of deciding precisely how the ordering should go, for there is a mingling of blood, race, and money—the three keys to her system—which upsets the easy classification of all humanity into types. The grotesque shape of this ordering is revealed in a leveling nightmare image that looks forward to the final revelation, but as its distorted and debased opposite: "Usually by the time she had fallen asleep all the classes of people were moiling and roiling around in her head, and she would dream they were all crammed in together in a box car, being ridden off to be put in a gas oven" (O'Connor, *CS* 492). Mrs. Turpin's classification system is driven by bigotry, self-satisfaction, and a condescension masquerading as false charity, given voice in an unconsciously parodic hymn of supplication issuing in thanksgiving to God: " '. . . Make me a good woman and it don't matter what else, how fat or how ugly or how poor!' Her heart rose. He had not made her a nigger or white-trash or ugly! He had made her herself and given her a little of everything. Jesus, thank you! she said. Thank you thank you thank you!" (O'Connor, *CS* 497).

These thoughts occupy Mrs. Turpin in the doctor's office as she considers and classifies the various people in the waiting room. As her thoughts are revealed in the conversation which unfolds, one of those seated there, Mary Grace, is alone in recognizing Mrs. Turpin's patronizing beneficence. Both her name and the aspect of her gaze reveal Mary Grace as possessed of a peculiar form of discernment, as her "eyes seemed lit all of a sudden with a peculiar light, an unnatural light" (O'Connor, *CS* 492), with her knowledge extending beyond the scope of her own experience, "looking at her as if she had known and disliked her all her life— all of Mrs. Turpin's life, it seemed too, not just all the girl's life" (O'Connor, *CS* 495). As she hurls her *Human Development* book and leaps at Mrs. Turpin, seizing her by the throat, Mary Grace discloses the grotesqueness of Mrs. Turpin's soul. Mary Grace's hold on her throat is a hold on Mrs. Turpin's entire being; thus ensnared, she seeks a revelation that might release her from the grip of terror:

> The girl raised her head. Her gaze locked with Mrs. Turpin's. "Go back to hell where you came from, you old wart hog," she whispered. Her voice was low but clear. Her eyes burned for a moment as if she saw with pleasure that her message had struck its target. (O'Connor, *CS* 500)

Mrs. Turpin, in recognizing the truth of Mary Grace's startling charge, reveals an integrity that issues in self-examination. But in her moment of recognition, she rebels against making a full confession of guilt. Unable to avoid the truth, but unable to accept its full force, Mrs. Turpin enters into an exercise of self-examination that discloses the form of her soul in the figure of the grotesque. No longer in thanksgiving but in wrath and with a sense of having suffered injustice, Mrs. Turpin rages against the

God who has made her what she is: "'What do you send me a message like that for?'" she said in a low fierce voice, barely above a whisper but with the force of a shout in its concentrated fury. "'How am I a hog and me both? How am I saved and from hell too?'" (O'Connor, *CS* 506) In the figure of the hog and human combined, the classical form of the grotesque is employed—a hybrid creature of debased physicality revealing an underlying spiritual corruption.

Mrs. Turpin's rage against God overturns her self-satisfied piety, replacing it with a fury that meets the fury of the revelatory charge made against her. The struggle of Mrs. Turpin's will against full self-realization of the true state of her soul becomes a struggle against the grace of God's mercy—the violent and undeniable dawning of self-knowledge which shatters the idol of self-righteousness. This struggle is drawn in the allegorical signification of the hogs on her farm internalized as a form of self-knowledge, and in the landscape of the sublime, seen through its emptiness to a revelation of God's saving grace. In finally accepting the appellation, Mrs. Turpin realizes, perhaps dimly, the altered state of hierarchy entailed by her revelation: "'Go on,' she yelled, 'call me a hog! Call me a hog again. From hell. Call me a wart hog from hell. Put that bottom rail on top. There'll still be a top and bottom!'" (O'Connor, *CS* 507). The fragility of her life is disclosed in a vision of sublime apprehension in which human activity appears always on the verge of destruction: "A tiny truck, Claud's, appeared on the highway, leading rapidly out of sight. Its gears scraped thinly. It looked like a child's toy. At any moment a bigger truck might smash into it and scatter Claud's and the niggers' brains all over the road" (O'Connor, *CS* 508). This prepares the way for the moment of the grotesque to be purged by God's redemptive action, disclosed in Mrs. Turpin's contemplation of the hogs after she has cleaned them down in a scene in which her rage becomes directed at them: "Then like a monumental statue coming to life, she bent her head slowly and gazed, as if through the very heart of mystery, down into the pig parlor at the hogs. They had settled all in one corner around the old sow who was grunting softly. A red glow suffused them. They appeared to pant with a secret life" (O'Connor, *CS* 508). In this vision the realization that all are in need of God's cleansing power is revealed as the secret life that unites all in their grotesque uncleanness. Her gaze returns to the landscape, a sublime symbol of vacuity, mingled with profound beauty that is unrecognized by Mrs. Turpin in her self-absorbed reflection: "Until the sun slipped finally behind the tree line, Mrs. Turpin remained there with her gaze bent to them as if she were absorbing some abysmal life-giving knowledge. At last she lifted her head. There was only a purple streak in the sky, cutting through a field of crimson and leading, like an extension of highway, into the descending dusk" (O'Connor, *CS* 508).

The final vision of souls on their way to heaven, seen through the transparency of the empty landscape, subverts the inverted horror of base materiality (Mrs. Turpin's standard for judging divine merit) disclosed in the dream vision of limbs mingled and shipped to be gassed, thereby subverting Mrs. Turpin's own spiritual hierarchy. The looks on the souls as they march to heaven disclose the wonder of God's grace, and the source of sin in pride that is in need of being purged: "Yet she could see by their shocked and altered faces that even their virtues were being burned away" (O'Connor, *CS* 508). Forced into facing her pride in the form of the grotesque, and purged of the illusory notion of the hierarchy of souls in God's divine order, Mrs. Turpin hears in the closing scene the true sound of praise, not in the false notes of condescension and disguised superiority, but in charity and thanksgiving for a mercy that none deserve: "In the woods around her the invisible cricket choruses had struck up, but what she heard were the voices of the souls climbing upward into the starry field and shouting hallelujah" (O'Connor, *CS* 509).

In this essay I have attempted to trace in the figures of the grotesque and the sublime the tropology of grace in a number of short stories of Flannery O'Connor. The originality of O'Connor's use of the grotesque appears in its deployment as a literary figure in proximity to the sublime, and in the context of a hermeneutic that is scripturally determined. The grotesque is the shape of the soul, seen as an action with moral significance. The grotesque in Flannery O'Connor's work is sin reduced to its essential form in pride; the grotesque is the idol of pride, the distortion of the soul in its transgression against its own natural form; it is the creature in its limitations attempting to become a god. The sublime is the death mask of the grotesque, a form emptied into a negation that discloses the ultimate aim of a soul distorted beyond recognition by sin. The sublime as a rupture in the world bursts forth from within the limited as a raging point from the very heart of a controlling will. The very effort of such a will releases a violent energy that shatters the surface of the literal and exposes the horizon of eternity. This is the point at which spirit intrudes upon the narrative, met by the overshadowing power of grace. It is in this point of energy that the idols of human construction are shattered; it is in the aspect of this violent gesture that an apocalyptic iconography is drawn.

Flannery O'Connor's work is allegorical not as an abstraction of moral character personified, but in the scriptural sense, as the literal disclosed symbolically through the grotesque and the anagogical revealed negatively through the sublime. It is allegory stretched to reveal the tension between the will and grace, wherein grace goes to all lengths to confront the will and lead it back to itself in God. It is in this dynamic interplay between the grotesque and the sublime that the lines of spiritual significance are disclosed in Flannery O'Connor's work, releasing an original and powerful form of creative energy that stamps the mark of the allegorical upon the landscape of the literal, and the significance of the eschatological upon the form of the concrete.[22] In a talk just a year and half before she died, Flannery O'Connor stated that "the real novelist, one with an instinct for what he is about, knows that he cannot approach the infinite directly, that he must penetrate the natural human world as it is. The more sacramental his theology, the more encouragement he will get from it to do just that" (*Mystery* 163). It is in the lines of the figurative made real, and the symbolic issuing from the core of the concrete, that Flannery O'Connor's sacramental vision is revealed.[23] For an age

---

[22] From the standpoint of the prophetic imagination, Karl Martin sees this duality in O'Connor's work as offering a criticism of the reigning Zeitgeist of the age, while at the same time offering hope to the marginalized in society. See Karl Martin, "Flannery O'Connor's Prophetic Imagination." For Martin, O'Connor's work, through employing what he calls the language of grief coupled with the language of amazement, is a call "to awaken her numb audience to both the judgment of God and the action of his grace in the world, to offer symbols of both suffering and hope based in the activity of God in history" (46). From this perspective, modern prophecy is set upon revealing the supernatural origin of God's Providence, which has been internalized in the Enlightenment idea of immanent progress, thus eliding God and arrogating to human history all forms of successful endeavor.

[23] The tropological analysis offered in this essay is a rejection of the claims

which does not recognize the natural as a sign of God's glory or the soul as the image of God, but deifies both in grotesque forms of self-adulation, the sacramental must appear as a perfection, but first through subtraction of imperfection. At bottom, Flannery O'Connor's vision is informed by the Incarnation. In the words of her greatest figure of personified evil, The Misfit: "He [Jesus] thrown everything off balance" (O'Connor, *CS* 132). In a world in which the grotesque has become the norm, "large and startling figures" must be drawn in order to put things in their proper perspective. For Flannery O'Connor, "it is the virgin birth, the Incarnation, the resurrection which are the true laws of the flesh and the physical. Death, decay, destruction are the suspension of these laws. . . . The resurrection of Christ seems the high point in the law of nature . . ." (O'Connor, *Habit* 100). Even with the focus on sin and spiritual death, the center of Flannery O'Connor's aesthetic vision lies in this: that although the human will is bent on self-destruction, in the emptying of nature of all spiritual significance, nevertheless redemption is possible, "Because the Holy Ghost over the bent / World broods with warm breast and with ah! bright wings."

WORKS CITED

Asals, Frederick. *Flannery O'Connor: The Imagination of Extremity.* Athens: U of Georgia P, 1982.
Baker, J. Robert. "Flannery O'Connor's Four-Fold Method of Allegory." *The Flannery O'Connor Bulletin* 21 (1992): 84–96.
Bleikasten, André. "The Heresy of Flannery O'Connor." *Critical Essays*

---

that the force of Flannery O'Connor's art entirely overwhelms the allegorical significance of her characters, and that religious significance does not arise out of concrete situations in her work. See Josephine Hendin, *The World of Flannery O'Connor.* My essay is also an attempt to show how O'Connor employs traditional hermeneutic strategies as a way of undercutting the flatness of literal readings imposed by modern sensibility, through exposing the idolatry of materiality as an absolute ideology. See Carol Schloss, *Flannery O'Connor's Dark Comedies: The Limits of Inference.* O'Connor's fiction, notwithstanding Schloss's claims to the contrary, is not a failure because it employs an allegorical framework rejected by her readers. It is precisely the allegorical in her work that exposes the inherent need of redemption by characters which stand as types of the modern. The large numbers of readers powerfully moved by O'Connor's fiction renders Schloss's claims de facto unintelligible.

on *Flannery O'Connor*. Ed. Melvin J. Friedman and Beverly Lyon Clark. Boston: Hall, 1985. 138–58.

Burke, Edmund. *A Philosophical Enquiry into the Origin of Our Ideas of the Sublime and the Beautiful*. Ed. J. T. Boulton. Notre Dame: U of Notre Dame P, 1958.

Clark, Michael. "Flannery O'Connor's 'A Good Man Is Hard to Find': The Moment of Grace." *English Language Notes* 29 (Dec. 1991).

Coleridge, Samuel Taylor. *Biographia Literaria, or, Biographical Sketches of My Literary Life and Opinions*. Vol. 2. Ed. James Engell and W. Jackson Bate. Princeton: Princeton UP, 1983.

Desmond, John F. *Risen Sons: Flannery O'Connor's Vision of History*. Athens: U of Georgia P, 1987.

DiRenzo, Anthony. *American Gargoyles: Flannery O'Connor and the Medieval Grotesque*. Carbondale: Southern Illinois UP, 1993.

Eggenschwiler, David. *The Christian Humanism of Flannery O'Connor*. Detroit: Wayne State UP, 1972.

Gardner, W. H., and N. H. MacKenzie, eds. *The Poems of Gerard Manley Hopkins*. New York: Oxford UP, 1970.

Gentry, Marshall Bruce. *Flannery O'Connor's Religion of the Grotesque*. Jackson: U of Mississippi P, 1986.

Giannone, Richard. *Flannery O'Connor and the Mystery of Love*. Urbana: U of Illinois P, 1989.

———."Flannery O'Connor Tells Her Desert Story." *Religion and Literature* 27.2 (Summer 1995): 47–57.

Hawkes, John. "Flannery O'Connor's Devil." *Critical Essays on Flannery O'Connor*. Ed. Melvin J. Friedman and Beverly Lyon Clark. Boston: Hall, 1985. 92–100.

Hendin, Josephin. *The World of Flannery O'Connor*. Bloomington: Indiana UP, 1970.

Katz, Claire. "Flannery O'Connor's Rage of Vision." *American Literature* 46 (1974): 54–67.

Kessler, Edward. *Flannery O'Connor and the Language of Apocalypse*. Princeton: Princeton UP, 1986.

Lyotard, Jean-François. *Lessons on the Analytic of the Sublime*. Trans. Elizabeth Rottenberg. Stanford: Stanford UP, 1994.

Malin, Irving. "Flannery O'Connor and the Grotesque." *The Added Dimension: The Art and Mind of Flannery O'Connor*. Ed. Melvin J. Friedman and Lewis A. Lawson. 2nd ed. New York: Fordham UP, 1977. 108–26.

Martin, Karl. "Flannery O'Connor's Prophetic Imagination." *Religion and Literature* 26 (1994): 33–58.

Muller, Gilbert H. *Nightmares and Visions: Flannery O'Connor and the Catholic Grotesque*. Athens: U of Georgia P, 1972.

O'Connor, Flannery. *The Complete Stories of Flannery O'Connor.* New York: Farrar, Straus, Giroux, 1971.

——. *The Habit of Being.* Ed. Sally Fitzgerald. New York: Farrar, Straus, Giroux, 1978.

——. *Mystery and Manners: Occasional Prose.* Ed. Sally Fitzgerald and Robert Fitzgerald. New York: Farrar, Straus, Giroux, 1987.

Parker, Blanford. *The Triumph of Augustan Poetics: English Poetry from Butler to Johnson.* Cambridge: Cambridge UP, 1997.

Rath, Sura P. "Roby Turpin's Redemption: Thomistic Resolution in Flannery O'Connor's 'Revelation.'" *The Flannery O'Connor Bulletin* 19 (1990): 1–8.

Ruskin, John. *The Stones of Venice.* Vol. 3. Boston: Estes, 1898.

Schlafer, Linda. "Pilgrims of the Absolute: Léon Bloy and Flannery O'Connor." *Realist of Distances: Flannery O'Connor Revisited.* Ed. Karl-Heinz Westarp and Jan Nordby Gretlund. Aarhus, Denmark: Aarhus UP, 1987.

Schleifer, Ronald. "Rural Gothic: The Stories of Flannery O'Connor." *Critical Essays on Flannery O'Connor.* Ed. Melvin J. Friedman and Beverly Lyon Clark. Boston: Hall, 1985. 158–68.

Schloss, Carol. *Flannery O'Connor's Dark Comedies: The Limits of Inference.* Baton Rouge: Louisiana State UP, 1980.

Scouten, Kenneth. "'The Artificial Nigger': Mr. Head's Ironic Salvation." *The Flannery O'Connor Bulletin* 9 (1980): 87–97.

Stevens, Martha. *The Question of Flannery O'Connor.* Baton Rouge: Louisiana State UP, 1973.

Strickland, Edward. "The Penitential Quest in 'The Artificial Nigger.'" *Studies in Short Fiction* 25 (1988): 453–59.

Taylor, Charles. *Sources of the Self: The Making of Modern Identity.* Cambridge, MA: Harvard UP, 1989.

14

Sour Grapes: Ezekiel and the Literature of Social Justice

Henry Louis Gates, Jr.

The Fathers have eaten sour grapes, and the children's teeth are set at edge: no more shall this be said in the land (Ezekiel 18:2–3). This is, as conventionally glossed, an admonition against collective guilt, the ascription of guilt to a group by virtue of the sins of only some of its members. But it is equally a caveat on the subject of historical guilt, the notion of the heritability of guilt across generations and across time.

"No more shall this be said in the land," Ezekiel tells us. And yet both notions, of collective responsibility and of historical guilt—a notion that is parasitic on the idea of collective identity—continue to haunt the public language of morality to this day. It vexes the notion of memory, the way we apprehend the historic-ity—the historical rootedness—of who we are. For in a world fissured by ethnic strife, we know that cultural identity is so often bound up in memories of who has wronged us and, less often, whom we have wronged.

The passage with which I began presents itself as a repudiation of an aphorism, the cancellation of received wisdom, of an idea to be found elsewhere and earlier in the Pentateuch. We might think, in Genesis, of the transgenerational curse visited to the sons of Ham, retribution for his having seen his father's nakedness.

Or—following another tradition of biblical exegesis—we might think of one of the most mordant passages in the Book of Genesis, in which Abraham argues with God for the preservation of Sodom and Gomorrah, whose inhospitality is to be grievously punished. To a modern reader, raised in the traditions of norma-tive Christianity, what is so striking is the impudence of Abraham arguing, negotiating with the Almighty. Most people get tongue-tied when they try to win concessions from the college dean; and yet here is Abraham appealing to the Almighty to reconsider his decision. And the principle on which Abraham bases his appeal is precisely that expressed in the Book of Ezekiel: collective justice is not justice.

In fact, a profound ambivalence about this matter is hardly restricted to biblical tradition. Both the concept of historical guilt, often figured as a transgenerational curse passed down like ritual pollution, and the protest against its fundamental injustice have proven surprisingly enduring. We could turn to Sophocles's late tragedy *Oedipus at Colonnus*, in which Oedipus must confront the fact that in the end his suffering is the outcome of a curse placed upon his lineage before he was born, a prefigurement of later discussions of theodicy.

But why labor the point? Perhaps this is something we all know. Why, after all, should children suffer from their parents' misbehavior? Why should we inherit the enmity of history as an heirloom to be carefully preserved intact? And yet should the suffering of our ancestors be as nothing? Is not the world we inhabit profoundly shaped by the struggles of our forebears? Can we make sense of our own legacies if we erase the past and pretend the world was created anew at our birth?

Plainly, Ezekiel does not tell us to forget the past, as if this had ever been possible. We may survey the bloodshed among the Serbs and Croatians, among Azerbs and Kazakhs, Armenia and Turkistan, with dismay. And yet who among us would tell the Armenian, for example, to forget that his people were massacred in this very century? The past leaves scars, scars that cannot be wished away with the bland counsel to forgive and forget.

Nor should anyone tell us to forget the bitter history of slavery. It is a tragic aspect of a shared American history that both black and white America must preserve in our national memory, the amber of history. Jew and Gentile alike must always remember the atrocities of the Nazi death camps, of that brief span of time in which one out of every three Jews on the planet was murdered.

No, Ezekiel's message is not to forget the wounds of history. It is predicated, after all, on the collective memory of a people. And the past cannot be put to rest until we have been. Ezekiel does not tell us to close the book of history; rather, his message is to abjure the doctrine of historical guilt. Of guilt, and therefore punishment incurred by the accident of birth. The Bible contains two well-known moments that appear to contravene this ordinance. One, to which I have alluded, is the curse placed upon the sons of Ham in a passage that has been misappropriated to provide biblical sanction for slavery, for the subjugation of the African, for racism. The other passage I have in mind is, of course, to be found in the New Testament, in which the Jews, so we are told, accept the guilt for Christ's death, taking it upon themselves and upon all the generations to come. It is this passage that was used to provide biblical sanction for anti-Semitism, the persecution of Jewry across the generations.

Two passages, two lineages of oppression link the Jew and the Negro. Whether the fathers ate of sour grapes, we can only conjecture; all we have certainty of is that the children's teeth are set at edge. Only too often has Ezekiel's ordinance fallen on deaf ears.

Ezekiel is on my mind these days for a more immediate reason. For today one of the best-selling books in the black community is entitled *The Secret Relationship Between Blacks and Jews*. It is for sale in black-oriented shops in cities across the nation, even those that specialize in Kente cloth and jewelry rather than books. It can be ordered over the phone by dialing 1–800–48–TRUTH. At a recent press conference, one of the most successful recording artists in history, the rap performer Ice Cube, proclaimed that it was urgent that everyone get hold of a copy.

The book, a sophisticated updating of the protocols of the elders of Zion, was prepared by the historical research department of the Nation of Islam. It charges that the Jews dominated the slave trade, both as merchants of the middle passage and as slave traders and slave holders in this country. It charges that the Jews bear a "massive and disproportionate" culpability in the historic crime of slavery. And among significant portions of the black community it has by itself established the terms of a new argument, insinuating itself as a basic tenet of a new philosophy of self-affirmation.

Not surprisingly, the book massively misrepresents the historical record through a process of selective quotation and outright misquotation of its reputable sources. But in peppering the text with 1,275 footnotes, its authors could be confident that few if any of its readers would go to the trouble of actually finding a library and reading the works cited. For if readers actually did so, they might discover a rather different picture. They might find out—from the book's own vaunted "authorities"—that of all the African slaves imported into the New World, Jewish merchants accounted for less than two percent, a finding sharply at odds with the Nation's claim of Jewish "predominance" in this traffic. They might find out that, in the domestic trade, all the Jewish slave traders combined "did not buy and sell as many slaves" as the single (Gentile) firm of Franklin and Armfield. They might learn, in short, that the book's repeated insistence that the Jews "dominated" the slave trade depends on a farrago of lies and recycled myths.

And yet I wonder whether the spuriousness of the book's historical research may not distract us from the larger and more troubling issue that such works raise. Irrespective of the historical record, that is, we must interrogate the premise that culpability is heritable. For the doctrine of this resurgent movement is, ironically, a doctrine of racial continuity, in which the racial evil of a people is merely manifest (rather than constituted) by their historical misdeeds. The reported misdeeds are then the signs of an essential nature that is evil. As the Afro-American moral philosopher Laurence Thomas notes, there is "a difference of no small order between simply judging a people to be inferior and judging a people to be inferior because their being evil or, at any rate, morally depraved is an inherent part of their constitution." This last he identifies as a conceptual feature of anti-Semitism, and one that is, perhaps, unique to it.

But how do these assumptions surface in our everyday moral discourse? In New York last spring, a forum was held at the Church of St. Paul and Andrew with the Passover holiday in mind. It was to provide an occasion for blacks and Jews to engage in dialogue on such issues as slavery and social injustice. Both Jewish and black panelists found common ground and common causes. But representatives of a certain black professor at City College, Dr. Leonard Jeffries, were in the audience and took strong issue with the tone of the proceedings. They said they demanded an apology. They wanted the Jews to apologize to the "descendants of African kings and queens." And the organizer of the event, Melanie Kaye Kantrowitz, did so. Her voice quavering with emotion, she said: "I think I speak for a lot of people in this room when I say 'I'm sorry.' We're ashamed of it, we hate it, and that's why we organized this event."

Ms. Kantrowitz is, no doubt, a member of that endangered species, the bleeding heart liberal. Did she descend from Simon Legree? Not likely. The question is whether a woman whose ancestors survived pogroms, Cossacks, and, latterly, the Nazi Holocaust, should be the primary target of our wrath. Is it for the Ms. Kantrowitzes of the world to apologize? And what is granted us in this hateful sport of victimology? That was on the mind of another audience member. "I don't want an apology," a dreadlocked woman told her angrily. "I want reparations. Forty acres and a mule, plus interest."

Did her father eat of sour grapes? Who knows? But how easy it is to set her teeth at edge. It is because we have learned from Ezekiel that we know that social policies cannot be indexed to historical reparation, but to contemporary social justice. The past can never be forgotten, but it cannot be indemnified either. That is a fundamental truth that we still must wrestle with. I said a little earlier that the Negro and the Jew know about transhistorical guilt, because both have been so accursed. But the apostles of bigotry today have been astonishingly effective in disguising the historical kinship of persecution. A recent Yankelovich poll shows that over the past twenty-five years anti-Semitism has diminished among white Americans and increased among black Americans: "Blacks are twice as likely as whites to hold significant anti-Semitic attitudes and, even more alarming, it is younger and better educated blacks who tend to be the most bigoted."

How far this all seems from the days when Martin Luther King, Jr., protested the unjust treatment of Soviet Jewry, as he did in 1964, with a fervent admonition: "Injustice anywhere is a threat to justice everywhere. Injustice to any people is a threat to justice to all people—and I cannot stand idly by, even though I live in the United States and even though I happen to be an American Negro, and fail to be concerned about what happens to my brothers and sisters who happen to be Jews in Soviet Russia. For what happens to them, happens to me—and to you; and we must be concerned." So Dr. King told us.

We now face the end of a most tragic century—a century of two world wars, of apartheid, of gulags, death camps, and police states. A century that should remind us that bigotry is an opportunistic infection, attacking most virulently when the body politic is in a weakened state. Today we all can look upon lawlessness and anomie and hopelessness, if we can bear to, in our own cities. And King's insistence—that "we must be concerned"—has a special trenchancy for us. Already the winds are shifting; in the black community an alarming wave of separatist, neo-nationalist posturing is in the making, one that esteems rage rather than compassion as our noblest emotion. I am not entirely optimistic. As the poet says, we must love one another or die.

But if we cannot break out of the regress of score settling, of grievance and counter-grievance, then there is no hope for us. The past must be a wellspring of moral courage, which is to say, we poison its well if we reduce it to a sump of hatred, a renewable resource of enmity everlasting where the sins of the past are visited upon the children, and their children, and their children, until, perhaps, there are no children left.

"No more shall this be said in the land," Ezekiel warns us.

No more.

15

Wallace Stevens's Spiritual Voyage: A Buddhist–Christian Path to Conversion

Dorothy Judd Hall

> Love is the epiphany of God in our poverty.
>
> —THOMAS MERTON

> [T]the wonder and mystery of art, as indeed of religion in the last resort, is the revelation of something 'wholly other' by which the inexpressible loneliness of thinking is broken and enriched.
>
> —WALLACE STEVENS

MY END IS IN MY BEGINNING: I intend to come full circle to a deeper appreciation of the epigraphs I have selected for this essay.[1] Let me start with a few basic propositions:

(1) *Zen* (meaning "meditation") is a mode of consciousness in the contemplative religious tradition—Buddhist and Christian. (Graham, *Zen* xi)

---

[1] This essay represents a condensed version of a book–length study (in progress), "Wallace Stevens: A Spiritual Voyage to the Center," a project that had its genesis in a talk I gave in April 1994 at the Jesuit Institute, Boston College. I wish to express my gratitude to Rev. Michael J. Buckley, S.J., Director of Jesuit Institute, for inviting me to give that talk; to Sister Bernetta Quinn, O.S.F., for her encouragement from afar, and to my friend William Alfred (Professor Emeritus, Harvard University) for his guidance along the way.

I wish also to thank Professor Roger J. Corless, Department of Religion, Duke University, for his painstaking reading of an earlier version of this essay. His understanding of Buddhist thought and his dedication to the ongoing Buddhist–Christian dialogue are reflected in numerous scholarly publications. I particularly recommend his *Vision of Buddhism* and his recent essay, "Idolatry and Inherent Existence: The Golden Calf and the Wooden Buddha." in David Loy, ed., *Healing Deconstruction: Postmodern Thought in Buddhism and Christianity*. The following footnotes reflect his comments in a letter to me dated June 19, 1996.

(2) In Buddhism, Form = Emptiness (*Ku; Sunyata*) = Silence. Ignorance and Enlightenment are one. (Graham, *Conversations* 8, 105, 192)

(3) Wallace Stevens is an essentially meditative poet whose kenotic images empty-out reality. "This is form gulping after formlessness. . . ." ("The Auroras of Autumn")

In 1948 Stevens conceded, with characteristic obliqueness, the implicitly autobiographical nature of his poetry:

> It is often said of a man that his work is autobiographical in spite of every subterfuge. It cannot be otherwise . . . even though it may be totally without reference to himself. (*Necessary Angel* 121)

This guarded admission invites us to chart Stevens's spiritual voyage within the poetry—to discover his inner turnings as he tacks around various markers, "Glozing his life with after-shining flicks" ("The Comedian as the Letter C," Stevens, *Palm* 75).

MEDITATIVE VISION

It was Louis Martz who first called attention to Stevens's meditative temperament and linked him to the monastic tradition. In the words of François de Sales, the tradition embraced the belief that

> Every meditation is a thought, but every thought is not a meditation; . . . when we think of heavenly things, not to learn, but to delight in them, that is called . . . meditation. (Martz 146)

In Stevens, of course, "delight" shifts from heaven to earth, a place where "resemblances converge." "For a moment," Martz wrote, "the [poetic] object becomes a vital center through which the sense of life is composed" (150). Yet we may wonder if such *momentary poetic centers* ultimately satisfy the human need for an *eternal spiritual center*. In 1951, four years before his death, Stevens seems to suggest this possibility, as he summons the poet to the office of secular priest: "In an age of disbelief . . . it is for the poet to supply the satisfactions of belief, in his measure and in his style" (Bates, *Opus* 259). The passage is open to misreading. Is the real subject in Stevens's own poetry "the secular mystery," as Robert Pack assumed (Stevens, *Letters* 863)? Or is there a hidden agenda? Was he traveling concurrently along two paths: (1) the way-of-art, where poetic fictions circle around shifting symbolic centers; (2) the way-of-life, never fully articulated in the poetry, but nevertheless the underlying direction in which his spirit moved—the true bearing which all his fictive moments approximate? Was he perhaps capable of an act of the imagination, a kind of leap, reaching beyond what some critics have considered his limits? Did he, in fact—on his deathbed—ask to be baptized into Roman Catholicism, as Peter Brazeau's oral biography, *Parts of a World*, reports? While some major critics dismiss or dispute the conversion, I think it must be reckoned with. My friend, Harvard professor William Alfred, told me recently:

> A questioning soul is a questing soul all the time. The inner biography dictates the final poem—the unwritten poem which the audience can only imagine. A poet needs a poetic conviction in order to write a poem. His poetic quest is similar to the search for God, and the two can go on simultaneously. (August 17, 1995)

In "Notes Toward a Supreme Fiction" (Stevens, *Palm* 230) Stevens acknowledges a discrepancy between the hidden truth of reality and the symbolic truth we imagine:

> . . . But to impose is not
> To discover. To discover an order as of
> A season, to discover summer and know it.
>
> To discover winter and know it well, to find,
> Not to impose, not to have reasoned at all,
> Out of nothing to have come on major weather,
>
> It is possible, possible, possible. It must
> Be possible. it must be that in time
> The real will from its crude compoundings come,
>
> Seeming, at first, a beast disgorged, unlike,
> Warmed by a desperate milk. To find the real,
> To be stripped of every fiction except one,

The fiction of an absolute—Angel,
Be silent in your luminous cloud and hear
The luminous melody of proper sound.

Stevens had a deep sense of what the questions in poetry were; he would not falsify by making them easy. He was so serious about his fixed conviction—his search for "The real" which *must* "in time / . . . from its crude compoundings come"—that all his poetry avoids specifying it. Nevertheless, I shall attempt to track Stevens's spiritual path through the vanishing centers of his poetic moments as he moved gradually toward the invisible and real "order" that lies beyond time.

BRAZEAU'S DISCLOSURES

With the publication of Brazeau's book, Stevens's baptism into Roman Catholicism became public knowledge. Some years earlier a rumor circulating in the Jesuit community—word the poet had come into the Church—had reached my ears. At first, I was surprised, puzzled, for it did not square with the views of leading literary critics: Marie Borroff, Harold Bloom, Helen Vendler. Then, gradually, the conversion story began to take amorphous shape in my imagination.

Brazeau's book reveals an intensely private poet. We catch glimpses of Stevens's guarded friendships, familial estrangements, ritualistic walking habits, and furtive visits to Saint Patrick's Cathedral in New York City. The entry that sparked most controversy was the author's conversation with Rev. Arthur Hanley (294–96), chaplain at St. Francis Hospital in Hartford at the time of Stevens's hospitalizations: the first, in April 1955, when he was diagnosed with what turned out to be his final illness; the second, when he was readmitted in July. He died August 2, 1955. The priest reminisces about his daily visits to Stevens's hospital room, recalling the poet's discomfort over his estrangement from Elsie, his wife, and his qualms about religious belief—in particular, the problem of evil and the apparent contradiction between "a merciful God" and the idea of "Hell."

The time-bomb in the conversation was the priest's disclosure of Stevens's baptism the second time he was in—just a few days before he died. "He seemed," says Father Hanley, "very much at peace, and he would say, 'Now I'm in the fold.' " The priest, belatedly setting matters straight, explains why the baptism went unrecorded: "because [Stevens's] wife was not a Catholic and because it might seem that we got people into the hospital to drag them into the Church at the last minute, Archbishop O'Brien told me not to let it be known. Sister Philomena, who was on the floor, knew; she came in for the baptism" (295).

A few years after Brazeau's book appeared, Joan Richardson's biography, *The Later Years*, reported the baptism story in a manner that trivialized it:

> Is it possible that as his final prank the comedian had led both Father Hanley and Holly [Stevens's daughter] to believe two different things, that the poet did, in fact, ask for Communion and Extreme Unction as part of the final act of his comedy without telling Holly, so that we now still wonder how he resolved the greatest problem of his age, the will to believe? (427)

OTHER CRITICAL VIEWS

Needless to say, Richardson's ambivalence did little to shake established critical notions of Stevens as a confirmed secularist. In their various ways Marie Borroff, Harold Bloom, and Helen Vendler portrayed him as a poet in quest of changing, impermanent "fictions" that might suffice, filling the human need for God in an age of disbelief. That image—crystallized by the end of the sixties—long went unchallenged. Borroff hails Stevens's talent as a "triumph of the imagination over the forces of cosmic destruction" (22). Bloom celebrates the "tentativeness" of Stevens's assertions—his "attempt," in "Notes Toward a Supreme Fiction," "at a final belief in a fiction known to be a fiction, in the predicate that there is nothing else" (Borroff 76–77). Vendler paints a more somber picture. Taking her title, *On Extended Wings* (1969), from Stevens's early poem "Sunday Morning," she charts a downward curve: Stevens's gradual descent into darkness—"his withering into the truth" (311). Aware that "the problem of pain and evil" was from the beginning ("Domination of Black," 1916) "an un-

congenial subject" for him (229), she questions his sustained ability to "re-create the world, turning Hesper into Phosphor by
turning himself from a mirror to a lamp" (308). Vendler's later
book, *Words Chosen Out of Desire* (1984), reinforces her view of
Stevens's progressive spiritual disillusionment.

However, alongside these secular readings, others were emerging which gave some credence to the baptism story: James Baird's
The Dome and the Rock (1968—before Brazeau) and Milton
Bates's *Wallace Stevens: A Mythology of Self* (1985). Then two more
voices joined the chorus: Sister Bernetta Quinn and Father Cassian J. Yuhaus (1989).

Finally, in 1993, David Jarraway met the issue head-on in his
book *Wallace Stevens and the Question of Belief*. His subtitle, *Metaphysician in the Dark*, indicates the philosophical bent of a tightly
reasoned argument that concludes, "Stevens's textuality ultimately draws a blank." Jarraway's study trails off into non-clo-
sure—no final period, just three dots:

> we can be sure that the Form of belief will never count for more
> than the force of its question, and there, too, that the force of the
> question will never promise less than *another* ordinary evening, in a
> world without end . . . (315)

Jarraway's punctuation, like his argument, consigns Stevens to a
pattern of eternal recurrence—"world without end." After following Jarraway's scrupulous logic, a question still remains: What
are we to make of Stevens's tactfully candid disclosure in a letter
to Sister Bernetta Quinn, around Easter 1948, seven years before
he died?

> Your mind is too much like my own for it to seem to be an evasion
> on my part to say merely that I do seek a centre and expect to go
> on seeking it. I don't say that I shall not find it or that I do not
> expect to find it. It is the great necessity even without specific
> identification. (Stevens, *Letters* 584)

STEVENS'S VOYAGE TO THE "CENTRE"

Assuming that Stevens's poetry is in some sense the record of his
inner life, how shall we chart his spiritual journey—in Borroff's

figure: *ascent of triumphal imagination*? In Vendler's *descent into stoic endurance*? Or in Jarraway's metaphor: entrapment in *eternal recurrence*? Did Stevens circle interminably on Nietzsche's Sea of X—or did he come to port? Consider the early Stevens, setting sail on the infinite deep with his pilot, imagination, at the helm. How might he navigate between the Scylla and Charybdis of modern thought: the specter of *nihilism* on one side, skepticism of Platonic *transcendence* on the other? His discomfort with spurious Romantic dreams is heard in the voice of "Crispin" ("The Comedian as the Letter C," 1922), who rejects the "niggling nightingale" and "Moonlight . . . evasion" of nineteenth-century poetry:

> Thus he conceived his voyaging to be
> An up and down between two elements,
> A fluctuating between sun and moon,
> A sally into gold and crimson forms.

How does imagination, inherently untrustworthy, steer the poet through the uncertain waters of modernity?

This essay has three major concerns: (1) *nothingness* and loss of the deific dream; (2) the desire for *transcendence*; (3) the peregrinations of *imagination*, an enigmatic figure at once revelatory and delusive, fickle and salvific, that frequently assumes feminine guise: day-dreaming lady in "Sunday Morning"; "mother of pathos and pity" in "Lunar Paraphrase"; singer-beside-the-sea in "The Idea of Order at Key West"; surreptitious lover in "Final Soliloquy of the Interior Paramour"; faithful Penelope awaiting the return of wandering Ulysses in "The Sail of Ulysses." I shall begin with "Sunday Morning." After moving through some troubled waters, around various poetic markers, I shall close with "the lady's" final transformation, which presages the retrieval of the dream in a deeper reality.

Loss of the Deific Dream: "Sunday Morning" (1915)

In "Sunday Morning" we encounter a woman who stays home from church on the sabbath to enjoy sensuous pleasures—

> late
> Coffee and oranges in a sunny chair,
> And the green freedom of a cockatoo
> Upon a rug . . .

On "her dreaming feet" the poet travels "Over the seas, to silent Palestine"—backward in time to the crucifixion, "Dominion of the blood and sepulchre."

> She hears, upon that water without sound,
> A voice that cries, "The tomb in Palestine
> Is not the porch of spirits lingering.
> It is the grave of Jesus, where he lay."

Beneath the surface "Complacencies of the peignoir" we sense disturbance:

> What is divinity if it can come
> Only in silent shadows and in dreams?

Through his dreaming lady, Stevens imagines the death of the deific dream. In her persona he rejects outworn religious myth, pagan and Christian alike—the myth of "Jove in the clouds" and of "Jesus." His lady dreams a dream of earth: "We live in an old chaos of the sun." Discounting ancient belief as mere romantic illusion,

> She says, "I am content when wakened birds,
> Before they fly, test the reality
> Of misty fields, ... ["]

Yet she questions,

> ["]But when the birds are gone, and their warm fields
> Return no more, where, then, is paradise?"

The lady in "Sunday Morning" shares our modern anxiety, our fear that what we call "divinity" is a mere psychological projection, a counterfeit born of unfulfilled yearning for a fugitive God: "Death is the mother of beauty." Questioning immortality and Jesus's resurrection, the lady turns inward, to her own psyche:

> Divinity must live within herself:
> Passions of rain, or moods in falling snow;
> Grievings in loneliness, or unsubdued
> Elations when the forest blooms; . . .

Her daydreams carry her back to a vanished age of faith. But, as the poem closes, she leaves the ancient holy ground. Skepticism intrudes upon belief, and the hopeful vision of Easter morning dissolves:

> . . . in the isolation of the sky,
> At evening, casual flocks of pigeons make
> Ambiguous undulations as they sink,
> Downward to darkness, on extended wings.

"Pigeons," drab birds of ordinary reality—not the annunciatory dove of Noah—sink "Downward to darkness," inverting the lady's yearning for spiritual transcendence. Her secular turn anticipates the triple negations of "The Snow Man."

THE ENIGMA OF NOTHINGNESS: "THE SNOW MAN" (1921)

Stevens's "The Snow Man" (five stanzas in a single sentence) is a complex lyric which explodes the romantic lie—the "pathetic fallacy," as Ruskin called it—that nature shares our human feelings of joy and sorrow:

> One must have a mind of winter
> To regard the frost and the boughs
> Of the pine-trees crusted with snow;
>
> And have been cold a long time
> To behold the junipers shagged with ice,
> The spruces rough in the distant glitter
>
> Of the January sun; and not to think
> Of any misery in the sound of the wind,
> In the sound of a few leaves,
>
> Which is the sound of the land
> Full of the same wind
> That is blowing in the same bare place

> For the listener, who listens in the snow,
> And, nothing himself, beholds
> Nothing that is not there and the nothing that is.

The triple negations in the final lines point toward the enigma of nothingness, a paradox that has vexed Western thought—especially since the nineteenth century when Nietzsche called into question the status of Being. In his reading of the poem, J. Hillis Miller offers this cogent insight:

> Being is a pervasive power, visible nowhere in itself and yet present and visible in all things. It is what things share through the fact that they are. Being is not a thing like other things and therefore can only appear to man as nothing, but it is what all things must participate in if they are to exist at all. (Bloom, *Wallace* 62)

Confusion over the status of Non-being points in two quite opposite directions: through the collapse of reason into *nihilism,* or beyond rational structures to the *via negativa* of mysticism. Bernard McGinn aptly states:

> If the modern consciousness of God is often of an absent God . . . many mystics seem almost to have been prophets of this in their intense realization that the "real God" becomes a possibility only when the many false gods (even the God of religion) have vanished and the frightening abyss of total nothingness is confronted. (xviii)

Some years back, I tended to interpret "The Snow Man" in strictly nihilist terms. Like many Western thinkers, I confused a rejection of romantic sentimentality with absence of cosmic meaning. Then I encountered the Buddhist Void.[2] Picking up a copy of Thomas Merton's *Zen and the Birds of Appetite*, I saw, on

---

[2] Professor Corless finds "Void" a "misleading" translation of "shunyata." He cites his preference for "Transparency"—even over the more common English rendering, "Emptiness." While I agree that "Transparency" captures the essence of Stevens's *poetic vision*, the crux of Stevens's spiritual predicament (in "The Snow Man" and elsewhere) is, I believe, rooted in a *metaphysical confusion* that pervades Western thought: the fallacious tendency to reify Being and to confuse non-Being (no-thingness) with nihilism. In accordance with this faulty thinking, the Buddhist "Void" becomes entangled with the "Abyss" in Western philosophy—with the sense of cosmic "meaninglessness" that informs existential *angst.*

its paperback cover, fog-shrouded Mount Fuji: Being emptying-
out into Non-being. Suddenly I was struck by a likeness between
Buddhist "emptiness" and Wallace Stevens's kenotic imagery—
for example, in "The Man with the Blue Guitar" where the mu-
sician decreases the world in the manner of "Picasso's . . .'hoard /
Of destructions.' " I decided to take a Buddhist path into Stevens's poetry. But before long I realized that another critic had
already turned eastward. William Bevis (*Mind of Winter*, 1988)
provides a Buddhist perspective on Stevens. He ignores, however,
the final conversion to Catholicism. Linking Stevens's vision to
the orientalism of Emerson and Thoreau, he connects the negations in "The Snow Man" to Buddhist meditative awareness (54–
55)—in particular "to the fourth stage of meditative
consciousness [during Zazen meditation], when 'satisfaction de-
parts and indifference begins,' or perhaps to a higher state, when
one says, 'There exists absolutely nothing' ":

> it is a state of mind quite different from the detachment of Western
> objectivity, or Western irony. This detachment is not a distancing
> of the intellect but a total disappearance of intellect.[3] . . . We will
> call excited self-loss, *ecstasy*, and detached self-loss, *meditation*.
> (32–33)

Distinguishing "rapture" (Western ecstatic sublime) from the qui-
eter mode of Buddhist "enlightenment," Bevis separates "excited
transcendentalists or visionaries"—Blake, Yeats, Emerson—from
"overlooked . . . mystics"—Stevens, Salinger, Virginia Woolf
(48).

But Stevens's Emersonian roots are tangled, for time and loss
darkened Emerson's own youthful optimism. Harold Bloom
traces Stevens's thinking to Nietzsche (*Wallace* 59) and to the
older, less rhapsodic Emerson of 1866 who declared, "For every
seeing soul there are two absorbing facts,—I and the Abyss" (62).
Bloom asserts emphatically that "the Snow Man . . . beholds as a
nihilist beholds" (62). Indeed, there is a pervasive intellectual kin-

---

[3] Corless offers this corrective to Bevis: "Nowhere in Buddhism do I know of
a 'total disappearance of the intellect'—that is something Buddhists accuse their
opponents of teaching, e.g., if no-thinking is best, then a stone is the wisest of
beings. What is taught in Buddhism is the *calming* of discursive mind, the *focusing*
of consciousness, which then becomes more penetrating."

ship between the German philosopher and the American poet, as George Stack shows in his penetrating study *Nietzsche and Emerson: An Elective Affinity* (1992).

From whatever perspective we approach "The Snow Man," the poem leaves the paradox of nothingness unresolved. Thomas Merton, in his meditation for Good Friday, April 16, 1965, the last year of his life, places resolution of the paradox beyond human consciousness and beyond time itself. "But God, the abyss of being beyond all division of being and nothingness, can neither be made to be nor reduced to nothing." He concludes, "The way to 'being' is then the way of non-assertion. This is God's way. Not that He has a way in Himself, but it is the way He has revealed for us" (Merton, *Vow* 174).

"The Snow Man" remains an intransigent "marker" on Stevens's voyage. Yet, circling around it, we discern a rough correspondence between the *tao* of Zen meditative detachment and the Christian contemplative path, the *via negativa*. And we may chart the triple negations in the poem as follows:

"nothing himself"	= meditative self-detachment
"Nothing that is not there"	= rejection of the romantic lie
"the nothing that is"	= the Buddhist Void or God-beyond-all division-of-being-and-nothingness

A poem for Stevens was an act of the mind discovering itself —clarifying the relation of self to world. In "The Snow Man" he struggles to stay on course as he steers by the Scylla of nothingness. He would revisit that paradox in later poems. But first he had to make his way past the Charybdis of Platonic transcendence.

ENLIGHTENMENT: "SAILING AFTER LUNCH" (1935)

As Helen Vendler correctly discerns, "transcendence" is a problem for Stevens. "The Man with the Blue Guitar" (1937) asserts: "Poetry / Exceeding music must take the place / Of empty heaven and its hymns." And "A Quiet Normal Life" (1952), written just three years before his death, reaffirms his suspicion of Platonic idealism:

> There was no fury in transcendent forms.
> But his actual candle blazed with artifice.

Vendler finds that, unlike Keats, who "emphasized . . . Platonic entities in a transcendent world where . . . Beauty is Truth, Truth Beauty," Stevens "shifts the locus of attention away from the transcendent to the actual, from the object of desire to desire inventing its object; and, most centrally, to the change over time of the desired object" (*Words* 29). Thus Vendler limits Stevens's options to: (1) Platonic transcendence ("the object of desire") or (2) Freudian projection ("desire inventing its object"). While it is true that Stevens rejected Platonic absolutes, he gradually discovered an alternative to solipsism, a Buddhist-like "middle way" which Nathan Scott calls "transcendence downward":

> It is in the moment of what the Greeks called *aletheia*, in the moment of revelation, when the candor in things leads them to unveil themselves, that we find ourselves savoring [the] "bouquet of being" [Morse 109]. . . . To win the great gift of *aletheia* there must, of course, be a right disposition of the mind and heart, such as the disciplines of decreation and abstraction prepare. (Scott 22–23)

Stevens's kenotic inclination, his tendency (as in "The Man with the Blue Guitar") to decrease the world, enables him to recognize transcendence *within the actual*.[4]

Modern consciousness is struggling to recover an immediacy that was lost long before Descartes, though he is often targeted for blame in the schism between self and world. The cure lies in a redefinition of "self," as Gerard Manley Hopkins discerns in his retreat notes on Ignatius Loyola's *Spiritual Exercises*:

> . . . whatever can with truth be called a self . . . is not a mere centre or point of reference for consciousness or action attributed to it. . . . Parts of this world of objects, this object-world, is also part of the very self in question. . . . A self then will consist of a centre and

---

[4] Corless affirms: " 'Transcendence within the actual.' Yes! This is it! That is *samsara* in *nirvana*, that is how you solve the koan, that is non-duality rather than (heretical, from a Buddhist point of view) monism."

a surrounding area or circumference, of a point of reference and a belonging field. (Ong 39–40)

By the time he came to write "Landscape with Boat" (1940), Stevens had cleared a phenomenological path where self and world are integrally related. The ironic voice in the poem obliquely disclaims the quest for absolutes:

> He never supposed
> That he might be truth, himself, or part of it,
> That the things that he rejected might be part
> And the irregular turquoise, part, the perceptible blue
> Grown denser, part, the eye so touched, so played
> Upon by clouds, the ear so magnified
> By thunder, parts, and all these things together,
> Parts, and more things, parts. He never supposed divine
> Things might not look divine, nor that if nothing
> Was divine then all things were, the world itself,
> And that if nothing was the truth, then all
> Things were the truth, the world itself was the truth.

But it was earlier, in "Sailing after Lunch" (1935), that the *meta-noia*—the turn to "downward transcendence"—occurred. William Alfred once said of this poem, "Stevens wasn't looking for transcendence, but he was glad when he found it!" What Stevens seems to mean by "transcendence" is something like exuberance: "the way one feels, sharp white," as—quite unexpectedly—"the light wind worries the sail" and the sailboat "rush[es] brightly through the summer air." The experience closely resembles Buddhist Satori (Enlightenment)—a spontaneous illumination that grounds the feeling of "transcendence" in the physical senses without recourse to Platonic Forms.

Stevens's sailboat poem is an elegy on the death of romantic dreaming:

> It is the word pejorative that hurts.
> My old boat goes round on a crutch
> And doesn't get under way. It's the time of the year
> And the time of the day.
> Perhaps it's the lunch that we had
> Or the lunch that we should have had.
> But I am, in any case,

> A most inappropriate man
> In a most unpropitious place.
> Mon Dieu, hear the poet's prayer.
> The romantic should be here.
> The romantic should be there.
> It ought to be everywhere.

"But the romantic must never remain," the poem laments. Can we trust, as the Romantics aspired to do, the synthesizing power of the imagination? One may become a bit dizzy, a little seasick from "sailing after lunch." Stevens rejects both Platonic transcendence and Romantic sentimentality. In fact, "Sailing after Lunch" is one of the few poems where the word *transcendence* occurs. A passage in his posthumous works clarifies the puzzling *pejorative* (in the first line of the poem) as referring to the weak, sentimental aspect of Romanticism:

> Although the romantic is referred to, most often, in a pejorative sense, this sense attaches, or should attach, not to the romantic in general but to some phase of the romantic that has become stale. Just as there is always a romantic that is potent, so there is always a romantic that is impotent. (Morse 180)

The sentimental romantic is "stale," "impotent." But there still may be a vital romantic spirit, one that takes us unaware—as the wind catches the "dirty sail"—carrying our imagination beyond the realm of the senses:

> This heavy historical sail
> Through the mustiest blue of the lake
> In a really vertiginous boat
> Is wholly the vapidest fake. . . .
> It is least what one ever sees.
> It is only the way one feels, to say
> Where my spirit is I am,
> To say the light wind worries the sail,
> To say the water is swift today,
>
> To expunge all people and be a pupil
> Of the gorgeous wheel and so to give
> That slight transcendence to the dirty sail,
> By light, the way one feels, sharp white,
> And then rush brightly through the summer air.

"Where my spirit is I am": "Sailing After Lunch" celebrates the human spirit in all its physicality. In "Sunday Morning" (1915) the deific dream had vanished with "Jove in the clouds," and two decades later, in "Sailing After Lunch," Stevens was exulting in those capricious winds that swept him across bright waters. As late as 1951—in an address to the College English Association, just a few years before his death—Stevens still rejoiced in the challenge to human imagination in a world bereft of myth:

> To see the gods dispelled in mid-air and dissolve like clouds is one of the great human experiences. It is not as if they had gone over the horizon to disappear for a time; nor as if they had been over-come by other gods of greater power and profounder knowledge. It is simply that they came to nothing. (Bates, *Opus* 260)

Was it coincidence—or did Stevens know—that in the very same year (1951) Heidegger, in Munich, had posited God-without-Being? When someone asked, "Is it proper to posit Being and God as identical" Heidegger responded:

> Being and God are not identical and I would never attempt to think the essence of God by means of Being. . . . Faith does not need the thought of Being. When faith has recourse to this thought, it is no longer faith. . . . I believe that Being can never be thought as the ground and essence of God, but that nevertheless the experience of God and of his manifestedness . . . flashes in the dimension of Being. . . . (Marion 61)

We sense a link between Heidegger's "flashes" and Stevens's "after shining flicks" ("The Comedian as the Letter C"). Stevens, impatient with pretentious philosophical rhetoric (the "beards" at "the Academy of Fine Ideas" [Stevens, *Palm* 179]), jingles the bells on his poet's cap and surveys the range of theological dream-ing—from mythic Zeus to Buddhist nothingness. How might poetry sustain the human spirit in a time of metaphysical crisis? Were the sacred presences of Judeo-Christian vision to be eradi-cated by nihilism? Or might the West rediscover, in Zen masters and Christian mystics, the contemplative path that leads, as Thomas Merton suggests, to "God, the abyss of being beyond all division of being and nothingness"?

IMAGINING ABSENCE: "THE PLAIN SENSE OF THINGS" (1952)

But how does human imagination cope with nothingness, with the Void after sacred images have evaporated? Stevens's kenotic temperament comes into play. His fine strokes disappear before our eyes like the delicate colors in a Japanese print—decreasing the world, opening out our field of view. On Stevens's voyage, "The Plain Sense of Things"—its sparse style reminiscent of the itinerant Zen poet Basho—is a turning point, a *metanoia* leading through the vanishing presences of imagination to Absence:

> Yet the absence of the imagination had
> Itself to be imagined. The great pond,
> The plain sense of it, without reflections, leaves,
> Mud, water like dirty glass, expressing silence
>
> Of a sort, silence of a rat come out to see,
> The great pond and its waste of the lilies, all this
> Had to be imagined as an inevitable knowledge,
> Required, as a necessity requires.

The Void is a place of infinite freedom—an unmapped inner geography where, like ice dancers on a limitless frozen pond, we may trace arcs forever. As Stevens wrote to Henry Church in October 1942, "If you take the varnish and dirt of generations off a picture, you see it in its first idea. If you think about the world without its varnish and dirt, you are a thinker of the first ideas" (Stevens, *Letters* 426–27). To use a *T'ien-t'ai* image, Stevens "clears the dust off the mirror of the mind,"[5] revealing an original

---

[5] Corless notes: "The image of clearing the dust off the mind is actually Yogachara (see *Visions of Buddhism*, 174–84) and from there is got into the vast packrat system of T'ien-t'ai. Also note . . . that whether enlightenment is gradual or sudden is a major issue *within* Buddhism (see *Vision of Buddhism*, 223–24)."

The controversy between Subitists and Gradualists is, indeed, so distinctive a feature of Chinese Buddhism that when the Tibetans staged a debate between an Indian and a Chinese Dharma Master, in order to decide which tradition to accept, they saw the issue in terms of Subitism and Gradualism. Most Tibetan lineages opted for Gradualism. The nyingma lineage has retained the Subitist position, but Subitist lineages (some forms of Zen and of Pure Land Buddhism) are found chiefly in Far Eastern Buddhism (223).

It would appear that the "Beat" poets, in the hope of achieving a Zen-like sudden enlightenment, opted for spontaneity of creative expression. By contrast, Stevens (with a few exceptions, such as the momentary "transcendence" in "Sailing After Lunch") inclined toward a meditative graduate enlightenment.

purity—a transparency like the imageless path of Zazen medita-
tion, or the *via negativa* of Christian mysticism. In the words of
William Alfred, "Transcendence is the shadow of our longing for
God."

An ardent connoisseur of modern art, Stevens employs the im-
pressionist lost-and-found line that forces the eye to follow beyond where the line disappears on the canvas. Avoiding hard
edges, he plays with light and shadow. He seems to be saying:
"See what the light does—instead of what the subject is." I once
heard a painter remark: "I do not draw an outline. Yet I end up
with one by showing where the light falls. I'm not dealing with
the subject. I'm dealing with my paint." He was sketching the
Venus de Milo: "You have to see where she's casting a shadow."
So it was with Stevens; he was casting a shadow in the direction
of transcendence. Like Buddhist *Satori* (Illumination), the experience of transcendence may occur suddenly (the gust of wind in
"Sailing After Lunch"). Or it may emerge gradually, with the
subtle luminosity of a Japanese watercolor ("The Poems of Our
Climate," 1938):

> Clear water in a brilliant bowl,
> Pink and white carnations. The light
> In the room more like a snowy air,
> Reflecting snow. A newly-fallen snow
> At the end of winter when afternoons return.
> Pink and white carnations—one desires
> So much more than that. The day itself
> Is simplified: a bowl of white,
> Cold, a cold porcelain, low and round,
> With nothing more than the carnations there.

Stevens's "cold porcelain" resonates to the "Cold Pastoral" in
Keats's "Ode on a Grecian Urn," but Stevens refuses the Platonic
split between frozen forms and human passion. With Zen-like
serenity, his shadow emerges:

> Still one would want more, one would need more,
> More than a world of white and snowy scents.

The intricate length of his spiritual journey bears witness to the care he took
navigating the shoals of doubt before coming into port.

Acknowledging the presence of Stevens's "shadow," Robert Bly observes that, unlike Stevens, many "American haiku poets do not grasp the idea that the shadow has to have risen up and invaded the haiku poem, otherwise it is not a haiku. The least important thing about it is its seventeen syllables or the nature scene" (70).

"Bitterness" and "delight" commingle in Stevens's essentially Zen poem. "Pink and white carnations" embody ephemeral beauty—the fragility of transience that Japanese painters discover in snow flakes and falling cherry blossoms. To see the world clearly is to see our original and "imperfect . . . paradise." For sorrow and impermanence are integral to life, and, as Aldous Huxley notes, the error of Platonic thought is its inability to see Be-ing in its changing iridescence:

> I was not looking now at an unusual flower arrangement. I was seeing what Adam had seen on the morning of his creation—the miracle, moment by moment, of naked existence. . . . *Istigkeit*—wasn't that the word Meister Eckhart liked to use? "Is-ness." (Neumann 176)

"Plato," says Huxley, "seems to have made the enormous, the grotesque mistake of separating Being from becoming and identifying it with the mathematical abstraction of the Idea"; "He could never, poor fellow, have seen a bunch of flowers shining with their own inner light and all but quivering under the pressure of the significance with which they were charged" (Neumann 176). Almost as if Huxley had read Stevens's "carnation" poem, he pursues his critique of Plato, who

> could never have perceived that what rose and iris and carnation so intensely signified was nothing more, and nothing less, than what they were—a transience that was yet eternal life, a perpetual perishing that was at the same time pure Being, a bundle of minute, unique particulars in which, by some unspeakable and yet self-evident paradox, was to be seen the divine source of all existence. (Neumann 176)

THE LADY: "FINAL SOLILOQUY OF THE INTERIOR PARAMOUR" (1950); "THE SAIL OF ULYSSES" (1954)

We turn once more to Stevens's "lady" and trace the shadow of her longing. Her "dreaming feet" had carried him to the holy land. At Key West she had sung with him "beside the sea." She becomes, at last, his "Interior Paramour," lighting "that highest candle" (imagination) in our modern darkness:

> Light the first light of evening, as in a room
> In which we rest and, for small reason, think
> The world imagined is the ultimate good.
>
> This is, therefore, the intensest rendezvous.
> It is in that thought that we collect ourselves,
> Out of all the indifferences, into one thing:
>
> Within a single thing, a single shawl
> Wrapped tightly round us, since we are poor, a warmth,
> A light, a power, the miraculous influence.
>
> Here, now, we forget each other and ourselves.
> We feel the obscurity of an order, a whole,
> A knowledge, that which arranged the rendezvous,
>
> Within its vital boundary, in the mind.
> We say God and the imagination are one . . .
> How high that highest candle lights the dark.
>
> Out of this same light, out of the central mind,
> We make a dwelling in the evening air,
> In which being there together is enough.

In an age of disbelief can Stevens's "Interior Paramour" intercede, like Dante's Beatrice, with the divine? Dante could imagine Beatrice, transformed and sanctified, leading him up to Paradise—to the Beatific Vision. But the medieval world-view has collapsed. Heaven, once pictured beyond fixed stars, has no locus in our no-bound cosmos. Can Stevens's "lady" function as spiritual guide in a world of exploded myth and secular vision? Is she merely a figment of solipsistic dreaming—a Freudian projection or Jungian archetype? Such questions intrude upon our understanding of Stevens's "Final Soliloquy." "That which arranged the rendez-vous"—the power, the light in-flowing. In that "miraculous in-fluence" we may still feel "the obscurity of an order, a whole." But what is the nature of this "obscurity"? Robert Lowell's com-

ment on the hidden agenda in poetry is pertinent: "My own feeling is that union with God is somewhere in sight in all poetry,
though it is usually rudimentary and misunderstood" ("Four
Quartets" 432–33).

Observing that "The term paramour occurs only four times in
the whole of [Stevens's] poetry," Barbara Fisher offers this insight:
"Stevens's paramour, like Dante's, suggests a trinity of selves, or
strongly experienced aspects of the self: the male, the female, and
love as a mystical energy and influence" (104).

Back in medieval Florence, the boy Dante was transformed
when he caught a glimpse of the young Beatrice: "From then
on," says Dante, "Love ruled over my soul." Recalling Stevens's
letters to Elsie during their courtship—Dear Buddy, Dear Bo-bo,
Dear Bo (105)—Fisher links his "sacral eroticism" to the *Vita
Nuova* (100). "For Dante," she argues, "as for Stevens, the beloved is *ingested* in some way and transformed into 'the lover that
lies within' " (102). While Fisher's psychologizing is persuasive, I
disagree with her conclusion:

> Stevens is careful to avoid the possibility of appropriation. What he
> nevertheless inherits from Dante, most particularly, is a complex
> dynamics of merger and interchange. One finds in both poets the
> ability to merge the sexual with the spiritual and the emotional; an
> easy intersubjectivity, the interchange of gender identity; a remark-
> able internalization of what is outside and externalization of what
> is inside. (106)

Fisher routes us through the archetypal unconscious and links Stevens's "interior paramour" to Jung's *anima*. Disregarding inten-
tionality, she reduces the "power of the Word" to a mere "gaiety
of language . . . our Seigneur" (105). Faced with her assertion
that Stevens "avoid[s] the possibility of appropriation," I ask: *For
how long?*

Appropriation—making something one's own—is key to conversion. The human creature, unique among animals, questions
its own existence. *Homo interrogans* is a "carrier of transcendence,"
says Merleau-Ponty, but transcendence is, as we have seen, a
stumbling-block for modern thought. Stevens, rejecting Platonic
absolutes, turned to what Santayana, in *The Last Puritan*, calls
"spontaneous fictions" (601). He looked for transcendence in

"the wonder and mystery of art"—in glints of light upon the waters, flecks and flickerings of phenomenal reality. In the changing "fictions" of poetry, he sought an antidote to "the inexpressible loneliness of thinking" (Morse 237). But, in the end, did art suffice? And here we arrive at the crux of the matter: religion, to be a viable alternative to art, must reveal the "wholly other," the *totaliter aliter.* We must now try to fit this last piece into the puzzle.

In the "Final Soliloquy" Stevens maintains his reticence through a strategic rhetorical maneuver: "We say God and the imagination are one." "We say" is casual, throw-away. Syntax approximates and then diverts—comes close, then turns away, simultaneously owning and disowning. But the "Soliloquy" is not the end of Stevens's voyage. The crucial transformation occurs in "The Sail of Ulysses" (1954), written a year before he died. Notice how he navigates this poetic marker as he heads into port:

> What is the shape of the sibyl? Not,
> For a change, the englistered woman, seated
> In colorings harmonious, dewed and dashed
> By them: gorgeous symbol seated
> On the seat of halidom, rainbowed,
> Piercing the spirit by appearance,
> A summing up of the loftiest lives
> And their directing sceptre, the crown
> And final effulgence and delving show.
> It is the sibyl of the self,
> The self as sibyl, whose diamond,
> Whose chiefest embracing of all wealth
> Is poverty, whose jewel found
> At the exactest central of the earth
> Is need. For this, the sibyl's shape
> Is a blind thing fumbling for its form,
> A form that is lame, a hand, a back,
> A dream too poor, too destitute
> To be remembered, the old shape
> Worn and leaning to nothingness.

Imagination, once "the englistered woman," is transformed into "the sibyl of the self" (as Stevens says elsewhere) "naked of any illusion, . . . / In the exactest poverty" (*Palm* 184). One might be tempted to give the "interior paramour" a Jungian face, but it does not suit her. Father Walter Ong's observation on Hopkins would apply as well to Stevens:

> a Jungian reading . . . is deeply informative, yet at points [it] will not fit, since [in Christian belief] God is not, as God seems to be for Jung, simply identified with psychic content, but quite separate from the psyche, even though within it. . . . The numinous God is the ultimate "not-I." (4)

THE INVISIBLE MARKER

In "The Snow Man" (1921) the "not-I" became manifest. But it was unmediated, tangled in conflicting negations. Stevens's eventual conversion involved a mediation of the "I" and the "not-I"—a reconciliation with "the ultimate 'not-I,' " God. It is true, of course, that the epiphanic feminine is inherently transformative. (Recall her various cultural manifestations: fair Aphrodite on the Aegean; merciful Kwanyin in ancient China; the *mater dolorosa*, lady of sorrows "full of grace" in Catholicism.) However, to understand Stevens's conversion we must move beyond the configurations of archetypal consciousness—toward the invisible "centre" that Stevens called "the great necessity even without specific identification" (*Letters* 584). And we must recognize, as he apparently did, that the sacrament of baptism implies consent to the inflection of divine love, to a mystery beyond human understanding.

The poem "Dolls" speaks of "Another, whom I must not name" (Bates, *Opus* 4). But it would seem that Stevens did, at last, name that other. Sister Bernetta Quinn has very kindly shared with me an audiotape (made January 21, 1976) on which Father Arthur Hanley recalls his visits to Stevens's hospital room in the spring and summer of 1955. Through their conversations the priest became acquainted with the kind of God the poet came to believe in—his conception of the unnamable, the *totaliter aliter*, the "ultimate not-I": "He had such a marvellous idea of what God was, the absolute idea of God—'the Uncreated.' Everything has been created. There's only one Uncreated and that for him was God."

Seven months before he died Stevens wrote an important letter to Robert Pack—responding to Pack's comment in a draft of his "secular mystery" essay: "Mr. Stevens's work does not really lead anywhere." Stevens replied: "Say what you will. But we are dealing with poetry, not with philosophy. The last thing in the world that I should want to do would be to formulate a system" (*Letters* 863–64).

As poet, Stevens knew that imagination requires a "revelation" to offset "the inexpressible loneliness of thinking"—something "wholly other" which, in the end, he called "the Uncreated." Yet the two paths—the way-of-art and the way-of-life—remain distinct, and silence descends upon the final question: how his mind closed the gap between the fictions of human longing and the revelation of divine love, "the epiphany of God in our poverty."

POSTSCRIPT

I should like to share some insights that have occurred to me in the interval between my submission of this essay to the editor, Professor John Mahoney, and its acceptance by the publisher. My insights grow out of further pondering the matter of Stevens's conversion to Roman Catholicism at the end of his life. Since, as my essay contends, Stevens's poetry manifests a spiritual kinship with Buddhism, some may wonder *why he did not turn toward Buddhism* for spiritual fulfillment, as did the "Beat" poets a generation later.

My response is threefold. The first and most obvious is chronological. Stevens died in 1955; his formative years were behind him by the time (in the aftermath of World War II) Buddhist and Native American spirituality effected a shift-of-consciousness among East and West Coast literary artists such as Jack Kerouac, Allen Ginsberg, and Gary Snyder. Stevens was a "Buddhist" by *temperament,* not by intent. His meditative manner, the transparency of his images, his awareness of emptiness—all these were aspects of his art, of his way of seeing reality.

The second part of my response is psychological. It concerns what I shall call "the homing instinct"—our (innate?) human tendency to come back to our origins. Raised a Lutheran, Stevens would very likely have found the sacramental emphasis in Roman

Catholicism congenial and comforting in his final illness. Para-doxically, Stevens's long-standing friendship with George Santa-yana (a temperamentally devout, if somewhat wayward, Spanish Catholic) seems to have played a role in his return to the church that Luther left. Indeed Stevens's imagery suggests the *homing* pat-tern: the long "candle" blown out by the wind in the early "Val-ley Candle" burns once again, after the passage of many years, in "To an Old Philosopher in Rome" where Stevens's aging mentor finishes his days in a Roman convent among ""books," "moving nuns," and a "candle" that "evades the sight":

> A light on the candle tearing against the wick
> To join a hovering excellence, to escape
> From fire and be part only of that of which
>
> Fire is the symbol: the celestial possible.

Finally, at the spiritual level, I must appeal to a mystery: the ways our human minds imagine (or fail to imagine) "God." Robert Magliola delves the complexity of that mystery:

> . . . 'God'— as Raimundo Panikkar and Karl Rahner remind us—is impersonal as well as personal. Indeed, . . . 'God' is sometimes frighteningly *impersonal* and . . . this *impersonality* double-binds into Divine *personality* in erratic, ever-altering ways that do not close into unity. (Which, by the way, is not at all to say that God is not a *loving* God.) That such a God is not encompassed, is not *captured* by either the formula or experience of a 'unifying source' *is* unsettling, *is* frightening for most Christians. (Loy 109)

Stevens's avowed search for "a centre" (in his letter to Sister Bernetta Quinn) is tantamount to a cry for a "unifying source"— for *spiritual closure*. This need, which the open-endedness of Bud-dhism cannot satisfy, is met in acceptance of Christ as the divine Logos. Thomas Merton has carefully delineated the question of *the centre* in Eastern versus Western thought:

> . . . in certain religions, Buddhism for instance, the philosophical or religious framework is of a kind that *can* more easily be discarded, because it has in itself a built-in "ejector," so to speak, by which the meditator is at a certain point flung out from the conceptual apparatus into the Void. It is possible for a Zen Master to say non-

chalantly to his disciple, "If you meet the Buddha, kill him!" But
in Christian mysticism the question whether or not the mystic can
get along without the human "form" (*Gestalt*) of the sacred Humanity of Christ is still hotly debated, with the majority opinion
definitely maintaining the necessity for the Christ of faith to be
present as ikon at the center of Christian contemplation. (Cunningham 409)

WORKS CITED

Baird, James. *The Dome and the Rock: Structure in the Poetry of Wallace Stevens*. Baltimore: Johns Hopkins UP, 1968.

Bates, Milton J., ed. *Opus Posthumous by Wallace Stevens*. Rev. New York: Knopf, 1989.

———. *Wallace Stevens: A Mythology of Self*. Berkeley: U of California P, 1985.

———. "Wallace Stevens's Final Yes: A Response to Sister Bernetta Quinn." *Renascence* (Summer 1989): 205–208.

Bevis, William W. *Mind of Winter: Wallace Stevens, Meditation, and Literature*. Pittsburgh: U of Pittsburgh P, 1988.

Bloom, Harold. "Notes Toward a Supreme Fiction: A Commentary." Borroff, ed. 76–95.

———. *Wallace Stevens: The Poems of Our Climate*. Ithaca: Cornell UP, 1976.

Bly, Robert. *A Little Book on the Human Shadow*. San Francisco: Harper, 1988.

Borroff, Marie, ed. *Wallace Stevens: A Collection of Critical Essays*. Englewood Cliffs: Prentice-Hall, 1963.

Brazeau, Peter. *Parts of a World: Wallace Stevens Remembered*. San Francisco: North Point P, 1985.

Corless, Roger J. "Idolatry and Inherent Existence: The Golden Calf and the Wooden Buddha." Loy, ed. 11–32.

———. *The Vision of Buddhism: The Space Under the Tree*. New York: Paragon House, 1989.

Cunningham, Lawrence S. *Thomas Merton: Spiritual Master*. Mahwah, NJ: Paulist, 1992.

Fisher, Barbara M. *Wallace Stevens: The Intensest Rendezvous*. Charlottesville: UP of Virginia, 1990.

Graham, Dom Aelred. *Conversations: Christian and Buddhist*. New York: Harcourt, 1968.

———. *Zen Catholicism*. New York: Harcourt, 1963.

Jarraway, David R. *Wallace Stevens and the Question of Belief: Metaphysician in the Dark.* Baton Rouge: Louisiana State UP, 1993.

Johnston, William. *Christian Zen: A Way of Meditation.* New York: Fordham UP, 1997.

Leggett, B. J. *Early Stevens: The Nietzschean Intertext.* Durham: Duke UP, 1992.

———. *Wallace Stevens and Poetic Theory: Conceiving the Supreme Fiction.* Chapel Hill: U of North Carolina P, 1987.

Lowell, Robert. Review: "Four Quartets." *Sewanee Review* (Summer 1943): 432–35.

Loy, David, ed. *Healing Deconstruction: Postmodern Thought in Buddhism and Christianity.* Atlanta: Scholars P, 1996.

Marion, Jean-Luc. *God Without Being.* Chicago: U of Chicago P, 1991.

Martz, Louis L. "Wallace Stevens: The World as Meditation." Boroff, ed. 133–50.

McGinn, Bernard. *The Foundations of Mysticism: Origins to the Fifth Century.* New York: Crossroad, 1992.

Merton, Thomas. *A Vow of Conversation.* New York: Farrar, 1988.

———. *Zen and the Birds of Appetite.* New York: New Directions, 1968.

Morris, Adalaide Kirby. *Wallace Stevens: Imagination and Faith.* Princeton: Princeton UP, 1974.

Morse, Samuel French, ed. *Opus Posthumous by Wallace Stevens.* New York: Knopf, 1957.

Neumann, Erich. *Art and the Creative Unconscious.* Princeton: Princeton UP, 1959.

Noon, William T., s.j. *Poetry and Prayer.* New Brunswick: Rutgers UP, 1967.

Ong, Walter J., s.j. *Hopkins, the Self, and God.* Toronto: U of Toronto P, 1986.

Quinn, Sister M. Bernetta, o.s.f. *The Metamorphic Tradition in Modern Poetry.* New Brunswick: Rutgers UP, 1955.

———. "Wallace Stevens: 'The Peace of the Last Intelligence.'" *Renascence.* (Summer 1989): 191–204.

Richardson, Joan. *Wallace Stevens: The Later Years, 1923–1955.* New York: Morrow, 1988.

Santayana, George. *The Last Puritan.* New York: Scribner's, 1936.

Scott, Nathan A., Jr. *Visions of Presence in Modern American Poetry.* Baltimore: Johns Hopkins UP, 1993.

Stack, George J. *Nietzsche and Emerson: An Elective Affinity.* Athens: Ohio UP, 1992.

Steiner, George. *Real Presences.* Chicago: U of Chicago P, 1989.

Stevens, Holly, ed. *Wallace Stevens: The Palm at the End of the Mind.* New York: Vintage-Random, 1990.

Stevens, Wallace. *Letters of Wallace Stevens*. Ed. Holly Stevens. New York: Knopf, 1970.

———. *The Necessary Angel: Essays on Reality and the Imagination*. New York: Vintage-Random, 1951.

Vendler, Helen Hennessy. *On Extended Wings: Wallace Stevens's Longer Poems*. Cambridge: Harvard UP, 1969.

———. *Wallace Stevens: Words Chosen Out of Desire*. Cambridge: Harvard UP, 1986.

Yuhaus, Cassian J., Father. "A Personal Letter to the Editor." *Renascence* (Summer 1989): 209–10.

16

Poetry, Language, and Identity: A Note on Seamus Heaney

Richard Kearney

IRISH LITERATURE HAS FREQUENTLY BEEN SUBJECT to the pressures of cultural stereotyping. Particularly abroad, but also in Ireland itself, one is often led to believe that a typically "Irish" work is one in which one or more of the following stock motifs are to be found: the idealization of the past; the lure of a primitive landscape; the compelling power of violence and its almost mystical rapport with feminine sexuality and Catholic spirituality; and finally an aboriginal fidelity to motherland, tribe, nation, community, and family. Phrased in more extreme and less kind terms, the caricatural attitude to Irish culture is one which expects to find a "land of Popes and Pigs and Bogs and Booze" (to quote the racist verse of Stuart Howard-Jones on the Irish, inexcusably selected by Kingsley Amis for *The New Oxford Book of Light Verse*)—and, one might add, of "poetry." As the colonial portrait goes, though the Irish are irresponsible, insalubrious, and irrational "Celts," they are at least, at their quaintest and most harmless, poetic "dreamers of dreams."

I

Seamus Heaney is often hailed as Ireland's greatest poet since Yeats. While such praise generally adverts to Heaney's remarkable sense of craft, his verbal and formal dexterity, it frequently betrays another kind of evaluation: one concerned less with Ireland's greatest *poet* than with *Ireland's* greatest poet. Here the emphasis falls on the typically and traditionally Irish quality of Heaney's writing. He is enlisted as the stereotypical poet of the *patria*, a home bird, an excavator of the national landscape devoted to the recovery of lost pieties. His primary inspiration, we are told, is one of place; his quintessentially Irish vocation, the sacramental naming of a homeland. Hence the preoccupation with images of mythology, archaeology, and religion, of returning to forgotten origins.

This orthodox view would have us believe that while certain other contemporary Irish poets embraced the modernist idioms of social alienation or the crisis of language, Heaney remained faithful to the primacy of the provincial. He did not need to take his tune from current trends in Continental or Anglo-American poetry; for he had discovered the cosmos, as it were, in his own backyard. But Heaney stuck to the home patch. He resisted the modernist impulse and remained, inalienably, a good old home-spun Catholic.

Some commenters have offered a more ideological interpretation of the nostalgia for lost traditions which is said to exemplify the "native" strain of Irish literature. The harking back to an abandoned, or at least threatened, spiritual lifestyle in tune with all that is best in the national heritage has been seen as an attempt to reconstruct a cultural harmony which would overcome, by overlooking, the actual divisions which torment modern Irish society—what Yeats referred to as the "filthy modern tide." As one critic remarked: "An emergent Catholic capitalist class espoused a myth of natural pious austerity in opposition to the profane forces of modernity, while the Anglo-Irish *déracinés* sought harmony with nature and a people characterized by wild, irrational, asocial energies" (Brown 90). Viewed in such perspective, Heaney's poetic efforts to bring Irish culture "home" to itself, might be dismissed as a conservative return to antiquated spiritualities of "tradition" and "nature."

II

But the stereotyped portrait of Heaney, whether it serves the interests of popular consumption or ideological suspicion, is untenable. The theme of "homecoming" in his work, for instance, involves a complex conflict of sensibility which has nothing to do with insular piety or parochial sentimentalism.

First, it should be noted that Heaney's poems are not in fact primarily about place at all; they are about *transit*, that is, about transitions from one place to another. One need only look to the titles of some of his major works to see just how fundamental this notion of poetry as transitional act is: *Wintering Out, Door into the Dark, Field Work, Sweeney Astray, Station Island.* One of the central reasons for Heaney's preference for journey over sojourn, for exodus over abode, is, I suggest, a fidelity to the nature of *language* itself. Far from subscribing to the traditional view that language is a transparent means of representing some *identity* which preexists language—call it self, nation, home, or whatever—Heaney's poetry embraces the modernist view that it is language which perpetually constructs and deconstructs our given notions of identity. As such, poetic language is always on the move, vacillating between opposing viewpoints, looking in at least two directions at once.

Heaney has been criticized for refusing to adopt a fixed unambiguous position, for not nailing his colors to the mast, particularly with regard to the "national question" (i.e., his attitude to his native North). One Irish politician described him as an "artful dodger" who displays "all the skills of the crafty tightrope walker . . . sidestepping and skipping his slippery way out of trouble" (Kemmy 21). Bemoaning the fact that his work is a "job of literary journeywork," this same politician admonishes him to "seek a less ambivalent position." The point is, however, that Heaney is a poet, not a party politician. He does not deny that his work has political connotations—for that would be to deny that it is concerned with life as it is lived. But this does not mean that he is compelled to subscribe to a definitive ideological standpoint. Heaney's refusal to be fixed, to be *placed* in any single perspective is no more than a recognition that poetry's primary fidelity is to language as an interminable metamorphosis of conflicting identities. Heaney himself states his position on language as dual or multiple perspective in the following passage from *Preoccupations*:

> When I called my second book *Door into the Dark* I intended to gesture towards this idea of poetry as a point of entry into the buried life of the feelings or as a point of exit from it. Words themselves are doors: Janus is to a certain extent their deity, looking back to a ramification of the roots and associations and forward to a

clarification of sense and meaning. . . . In *Door into the Dark* there are a number of poems that arise out of the almost unnameable energies that, for me, hovered over certain bits of language. . . . (52)

Heaney frequently endorses the modern view that literature is essentially about language itself. Mallarmé and Rimbaud made this view the central plank of their modernist program, as did, in another context, Heaney's compatriots Joyce and Beckett. This is not to suggest for a moment that Heaney—or his fellow-modernists—approach literature as some elitist art for art's sake; or that his fascination with words degenerates into self-regarding formalism. Heaney simply recognizes that reality as we perceive it is always profoundly informed by the words we use. And these words carry *several* meanings, for language is an endless creation of new worlds, possible worlds which remain irreducible to the univocal slide rule of a one-to-one correspondence between work and thing. That is why the double-faced Janus is the deity of Heaney's literary "journeywork."

III

Heaney's commitment to the ambivalence of poetic language is, I submit, plainly manifest in his exploration of the pivotal motif of "homecoming."

Whereas in the early works, Heaney usually talks of home in terms of a personal quest for self-identity, in his later collections—and particularly *North* (1975) and *Station Island* (1984)—he begins to interpret homecoming more in terms of a linguistic search for historical identity. As he himself remarks in *Preoccupations*, words cease to be fingerprints recording the unique signature of the poet and become "bearers of history." But if Heaney insists that one of the tasks of the poet is to recover a sense of belonging to a shared past—"an ancestry, a history, a culture"—he construes this task as a linguistic *project* rather than a tribal possession, as a spiritual exploration of language rather than some ideological appropriation of national identity.

Poetry, in short, comes to express the sense of "home" less as a literal (i.e., geographical, political, or personal) property than as a metaphysical preoccupation. Home is something that cannot be taken for granted as present. It must be sought after precisely because it is *absent*. For Heaney, homecoming is not the actuality of an event but the possibility of an advent. And here he would surely agree with Hugh, the schoolmaster of Friel's *Translations*, who recognizes that "words are signals, not immortal" and that a "civilization can be imprisoned in a linguistic contour which no longer matches the language of fact." Hence the need, as Hugh puts it, to negotiate a transition from the old language to the new, to learn the "new names" and to make them our "new home."

At this point it may be useful to take a brief look at some poems in the collection *North* which deal with this theme. In a poem entitled "Homecomings," Heaney would seem to be affirming the experience of home as a *positive* goal. He meditates upon the "homing" maneuverings of a sandmartin as it circles back to its nest:

> At the worn mouth of the hole
> Flight after flight after flight
> The swoop of its wings
> Gloved and kissed home.

The poet sees this instinctual, almost atavistic, homecoming of the sandmartin as an analogy for his own vocation to return to an originating womb of earth where he may regain a sense of prenatal silence, unity, and belonging:

> A glottal stillness. An eardrum.
> Far in, featherbrains tucked in silence,
> A silence of water lipping the bank
> Mould my shoulders inward to you.
> Occlude me.
> Be damp clay pouting.
> Let me listen under your eaves.

This experience recalls the opening passage from *Preoccupations* where Heaney invokes the sacred image of the *omphalos* as a hidden underground well of childhood memory. "I would begin," he writes,

> with the Greek word, *omphalos*, meaning the navel, and hence the
> stone that marked the centre of the world, and repeat it, *omphalos*,

omphalos, omphalos, until its blunt and falling music becomes the music of somebody pumping water at the pump outside our back door. . . . The pump marked an original descent into earth, sand, gravel, water. It centred and slaked the imagination, made its foundations the foundations of the *omphalos* itself. So I find it altogether appropriate that an old superstition ratifies this hankering after the underground side of things. (21)

These positive images of home are identified with nature, mother earth, and childhood. They describe the experience of an edenesque dwelling in harmony with the natural environment. And, as such, they might be thought to invoke a theological time before time, a primordial identity pre-existing language, self-consciousness, and death. But we must not forget that Heaney's first collection of poems is entitled *Death of a Naturalist.* All Heaney's writing is informed by the awareness that the poet as a resourceful dweller in language has replaced the naturalist as an innocent dweller in nature. So that if Heaney occasionally seeks to retrieve the experience of the "naturalist," it is always as a "post-naturalist": as someone who is, at best, hankering after something which he knows full well is irretrievably lost. Homecoming thus becomes a dialectical search for some forfeited or forbidden presence in and through the awareness of its absence. We should not be surprised therefore to find Heaney, in a poem called "Kinship," referring to the *omphalos* as a grave, or to mother earth as the inevitable casualty of autumnal death and decay. Language has now, it seems, adulterated the pristine innocence of nature. The vowel of earth can do no more than "dream" its root. Home can be spoken of only as some ground from which we have become irreparably uprooted.

In other poems in *North* (the title of this collection itself is a symbol, amongst other things, for Heaney's own lost homeland or motherland), the theme of homecoming assumes an explicitly ominous tone. The very attempt to return home is now equated by the poet with necrophiliac nostalgia; it assumes the character of a sacrificial death rite which provokes sentiments of recoil. In a poem called "Stump," Heaney surmises that his homing instinct may well become a parasite of plague and putrefaction as soon as it presumes to make of home a tribal acquisition. "I am riding to plague again," he rebukes himself. "What do I say if they wheel

out their dead? / I'm cauterized, a black stump of home." And in
yet another poem, "Roots," Heaney's suspicion of necrophilial
impulses reaches even more self-recriminatory proportions. Here
he conceives of the tribal hankering after dispossessed origins or
"roots" as a sanguinary pagan cult bedeviling his Northern province and intruding upon the private intimacies of love. Outside
in the terraced streets the earth's "fault is opening" as the gunshots
of the sniper and the sirens of the army scream at each other.
Inside in the bedroom, the poet tries to take refuge in love; but
his dark bloodletting dreams, echoing the slaughter in the streets,
contaminate the lovers' communion and deform it into the image
of a mandrake—a poisonous plant whose root is thought to re-
semble a human form and to shriek when plucked:

> I'm soaked by moonlight in tidal blood
> A mandrake, lodged human fork,
> Earth sac, limb of the dark;
> And I wound its damp smelly loam
> And stop my ears against the scream.

IV

Heaney's celebrated "bog poems" provide arresting examples of
the critical dialectic of "homecoming" and "estrangement." For
Heaney, the northern bog is a sort of placeless place; it is a shifting
palimpsest of endless layers and sublayers, an archival memory of
lost cultures.

  In one of the first of his bog poems—the last poem of *Wintering
Out* (1972)—Heaney describes how a great elk and a morsel of
butter, having been preserved for centuries in the dark and watery
peat, were recovered from Irish bogs. The poem concludes with
the following image of an interminable excavation for a vanished
omphalos:

> Our pioneers keep striking
> Inwards and downwards,
> Every layer they strip
> Seems camped on before.
> The bogholes might be Atlantic seepage
> The wet centre is bottomless.

Heaney explains that while this bogland motif began as a germ of childhood association, it gradually assumed the status of a sacred myth. "We used to hear about bog-butter," writes Heaney of his early childhood,

> butter kept fresh for a great number of years under the peat. Then when I was at school the skeleton of an elk had been taken out of a bog nearby and a few of our neighbours had got their photographs in the paper, peering out across its antlers. So I began to get an idea of a bog as the memory of the landscape, or as a landscape that remembered everything that happened in and to it. In fact, if you go round the National Museum in Dublin, you will realize that a great proportion of the most cherished material heritage of Ireland was "found in a bog." Moreover, since memory was the faculty that supplied me with the first quickening of my own poetry, I have a tentative unrealized need to make a congruence between memory and bogland and, for want of a better word, our national consciousness. (*Preoccupations* 55)

But if the bog becomes a symbol of national consciousness, it is not in the manner of an insular, self-righteous nationalism. Heaney is mindful of the fact that the lost homeland is less a territorial locality than an eschatological dream whose universal dimensions forever elude the boundaries of a particular nation. The closer we get to home in this sense, the more distant it becomes; its very construction is its deconstruction. "The wet centre," as Heaney concedes, is *"bottomless."* The bogholes of receding memory lead back to a fathomless ocean flow which transcends our contemporary grasp. Homecoming, poetically understood, means therefore that our literal or geographical home is actually decentered. The very process of homecoming reminds us, paradoxically, that we are displaced, in exile, estranged (*unheimlich*). So that just as the fundamental questions of Being and God, according to Heidegger, can be retrieved from oblivion only by "deconstructing" the pretension of Western metaphysics to represent some unbroken continuous tradition; so too with regard to the more general question of our cultural and spiritual heritage. Or as another deconstructionist thinker, Michel Foucault, puts it: "In attempting to uncover the deepest strata of western culture, I am restoring to our silent and apparently immobile soil, its rifts, its instability, its flaws; and it is the same ground that is once more stirring under our feet" (7).

But it would be a mistake to interpret this "defamiliarization" of the experience of tradition as meaning that Heaney abandons all concern for the political plight of his native Ulster. Heaney insists that his bog poems are also a reaching after "images and symbols *adequate to our predicament.*" He explains that he felt it imperative to discover "a field of force in which, without abandoning fidelity to the processes and experiences of poetry . . . it would be possible to encompass the perspectives of a humane reason and at the same time to grant the religious intensity of the violence its deplorable authenticity and complexity" (*Preoccupations* 56). In other words, Heaney sees the contemporary conflict in Northern Ireland as, amongst other things, a symptom of a collision between the opposing claims of rationalistic order and religious atavism. He makes it quite clear, of course, that he is using the term "religious" not just in the more current sense of sectarian division between Catholic and Protestant, but in the anthropological sense of an ancient enmity between "the cults and devotees of a god and a goddess." There is, Heaney observes,

> an indigenous numen, a tutelar of the whole island, call her mother Ireland, Kathleen Ni Houlihan, the poor old woman, the Shan Van Vocht, whatever; and her sovereignty has been temporarily usurped or infringed by a new male cult whose founding fathers were Cromwell, William of Orange and Edward Carson, and whose godhead is incarnate in a *rex* or Caesar resident in a palace in London. What we have here is the tail end of a struggle in a province between territorial piety and imperial power. (*Preoccupations* 57)

By tracing the capillaries of our current political and social ideologies back to their roots in a hidden sublayer of sacred mythologies, Heaney is attempting not to revive these mythologies, but to critically explore and expose them.

Nor does Heaney confine himself to Celtic myth. Indeed, one of the most striking emblems of this dialectic between critical distance and religious belonging is borrowed from the Greek myth of Antaeus and Hercules. Heaney casts Hercules in the role of triumphant reason, "sky-born and royal . . . his future hung with trophies." Antaeus, by contrast, is portrayed as a mould-

hugger, clinging to his sacrosanct terrestrial past. By dispossessing
Antaeus of his tribal fixation with ancestral origins, Hercules drags
him:

> Out of his element
> Into a dream of loss
> And origins—the cradling dark,
> The river-veins, the secret gullies
> Of his strength,
> The hatching grounds
> Of cave and souterrain,
> He has bequeathed it all
> To elegists. . . .

And so it is, in Heaney's own elegiac bog poems, that the homeless and vanquished Antaeus can be recovered—if at all—only in
the suspended animation of his ancient slumber, brought home to
us again as a "sleeping giant pap, for the dispossessed." Heaney
comments on this key dialectic between rational consciousness
and the mythico-religious unconscious as follows:

> Hercules represents the balanced rational light while Antaeus repre-
> sents the pieties of illiterate fidelity. The poem drifts towards an
> assent to Hercules, though there was a sort of nostalgia for Antaeus.
> . . . This is a see-saw, an advance–retire situation. ("Unhappy" 63)

To reformulate this position in "temporal" terms, we might
say that the poetics of homecoming require us to juxtapose the
prospective glance of Hercules and the *retrospective* glance of Antaeus. Otherwise put: it is the Herculean act of estranged detachment which enables us to remember the Antaean origin of "cave
and *souterrain*." To dispense with the distancing detour of elegy
would be to diminish the possibility of homecoming as a liberating advent, cultivating it instead as a reactionary return to the
past. For it is thanks to the critical challenge of the homeless Hercules that Antaeus's homing instinct can be transformed from
tribal nostalgia into an authentic quest for a new cultural community. In this dialectical vacillation between the claims of Herculean
reason and Antaean piety, the *topos* of the past can come toward
us as a utopia of the future. Heaney remains mindful of the fact
that the act of poetic remembering must always observe a delicate

balance between the opposite risks of belonging to a home and being exiled in homelessness. To resolve this paradox by opting in absolute fashion for either extreme is to betray poetry itself.

V

This paradox of "homecoming" is powerfully sustained in Heaney's *Station Island* (1984), a collection which takes its name from the Northern place of Catholic pilgrimage, Lough Derg. Here Heaney returns to an exploration of the homing instincts of religious and political reverence. Perhaps more explicitly than in any previous work, Heaney interprets the fascination with "home" as a need for *sacred tradition, unity of being, cultural harmony, ancestry, community, memory, mythology, the collective unconscious*. In the long title sequence, the poet is assailed by several accusing voices from his past—usually victims of the bloody carnage in his native Ulster. These "ancestral ghosts" address him in dream or reverie as he rehearses the ritual stations of Lough Derg. Here is a privileged place and time for spiritual recollection, for coming to terms with what Joyce's Stephen Dedalus called the "night-mare of history"—the claims of motherland and mother church.

The sequence opens with the poet's alter-ego, Sweeney, shout-ing at him to "stay clear of all processions." But the poet persists on the "drugged path" of religious ceremony. He embraces the "murmur of the crowd," the pious solidarity of the living and the dead. The poet's visitor from beyond the grave is Carleton, an-other Irish writer who had experienced "gun butts cracking on the door" and whose rejection of both "hard-mouthed Ribbon-men and Orange bigots" (Catholic and Protestant northern gangs) had "mucked the byre of their politics." The poet confesses that he himself has "no mettle for the angry role" of ancestral revenge; yet he is compelled by Carleton's counsel to "remember every-thing and keep [his] head."

For Heaney, however, remembrance is racked with guilt—and particularly guilt about his lack of direct political involvement with the sufferings of his own Catholic tribe. One visitation from an assassinated childhood friend provokes the poet to seek forgiveness for "the way [he] has lived indifferent." And another murder vic-tim, a second cousin, chides the religious pilgrim for consorting with effete fellow-poets when he first heard the news of his death:

> I accuse directly, but indirectly, you
> Who now atone perhaps upon this bed
> For the way you whitewashed ugliness . . .
> And saccharined my death with morning dew.

Faced with this litany of tribal accusations, the author drifts toward sacramental repentance. He also realizes that his primary commitment as a poet is to the exploration of the buried truths of *language*—which mediates, records, and structures our experience—rather than to the immediate exigencies of political legislation or reprisal: "As if the eddy could reform the pool." The buried truths of language are revealed by poetry to the degree that (1) the poet steps back from our familiar use of words as means/end strategies, and (2) listens in silence to what language is saying in and through us. The poem is in this way a response, before all else, to the silent voices of language itself. This is what modern thinkers such as Heidegger, Derrida, and Lacan have taught us. As the last has remarked: "The subject is spoken rather than speaking. . . . It was certainly the Word that was in the beginning, and we live in its creation, but it is the action of our spirit that continues this creation by constantly renewing it. . . . It is the world of words that creates the world of things. . . . Man speaks them, but it is because the symbol has made him man" (Lacan). Heaney makes this point about his own work when he declares that "the creative mind is astraddle silence" (*Preoccupations* 78). And one finds a further echo of this mystical stance in the claim by Samuel Beckett that "silence is our mother-tongue."

The final visitation in the Lough Derg sequence of *Station Island* is Joyce's ghost. Joyce, like Carleton, serves as a *literary* conscience; he warns the poet that the obsession with collective guilt and tribal grievance is a mistake:

> That subject people stuff is a cod's game . . .
> You lose more of yourself than you redeem
> Doing the decent thing.
> Keep at a tangent.
> When they make the circle wide, it's time to swim
> Out on your own and fill the element
> With signatures of your own frequency . . .
> Elver-gleams in the dark of the whole sea.

Significantly, the figure of Sweeney Astray—the exiled wandering bard of Irish legend and the subject of a verse translation by
Heaney from the Gaelic—returns in the third section of the book
as symbol of the dissenting and disinherited poet. Sweeney's liberating impulses confirm the Joycean plea. But one of the main
strengths of *Station Island* is the refusal to choose between Heaney
and Sweeney—between the guilt-ridden pilgrim of history and
the carefree *émigré* of the imagination. As in the lines invoked by
the Janus-faced author early in the collection:

> I was stretched
> between contemplation
> of a motionless point
> and the command to participate
> actively in history.

This characteristic tension in Heaney's work between the sanctity of home and the skepticism of homelessness is perceptively
summed up by his fellow-northerner Seamus Deane:

> The poet turns, entering into conversation with his family, his
> friends, his dead, his various *personae* . . . asking for manumission
> from his enslavement to reverence, and fearful that it will be
> granted. As always with Heaney, there is a paradox here. Even in
> his caution there is risk, and one of the delights of his poetry is to
> see the variety of ways in which he can pungently embody the
> opposing attitudes. . . . "a cunning middle voice" learns to negoti-
> ate between the known and the foreign, the dialect of the local and
> the *lingua franca* of the world. Even in berating himself for his cau-
> tion, he recognizes that he enhances the feeling of veneration for
> everything that is private, love-worn, ancestral by the very act of
> suspecting it, of chastening its easily available consolations. On the
> other hand, this suspicion allows him to bring in the voice of the
> other, peremptory world of the present, with its political crises and
> its alien immediacies. *Station Island*'s three parts are phases in the
> intricate debate thus established. (34)

Heaney's ultimate fidelity to the ambiguity of opposing demands, and to the inner maneuverings of language which sustain
such demands, his refusal of any single place or position which
would permit the illusion of a final solution, is singular proof of
his commitment to the truth of spiritual paradox. As he observes

in a poem called "Terminus" (*Hailstones*, 1984), dedicated to the god of boundaries and borders:

> Two buckets were easier carried than one.
> I grew up in between.

WORKS CITED

Brown, Terence. *Culture and Ideology in Ireland*. Ed. Mary Kelly, Chris Curtin, and Liam O'Dowd. Galway: Galway UP, 1984. In *The Crane Bag of Irish Studies* 9.1 (1985): 90.

Deane, Seamus. "Noble Startling Achievement." *The Irish Literary Supplement* (Spring 1985): 34.

Foucault, Michel. *Language, Counter-Memory, and Practice*. Oxford: Blackwell, 1977.

Heaney, Seamus. *Preoccupations: Selected Prose, 1968–1978*. London: Faber, 1980.

———. "Unhappy and at Home: Interview with Seamus Deane." *The Crane Bag*. 1.1 (1977): 63.

Kemmy, Jim. *New Hibernia* (Dublin) 1.2 (1984).

Lacan, Jacques. *Écrits*. London: Tavistock, 1977.

17

Stevie Smith: Skepticism and the Poetry of Religious Experience

John L. Mahoney

I cry I cry
To God who created me
Not to you Angels who frustrated me
Let me fly, let me die,
Let me come to Him.

IT IS DIFFICULT TO KNOW exactly what drew me to Stevie (baptismal name Florence Margaret) Smith. It certainly was not, at least not at first, a conviction that her sense of some kind of ultimacy was so compelling that her work simply had to be mastered and presented in a volume like this one. All too often readers may find the voice and tone of the poems angry, rebellious, iconoclastic, indeed blasphemous. And it certainly was not the conviction that her poetry matched the artistry of twentieth-century masters like T. S. Eliot, W. H. Auden, Stephen Spender, Philip Larkin, and others. No, it started with the viewing of a film called *Stevie*, based on a play of the same name by Hugh Whitemore, with the distinguished British actress Glenda Jackson playing the title role in both.

The film was interesting and engaging in itself, presenting as it did Smith's story, she an unprepossessing, physically frail British secretary, editor, book reviewer, writer, poet, living with her maiden aunt in the London suburb of Palmer's Green. More striking, however, was the extraordinary cinematic technique of having Stevie—and the narrator—recite large chunks of her poetry to the camera in such a way that they seemed perfectly appropriate in advancing a story of her personal development, her professional life in London and her private life with her aunt, and her relationships with a mysterious friend/narrator called simply "The Man" and sometime boy friends Karl and Freddie. Yet fascinating though technique and performance were, they seemed both to frame certain key poems, particularly those preoccupied with death, God, the Church and Church teaching, and love human and divine, and to allow the audience to hear the sometimes melancholy, sometimes wonderfully witty turning of the poet's mind to the kinds of larger questions and issues which many would associate with religious experience.

But who is this Stevie Smith? Recent biographies by Jack Barbera and William McBrien and by Frances Spalding, and the Preface to the *Collected Poems* by Stevie's close friend and editor James MacGibbon have been most helpful.[1] Born two months premature to Charles Ward Smith and Ethel Spear in Hull, Yorkshire, on September 20, 1902, she almost died. Baptized some three weeks later as her health improved, she nevertheless spent a good many of her childhood years in and out of a convalescent home for children in Kent. Unable to maintain the large house in Hull, mother, aunt (who as "The Lion" was to be a strong force in Stevie's life), Stevie, and her elder sister, Molly, moved to No. 1 Avondale Road in Palmer's Green in 1906. As a child she enjoyed being read to, appreciating especially works like *Alice in Wonderland* and Kingsley's *Water Babies*. She later described childhood as seeming like "a golden age, a time untouched by war, a dream of innocent quiet happenings, a dream in which people go quietly about their blameless business . . . believing in God, believing in peace, believing in Progress . . . believing in the catechism" (Barbera, *Me Again* 84). Family life was complicated at best; her parents' marriage was clearly not a happy one. Stevie's mother, to whom she was very close, died on February 6, 1919, and her father, an absentee parent with a passion for travel who meant little to her, remarried and died many years later. Stevie grieved for her mother whom she lost during her teenage years, but failed even to attend her father's funeral. Her aunt was her true parent to the end of her life.

---

[1] See Barbera and McBrien, *A Biography of Stevie Smith*; Spalding, *Stevie Smith: A Biography*; and *The Collected Poems of Stevie Smith*, edited by MacGibbon. I am greatly indebted to these works for important biographical information. All quotations from Smith's poetry are from the *Collected Poems*.

Stevie was educated in the lower grades and in high school in Palmer's Green, and then attended North London Collegiate School. It was during her teenage years that she acquired her nickname (her aunt called her Peggy) as a group of boys who watched her horseback riding were reminded of the noted English jockey Stevie Donaghue. Never able to support herself from her literary efforts, she worked in London over the years as a secretary, and later as private secretary to the chairman of a large publishing house. From early on she was an inveterate reader, admiring greatly David Cecil's classic life of the Methodist poet William Cowper, finding Kafka's mysterious *The Castle* a riveting work, enjoying Proust, Woolf, Joyce, and Dorothy Richardson among many others (Barbera and McBrien 47; Spalding 114). And while my focus in this essay is on a range of poems early and late, it should be noted that Stevie was a novelist of some note, and her autobiographical *Novel on Yellow Paper* (1936), as well as *Over the Frontier* (1938) and *The Holiday* (1949), are still generally available.

Stevie traveled to Germany in 1929 and 1931, experiencing the ominous "between the Wars" atmosphere and finding short-lived romance with a young German named Karl. She was later to have a more serious and extended affair with Eric Armitage, the "Freddy" of her witty, satiric, and at times deeply emotional poem, whom she met at socials given by her St. John's Parish Church in Palmer's Green. But, as she reminds us again and again, she never married, and remained devoted to her Lion Aunt, attending local parties, participating in poetry readings, and reviewing enormous numbers of books for *The Tribune, John O'London's Weekly, Modern Woman, The Spectator, The Daily Telegraph, The Observer, The Listener,* and other periodicals. She attempted suicide on July 1, 1953, at her London office, only to be brought home—the scene in the film is touching—to the loving care of her aunt. Her last twenty years were filled with activities of all kinds—lectures, readings, the publication of her *Selected Poems,* a private audience with the Queen before receiving the Queen's medal for poetry in 1969. Diagnosed with an inoperable brain tumor, she died in Ashburton Hospital on March 7, 1971.

So much for who Stevie Smith is—a person obsessed with love and death, a strange combination of wit and melancholy, an innovative artist. But it is the poet who engages us most deeply. As two of her biographers put it, "she understood herself to be at truest pitch a poet. . . . More and more as time passed, Stevie hunted 'the beauty and subtlety of unuttered thought' in the guise of a poet" (Barbara and McBrien 99). Stevie herself, replying to a questioner in 1951, wrote that "poetry must be rooted in religion and philosophy" (Barbera, *Me Again*, 71). Joyce Carol Oates sees Smith writing novels "with the left hand." "She is," says Oates, "justly celebrated for her remarkable poetry, which magically combines the rhythms of light verse . . . with the unyielding starkness of a tragic vision" (70). Barbera and McBrien judge Smith to be an original, standing outside any tradition, the Georgians on the one hand, the Auden generation and Dylan Thomas on the other (101).

For me it is the poet's preoccupation with the large religious questions, her highly complex, impossible-to-reduce responses to these questions, and her vision of some ultimate meaning that command attention. Metrical virtuosity, wordplay, Blake-like illustrations of the poems—all these are important but secondary. As already noted, Stevie was baptized Christian, a member of a Church of England family who delighted as a child and as a young woman in the ceremony, ritual, and Prayer Book of that Church. Her sister, Molly, who later converted to Roman Catholicism, spoke of Stevie's sharing her "Roman fever" (Barbera and McBrien 35) for a while, but Stevie clung, however tenuously at times, to her Anglican faith and was resistant, as we see in her poem "Admire Cranmer!" to changes in the Prayer Book. "Admire the old man, admire him, admire him, / Mocked by the priests of Mary Tudor, given to the flames, / Flinching and overcoming the flinching, Cranmer," she writes. But admire him not just for his "flinching" but also for his "genius."

She had read Catholic apologists like Hilaire Belloc, Gilbert Keith Chesterton, and Ronald Knox, but could never accept the idea of divine sanction for the good life, an idea she associated with the Church of Rome. To her the Church of England was close to a true *via media* in a world of political, social, and religious extremes. And the bishops of that Church, as her poem goes, "do their best / To resolve wisely / To govern effectively." Stevie's funeral service on March 12, 1971, was celebrated in the Anglican Church of the Holy Trinity at Buckfastleigh, and on March 31 a memorial service, with an Anglican liturgy, was held in London at

St. Matthews, Westminster, with two close friends participating. Father Gerard Irvine gave the eulogy, and James MacGibbon, her friend and editor, read her haunting poem "Come Death (2)."

But to the matter at hand: Smith's poetry. That poetry, at times deeply sad, even half-in-love with Death as Friend, has a persisting religious dimension, if by "religious" one means a sense of something transcendent, of an ultimate reality beyond the worldly. In the Blake-sounding "Little Boy Sick," we hear the sadness, "I am not God's little lamb / I am God's sick tiger" and a plea "Consider, Lord, a tiger's melancholy / And heed a minished tiger's muted moan, / For thou art sleek and shining bright / And I am weary. / Thy countenance is full of light / And mine is dreary." And in "Come, Death (2)" she pleads for God's pity, but turns "to the one I know." Her prayer is simple, direct, powerful: "Ah me, sweet Death, you are the only god / Who comes as a servant when he is called, you know, / Listen then to this sound I make, it is sharp, / Come Death. Do not be slow."

Stevie's melancholy is nowhere more powerfully evoked than in perhaps her best-known and most-often-anthologized poem, "Not Waving but Drowning," with its contrast between the dead man's inner torment and the image of good nature his friends saw in his comings and goings. It is a vivid mini-drama with narrator, dead man, and friends as *dramatis personae*. "Nobody heard him, the dead man, / But still he lay moaning," says the narrator. Then quickly we hear the dead man's voice as he confesses his predicament: "I was much further out than you thought / And not waving but drowning." How different the attempts of friends to explain his death: "Poor chap, he always loved larking / And now he's dead / It must have been too cold for him his heart gave way, / They said." But the dead man will brook no explanations, no rationalizations, playing on the two key words of the poem's title: "Oh, no, no, no, it was too cold always / (Still the dead one lay moaning) / I was much too far out all my life / And not waving but drowning."

Yet Stevie's religious sense often mutes the despair; God is personified as Creator, Protector, Lover again and again. Michael Tatham says it well as he describes her as "a profoundly religious poet and speaks to our condition as modern piety can seldom hope to speak." And he further argues persuasively that her "remarkable achievement as a poet was to sustain a dialogue with

God in which there was no pretense that a comfortable response was possible" (133–34). Her longtime friend, the Reverend Gerard Irvine, seems to hit just the right note as he speaks of the complexity of her beliefs. "Stevie," he says, "was ambivalent: neither a believer, an unbeliever nor agnostic, but oddly all three at once. . . . One could say that she did not like the God of Christian orthodoxy, but she could not disregard Him or ever quite bring herself to disbelieve in Him" (qtd. in MacGibbon 9). And as far as early and later Smith poems go, Mark Storey is quite right in his contention that "She does not develop, in any helpful sense of the word: the first handful of poems announce her concern as do the final, posthumous poems" (Storey 177). Philip Larkin seems to agree (Larkin 115).

We again hear echoes of Blake in the deep yearning of "The Heavenly City": "I sigh for the heavenly country, / Where the heavenly people pass, / And the sea is as quiet as a mirror / Of beautiful beautiful glass." Or there is the sage counsel of her lines "To Dean Inge Lecturing on Origen": "Listen, all of you, listen, all of you, / This way wisdom lies, / To reconcile with the simplicity of God / His contingent pluralities." No facile theological speculation, no philosophical gymnastics will do for Stevie. In her long, restlessly questioning poem "How do you see?" she begins with the humblest, simplest profession of faith, eschewing any kind of spiritualism or supernaturalism. "How do you see the Holy Spirit of God?" she questions, and answers straightforwardly, "I see him as the holy spirit of good, / But I do not think we should talk about spirits, I think / We should call good, good."

Taking issue with what she regards as conventional, simplistic beliefs, Stevie bemoans what men and women have made of God, how they have shaped institutional configurations that belie the purity of the message, how they have twisted God's words into tortuous and stern creeds of good and evil, heaven and hell, rewards and punishments, into a forbidding, otherworldly asceticism. Her lifelong strain of sadness, her suicide attempt make Death a powerful figure in her mythology, Death as the supreme release, as the gateway to whatever eternity there may be. "Part of her quarrel with Christianity," argue Barbera and McBrien, "was that it absolutely forbids command over death, a power she found 'delicious'" (19). Yet no matter how strident her antireligious sentiments may seem at times, they do not hide a deep faith in an ultimate reality, in a God who loves and delights in Creation. In Sternlicht's words, "Stevie set about reconstructing God through her metaphysics into a more sympathetic, less autocratic and vengeful deity. She allowed God his maleness but feminized him too. He could rule the universe, but it had better be through love" (25). Frances Spalding sees Smith as voicing the tough questions that keep returning: "To committed Christians her arguments seem inadequate because they remain confined within the arena of rational discourse, whereas many of the religious statements that she is dealing with belong to the language of faith." Unlike many nonliteralistic Christians she was unable to make an easy distinction between the authority of the Bible and personal religious experience. She was "unable to accept biblical authority on a rational level" and yet at the same time "refused to make a commitment based on personal experience alone" (236).

Stevie's notable lecture on "The Necessity of Not Believing" to the Cambridge Humanists is instructive in getting close to the core of her love/hate relationship with Christianity. She described the lecture as "partly autobiographical, showing how very religious I was when young . . . and later how I became not religious, but consciously anti-religious" (qtd. in Spalding 233). Spalding offers the puzzling but intriguing observation that "Stevie's attitude to the Christian religion, like that of Emily Dickinson, was that of an agnostic who could not entirely abandon belief in a God of Love" (233–34). It is this God of Love that organized Christianity has distorted for Stevie, whose responses are consistently informed by a fairly rich knowledge of Church history, as well as of more specifically biblical and liturgical matters. Sternlicht contends that Stevie was "progressively disillusioned by Christianity. She saw dishonesty in the churches, and she disagreed with the conventional construct of God as demanding, vain, jealous, revengeful, eager to sacrifice the innocent, and very masculine" (25).

It is, I think, a mistake to attribute too quickly a kind of naked agnosticism to Smith, she who dramatizes a God of Love more powerfully than less authentic orthodox Christians and who once agreed with a friend about "how very imperfect an agnostic I am" (qtd. in Barbera and McBrien 271). Such Christians, Spalding observes, "remain confined within the areas of rational discourse" while many of Smith's religious sentiments "belong to the language of faith" (236). Stevie's December 1968 talk to the St. Anne's Society in London on "Some Impediments to Christian Commitment" raises the powerful question, "how can one's heart *not* go out to the idea that a God of absolute love is in charge of the universe" (Barbera, *Me Again* 153). And in an unpublished essay on death, she argues that "all love seeks its source and destiny in Love, in the idea of some great Love, that is beyond the human pattern. But that perfect love may be what I have often written of as the greatest of all blessings" (qtd. in Spalding 243).

Her poem "No Categories" laments all that comes between her desire to know God and the human constructs that intervene. Theologizing isolates humankind from God; love unites. "I cry I cry," she begins, "To God who created me / Not to you Angels who frustrated me / Let me fly, let me die, / Let me come to Him." The servant would come to the heavenly kingdom of the Creator. But the "Angels on the wing" are preoccupied with their own status, with their places in a great chain of power, and they offer only "severe faces," "scholarly grimaces," "exasperating pit-pat / Of appropriate admonishment." Certainly, says the speaker, "That is not what the Creator meant, / In the day of his gusty creation / He made this and that / And laughed to see them grow fat." Hers is a feisty God, delighting in His creatures. No, she adds, she will not "plod on" as the angels would like, would not become an angel. Summoning God as witness, pleading for some divine command and action, she cries, "See what your Angels do; scatter / Their pride; laugh them away / Oh no categories I pray."

We hear a divine voice in "God Speaks," a wonderfully decisive voice. "I made man with too many faults. Yet I love him. / And if he wishes I have a home above for him." But, says God, He wants no grim discipline, no macabre images of Him as a tormentor, as one who violently "had a son and gave him for their salvation." Wittily God concludes that such images and such actions lead to "nervous prostration." The poem concludes with God returning to His original wish for man, but with a special twist: "I should like him to be happy in heaven here, / But he cannot come by wishing. Only by being already at home here."

On the one hand, Stevie remained angry with the churches and their dogmas which unnecessarily complicate the simplicity of God and His message, advancing ideas like Incarnation, Redemption, the Divinity of Jesus, eternal punishment for sin, and more. On the other hand, she admired the ministry of Jesus on earth. Her poem "Oh, Christianity, Christianity" berates an institution that will not "answer our difficulties." In a series of rapid-fire questions the speaker powerfully engages the churches and their leaders for what she sees as contradiction and obfuscation. "You say He was born humble—but he was not, / He was born God— / Taking our nature upon Him. / But this you say, / He was perfect Man. Do you mean / Perfectly Man, meaning wholly; or man without sin? Oh / Perfect man without sin is not what we are." The speaker closes her monologue in a rage: "Oh what do you mean, what do you mean?"

But then there is the dazzling and haunting "The Airy Christ," written, as the subtitle tells us, "After reading Dr. Rieu's translation of St. Mark's Gospel." Here is a Christ who forces new questions and new answers: "Who is this that comes in splendour, coming from the blazing East? / This is he we had not thought of, this is he the airy Christ." Here is a Jesus unhappy with the image created by humans of a suffering Savior, a Jesus who frowns on "What they say he knows must be, but he looks aloofly down, / Looks aloofly at his feet, looks aloofly at his hands, / Knows they must, as prophets say, nailed be to wooden bands." But for those who truly hear the voice, there will never be need for sanctions, for "working laws to keep from doing wrong." Those who truly hear this airy Christ hear a joyous song and He is delighted, for "the sweet singer does not care that he was crucified. / For he does not wish that men should love him more than anything / Because he died; he only wishes they would hear him sing."

Stevie cannot bear the violent dimensions of Christianity's doctrines. As Spalding puts it, "The cruellest aspect of Christian teaching, for her, was the doctrine of hell: while proclaiming a God of Love, Christianity preaches also the severest indictment—eternal damnation" (234). Stevie's lines, "Thoughts about the Christian Doctrine of Eternal Hell" begin almost whimsically with "Is it not interesting to see / How the Christians continually / Try to separate themselves in vain / From the doctrine of eternal pain." But whimsy quickly gives way to anger as she affirms the folly of such attempts. "They cannot do it, / They are committed to it, / Their Lord said it, / They must believe it." It is not God's word but the Christian religion that offers such a god, and the only answer to such an image is to "Blow it away, have done with it."

But beyond the doctrine of eternal punishment there is her sharply negative sense of the doctrine of the Incarnation, especially its seeming sense of a bargain involving the suffering and death of a Savior in exchange for the redemption of sinful man. It is, says Stevie, "(the Monstrous Bargain, the Writ of Scandal to the unbelieving) . . . monstrous it must seem to unbelievers and a cause of sickness in the minds of Christians" (qtd. in Barbera and McBrien 216).

These pages represent but a beginning of what might very well be a larger project, the emergence of Stevie Smith as not only an important twentieth-century poet, but also as an important religious writer. Writing about the intersection of religion and passion is at best a difficult enterprise. Giles Gunn, certainly a pioneer in the field, puts it nicely when he asks "how does one discuss the religious elements, motifs, or characteristics of any given work of literature without either turning literature into a surrogate for philosophy or theology on the one hand, or reducing religion merely to any and every work's dimension of seriousness or depth on the other" (12). Gunn opts ultimately for a "principled eclecticism," for form which must "ultimately seem, if not altogether natural and inevitable, at least plausible and compelling to our deepest sense of ourselves" (24). It is this eclecticism I find attractive.

Mark Storey in "Why Stevie Smith Matters" finds Stevie a poet who can "challenge our preconceptions" (176). But Barbera and McBrien make the most telling point about both religious poetry and about Stevie in particular: "The purpose of a religious poem, as T. S. Eliot said, is not to convert, but to let us know what it feels like to behave in a certain way. And Stevie's poems on Christianity certainly do convey her passion" (226).

The 1960s brought Stevie Smith wider recognition not only in Europe, but also in America. James Laughlin of New Directions, her American publisher, was a strong promoter. And Philip Larkin in a crucial review of her poems in *The New Statesman* for September 26, 1962, countered "the suspicion that her work was dangerously close to light verse by insisting that her poetry was serious and spoke with 'the authority of sadness' " (qtd. in Spalding 257). Brendan Gill noted her work in *The New Yorker*, and other reviews appeared in prestigious publications like *The Atlantic Monthly* and *The New York Times Book Review*. Two interesting fans of her poetry express great enthusiasm. Sylvia Plath wrote to her on November 19, 1962, just a few months before her own tragic death, saying "straight out that I am an addict of your poetry, a desperate Smith addict" (qtd. in Barbera, *Me Again* 6). Also, the Trappist monk and noted spiritual writer Thomas Merton—Stevie had become friendly with several of the Benedictine monks at Buckfast Abbey—in a letter to a friend seems almost giddy in describing his response to her poems: "I love her. I am crazy about her." Her poems have "a lot of true religion" (qtd in Barbera and McBrien 227).

Stevie Smith, whose complex religious impulses find an outlet in poems varied in form, voice, and rhythm, puzzles some and angers other readers. An admirer of Gerard Manley Hopkins, "that sainted, awkward poet . . . always so tormented in his spirit . . . with never a beautiful word he wrote understood until he was dead, and everyone preferred before him" (qtd. in Barbera and McBrien 216), she is a poet who at her best catches the human quest for the deepest love, for the divine, and the frustrations and failures and torments that often are part of that quest. Holbert Weidner's response can serve as a pointed epilogue to this essay. "She," he writes, "like her image of Christ was not mild. Her poetry is prickly, and she dares to be as impatient and questioning as Job. It is a great gift to both believer and unbeliever that she cared enough to argue so well and so often" (490).

WORKS CITED

Barbera, Jack, and William McBrien. *A Biography of Stevie Smith*. New York and Oxford: Oxford UP, 1987.

Barbera, Jack, and William McBrien, eds. *Me Again: Uncollected Writing of Stevie Smith Illustrated by Herself*. New York: Farrar, 1981.

Gunn, Giles, ed. *Literature and Religion*. London: S.C.M., 1971.

Larkin, Philip. "Stevie Goodbye." Sternlicht. 75–81.

Oates, Joyce Carol. "A Child with a Cold, Cold Eye." Sternlicht 65–70.

MacGibbon, James, ed. *The Collected Poems of Stevie Smith*. Allen Lane: Penguin, 1975.

Spalding, Frances. *Stevie Smith: A Biography*. New York: Norton, 1988.

Sternlicht, Sanford, ed. *In Search of Stevie Smith*. Syracuse: Syracuse UP, 1991.

Storey, Mark. "Why Stevie Smith Matters." Sternlicht. 141–56.

Tatham, Michael. "That One Must Speak Lightly." Sternlicht. 132–46.

Weidner, Holbert. "Stevie Smith: Questioning Faith Through Poetry." *The Christian Century* 18 May 1983: 489–90.

18

Acts of God:
Film, Religion, and "FX"

Judith Wilt

MY MOVIE-GOING BEGINNINGS coincided with the age of the religious blockbuster, and I knew transcendence when I heard it. *Quo Vadis?*, *The Robe*, *Ben Hur* . . . The Choir! where was it? Later, *Guys and Dolls*, *The Sound of Music*: you climbed every mountain, sat down when you rocked the boat. You felt you were in The Choir, but it was not you, exactly. In late adolescence, on the late show, I thrilled to the depiction of the earthly production of the choir, *Angels with Dirty Faces*, *Going My Way*, *The Bells of Saint Mary's*, in parochial disciplines that pointed to but hardly accounted for, the choir, its epiphanic penetration, its unsponsored otherworldness, its protean "FX." There *was* another world, religion in film, religion and film, film, even, as religion.[1]

It is not surprising that the "special effect" I first marked in film was The Choir. In the early 1950s film was still in its robust first generation of deploying sound; indeed, as Parker Tyler has argued, the indelibly "ventriloquist" aspect of sound in a film always gives to the element of voice itself "a type of supernaturalism," no matter how long we have lived with the

---

[1] These three phrasings of the topic are distinct as well as related: writers interested in the spiritual often tend, as I will suggest, to feel that the more overt the religion *in* the film the less truly "religious" it can be, while writers interested in film and popular culture seem to feel, mixing approval with disapproval, that film itself, as the chief vessel of twentieth-century mass popular culture, *is* religion in the sense that it does for the mass audience the cultural work that religions have done, that is, supply models for ethical action and provide grounding images for ideals and desires (see especially John Wiley Nelson, and the essay by Darrol Bryant in May and Bird's *Religion in Film*, which makes the interesting argument that film is the preeminent form of modern technological culture which has "inherited the alchemical dreams of the past" [105]).

cinematic marriage of sound and picture (249). The classic visual form of Hollywood cinema, that shot/reverse shot, the looker generating the thing looked at, had already by the 1920s folded, or "sutured," film narrative into a comfortably inevitable momentum, a naturalized "seam of significance" within the infinite number of ways of seeing an action, but sound with picture is a suture that seems always just about ready to give out.

These sutures, collaborations in "continuity," projected an intrinsic and providential meaningfulness and concealed the fact that every separated frame of a film, with its grafted-on sound, was a manmade artifact, external intervention, special effect.[2] In classic Hollywood continuity structure, the effects that made things linearly match—shot angles that kept the eyelines, or liplines, of two talking or kissing actors of wildly different heights seemingly on a level, movements of waiters or birds or cars that naturalized a camera pan from a random area to "the" area of significance in a visual field—were conventionalized, despecialized: these were just the innocent operations of God's ordinary world, not "style." Ruptures in this order, the unconcealing of "effects" as "special," as "style," expose the unsettling presence of a trickster god with designs upon the viewer.

With so much artful effectlessness (artless effectfulness) grounding the production of the mundane in film, it is interestingly difficult to properly produce the effect of the extraordinary, the uncanny, the exalted, the transcendent, the holy. Hollywood czars and academic critics agree that it is particularly hard to depict a miracle, cast God, without unraveling the whole fabric of (the filmic illusion of) reality.

Now, both the aesthetically or politically radical and the transcendentally minded filmmaker may *wish* to unravel the artful film fabric of reality, mundaneity, narrative, for their different motives. But the starting place is always the "abundance" of cinema, an entanglement in the glamorous profusion of image and the momentum of narrative which constitutes (aesthetically) "realism" and (theologically) "world." Paul Schrader, working with categories supplied by Jacques Maritain and examples from filmmakers

---

[2] Robert B. Ray's *A Certain Tendency of the Hollywood Cinema* offers an accessible account of "suture" in his opening argument about the meshing of continuity cinema, the "seam of significance," and the thematic tendency in Hollywood films to elide the necessity of making choices, granting significance.

Yasujiro Ozu, Robert Bresson, and Carl Dreyer, proposed in a 1972 book that "transcendental style" typically "rides a thin line" between the abundant means of cinema (density of image and sound, verifiable material environment, action and experience, identification and empathy) and the "sparse means" which approach negation of these (silence, stasis, blank). In a "film of spiritual intent" (160) the filmmaker carefully withdraws from abundant toward sparse means and modes in a way that critiques but does not erase the abundance of (cinematically represented) worldly experience, creating the conditions for a moment of genuine alterity—in Wordsworthian parlance, a laying asleep of experience and an awakening to the (unrepresentable) Burden of the Mystery. Robert B. Ray, studying "a certain tendency of the Hollywood cinema" to defuse conflict and obscure the necessity for political or moral choice, proposes in a more recent book that a radical cinema would expose that urgent necessity not by allegiance to the (far from) innocent abundances of Hollywood realistic style, and not in the aggressive but largely unwatched counter cinema of stasis, estrangement, and disruption. Rather, such a cinema would design a film structure that withdraws from the certainties of classic formal "suture" and classic American freedom/tolerance themes in a series of sparsely ironic corrections to itself, a structure for which Schrader's own 1976 *Taxi Driver* ("There's no escape. I'm God's lonely man," says the protagonist) is the model.[3]

For both Schrader and Ray a film can in fact "hold off" cinema's conventional narrative "success" for a moment of transcendent potential, or political correction, through the eruption of style into story, unconcealed "effect" crossing "the real." This means in psychoanalytic terms the checking or changing in the Symbolic order of the powerful dream/screen thematics of a culture's Imaginary; in theological terms it means the admission of a miracle, the sight of an act of God.

There are all kinds of miracles. Like other established churches the Hollywood cinema is happiest with the sacralization of the mundane, the miracle of orderly dailiness. It is uneasiest with violent visitations of the Creator, who is, however, there, just off the fold of the frame, a preverbal utterance in the soundtrack, an act

---

[3] See especially pp. 362–65 of *Transcendental Style in Film.*

before the opening/middle of the story. Masters of the transcendental style deliberate with light, space, repetition, and retardation seeking to depict or create new states of being, but Hollywood cinema, in thrall to the devil of action, creates to conceal, abashed and abject, miracles.

Film effects began as a way to reproduce nature, continued as "a way of imitating the marvels of professional magicians," comment the writers of *Film Tricks*, "but by the 1920s, effects men were being asked to duplicate miracles previously performed only by God" (36). Many of these special effect miracles are biomechanical, uncanny beings of flesh, plastic, paper, wood, and electrons; many are purely optical, the mixing of two (or a dozen) representations in ink, paint, plaster, celluloid, and clay in one picture. All are realizable nowhere but in the ruthlessly directive glance of the film camera(s), deployed (to read some surly film critics, to recall the bragging of Cecil B. DeMille) by the Simon Magus who claims to be the Christ. If you can see it, says a familiar, icon-wary tradition in religious thought, it cannot be the true miracle.[4]

Yet one may think religiously even in the presence of miracles, even Hollywood ones. The proper tone for the cultural critic here is somewhere between the ebullience of John Wiley Nelson's *Your God Is Alive and Well and Appearing in Popular Culture* and the skepticism of those colleagues who claim, on hearing of my topic, that there is no real religion in mainstream film. Popular culture will neither save your soul nor damn it, but it *is* the place for a study of the interesting paradox of an American culture both secularized and religiously saturated, a state of affairs where religion, arguably, "finds new life embedded more discretely in cultural forms" and less directly in churches, as Conrad E. Ostwalt Jr., suggests in *Screening the Sacred* (158).

What will interest me particularly in this essay is the creation of the effect of interlocking simultaneous worlds of reality, memory, and prophecy in a group of classic to contemporary films of varyingly overt and covert religious intent, an effect which itself is, however sutured and despecialized by film convention and blunted by accompanying commercial intent (or designs on mass

---

[4] See Michael Bird's essay "Film as Hierophany" in May and Bird eds., *Religion in Film*.

pleasure), both true and miraculous, both perjured and real. Special effects play matter's tricks on the spirit, and receive spirit back, from the adolescence of "effects" in *The Hunchback of Notre Dame* and *The Bells of St. Mary's*, through their robust adulthood in the gladiator films of the 1950s and their descendants, the galactic epics, to the domestic religious genre pictures of our own multicultural time.

BELLS

Two high-grossing films from Hollywood's classical age offer an interesting integration of social and religious miracle, and special effects. Both *The Hunchback of Notre Dame* (1939) and *The Bells of St. Mary's* (1945) begin with the sound and sight of bells, choirs, and towers: each tells a story which "conserves" selected aspects of Christian religious feeling and practice even as it casts its lot with a selected version of Modernity. *Notre Dame*'s camera withdraws from the opening glass-painted and matte-enhanced belltower through a window frame into the interior of a studio-constructed mechanic's shop where the story's "transit" figure, King Louis XI, rises from Angelus prayer, praises the bellringer, and then studies and names as a "miracle" the medium in front of him that will replace the churchbells, the printing press.[5] Likewise, *St Mary*'s camera pans down from a painted tower to a card-

---

[5] It is easy for the simplest viewer to connect that withdrawal with the very first shot/fade of the film, which withdrew from the pages of Victor Hugo's nineteenth-century novel to the scenes of the 1939 film, folding king and viewer together as witnesses, and acolytes, to "progress." Even more interestingly problematic are the many rearrangements in the film of the novel's reality, most crucially the erasure of the priestly identity of the Gothic villain Frollo, and the awarding of life to the beautiful Esmeralda and death to the gloriously stupid male love object, Captain Phoebus. In the novel she dies and he lives: the film exactly reverses both Hugo's Romantic critique of Christian celibacy and his Romantic espousal of Aeschylean religious fatality. The 1996 Disney animated version of the story, interestingly, restores the priestly identity of Frollo for a long Gothic sequence-song on the sexual frustration of the desirous priest, and instead erases almost all the political content of both the Hugo novel and the earlier film which had been bound up in the alliance of king, poet, and printing press. Disney also reinvents Captain Phoebus as an intelligent and humorous knight, and makes Quasimodo something of an artist, his carvings of the characters in the story linking him not to the cathedral's gargoyles so much as to the sculptors of the gargoyles.

board street where the transit-to-Modernity figure, a troubleshooting priest-updater of old urban Catholicism, passes from church to rectory, eventually to the school, this film's printing press in need of a new miracle for its continued existence.

The High Justice in *Notre Dame*'s opening scene equates the printing press with heresy, witches, sorcerers, and gypsies. In the crowd scene that follows, the camera tracks the incursion of Maureen O'Hara's gypsy witch, but a thrilled and frightened townswoman cries that it is the sorcerer-fool, Quasimodo (named for the Sunday after Easter Sunday), who has crossed her path, and the drama of linking rescues and separating scapegoating between these two figures is joined. The salty old housekeeper of *St. Mary's* suggests in the opening scene that the previous pastor was driven out (and driven insane) by the spells of the nuns of the school, setting up the drama of combats and rescues between Ingrid Bergman's witch-saint, Sister Mary Benedict, and Bing Crosby's crooner-fixer, Father O'Malley. Bells literally represent the Order of each society, and the supernatural Dame, Our Lady, the power of order: special effects help tell the tale of her modernizing and, in the end, of her equivocal masculinization.

The two key special effects of *The Hunchback of Notre Dame* are the body of the title character and the rescue that he effects of the condemned and triply beloved heretic gypsy madonna who is his, as he is her, Sanctuary. Victor Hugo's Quasimodo is a protean figure of strength, intelligence, and moral pathos, psychically twisted rather like Mary Shelley's creature in *Frankenstein* because of the social reception of his outsize being, "like a giant broken in pieces and badly reassembled" (71). Charles Laughton's Quasimodo is a marvel of broken pieces: the camera catches a blind forehead, then an eye, a humped running figure, a full face with eye and tooth springing from the flesh, a suspicious then delighted then abashed king of fools alternately biting and laughing, but always, always watching—this one-eyed monster is both our spectacle and our surrogate. The film rides on alternate concealings and exposures of this body: the exposure progressively normalizes the body, and its watchings, and ours, and eroticizes it, and them. This body, massively virile with all its suggestive swellings, joyously bounces on the bellrope, embraces the bells, finally, surreally, beds down with them, happily pumping sound from them with its legs. On the cross-pillory ("To think that yesterday in the same spot they crowned him their king!") the huge stripped body absorbs its punishment and accrues social along with its religious meaning ("after the hundred years' war thousands of us went from door to door looking for honest work and were whipped for beggary").

And at the end of the story, discharged of all its dynamic climbings and ridings, pursuits and rescues, shudderings, liftings and hurlings, this "FX"-enhanced body shrinks and cools to the shape all along implied in the novel and the film, next to its stone brother on the belltower balcony. Matching the gargoyle's pensive gaze on the city from the belltower, Quasimodo speaks the film's last words, "Why was I not made of stone like these?" before The Choir ruthlessly redelivers the "alleluias" that were first generated as part of the film's climactic special effect, the hunchback's victorious snatching of the gypsy girl from the gibbet to the Sanctuary of the belltower.

Early in the film the cathedral deacon reassured the gypsy that her genetically alien body will not bar her from the Sanctuary, for it was as much "an act of God" as the body of the hunchback. As competing spectacles of beautiful ugliness, and (racially and religiously) ugly beauty, the hunchback and the gypsy are applauded in the festival-plaza before the cathedral as entertainment, but in the emptying streets afterward both become objects of fear or mockery, and both seek the Sanctuary of the church, becoming its characteristic sacred bodies. In a double alienation from these sacred constructions, however, Quasimodo pursues Esmeralda at the behest of the lustful High Justice, and Esmeralda develops a deadly worship for her false-god rescuer, Captain Phoebus, which first brings Quasimodo to the pillory in front of the cathedral and then Esmeralda to the gibbet in the same space after the High Justice kills the Captain.

Never did female body seem more "made" than in the miraculous rescue back to Sanctuary which follows. Covered in white cloth and wearing its rope, the body slumps bonelessly in the cart, on the church steps, against the stark wooden triangle of the hanging tree, passive in pre-Raphaelite composition. The camera cuts agitatedly, then purposefully, between this prepared Sacrifice and the agile body of the hunchback as it moves from among the stone bodies to scamper across the (plaster and paint) stone of the churchfront toward the rope and construction frame eternally standing against a cathedral eternally under construction.

By no kind of geometry can it be conceived that the arc of that swung rope hanging flat from the construction frame could reach the girl on the platform, or return the two outcast bodies to the belltower: the fulcrum of the rope is out of the frame, and out of this world, as the camera drops to shoot the incoming rescuer from between the legs of the unsuspecting hangman, moves to the middle distance to capture the return, drops below the construction frame to record the one-armed carrying of a stuffed dummy to the tower, and then zooms above the scene to look down upon the sacerdotal raising of the Sacrifice. This is Our Body, limp, bridal and shaken, consecrated, its twisted priest-rescuer invisible between the white body and the exulting crowd, whose voice, mute until priest grasps body, is explosively produced at that moment as The Choir's "alleluias."

The extraordinary consecration-communion of crowd, double-gendered priest-scapegoat sacrifice, and approving/enacting spectator is a special effect created by the cameras and The Choir, a representation of the climax of the Catholic Mass and an epiphanic manifestation of the meaning of the Sanctuary of Notre Dame, which includes, at least momentarily, the living Dame as well as the stone ones of statue and church. Classic Hollywood narrative, however, approves only heterosexual love as true "sanctuary." Hollywood Modernity is in love with the printing press, not the Mass. In the final scenes the Sanctuary and its two consecrated bodies become a quite incoherently anarchic battleground among royal, ecclesiastical, legal, and proto-proletarian forces: in the mêlée the evil High Justice is pitched from the tower in a representation of the abjection of Law, the beautiful girl rides off into Modernity with her new printer-poet-lover, and the hunchback hardens into the fabric of the now remasculinized cathedral Dame.

The bells of St. Mary's are school bells as well as church bells; in this film the sanctuary is Modernity's saving myth—education. But here too, interestingly, the film works to move the representative dame of power out of the sanctuary. Leo McCarey's second Father O'Malley film, an amiable comedy of urban manners and working women, achieves its miracle through a modest but recurring and important special effect, as school principal and witch,

Sister Mary Benedict, and capitalist banker-wizard, Mr. Bogardus, compete to impose on the screen a prophetic fade-in of their different desires about the space next to the church—corporate headquarters or new school. The new pastor, Father O'Malley, sees no visions himself, but he comes to the parish with Bogardus's offer to buy and tear down the current school in his pocket and the bishop's authority to sell: his support is crucial to the enactment of either miracle.

Not for a moment, of course, is the spectator encouraged to believe that Father O'Malley will aquiesce in the sale of the school, that expensive but sacred co-sanctuary of the twentieth-century American parish. The film dallies for half its length with oppositions between the nun ("Did anyone ever tell you that you have a dishonest face, for a priest, I mean?") and the priest ("Aren't we here to give the children a helping hand, or are we here to measure their brains with a yardstick?"). But the film knows its place in the mythos of American social religion: progress (a new school building, a socialized immigrant population) is our most important product.

O'Malley's real job in the narrative is to delay the practical acts of Bogardus—who wants to complete the new building that stands in the old playground, get the current old school condemned by the city council whose president he is, and make it a parking lot—long enough to make the businessman susceptible to the special effects/spells of Sister Mary Benedict. As the building nears completion, the nuns visit Bogardus for a tour and the camera inscribes their competing visions: the businessman looks at the school and it fades to a shining line of cars; the nun looks at the office and it fades to a line of shining student faces in new desks. "Can't you just picture that?" insinuates the wonderworking nun, and in the next scene, slowed by a heart attack and shaken by a hectoring intervention from The Choir practicing next door ("Tota pulchra est, O Maria" . . . "Can't you get 'em to stop that, father?"), Bogardus looks and sees the nun's picture, much to his horror. A little benevolent blackmail from priest and doctor about the stress-reducing quality of philanthropy turns the horror to conviction, and the victory of this Dame takes place in the Church Porch. The new philanthropist tries to surprise Sister Mary Benedict with the words she is represented as actually putting into his mouth, the camera catching her lip movements as the sound track follows a split second later with his words, "I was wondering if you would accept my building."

Here too, though, the victory of the Dame of power is followed by ejection, in a sequence evoking, chastely, the Hollywood sanctuary of Romance. Sister Mary Benedict's doctor suddenly reveals she has TB and insists she be sent away without explanation to a dryer climate and lighter duties ("Don't you people more or less go where you're told, without question?"). Father O'Malley's assent to the doctor's orders becomes the occasion for a last test of internal and interpersonal wills, as the woman struggles with her Obedience (The Choir helps in a chapel prayer scene) and the man struggles with the charade that makes him appear to her as if he's simply taking a cheap revenge in the long comic struggle between pastor and principal. She wins her struggle and obeys; he is the one who breaks and tells her the truth of her illness. On the soundtrack The Choir sings its approval as the two bend shining faces to each other in a shot you have to look twice at to see wasn't actually a kiss.[6] Nevertheless, she leaves the scene: he stays.

SWORDS

During the 1950s religious spectacle and American cultural politics came together in a series of high-profile film blockbusters which constituted an appealing and ambiguous genre all their own, the Cold War religious epic, with a recognizable and still more ambiguous subgenre, the gladiator film. The top-grossing films of eight of the years between 1949 (*Samson and Delilah*) and 1960 (*Spartacus*) were religious and biblical spectaculars.

At bottom this genre, like most of the action genres of the 1950s, fed the myth of the national self that Richard Slotkin calls

---

[6] The miracle of this *Bells* is that it seems as if there *was* a Romance, a message received by two important viewers depicted in *The Godfather*, where Don Corleone's Americanized son and his WASP girlfriend leave a Radio City showing of *Bells* playfully reliving that scene ("Michael, would you love me better if I were a nun?" "I would if you looked like Ingrid Bergman"). Unlike O'Malley, Michael Corleone never breaks from his priestly immersion in godhood once he takes up his vocation: keeping the truth from women for their own good allows him in the famous last shot of the film to close the door on the inquiring Kay, freezing her in her sacred role as Mafia wife.

"gunfighter nation," a myth of "savage warfare" and "regenera-
tion through violence," connected to "Christian eschatological
foundations."[7] Most of the 1950s religious and biblical epics trans-
lated easily into post–cold-war national defense, picturing the first
American hundred years of nation-building as the fight of the
chosen (white Christian) people against Philistine, Egyptian,
above all Roman Empires, even while the American Empire was,
of course, itself consolidating its own reach. As Gerald E. Forshey
comments, these films conflated "freedom" and "faith" (34) in a
particularly Western way licensed by the projecting of American
democracy as oppressed by the evil Empires of Russian and Third
World Communism.

The special effects of these post-Normandy, post-Auschwitz,
post-Hiroshima films were military and masculine. With directors
as generals, they recreated mass military action (often with supple-
mentary mass refugee movement) in extravagant boom shots of
wheeling battalions and whole societies on the move, while the
close-ups featured the near naked masculine body, painted to display kill-and-maim spots (*Spartacus*), chained and quivering with
repressed proletarian anger (*The Ten Commandments*, *The Robe*),
grappling in the flesh with beasts (*Quo Vadis?*), pillars (*Samson and
Delilah*), and wooden oars (*Ben Hur*), and, preeminently, with
other near-naked men (*Spartacus*, *Demetrius and the Gladiators*).

The existential theology of these narratives veers between "I
came not to bring peace but a sword" (Matthew 10:34) and "I
felt His voice take the sword out of my hand" (*Ben Hur*). The
social theology is at grips with the conundrum best stated by
Audre Lord: you cannot dismantle the Master's House with the
Master's Tools. Gladiator films are morally useful for forcing oppressed heroes into mastery of the Master's tools of violence: the
apparent thousands of smashed bodies and other properties which
fill the screens of these films are a prodigious special effect representing both the Just War and the even darker imperative for
1950s America, the freedom to smash its own excess wealth. As
Michael Wood notes, the one thing certain in these epics is that
things are destroyed; we can take clean comfort from the fact that
the dead bodies and the Red Sea–wrecked chariots, the toppling
temples and the burning ships are a trick of the eye, and dirty glee

[7] See especially pages 10–21 of *Gunfighter Nation*.

in the knowledge that millions were in fact spent to construct these replicas and then put them to Hollywood's flaming sword, if only in backlots and watertanks (180).

The best of the gladiator films are attentive to the ambiguities of these matters, the destruction that regenerates, the (liberating but corrupting) sword of the slave, the epidemiology of violence, the slippage of roles between the villain and the victim: "Judah, it is as if you had become Messala," "we who are about to die salute you." In *Ben Hur* (1959) and *Spartacus* (1960) the final place of honor is on the cross, but the films are built on the sword they desire to discredit, Roman in spite of themselves. *Ben Hur*, with its climactic chariot race and edge-of-frame treatment of the life of Jesus, seems religious but not a gladiator film; *Spartacus*, with its many blade-littered arenas and debates on political philosophy, seems a gladiator film but not "religious." Yet the merchant Judah Ben Hur reaches his fighting mastery as a slave under the military professional whom it amuses, "in my leisure time," to train "some of the best gladiators and charioteers in Rome." And the complicated material and emotional "effects" which produce the transcendent core to the secular political miracle of a mass identity, "I am Spartacus," unite the cry of the dead and the voice of the defeated in a military Gethsemane that nevertheless receives the sanction of a Crucifixion.[8]

In both these films the debate is one of ideas, and divinized ones at that: Rome *vs.* Jerusalem. "How do you fight an idea?" the tribune Messala challenges the Jehovah-weary Roman commander he is replacing: "with another idea!" Later, to Ben Hur himself, "it was fate that chose us to civilize the world." "Rome is an eternal thought in the mind of God," says the patrician Crassus in the later film; "If there were no gods at all, I'd revere them: if there were no Rome, I'd dream of her."[9] In *Spartacus* the skep-

---

[8] In a contemporary revisiting of this "I am Spartacus" effect, the Stephen Spielberg–produced *To Wong Foo, Thanks for Everything, Julie Newmar* depicts a frayed middle-American town reinvigorated by the visit of three quasi-Angelic drag queens; when a homophobic police officer calls on them to identify the person who assaulted him, person after person steps up to claim "I am the drag queen."

[9] Laurence Olivier's Crassus, an altogether more formidable "Roman" than the mad emperors of early 1950s films or Stephen Boyd's charmingly macho Tribune, is consciously reconstructing "reverence" for the pre-republican gods of Rome as the new instrument of social control needed for the newly proletari-

tics are God-desiring dreamers and so is the gladiator himself: even safe in his wife's bed, says Kirk Douglas's Spartacus, mystified, "I feel so alone. . . . I imagine a god for slaves, and I pray." In *Ben Hur* the man of faith trusts in "the god of my fathers" to save him even chained to a Roman oar, and he challenges the doubting admiral who tells him that "a sane man would have learned to lose" that unprovable faith, as the admiral has because of the early death of his son. Condemnation of his mother and sister to the living grave of leprosy drives away Judah's faith ("I don't believe in miracles") until witnessing/identifying with the Roman crucifixion of the Nazarene who once gave him water to drink makes the miracle, first in the heart and then on the body, that restores faith.

Both the glittering blades that Messala uses on his chariot wheels, and the sword wielded by the escaped slave Spartacus, are illicit "effects" memorably aimed at cutting bodies. Superb stunting and editing make us see Messala's "sword" turned upon himself as his wheel locks and breaks during his effort to slice his rival's hamstring in the last lap of the famous race. In a remarkable mid-battle effect Kirk Douglas's Spartacus turns on a Roman opponent and cuts off his sword-in-hand, leaving two pumping streams of gore where the hand was.

Gore is the political and even theological "effect" of Empire, say both these films, both the cause and the effect of the gladiatorial spectacle, the matching micro-"effect" of the macropolitical spectacle of assembling crowds, whole zoos of racing men and animals, the alternating solemn dance and Dionysian bacchanal of giant competing armies. The effect in both films is purgative and paradoxical: "Every man in Judea is unclean until we have scoured off our bodies the crust and filth of being at the mercy of tyranny," says Judah Ben Hur, "in blood" if necessary. Both films find a culminating cleansing in the blood of the crucified figure, washing the crust of Roman slavery off the body of the "free" male (and, in both films, of his female surrogates). In *Ben Hur* the hero wins free of his Roman rival but is emotionally paralyzed by the Roman violence he needed to master in order to win the victory. He spends the last part of the film lost in despair, rather,

---

anized peasantry of the nation, a Marxian analysis specified throughout Howard Fast's 1951 novel.

as Gerald Forshey comments, "like the returning veterans of world war, burnt out, worn out, perpetually in a crisis of faith" (28), until the miraculous "effect" of the Crucifixion, caught by the camera's created "lightning" as a part of every drop of water flowing between sky, Cross, and earth, restores him. In *Spartacus* the legendary hero never loses his faith in man, but must, in a strenuously paradoxical last gladiatorial spectacle, put a loving sword through his surrogate son-disciple in order to reserve for himself the shameful, but epic, atonement of crucifixion.

The religious blockbuster film, critics suggest, died in the 1960s, its American "chosen-nation" mythos a victim of Dallas, Vietnam, and Watergate, only to be reborn in the science fiction epics whose galacto-gladiatorial arena offers ever more glamorous new potential for "FX" of the sword. In 1976 George Lucas's *Star Wars* began the galacto-gladiatorial era, and six months later Stephen Spielberg's *Close Encounters of the Third Kind* parodied it in a final sequence in which the apparent sword-rattling of earth governments against anticipated Romans from the skies turns out to have been a welcome mat all along. *Star Wars*'s light swords became *Encounters*'s lights, and the first film's community of fighter pilots gave way to Spielberg's new manifestation of The Choir, with the ticket-buying millions of the earth singing the famous five-note anthem that came from the stars.[10] In the 1980s a grittier adult series of galacto-gladiatorials moved into view, but even here the ghost of the religious blockbuster hovered in such sacred cyborgs as *Blade Runner*'s pierced and life-loving Roy and the jauntily self- and world-redemptive mechanical man of *Terminator 2*. In the most recent of the *Alien* series in 1992, impregnated in a baleful Annunciation, pitted again against the slavering evil of the ultimate gladiator, the perfect killing machine, and backed up by "a bunch of lifers who found God on a prison planet at the ass-end of space," Sigourney Weaver's Ellen Ripley backdives with her emerging sacred "dragon" offspring, familiar "FX," into a boiling lead cauldron imaged as a gigantic blossom of light, to the approving sighs of The Choir.

---

[10] In a related analysis, Thomas Schatz describes the post-"classic" transition of Hollywood cinema as marked in three decades by three massive blockbusters, *The Ten Commandments* (1956), *The Sound of Music* (1965), and *Jaws* (1975), each of them saturated, in characteristically different ways, with religious imagery (see essay in *Film Theory Goes to the Movies*).

Domestic Visions

Too much galactic rollercoaster transcendence can produce vertigo. In 1984 the modest *Places in the Heart* dealt out a robust special-effects tornado in its center, but offered a single quiet moment of domestic transcendence at the end of a story of racial turmoil and family loyalty and productivity in a Depression-era Texas farm: in a little church where the parishioners are the (genuine) choir, a communion basket with tiny cups of wine passes from pew to pew, slowly including, hand to hand, side by side, the stalwart family who remained in the town, the black drifter who saved their farm but was driven to the road again by the Ku Klux Klan, and, finally, the sheriff-father killed at the beginning of the film and the black teenager who accidentally killed him and was murdered himself by angry townspeople.

While the epic blockbusters of the West create fictive cultures that inevitably repeat elements of the West's religious and mythical systems (that is, 1995's Noah's ark, *Waterworld*), another line of films with spiritual intent burrows deeper into contemporary American domestic life for a close-up look at the communities where ethnicity, religion, economic and bureaucratic history, and process make myriad "cultures." I want to look finally at two superb recent examples of this format, two quasi-independent but faithfully "Hollywood" narratives which opened to significant critical appreciation but failed to find an audience in mainstream theatrical release. They await in video form what I would hope is a critical and academic resurrection.

The films are *Pow Wow Highway*, a 1988 film, part American road-picture and part Cheyenne vision-quest, in which a political revolutionary and a gentle fool-prophet wrangle on the way to rescue a woman jailed by the Federal Indian Bureau as part of a scheme to gain control of reservation mining rights, and *Household Saints*, Nancy Savocca's 1993 film of Francine Prose's 1981 novel of Italian Catholic culture set in New York at mid-century, depicting its transitions and traditions and its struggle with desire and the sacred. Powerful treatments of their own cultural themes, these two films also recall in interesting ways the holy fools, epic and domestic, of *The Hunchback of Notre Dame* and *The Bells of St. Mary's*.

Under the chief of his tribe at the Lame Deer reservation in

Montana, A. Alvarez's Buddy Red Bow has settled down uneasily to work as agricultural agent after a career as a decorated Vietnam hero and an A.I.M. revolutionary. He remains enraged at the subordinate position of Native Americans, but his dream for his people is totally political, alienated from and impatient with the historical and spiritual reservoirs of Cheyenne culture: "I don't dance. I hate [pow wows]. Look at these people; they think a few lousy beads and some feathers is a culture or something." When the Indian Bureau has his sister jailed in Santa Fe on a fake drug charge to get this firebrand off the reservation while an important tribal vote on a mining sale takes place, Buddy commandeers the junkyard car of the gentle giant, Philbert (beautifully played by Gary Farmer), for the trip south. The agile, verbal, skeptical Buddy has been accustomed from childhood to bully the slower, reflective, dream-weaving Philbert, and pays no attention to the other's contention that he and his rattling old "war pony, Protector," are actually on a vision-quest to gather, or rather to be made worthy to receive, the tokens of power that will earn him his true name and stature.

The film believes Philbert. It offers in rich golden special-effects light Philbert's memory/vision of his plains-galloping spiritual self, his memory/reception of power from the Cheyenne prophet Light Cloud, and later offers in rich blue light his grieving memory/reception of stamina and purpose from the ancestral spirits who survived the starving forced trek from Oklahoma to Fort Robinson. In a half-mystic, half-comic ten-fouring conversation on the midnight ether with another truckdriving Cheyenne on the interstate highway, Philbert is reminded of the association of Light Cloud and the mountain of Sweet Butte in South Dakota, and he takes control of the journey, gathering power in a dream-weaving sequence on that undisturbed natural place of spirit located adjacent to, and silently compared to, the imperial, fragmented, mountain-blaspheming monumentalism of the presidential heads of Mount Rushmore.

Philbert draws his reluctant and increasingly haunted companion into the river for a dawn song, then further out of his way to a Pine Ridge Pow Wow. There Buddy meets a Vietnam vet friend shattered into near muteness by his war experiences and the social-racial rejection of the country he fought for (played in a stunning cameo by a pre-*Dances with Wolves* Graham Greene), who compels him further toward the culture he has lost with the one word he can muster: Dance. And Buddy does dance, while the Native American version of The Choir sings approval.

Spiritual, cultural, and political forces thus converging, a newly purposeful Philbert turns the quest again to its southward vector, the rescue of Bonnie Red Bow. Like some latter-day Hunchback of Notre Dame he picks a plan out of the culture around him, sees a TV western where a man's friends break him out of jail with a horse pulling a rope tied to the bars, and duplicates the rescue, the junkyard car magically performing indeed like Protector, the war pony.

The film paints the transfiguring alternate world of Cheyenne spirituality in four kinds of special effects: (1) the sudden cuts to specially lit frames of racial memory and prophecy; (2) the slight slow motion of several such scenes to contrast with (that is, partly to critique and partly simply to complement) the slightly speeded-up scenes where the politically enraged Buddy smashes the inimical white world with his fists; (3) the careful intrusion in key places of acts of the alternate world into the frame of the "real" world; and (4) the occasional framing of the "real" natural world from an angle that unmistakably suggests its imbrication with the alternate spiritual one. Racial memory irradiates the token stones Philbert acquires in his shirt pocket and guides his powerful hand when he sharply cuts his car to the side of the road to save the spider whom he sees as his alter ego, the Cheyenne trickster god. Fingering the gun he expects to use at Sante Fe but frightened of the spider, Buddy is thrown out of the car, his gun broken and rendered harmless.

As the car later that night drives from the jail with the rescued Bonnie, Buddy stays behind to stop pursuit somehow, with no weapon but the broken window of the car. He faces the oncoming police vehicles, emits a warrior's call of power, and holds the glass as a shield from and reflector to police violence: the camera cuts to a feathered warrior with Buddy's face leaping into the air in slow motion with a fighting tomahawk, follows the tomahawk through the air, and records the invisible but effective force from the world of prophecy breaking the "real" window of the first vehicle, causing an escape-generating police pileup.

More effective still in the painting of the presence of the world of spirit are effects like the long pan shot near the beginning of

the film from eagle height of the plain which passes into a com-
mingled reflecting water/sky world in its midst; and another
moving shot from mid-level of the car advancing down a midnight road traveling a strip of asphalt bordered by snow while thin
fans of white sweep the asphalt in patterns from left and right,
seeming to draw the car and its quest forward.

Shots like these last two create a watching presence of the spiritual in the film that invisibly grounds the visible "FX" which
represent memory, prophecy, and miracle. This presence is momentarily embodied in, but not exhausted by, the form of the
chief of the tribe, who turns up at the end of the film in Santa Fe,
to authorize his wandering sheep and make various protecting
moves for them, and to gather them into his truck when Philbert's "war pony" crashes and burns, safely "throwing him" first.
The united, extended, and reenculturated Native American
group will return north at the end of the film to the same problems they faced before the quest, but they unmistakably carry new
solidity in the eye of this established presence.

In the late 1940s in New York's Little Italy Mama Santangelo,
sausage-maker supreme, talks matter-of-factly to her dead husband, Vincenzo: their son Joseph in a drunken pinochle game has
won a wife whom he means actually to marry—a virgin, yes, but
no beauty; she can't cook and she clearly, given the pinochle
game, comes from a very bad-luck family. Enzo shrugs, saying
"Man deals the cards, God stacks the deck." From such origins
comes a marriage, then a child who desires Jesus, no more and no
less, and who dies an early death smelling like roses. Was this the
story of a saint? a scandal of female repression and madness? an
anthropologist's delight of community myth-building? Nancy Savocca's *Household Saints* opens with the community's elders and
youngsters in 1970, comfortable in the suburbs and missing the
ghetto-miracle taste of Santangelo's sausages, squabbling over the
meaning of the story and vying for the telling that makes alternate
meanings: at the end of the film the community still squabbles
and the spectator savors the brilliantly wrought suspension of
judgment. All the versions are true.

Household Saints is powered by the superb performances of Tra-
cey Ullman as a naïve girl of the 1940s become a thoughtful
mother of the 1970s, and Lili Taylor as the daughter who troublesomely, poignantly, ridiculously, thoroughly believably, wants to

be a saint. Ullman's Catherine begins as a romantic reader of *Photoplay* easily convinced by her old-country mother-in-law that her first child might be born as a chicken because she watched her butcher husband prepare a Thanksgiving bird. As she becomes her own woman, she moves the highly colored icons and crucifixes of her culture from walls to the back of closets, and modulates her faith, generously but comfortably, as we all are wont to do, toward the rationally ethical: miracles are all around us, the blossoming of flowers, the birth of babies, let us love one another and attend to the little acts of God and not expect the operatic romantic ones that may just as easily conclude in doom as in triumph. Her virile, goodhearted, and skeptical husband feels the same. He is content to love his wife and raise his daughter without spiritual fuss, projecting an amiably roguish but insistent control over his life by adding his thumb to the scale of every sale and action: he assumes that the mayor, the pope, and even God are doing the same.

His masculine sense that to cheat a little is sanity matches Catherine's feminine metaphorization of miracle. But both these accommodations are utterly disrupted by little Theresa's entirely pure and comically straight reception of Catholic Mystery, her hunger for "the secret" of Fatima, her repetition of the domestic vision-quest of Theresa of Lisieux, her pursuit of her own protean and troublesomely desiring self through the labyrinth of Christian "examination of conscience." Stalking the vision from near starvation to sex in the bed of St. John's University Lothario and "TV law" student Leonard Villanova, Theresa confides in voice-over to her spiritual journal: "I was sick with worry. What if this is all the devil's work? Or worse, what if it's only real life, plain and simple? Maybe God does not have a great plan for me. . . . How many others like me will come to judgment day saying, God, I did it all for you, only to have God say, for me? well, you were mistaken." Such piercingly exalted and sensible ruminations absolutely create the reality of the sacred addressee, who appears, in crown of thorns and stained shroud, one day as she stands there ironing a red checked shirt in Leonard's apartment.

The film has used modest special effects before this scene—the prosaic figure of the dead Vincenzo, a half-glimpsed flutter of wings as Catherine pondered the possibility she would deliver a baby chicken, a bubbling blue-lit underwater shimmer to the

scenes where Catherine, and later Theresa, first yielded their bodies to the god-call of sexual desire, the slow motion of the street
scene that suddenly convinced Theresa that "God is everywhere."

The effects in the apparition scene too are modest, held between the exalted and the sensible, as Theresa records, "my whole
life I used to wonder, what would I do if I really had a vision? if
Jesus came, would I have the sense to look for a soft place to fall?"
Lord and lover have a smiling chat over the ironing board as the
shadow of a figure carrying a cross passes: "I came to keep you
company." "Thanks." Theresa offers a household saint's service
in the way of shroud washing and ironing: she opens the closet
door to put her secondary lover's shirt in the closet and out pours
a startling blast, a cornucopia, a veritable loaves-and-fishes multi-
plication of red checked shirts, extending all through the closet
and out around the walls and windows of the room. Lord and
lover laugh in glee: The Choir joins in, and the spectator, exqui-
sitely held between laughter and tears, lands in transcendental
space for just the one minute that is allowed before the miracle
fades to the diagnosis of the spectator—it was a "special effect";
the diagnosis of the educated Carmelite mistress of novices—it
was "acute hallucinatory psychosis . . . no doubt aggravated by a
somewhat obsessional religious nature"; the diagnosis of the com-
passionate and bewildered parents—"You know what Jesus came
to tell her today? Thank you. That's all she wanted." "People say
thank you all the time. She's gotta have it from Jesus?" Apparently
so.

What we are watching, twenty years after the facts (whatever
they were), is a story told by the old man who grabbed the telling
in the frame, who wants to believe that the ethnic/religious community can be knit (irregularly) together still by a sense of mystery
and religious desire on a spectrum ranging from rank superstition
and the perfect pinochle hand to the Resurrection. A feminist
daughter in the frame story sees the narrative of this exalted,
floor-scrubbing, and shirt-ironing Little Flower differently: "I
could name a list of women as long as my arm who went crazy
washing and cleaning and trying to please everybody." Savocca's
film unfolds from Joseph Santangelo's insight that what makes
miracles is Desire, and it supports Joseph's roguish image of Desire, personal ambition, the thumb on the scale, sexual delight,

the hand on the body. It supports Catherine's image of Desire too, the blossoming of plants under attention. The wild card in the deck of Desire, Theresa's for (no less than) a thank you from Jesus, is fairly dealt as well, still on the table at the end of the film, its final "effect" to be calculated by the spectator as the credits roll. And The Choir sings.

THE END

The chief special effect of narrative, of course, is that it ends. The special effect of film narrative is that it wraps itself all together, concludes with a satisfying and inherently "religious" teleology a split second before the world of the film, coherence of color and sound, meaning and feeling, shatters, and the world of the seats and the screen and the crowds and the streets and the meaning still to be made returns. In 1989s *Crimes and Misdemeanors*, a filmmaker, played by Woody Allen (who is also the maker of the film), hears the confession of Judah Rosenthal, philanthropist, opthalmologist, murderer, offered as a possible story for a movie: a man ordinarily of good and secular ethical conscience is led by his ungovernable multiple desires to commit murder; he finds himself plagued by guilt; "little sparks of his religious background, which he has rejected, come back." Eagerly, professionally competent, the filmmaker/confessor supplies the conclusion: "In the absence of a God he is forced to assume that responsibility himself" and hold himself accountable. But the scientific vision specialist tells the filmmaker, "that's the movies," not real life. In real life, he argues, no "end" to the situation comes, the man simply continues to carry his contradictions along.[11] The filmmaker in the film continues to protest, but the maker of the film agrees with the criminal and, unmoved, watches him go freely out of frame into the world.

Or rather, not unmoved. Assuming responsibility, the filmmaker's camera actually does move from its bleak prospect fram-

---

[11] After all, remarks Ernest Ferlita, "the *motion* picture is the dramatic art best able to depict man on the move," to depict "that archetypal image for the furthest reach of the human spirit, the quest" (117, 131); by its nature, quest, and the moving picture, have no end (see his essay in May and Bird, eds., *Religion in Film*).

ing the emptied doorway to the populated ballroom next door. There a blind rabbi dances with his daughter while The Choir sings "I'll be seeing you" over the credits. In this shot the teleology that religion and film share organizes our pity, our irony, our effects, our ends. But, wrapped in endless interior vision with the rabbi and The Choir, or locked in undecidable debate with the filmmaker and the criminal, we do not, in this shot, merely end. The film has produced an effect both teleological (religious in the standard sense) and unsettlingly ongoing, religious in the postmodern sense that figures the sacred as the "trace" of "the other," always elusive, always a challenge to faith. In the final moment, viewers sharing the blindness of the teacher of faith while the song carries the burden of "seeing you," the film communicates that "element of indecipherability, of incorrigibility, of alterity" (196) that critic Paul Giles locates at the heart of the hunger for the sacred in this, our own knowledgeable, deciphering, penetrating, familiar time.

WORKS CITED

Collins, Jim, Hilary Radner, and Ava Preacher Collins, eds. *Film Theory Goes to the Movies*. New York: Routledge, 1993.

Fast, Howard. *Spartacus*. New York: Crown, 1951.

Forshey, Gerald E. *American Religious and Biblical Spectaculars*. Westport, CT: Praeger, 1992.

Giles, Paul. *The Culture of Criticism and the Criticism of Culture*. New York: Oxford UP, 1987.

Hugo, Victor. *Notre-Dame of Paris*. 1831. Harmondsworth, Middlesex: Penguin, 1986.

Martin, Joel W., and Conrad E. Ostwalt, Jr., eds. *Screening the Sacred: Religion, Myth, and Ideology in Popular American Film*. Boulder, CO: Westview, 1995.

May, John R., and Michael Bird, eds. *Religion in Film*. Knoxville: U of Tennessee P, 1982.

Nelson, John Wiley. *Your God Is Alive and Well and Living in Popular Culture*. Philadelphia: Westminster, 1976.

Prose, Francine. *Household Saints*. 1981. New York: Ballantine, 1993.

Ray, Robert B. *A Certain Tendency of the Hollywood Cinema, 1930–1980*. Princeton, NJ: Princeton UP, 1985.

Schechter, Harold, and David Everitt, eds. *Film Tricks: Special Effects in the Movies*. New York: Dial-Delacorte, 1980.

Schrader, Paul. *Transcendental Style in Film: Ozu, Bresson, Dreyer.* Berkeley : U of California P, 1972.

Slotkin, Richard. *Gunfighter Nation: The Myth of the Frontier in Twentieth-Century America.* New York: Athenaeum, 1992.

Tyler, Parker. *Magic and Myth of the Movies.* New York: Simon & Schuster, 1947.

Wallace, Lew. *Ben Hur: A Tale of the Christ.* New York: Harper & Bros., 1880.

Wood, Michael. *America in the Movies, or, "Santa Maria, It Had Slipped My Mind."* New York: Basic Books, 1975.

NOTES ON CONTRIBUTORS

JOHN ANDERSON is currently teaching at Boston College and specializing in British Romantic literature. His work on women writers of the period has appeared in *Studies in English Literature*, and he is currently working on the book *Beyond Calliope: Women Epic Writers of the Romantic Period*.

J. A. APPLEYARD, S.J., is Professor of English at Boston College. He is the author of *Coleridge's Philosophy of Literature* and the recent *Becoming a Reader: The Experience of Fiction from Childhood to Adulthood*.

J. ROBERT BARTH, S.J., is Professor of English and Dean of the College of Arts and Sciences at Boston College. He is the author of *Coleridge and Christian Doctrine*, *The Symbolic Imagination: Coleridge and the Romantic Tradition*, and *Coleridge and the Power of Love*.

JOHN BOYD, S.J., Professor Emeritus of English at Fordham University, is the author of *The Function of Mimesis and Its Decline* and of numerous articles on Religion and Literature.

STEPHEN FIX, Professor of English and Chair of the Department at Williams College, has written extensively on the literary criticism of Samuel Johnson. His articles have appeared in *Modern Philology* and *Journal of English Literary History*, and he is currently editing Johnson's *Life of Milton* for the Yale University Press edition of Johnson's works.

HENRY LOUIS GATES, JR., is Professor of Afro-American Studies and Chair of the Department at Harvard University. Among his recent books are *Colored People: A Memoir*, *Loose Cannons: Notes on the Culture Wars*, and *Black Literature and Literary Theory*. He has also co-edited *Gloria Naylor: Critical Perspectives Past and Present*.

DOROTHY JUDD HALL teaches Religion and Liberature at Boston University where she received her doctorate in literature. A published poet, she is the author of *Robert Frost: Contours of Belief* and is currently editing *The Pollen Path: Moments of Radiance in Life and Art*. Her appointment as Visiting Scholar (1992–1993) to the Jesuit Institute at Boston College was the impetus for two book-length studies (in progress) on the spiritual journeys of Robert Frost and Wallace Stevens.

RICHARD KEARNEY is Professor of English at University College, Dublin. He is the author of *Modern Movements in European Philosophy, The Poetics of Imagining from Husserl to Lyotard, Transition Narratives in Modern Irish Culture*, and *The Wake of Imagination: Toward a Postmodern Culture*.

ROBERT KIELY is Professor of English at Harvard University. His books include *The Romantic Novel in England, Beyond Egotism: The Fiction of James Joyce, Modernism Reconsidered*, and *Reverse Tradition: Postmodern Fictions and the Nineteenth-Century Novel*.

DAVID LEIGH, S.J., is Professor of English and Chair of the Department at Seattle University. His articles have appeared in the *Keats–Shelley Journal, Renascence*, and the *James Joyce Journal*, and he has recently completed a book on religious autobiography.

JOHN L. MAHONEY is Thomas F. Rattigan Professor of English at Boston College and the author of *The Logic of Passion: The Literary Criticism of William Hazlitt, The Whole Internal Universe: Imitation and the New Defense of Literature in British Criticism, 1660–1830*, and *William Wordsworth: A Poetic Life*. He has recently edited, with J. Robert Barth, S.J., *Coleridge, Keats, and the Imagination: Romanticism and Adam's Dream*.

MELINDA PONDER is Associate Professor of English, Chair of the B.A. program, and Coordinator of Women's Studies at Pine Manor College. She is the author of *Hawthorne's Early Narrative Art*, and is currently co-editing *Hawthorne and "Scribbling Women": Engendering and Expanding the Hawthorne Tradition*.

MICHAEL RAIGER is a candidate for the Ph.D. at New York University. His articles on Coleridge have appeared in *The Wordsworth Circle* and the *European Romantic Review*.

PHILIP RULE, S.J., Professor of English at Holy Cross College, has recently completed a book on Coleridge and Newman. He is also the author of the monograph *Something of Great Constancy: Uses of the Imagination.*

CHARLES RZEPKA is Professor of English at Boston University. A specialist in British Romantic literature, he is the author of *The Self as Mind: Vision and Identity in Wordsworth, Coleridge, and Keats* and the recent *Sacramental Commodities: Gift, Text, and the Sublime in DeQuincey.*

JANE RANNEY RZEPKA is Minister at the Unitarian Universalist Church in Reading, Massachusetts. She teaches at Harvard Divinity School and is the author of *A Small Heaven: A Meditation Manual.*

E. DENNIS TAYLOR is Professor of English at Boston College and editor of the recently-founded journal *Religion and the Arts.* He is author of *Hardy's Poetry, 1860–1928* and *Hardy's Literary Language and Victorian Philology.*

K. P. VAN ANGLEN has taught English at the University of Pennsylvania, Boston College, and Harvard University. He has edited both the *Translations* volume in the Princeton Edition of *The Writings of Henry David Thoreau* (1986) and the Thoreau volume of *The Columbia Library of Quotations* (1996). He is also the author of *The New England Milton: Literary Reception and Cultural Authority in the Early Republic* (1993).

JUDITH WILT is Professor of English at Boston College. Her books include *Ghosts of the Gothic: Austen, Eliot, and Lawrence, Secret Leaves: The Novels of Sir Walter Scott, The Readable People of George Meredith,* and *Abortion, Choice, and Contemporary Fiction.*

INDEX